Fuel Hedging
and Risk
Management

Fuel Hedging and Risk Management

Strategies for Airlines, Shippers, and Other Consumers

S. MOHAMED DAFIR
VISHNU N. GAJJALA

WILEY

This edition first published 2016
© 2016 S. Mohamed Dafir and Vishnu N. Gajjala

Registered office
John Wiley & Sons Ltd, The Atrium, Southern Gate, Chichester, West Sussex, PO19 8SQ, United Kingdom

For details of our global editorial offices, for customer services and for information about how to apply for permission to reuse the copyright material in this book please see our website at www.wiley.com.

Wiley publishes in a variety of print and electronic formats and by print-on-demand. Some material included with standard print versions of this book may not be included in e-books or in print-on-demand. If this book refers to media such as a CD or DVD that is not included in the version you purchased, you may download this material at http://booksupport.wiley.com. For more information about Wiley products, visit www.wiley.com.

A catalogue record for this book is available from the Library of Congress.

A catalogue record for this book is available from the British Library.

ISBN 978-1-119-02672-3 (hardback)   ISBN 978-1-119-02675-4 (ebk)
ISBN 978-1-119-02673-0 (ebk)   ISBN 978-1-119-02674-7 (obk)

Cover design: Wiley
Cover image: Airplane image: © 06photo/iStockphoto; Sunset/Ship image: © zeroin/iStockphoto;
          Bottom image: © GeoPappas/iStockphoto

Set in 10/12pt Times by Aptara Inc., New Delhi, India
Printed in Great Britain by TJ International Ltd, Padstow, Cornwall, UK

To my dear parents, Lin Yi, and my nieces, princesses Malak, Omayma, Myriam, and Asma, without forgetting Captain Zachary Yacin and all the family Dafir.
- S.M.D.

To my parents, Sairoopa and Prasad.
- V.G.

Contents

Preface

"The day the hippopotamus left the pool…"

If you had asked me 15 years ago what kind of book I would have liked to write, my answer would have been philosophy, politics, or poetry. I never would have imagined that the day would come that would find me writing about a topic such as fuel oils: substances still associated with childhood memories of images of oiled seabirds or with the smell of gasoline that instantly calls to mind car sickness.

But if you were to next ask me why I have written a book about fuel hedging, the first answer that might come to my mind would be because I am good at it and that experience has shown me that there are so many people out there who would benefit from learning about it, otherwise remaining disadvantaged and at the mercy of ruthless and sophisticated fuel derivatives practitioners. After giving the question a second thought, I might realize that I shouldn't try to protect any party. After all, there are, there have been, and there will always be fat cats and hungry dogs in this world. My subsequent answer would be that by writing this book, I might be unconsciously trying to defend the truth that this practice has merit, that there is a science behind it, and that mishaps of the past should in no way diminish fuel risk management techniques, but rather reveal the omissions of the unvigilant, the mistakes of the careless, and the incompetence of charlatans.

In 2013, when I first got in touch with Wiley, my intention was to write a book about commodity derivatives. But after long discussions with Vishnu, it became clear to us that a book focused on fuel hedging would be particularly useful. Vishnu Gajjala is not only my coauthor; Vishnu and I worked together in commodities structuring for seven years and because of that, I know Vishnu has a unique blend of expertise, discipline, and patience – essential to writing an outstanding book. We also share the hope that this book will serve as a continuing encouragement, reminder, and, when necessary, an exhortation for fuel hedging practitioners to think off the beaten path. We made it to this finish line together, and I cannot imagine going through this book-writing journey with anyone else.

During the time it took to write the book, many market and geopolitical events unraveled, impacting the energy market landscape. It was therefore important to refrain from chasing events but rather to focus on how to help the reader anticipate and participate in the dynamic energy market. This exercise was equally enriching for me, especially due to the warm discussions that I had with people close to me who were interested in knowing more about the book and the rationale behind it.

After Rab Arous, a friend of mine, once asked me how I had ended up working in this field, my candid answer was that the smell of the petrodollar might not be as bad as that of petrol. By indexing the compensation for protection and security of trade routes to the most traded commodity, the petrodollar system allows the smooth projection of power, oiling rusty human relationships. Having played a central role in the geopolitics of the last 30 years, oil has not only become an underlying reason for many territorial conflicts, but also a means of coercion and pressure. This was remarked on by President Vladimir Putin in the midst of the Ukrainian crisis and spectacular decline of oil prices, when he stated that "A political component is always present in oil prices. Furthermore, at some moments of crisis it starts to feel like it is the politics that prevails in the pricing of energy resources." The use of this perception of oil to justify economic war could only sound legitimate in light of the statement made by President Reagan's son, who, in March 2014, said, "Since selling oil was the source of the Kremlin's wealth, my father got the Saudis to flood the market with cheap oil... Lower oil prices devalued the ruble, causing the USSR to go bankrupt, which led to perestroika and Mikhail Gorbachev and the collapse of the Soviet Empire." Even though such an unverified claim might not provide a complete explanation of the fall in oil prices back then, there is a strong sentiment that even the recent change of tack on oil prices by Gulf States was designed to use oil prices to pressurize Iran and Russia to come to the bargaining table.

My discussion with Mr Arous began with a simple question, which quickly developed into an interesting conversation, a part of which is worth recounting here.

R. Arous	Why are you focusing on oil consumers, given that the drivers and factors impacting the supply side of the equation sound more exciting and thrilling, especially when combined with the geopolitics of trade routes and maritime security?
S.M. Dafir	When all is said and done, it is the consumer who pays for the consumed good, thereby providing the fundamental incentive for producers to produce. Furthermore, consumers can consolidate market power with the help of regulations or legislation, like consumer protection laws that aim to defend the bargaining power of end consumers in recognition of their political power as potential voters. The same applies to the demand for a book, as there are more consumers than producers interested in a book about fuel risk management. Quite often, we hear friends, taxi drivers, or even restaurant owners complaining about high oil prices or justifying the high cost of their services. However, we seldom hear any feedback from these same people when oil prices collapse, save when they have fuel hedges in place and become very vocal about any associated financial losses.
R. Arous	Isn't that how hedging mechanisms work?
S.M. Dafir	Yes, but when a risk manager takes credit for the positive payout of a hedge that he/she has put in place, he/she should also accept blame for future negative payouts. So many risk managers praise themselves for the market timing of their hedges and seek appropriate recognition from senior management. It is a very common human behavior to take credit for good luck and associate it with skill, while negative outcomes are usually explained by bad luck. In financial markets, losses are very often blamed on "volatility," but high profits from price spikes are usually presented as good market timing.
	For example, take the spectacular decline of oil prices witnessed in 2008. Many Asian airlines reported significant losses on fuel hedging derivatives, eliciting strong reactions from top management, tremendous concern from banks about the risk of default on hedging derivatives, and a tsunami of bad publicity

regarding structured hedging derivatives. It was very easy back then for any layperson to raise his or her voice and designate structured and exotic derivatives as too complex, warranting their avoidance or even prohibition, as if complexity could be accepted as reasonable grounds for culpability. That was an easy way out for many stakeholders. However, the recent dramatic decline of oil (2014–15) amounted to a replay of past events that proved how the allegations made in 2008–9 overlooked the underlying culprit behind the unfortunate mishaps. In other words, the last five years of change in airlines' hedging policies, which were designed to avoid complex exotic and structured products, could not prevent large losses in 2015. Unfortunately, the media and many so-called experts have been recycling the same narrative of the past as if the market suffers from amnesia.

R. Arous   When money is lost, people need an "acceptable" explanation and a scapegoat. Isn't it the same here?

S.M. Dafir   Yes. This is no different from how the concept of witchcraft was used to identify scapegoats for natural disasters or newborn malformation. For some religious leaders to reconcile the concepts of omnipotence and an all-loving deity, they might have invented "witches" in order to explain the existence of evil.

The recent decline of oil prices was good news for the airline industry, although many airlines reported big realized/expected losses from fuel hedges in 2015, including Southwest Airlines (over \$1 billion), Cathay Pacific (over HK\$3 billion), Singapore Airlines, and Delta Airlines. The problem is that without hedging, you can always blame the market, but if you make losses because of your hedging, then it is your fault. As I explained earlier, this is only fair if a risk manager chooses to take credit for the hedging gains without considering the performance of the business as a whole. In fact, those airlines that had fuel hedges in place saw this benefit muted by hedging losses. In my opinion, what is commonly perceived as evil is nothing but the absence of good, in the same way that blindness is the absence of sight and deafness is the absence of hearing. Those who describe these risk management instruments as "casino-like hedges" show a profound misunderstanding of how financial markets and price discovery mechanisms work. They fail to accept that, in the absence of value creation, one person's gain is another person's loss. When fuel prices keep rising, those who make money, including producers, investors, speculators, and even certain hedgers, make huge gains that must come from someone else. When these gains are not reinserted into the economy in the form of consumption, a transfer of wealth takes place. One party in the economic equation will experience financial bleeding that can't be sustained forever. When such status quo gets challenged, extreme and rough events occur!

R. Arous   Are you referring to mean reversion?

S.M. Dafir   In a sense, yes. Mean reversion might reflect the rebalancing of the distribution of value that is finite. Let me tell you a story. My father visited me once and kept himself happily engaged taking care of the potted plants on the roof terrace. Among the things he planted was a pumpkin seed, which grew quickly into a pumpkin tree and even bore small fruit. My dad was so excited and enthusiastic that he started telling me how we would no longer need to buy pumpkins from the supermarket. That was until I reminded him that the tree that he expected to produce a dozen pumpkins was planted in a small pot not even the size of one ripe pumpkin!

R. Arous	But you could still add more soil and water to sustain its growth.
S.M. Dafir	Exactly! That is precisely what happens with rising oil prices. Increasing debt makes energy products affordable and allows the economy to continue to grow. Without debt, oil prices would plummet. Similar to the potted pumpkin tree, recycling the petrodollar helps reinject some of the liquidity through a well-functioning financial system. However, if the outstanding credit drops, growth gets impacted and oil prices plummet. Quantitative easing was nothing but a response to this phenomenon.
R. Arous	What about volatility?
S.M. Dafir	In my opinion, volatility spikes are akin to revolutions; they are prompted by a demand for decorrelation, regime change, or a more equitable division of created wealth. For example, a sharp decline in the price of oil has the effect of boosting consumers' spending. Unfortunately, just as with the case of revolutions, volatility spikes are usually more profitable for those who possess solid capabilities, information, and resources. For example, in the commodities market, falling prices are usually accompanied by a futures market in "contango" (steep forward curve) that offers arbitrageurs the opportunity to buy the physical commodity, store it, and secure a high selling price in the future. However, weak players might not have the access to funds and storage facilities to execute this. Even worse, they might struggle to meet margin requirements on their existing hedges or derivatives. Short of funds, many fuel hedgers are obliged to early-terminate their hedging trades at unfavorable exit levels. This book dedicates an entire chapter to discussing unwanted risks associated with fuel hedging to help hedgers learn how to assess risks, negotiate ISDA and CSA, and formulate solid strategies to harness volatility.
R. Arous	You explained earlier how macroeconomic and geopolitical factors affect oil prices. Can't fuel hedgers focus on these macro factors in order to anticipate and navigate volatility?
S.M. Dafir	That is not enough. The macroscopic and the microscopic are intertwined. The more we learn about the macro picture, the better we understand the microscopic details and vice versa. Take for example the pricing models of derivatives; they are based on our understanding of the dynamics of price movement, which includes mean reversion, regime changes, correlations, and other assumptions borrowed from our knowledge at the macroeconomic level. At the same time, knowledge of derivatives' valuation, risk management, and collateralization helps us understand the market reaction to price movement, triggers of liquidity drainage and credit crunches, and the impact of derivatives replications on the price determination process.
	During the five years preceding the peak of the credit crisis and the collapse of Lehman Brothers, commodities markets witnessed a phenomenal development of financial commodity products giving birth to innovative solutions, some of which were borrowed from other asset classes. Unfortunately, much of the accumulated experience and know-how seems to have been lost during the years following the credit crisis, which was capitalized upon by some participants to start a witch-hunt regarding structured derivatives products. During the same period, many experienced commodities derivatives practitioners left the field to pursue other interests. Hopefully, this book will help record some of the know-how and lessons learned, making them available for people to come.

R. Arous	I understand that there is a lot to comprehend from past experiences in commodities derivatives and derivatives in general. But, the biggest risks might not be a replay of the past. What is the market uncertainty that concerns you the most?
S.M. Dafir	Mehdi Elmandjra once said, "The illiterate of today is one who does not know how to unlearn in order to learn how to learn again."

****

Let me tell you my little story about the "hippopotamus." There was once a man named BenBer who lived in a huge villa. As a fan of animals, he even kept a hippopotamus in his pool. He was fond of seeing that other smaller animals, such as ducks, cohabited together and shared the same pool.

One morning, BenBer woke up to the surprise that the hippopotamus had left the pool and disappeared. As a result, the water level decreased significantly. Worried about the survival of the animals that became exposed, BenBer rushed to his hose and kept pouring water into the pool until it reached its usual level. Thanks to BenBer's rescue operation, most of the animals remaining in the pool survived…

… **But what if the hippopotamus comes back?**

S. Mohamed Dafir

Acknowledgments

I would like to offer my sincere gratitude to everybody at Volguard Private Limited, Timothy Sung, Melissa Chia, Kevin Fazaeli, Ouchnid, Junia Sulaiman, and all my friends in Singapore for their advice, counsel, and support during the last 12 months.

I would like to thank Rania Soppelsa from the SORBONNE-ASSAS and all my students for their strong interest and enriching debates.

I extend a special thank you to Uncle Lin Duo and Aunt Lu Lanting for taking care of me when I come to Hainan, without forgetting Qi Guo, You Yingyu, and all my friends in China.

I would also like to thank Mostafa for driving me all the way down to my home town, to Beni-Mellal and beyond.

S. MOHAMED DAFIR

We would like to thank Samantha Hartley and Thomas Hyrkiel for their invaluable support throughout the publishing process.

We are especially indebted to the International Energy Agency, the International Air Transport Association, and BP for providing their historical data.

I would also like to express my gratitude to my colleagues, Sashi Anumula and Abhinav Jain, for several thought-provoking discussions on physical commodities and refined products markets that were very enriching. I am thankful for the kind words of encouragement and support provided at every stage of the project by my family, friends, colleagues, and well-wishers.

VISHNU N. GAJJALA

About the Authors

Simo Mohamed Dafir is Managing Director at Volguard, a financial consulting firm specialized in Capital Markets, Wealth Management and Derivatives. He has over 14 years of experience during which he held senior positions in a number of major international banks in Hong Kong and Singapore.

He was Regional Head of Commodity Structuring at Standard Chartered Bank, Head of Commodity Exotics and Hybrids at Merrill Lynch Asia and Trader of Credit Derivatives at Credit Suisse. He is also professor of Global Financial Markets at Sorbonne Assas International Law School and an expert witness for Financial Markets litigations.

Mr Dafir started his career in Aerospace and Telecom at the European Space Agency and Alcatel.

He holds an MBA from INSEAD, a Post Graduate Research Degree from the National Polytechnic Institute of Toulouse, an MSc in Automation from ENSEEIHT and a Bachelors degree in Mathematics.

Vishnu Gajjala is a commodity derivatives professional and is currently a consultant for Volguard, responsible for financial markets analytics. He has extensive experience in commodity derivatives and structured products.

Mr Gajjala started his career at Merrill Lynch in Hong Kong, working on commodities structured notes, exotics and hybrids. He developed many innovative structures catering to commodity investors and hedgers, including airlines, mining companies, private banks, and sovereign wealth funds.

At Standard Chartered Bank in Singapore, Mr Gajjala held positions in commodities sales and structuring, providing commodity hedging and financing solutions to major corporate clients in Asia. He holds a Bachelor's degree in Engineering from IIT Madras and an MBA from IIM Bangalore.

CHAPTER 1

Energy Commodities and Price Formation

"If a commodity were in no way useful…, it would be destitute of exchangeable value, however scarce it might be, or whatever quantity of labour might be necessary to procure it."

—David Ricardo

T hroughout history, the availability of sources of energy and the means to produce, transport and harness it efficiently have been a necessary conditions for the growth of civilizations. Over the last century, fossil fuels have become the dominant source of energy globally, and companies have explored new sources and developed new technologies to access these reserves. But what is fuel without fuel consumers? Fossil fuels could have remained a topic confined to geologists' circles if it were not for the development and popularity of fossil fuel-based transportation machinery – such as cars, planes, and ships – has made these fuels essential to human life. It has been suggested that the usage of fossil fuels is an important factor behind the doubling of the world's population over the last century. Over the past few decades, the scarcity or abundance of these resources has been significantly influenced by the demand for these fuels, as consumers develop new uses for fuels, use fuels more efficiently, or substitute them with other energy sources.

This chapter emphasizes the strategic nature of energy commodities and introduces the energy markets by discussing the principal fuels transacted, the uses of these fuels, their origin, and how they are brought to market. Thereafter, the chapter examines the factors that influence fuel prices, including geopolitical risks and short-term supply/demand balances, as well as long-term fuel market considerations that contribute to the volatility of energy prices.

ENERGY AS A STRATEGIC RESOURCE

The importance of energy for present-day society cannot be understated. Energy is ubiquitous in the modern world, with every conceivable product and service utilizing energy for its production and delivery. Consequently, fluctuations in energy prices affect entities at all levels – from households and small businesses to large companies and governments – and the impact of price volatility is easily apparent. Rising energy prices impact a family's consumption basket, causing everything from transportation to groceries to become more expensive, thereby reducing their purchasing power. Higher fuel prices also mean that companies need to either absorb higher costs, raise output prices to maintain profitability, or otherwise manage the rise in costs. Finally, governments need to balance the subsidies given to energy consumers against deterioration in trade and budget metrics (e.g., fiscal and trade deficits) and potential social unrest. Even governments of energy-rich countries need to calibrate the amount of social support provided during periods of high energy prices in order to maintain a buffer for years when energy prices are low.

This increased awareness of the centrality of energy resources has been accompanied, over the last 30 years, by the development of sophisticated financial markets, the advent of the Internet, and electronic trading technologies allowing for more "democratic" access to commodities trading. Nowadays, investors, hedgers, and speculators are able to take control of thousands of oil barrels without leaving their chairs. Very often, the person trading these commodities has no personal experience with the physical commodity. Anyone can buy and sell commodities on trading platforms without even knowing the color of palladium, the location of gas pipelines, or the sea lanes used by very large crude carriers (VLCCs). Such abstraction from the details of the underlying physical commodity and its supply chain may be tolerable for some commodities, but is not advisable in the case of a "strategic" resource such as energy. The issue of security of production and supply is especially important for energy commodities, and this gives them a strategic dimension. Even experienced professionals like energy economists, who do a good job explaining energy prices in terms of supply and demand, can falter if they overlook the cost of securing supply and the security of trade routes.

To understand the importance of these details in the case of energy markets, let us use the analogy of a computer or a tablet. One can think of the commodities' physical platform as the hardware and the financial system as the software installed on it. The luxury of the touch screen and user-friendly graphic interfaces makes electronic technology easily accessible to everybody, to the point that one forgets about the existence of electronic circuits. It is perfectly understandable that more and more users find the workings of the hardware irrelevant, as long as they can use the apps. However if, hypothetically, the computer were to be used in conjunction with other devices to control the heartbeat or any other vital organ in the body, the concerned person would insist on learning about the safety mechanisms of the hardware, reading the manufacturer reviews, and even renegotiating his/her insurance scheme. Similarly, energy security cannot be discussed without a proper understanding of the commodities' physical platform. In a world where major energy chokepoints are prone to instability or turbulence, it is reasonable to assume that consuming nations must, directly or indirectly, bear the cost of securing energy supplies.

To further illustrate the strategic nature of energy, let us consider the case of China, which has become a major part of the energy equation, accounting for a significant fraction of oil demand growth. As a major oil consumer, China now commands the attention of market participants, who keep a close eye on the growth rate of the Chinese economy as any signs of a slowing of growth could send oil prices south. This simplistic analysis sometimes depicts China as mainly responsible for recent oil price volatility, either due to inappropriate monetary policy or industrial overcapacity, among other reasons. However, the situation looks quite different when viewed in the context of the petrodollar system.

Since the onset of the petrodollar system in the 1970s, most Asian oil-importing economies, including China, were obliged to export goods to the United States to lay their hands on the US dollars that were necessary to procure oil from Saudi Arabia and other Organization of Petroleum Exporting Countries (OPEC) members. China has been successful in leveraging its large workforce to build a significant manufacturing infrastructure capable of meeting (or exceeding) the US market demand for manufactured goods. This status quo has helped China to build an industrial complex, the OPEC countries to enjoy unprecedented purchasing power, and the USA to pay for goods and services in a currency it can control or even "print." The consequence of this system is that, in the absence of credible alternative counterparties, economies like China are very vulnerable to contractions in US imports, while the USA keeps the option to shift manufacturing to other countries like Bangladesh or Vietnam. As China's internal market cannot absorb its industrial production at international prices to cover US dollar-denominated commodity costs, any contraction of US imports can have a social impact (such as unemployment) in China and similar repercussions for neighboring economies. With a very large population aspiring to participate in its economic growth, China needs to maintain a minimum level of gross domestic product (GDP) growth, which requires incremental commodities that can only be purchased when margins from exports are significant. If this were not the case, then growth would likely be borrowed from the future in the form of bad loans. Such complex challenges faced by China and other exporter nations are intimately related to the energy market but are not readily apparent just from trading screens.

Therefore, it is important for market participants to be alert to the geopolitical factors impacting energy prices and the importance of maritime route security and energy chokepoints. In this regard, we will take a closer look at China and how it is reducing its exposure to the petrodollar system through the use of oil and gas trade-offset mechanisms with Russia. We will also discuss how it aims to limit its reliance on the Strait of Malacca and the troubled South China Sea for its energy imports. But before that, we will look at different types of commodities, some characteristics of energy commodities, their provenance, and how they are refined and transported.

ENERGY AS A TRADABLE COMMODITY

The commoditization of energy resources unfolded in an accelerated fashion after the collapse of the Bretton Woods system, which ultimately led to the inauguration of crude oil trading on the Chicago Board of Trade (CBOT) and the New York Mercantile Exchange (NYMEX) in 1983. The Bretton Woods system of fixed exchange rates was replaced by a floating exchange rate system that gave rise to increased volatility in financial markets in the 1970s. The need to manage exchange rate volatility led to the development of markets for foreign exchange. Concurrently, oil-producing countries were very concerned about the declining US dollar and started adjusting oil prices to match changes in gold price. In other words, there was reluctance in the oil market to break from the old Bretton Woods system that was pegged to gold. This kept oil prices stable when expressed in the old, "gold-backed dollars" but led to volatility spikes in actual oil prices (expressed in post-Bretton Woods US dollars). Thus, the evolution of the oil market from a regulated market with price controls to a free market necessitated the development of instruments for oil price risk management, akin to agricultural commodities markets. The development of this market depended heavily on the successful commoditization of these energy resources.

A commodity can be defined as any good or service for which there is demand and which is indistinguishable from other goods of the same type. That is, there is no special feature or additional utility provided by a particular good that is not available from another good of the same type. For example, crude oil produced in the USA is fungible with crude oil produced elsewhere in the world and can be used for similar purposes. Thus, all goods of the same type are treated as equivalent and this facilitates the formation of markets as commoditized goods become substitutable for each other. In practice, commodities which are traded on commodity markets have to adhere to a minimum standard or grade in order for them to be widely traded.

In this book, the use of the term "commodity" will refer to physical goods, usually natural resources, which are grown, mined, or extracted and are traded in a marketplace. The price of the commodity is generally determined by the market as a whole and not by individual producers or consumers. This assumes that a commodity is not differentiable by source, quality, or other specifications. However, in real life, there are minimum standards of quality and quantity that need to be observed for products to be traded in a marketplace. These minimum standards enable trading of large quantities of commodities as buyers do not have to bear the costs of analyzing the provenance of underlying commodities for each transaction. Markets also assign value to quality differences and, by extension, to the sources of commodities. For example, crude oil with low sulfur content and higher fractions of high-end products such as gasoline and kerosene (called light sweet crude oil) is usually assigned a higher price than crude oil with higher sulfur content.

As opposed to other asset classes such as stocks or bonds, which represent claims on a corporation or entity, commodities are more difficult to define as an asset class. They can range from precious metals, such as gold and silver, to agricultural products like corn and wheat, as well as energy products such as crude oil and natural gas. Commodities can trade across physical markets, where participants exchange the actual commodity, or financial markets, where participants exchange claims to underlying commodities (akin to stocks and bonds). In this respect, commodities are better understood by observing the markets in which they are traded.

Commodities can have multiple sources, making classification on this basis impractical. For instance, gold mined in Australia is substantially similar to gold mined elsewhere in the world. It is easier to classify commodities based on shared characteristics such as physical state, method of production, and primary end use. Commodities can be broadly classified under four major classes.

1. *Precious metals*. Metals such as gold, silver, platinum, palladium, rhodium, etc. can be classified as precious metals. This classification derives from their historical usage as currency, and their scarcity relative to other metals.
2. *Base metals/industrial metals*. Metals such as copper, aluminum, zinc, nickel, lead, and tin are some of the major base metals traded in global markets. The name "base metals" derives from their tendency to oxidize or corrode, as opposed to noble or precious metals. In mining, the term "base metals" generally refers to non-ferrous metals, excluding precious metals, while the term "industrial metals" expands the definition to include other commonly used metals such as iron and steel.
3. *Energy commodities*. Commodities that are used for the production of energy come under this category. They include crude oil, derivatives of crude oil such as naphtha, gasoline, gasoil, heating oil, and fuel oil, in addition to natural gas, coal, electricity, biodiesel, and

other commodities. Petrochemicals, emissions, and freight, which have close linkages to the energy market, can also be considered as energy commodities.

4. *Agricultural commodities.* Agricultural commodities encompass a wide range of commodities produced by farming. They can be further divided into sub-classes, based on their usage, availability, and the similarity of their markets.

   a. *Food grains.* Commodities mainly used for human consumption, like rice, wheat, corn, etc.

   b. *Edible oils and oilseeds.* Oils fit for human consumption, including soybean oil, palm oil, soybeans, soybean meal, rapeseed (canola) oil, sunflower oil, etc.

   c. *Livestock.* Live animals, which are mainly live cattle, feeder cattle, and lean hogs.

   d. *Soft commodities.* Other agricultural commodities such as cotton, coffee, cocoa, sugar, orange juice, rubber, etc.

Increasingly, there are linkages between classes of commodities such as energy and agricultural commodities. Commodities such as sugar or palm oil are used not only as food, but also to generate energy in the form of biodiesel. However, we use the aforementioned classification as it is based on the primary usage of the commodity and the major driver of demand for that particular commodity.

ENERGY COMMODITIES

Energy commodities come in different physical forms: solids such as coal and wood, liquids like petroleum, and gases such as natural gas and propane and butane (that are converted into Liquefied Petroleum Gas (LPG)). Most energy commodities in use are hydrocarbons, although nuclear energy and hydroelectric power are notable sources of power that are not hydrocarbon-based.

The main sources of primary energy are oil, natural gas, coal, nuclear energy, hydroelectric power, and renewables. Many of these primary sources are used in the generation of electricity, a secondary form of energy. The International Energy Agency (IEA) provides details on the supply and consumption of oil and other energy commodities. A breakdown of the total primary energy supply (TPES) of the world is shown in Figure 1.1. Oil and coal are the biggest sources of energy, with natural gas not far behind. Of these forms of energy, oil, coal, natural gas, and biofuels are traded in regional and global markets.

The total final consumption of energy provides a picture of the end uses of primary energy (without including backflows from the petrochemical industry). It can be inferred by comparison with primary energy supply that a significant proportion of primary energy sources, especially coal and natural gas, are converted into electricity for final use. As per the IEA, 63.7% of oil is consumed for transportation, while industrial use of coal accounts for 80% of its annual consumption (Figure 1.2).

Let us now briefly consider individual energy commodities, starting with crude oil.

Crude Oil

Crude oil or petroleum, derived from the Latin: petra (rock) + oleum (oil), refers to the thick, usually dark-colored liquid that occurs naturally in different parts of the world and is commonly retrieved by drilling. Petroleum is a fossil fuel, which was formed when a large

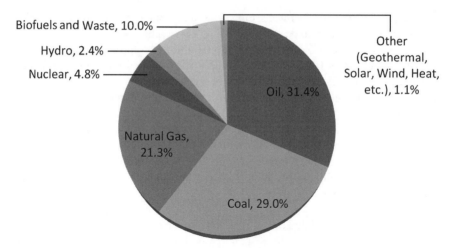

FIGURE 1.1   Total primary energy supply for 2012; TPES totaled 13,371 Mtoe (million tons of oil equivalent)
Source: International Energy Agency, © OECD/IEA 2014, Key World Energy Statistics, IEA Publishing; modified by John Wiley and Sons Ltd. License: www.iea.org/t&c/termsandconditions.

number of dead organisms were buried under sedimentary rock and subjected to enormous heat and pressure over millions of years. Crude oil is the most prominent of the hydrocarbon-based fuels, compounds composed mainly of carbon and hydrogen in varying proportions.

Since crude oil on its own is not of much use and needs to be processed for most modern applications, the value of crude oil is derived from the value of the underlying refined products that are obtained after processing. The products that can be obtained from refining a particular grade of crude oil depend on the chemical characteristics of the crude oil. Since crude oil obtained from an oil well will differ slightly in quality from oil drilled from any other well, it is instructive to look at the overarching physical properties and characteristics that determine the value of a particular grade of crude.

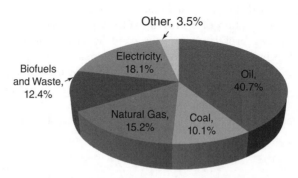

FIGURE 1.2   Total final consumption for 2012; TFC totaled 8979 Mtoe (million tons of oil equivalent)
Source: International Energy Agency, © OECD/IEA 2014, Key World Energy Statistics, IEA Publishing; modified by John Wiley and Sons Ltd. License: www.iea.org/t&c/termsandconditions.

The major properties of crude oil that are referenced in most contracts and specifications are the density, sulfur content, viscosity, pour point, volatility, water content, and sediment and other impurities. Other properties that are applicable to oil products include the flash point, cloud point, stability, dye, etc.

Density is measured using the American Petroleum Institute (API)s gravity scale, which is a measure of how much heavier or lighter the petroleum liquid is compared with water. A reading of above 10 indicates that the liquid is lighter than water and floats on it. Crude oil with a high API gravity value is referred to as light crude oil and would yield a higher percentage of lighter or less-dense products such as gasoline and kerosene upon refining. Crude oils with a low API gravity value are termed heavy crudes and are more difficult to refine, yielding lesser quantities of the high-value lighter products.

Sulfur is an undesirable impurity as it is corrosive and foul smelling, and it needs to be removed during the refining process. Crude oils with a sulfur content of less than 0.5% are referred to as "sweet" crude oils, while those with a sulfur content greater than 0.5% are termed "sour" crudes.

Viscosity is a measure of the thickness of the fluid or the resistance that it offers to pouring. It is measured in centistokes or Saybolt universal seconds. The pour point is the lowest temperature at which the crude oil retains its flow characteristics and below which it turns semi-solid. These measures are essential to determine the means of storage and transportation for liquids.

Volatility of crude oil and other products is measured using the Reid vapor pressure test and is important for handling and treatment considerations. Vapor pressure is especially important for gasoline as it affects starting, warm-up, and vapor locking tendency during use. Water content and sediment content are measured, as they are indicative of the effort needed to remove these impurities.

The main crude oil benchmarks are West Texas Intermediate (WTI) Crude Oil, which is a US crude oil, and Brent Crude Oil (North Sea crude oil). Both of these crudes are light sweet crude oils, where the API gravity is greater than 31.1°. Dubai Crude Oil is a major benchmark in the Asian region and is classified as a medium crude oil (API between 22.3° and 31.1°). Some of the major crude oil streams, along with their properties, are shown in Table 1.1.

TABLE 1.1 Major crude oil streams and their properties

	Crude oil stream	Country	API gravity	Sulfur (%)
1	West Texas Intermediate	USA	38.7	0.45
2	Brent Blend	UK	38.5	0.41
3	Arab Light	Saudi Arabia	32.7	1.8
4	Urals	Russia	31.8	1.35
5	Bonny Light	Nigeria	33.6	0.14
6	Maya	Mexico	21.8	3.33
7	Tapis	Malaysia	45.2	0.03
8	Kuwait	Kuwait	30.5	2.55
9	Basrah Blend	Iraq	34.4	2.1
10	Iran Light	Iran	33.4	1.36
11	Dubai	Dubai – UAE	30.4	2.13
12	Bow River	Canada	19.6	2.92
13	Murban	Abu Dhabi – UAE	39.6	0.79

Oil Products

Crude oil is too volatile to be used on its own, and hence distillation of crude oil into various fractions of different volatility is needed. The main types of oil products in descending order of volatility are:

- gases and LPGs
- gasolines/naphthas
- kerosenes
- gasoils/diesels
- fuel oils
- lubricating oils, paraffin wax, asphalt, tar, and other residuals.

Methane and ethane are gases found with petroleum. Methane, which is also referred to as "natural gas," is used for energy generation while ethane is used as a feedstock for petrochemical production, where it is converted into plastics. LPGs refer to propane, butane, or and a mixture of the two. They are used for cooking and industrial purposes. Gasoline is used mainly for motor transportation. Gasolines or naphthas are also used as feedstock for the petrochemical industry and refineries.

Kerosenes are mainly used as aviation turbine fuel (ATF). They are also still used for lighting and cooking in some parts of the world. Gasoils are used principally for home heating or as diesel engine fuel. They are also used as petrochemical feedstock. Fuel oils are used in marine transportation (also known as bunker oil) or as a source of fuel at refineries or power stations.

The refining process involves the separation of hydrocarbons by state and size, processing and treating individual products for the purpose of removing impurities and converting, or cracking, heavier hydrocarbons into lighter, more desirable compounds (Figure 1.3). The first stage of refining involves fractional distillation, whereby the crude oil is heated to a high temperature, usually around 350°C, and pumped into a distillation column where a temperature gradient is maintained between the top and the bottom. Lighter components of the crude oil, which boil at lower temperatures, condense at higher levels of the column while heavier compounds settle at lower levels of the column. Off-take pipes at different heights of the column withdraw fractions of different compounds, with gases and LPG at the top of the tower and fuel oils and residuals at the bottom. This residue from atmospheric distillation can further be subjected to vacuum distillation to remove more volatile components of the residue, leaving behind asphaltenes and other heavy residues.

Following distillation, the oil products are subjected to hydro-treating or Merox treating, whereby the sulfur present in the products is removed. Hydro-treating involves mixing hydrogen gas with the oil product (usually naphtha or gasoline) and passing the mixture over a catalyst at high temperature and pressure, resulting in the sulfur being removed as hydrogen sulfide gas.

The next major step in the refining process is the conversion of fractions into lighter, more desirable compounds. Naphthas are subjected to a process of catalytic reforming or platforming, whereby the "octane number," a measure of performance of motor fuels, is increased using a catalyst like platinum. Heavy residues are subjected to thermal cracking (heating to temperatures in excess of 400°C) or catalytic cracking, where a finely divided catalyst is mixed with the feedstock and heated, to produce catalytic-cracked gasoline and other light products. Hydro-cracking, another catalytic cracking process that uses hydrogen, can also be used for this purpose.

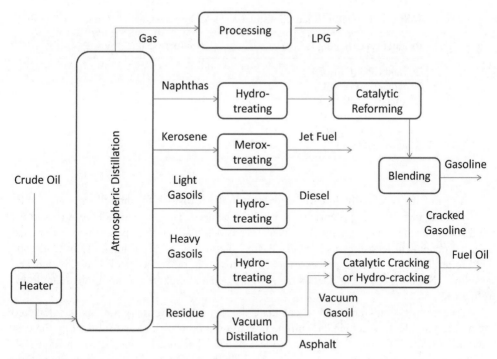

FIGURE 1.3 Simplified refining process diagram

The final step in the process is blending, where different products produced at the refinery are mixed in certain proportions to form the finished products, which conform to certain standards. For example, oxygenates are blended with motor gasoline to reduce the lead content and increase the octane number of the fuel.

Prior to refining, a crude oil assay is conducted to get a good idea of the product yield (i.e., the fraction of each product that can be obtained from the particular grade of crude oil). With crude oils of a similar origin, the crude grade with a higher API gravity value is likely to yield higher-end products; however, an assay is the best means of getting a reliable estimate of product yield. Sample product yields from primary distillation of Brent Crude Oil and Dubai Crude Oil are shown in Tables 1.2 and 1.3.

TABLE 1.2 Brent Crude Oil distillation yields by percentage of weight

Product type (boiling range)	Product yield (% by wt.)
Gas and LPG (C1 to C4)	2.4
Naphtha (C5 to 149°C)	19.1
Kerosene (149°C to 232°C)	14.2
Gas oil (232°C to 342°C)	20.9
Atmospheric residue (342°C+)	43.4

TABLE 1.3 Dubai Crude Oil distillation yields by percentage of weight

Product type (boiling range)	Product yield (% by wt.)
Gas and LPG (C1 to C4)	1.5
Naphtha (C5 to 180°C)	18.6
Kerosene (180°C to 240°C)	10.4
Gas oil (240°C to 380°C)	28.1
Vacuum gas oil (380°C to 550°C)	21.3
Residue (550°C+)	20.1

A test of the types of hydrocarbons present in the feedstock for the refinery can also be conducted to identify the appropriate feedstock to be used. This is called a PONA (paraffins, olefins, naphthenes, and aromatics) analysis. Feedstock that is rich in paraffins is better used as a petrochemical feedstock as it cracks easily. Olefins do not occur naturally in crude oils but are produced by refining processes and are present in other feedstock like naphthas and gasolines. Naphthenes and aromatics have higher octane numbers and are more suitable for refineries.

The product yields are used to calculate the gross refining margin. This is calculated by multiplying the product yields with the prevailing product prices and subtracting the cost of crude oil used. Some of the popular local product benchmarks are listed in Table 1.4. Calculating refining margins is essential to maintain the profitability of the refining operation, as refineries have flexibility in terms of choosing the optimum crude oil grade to use, changing the operation of the refinery to produce different fractions of products, blending, and the storage of products.

TABLE 1.4 Selected local product benchmarks

Region	Asia Pacific & Middle East	Europe	Americas
Crude oil	Dubai Crude Oil	Brent Crude Oil	WTI Crude Oil
Naphtha	MOPJ (Mean of Platts Japan) Naphtha; Singapore Naphtha	Naphtha CIF NWE (North West Europe); Naphtha Med (Italy) or Rotterdam Barges	Naphtha FOB USGC
Kerosene	Singapore Jet Kero	Jet NWE	Jet 54 USGC; Jet Fuel LS New York Harbor
Gasoline	FOB Singapore Gasoline 92 RON	Gasoline 10 ppm FOB MED; Eurobob Gasoline FOB ARA (Amsterdam Rotterdam Antwerp)	US Gulf Coast Gasoline
Gasoil	Singapore Gasoil	ICE Gasoil	No. 2 Heating Oil
Fuel oil	Singapore High Sulfur Fuel Oil (HSFO) 180 CST and HSFO 380 CST	Fuel Oil 3.5% Rotterdam Barges	FO RMG 380

Natural Gas

Natural gas is another fossil fuel, which is naturally found along with crude oil or coal and is formed in a similar manner (i.e., the exertion of high pressure and temperature over millions of years, by geological processes, on the remains of plants and animals). The main constituent of natural gas is methane (CH_4). Natural gas, when produced along with crude oil, is called associated gas. When crude oil is found in small quantities along with primarily natural gas, it is called condensate. Natural gas can also be extracted from coal reservoirs (known as coalbed methane), and landfill gas and biogas also contain high quantities of methane. Natural gas usually occurs with impurities such as water vapor, carbon dioxide, mercury, nitrogen, and hydrogen sulfide, as well as other gases such as ethane, propane, butane, and heavier hydrocarbons, which when liquefied are called natural gas liquids (NGLs). These impurities need to be removed before natural gas can be transported.

Natural gas is transported through pipelines or is liquefied to transport using liquefied natural gas (LNG) carriers. In this case, regasification facilities are required at the terminal where LNG is transported to. Since the heating use of natural gas is seasonal, gas needs to be stored for the winter season. Natural gas is "injected" into underground facilities like depleted gas reservoirs, salt caverns, and aquifers or stored within pipelines or as LNG.

Natural gas is the cleanest-burning hydrocarbon and is increasingly being used for electricity generation. It is used for heating and cooking and as feedstock for chemical manufacturing. It is also used as fuel for vehicles, which run on either compressed or liquid natural gas, and it can further be converted to other fuels using gas-to-liquid processes. Ethane is used for manufacturing plastics, while propane and butane are used as LPG. Heavier NGLs consist of gasoline, naphtha, and kerosene fractions and can be blended with crude oils.

Natural gas markets are much more localized than other energy markets and multiple pricing methods prevail globally; this has allowed only a few benchmark prices to attract sufficient market liquidity. The benchmarks that have gained popularity include Henry Hub Natural Gas in the USA, the National Balancing Point (NBP) in the UK, and Zeebrugge and TTF (Title Transfer Facility) in Continental Europe.

Coal

Coal is a black or dark-brown combustible sedimentary rock that is formed by the carbonization of vegetation and is composed primarily of carbon, along with varying proportions of hydrogen, nitrogen, sulfur, and oxygen. It generally occurs in rock strata, in layers called coal beds or coal seams. There are various grades of coal, classified based on the amount of time spent under intense heat and pressure, which affects their chemical properties. Lower-rank coals such as peat, lignite, and sub-bituminous coals have lower amounts of carbon by weight and are more volatile. Higher-rank coals include anthracite and bituminous coal, which have higher carbon and, thus, higher heat content.

Anthracite coal is primarily used for heating. Bituminous coal can be divided into two types – thermal or "steam coal" and metallurgical or "coking coal." Steam coal is mainly used for power generation and as an energy source for cement production, while coking coal is used to produce coke, which acts as a reducing agent in the production of pig iron and subsequently, steel. Lignite and sub-bituminous coals are mainly used for power generation. Coal can be converted into liquids to use as alternate fuels for transport, cooking, power generation, and in the chemicals industry. Coal can also be converted to syngas, a mixture of carbon monoxide and hydrogen gas, and subsequently used to produce electricity or other transport fuels.

Global coal markets can be split into two major regions – the Pacific basin and the Atlantic basin. The major benchmarks for thermal coal are based on delivery at ports where coal is exported from or imported to, and include Newcastle coal (Australia), API4 coal (Richards Bay, South Africa), and API2 coal (Amsterdam Rotterdam Antwerp, ARA). Further, local coal markets like the USA have their own benchmarks.

PRICE DRIVERS IN ENERGY MARKETS

Prices in physical markets are influenced by a myriad of factors. As in most markets, supply and demand play a major role in price determination. Commodity prices are also generally linked to economic performance, with growing economies consuming more commodities, and thus raising prices. Commodity prices are also influenced by events affecting the supply chain of the product, from producers and refiners to distributors and consumers.

As a number of energy commodities are considered strategic assets and their production is concentrated in the hands of a few countries, which are largely emerging economies that can be prone to instability, there is a geopolitical aspect to price determination as well. As commodities get increasingly financialized, with major financial players like banks and hedge funds trading in these markets, commodity prices have also become linked to other asset prices.

Let us examine some of these factors briefly, using the oil markets as an example.

Geopolitical Risks

Oil prices are particularly vulnerable to events such as war, internal strife, or terrorist attacks, especially in the sensitive Middle East region. For example, oil prices spiked in the wake of the Gulf War and the Iraq War of 2003, as well as during the "Arab spring" rebellions across a number of countries in North Africa and the Middle East. In such environments, oil prices trade at a premium to prices implied by supply/demand balance, and this is sometimes dubbed the "fear premium." In contrast, resource nationalism, in the form of higher royalties or outright nationalization of assets, has been decreasing in recent years and many national oil companies are opening up to collaboration with global oil companies due to the scarcity of capital and technological know-how needed to exploit new reserves.

The Geopolitical Chessboard – The Petrodollar System and Rising China

Earlier in this chapter we discussed the strategic role played by energy resources and touched on how the pricing of this commodity can impact the destiny of large nations. The fact that more than 60% of the global production of oil moves on maritime routes makes naval power integral to securing the supply of oil and thereby shaping the world's geopolitical chessboard. By far, the USA is the mightiest naval power in the world and has been successful in providing protection to major oil producers and securing the maritime routes, thereby deserving the privileges of the petrodollar system. Other rising powers, like China, have also relied on US-led maritime route security to secure the energy imports required to build an industrial complex and accelerate their economic growth. However, it is only recently that these nations have begun viewing these energy maritime routes as the source of vulnerability that they are and have taken steps to address these weaknesses and reduce their exposure to the petrodollar system.

The Strait of Hormuz, the Strait of Malacca, the Suez Canal, Bab El Mandab, the Danish Straits, the Bosporus and, to a lesser extent, the Panama Straits are the major oil chokepoints, representing the most strategic locations that have shaped the geopolitics of the last 40 years. The most strategic and troubled chokepoint remains the Strait of Hormuz, which has been used as a bargaining card by Iran to negotiate with the West and put pressure on neighboring oil-producing countries.

In the case of China, the world's second-largest oil-consuming nation, the situation is much more complicated, because its oil imports need to move through two major chokepoints and a troubled South China Sea, as shown in Figure 1.4.

China imports over 70% of its crude oil from the Middle East and the traditional sea route has been through the Indian Ocean, the Strait of Malacca, and the South China Sea. China remains concerned about its security of sea lanes, especially those passing through the Strait of Malacca and the South China Sea, through which an estimated 80% of its oil imports transit. Also, in the absence of a significant global naval presence, China is not comfortable relying on oil imports passing through the South China Sea, which is surrounded by countries that are perceived to be part of a US-led containment coalition. These potentially hostile countries include the Philippines, Japan, and Taiwan, which were once referred to as an "unsinkable aircraft carrier" by General MacArthur. As a nation that is not a US ally, China fears the disruption of its oil imports in the case of hostilities in the region.

In order to alleviate the disruption risks, China has done a formidable job developing trade links with its Central Asian neighbors and building infrastructure in close South Asian neighbors to gain access to the Indian Ocean. Together with Pakistan, China has been developing a megaproject called the China Pakistan Economic Corridor (CPEC) consisting of a network of highways, railways, and oil and gas pipelines over 3000 km running from the port of Gwadar all the way to Kashgar in China. The CPEC will give China access to the Arabian Sea not far from the Strait of Hormuz. Similarly, China gained access to the Bay of Bengal via Sino-Burma pipelines, which transport oil and gas from the port of Kyaukphyu to Kunming (Yunnan Province). In addition to cutting the shipping time of Middle Eastern and African crude oil significantly, these two shortcuts are game-changers on the chessboard as they help avoid crowded South China Sea waters and any unexpected hostilities in transit. Additionally, as mentioned earlier, China has also been working closely with its neighbors in the east and the north, signing megaprojects allowing Russia to trade its oil and gas in Yuan or Roubles using trade-offset mechanisms to minimize its dependence on the US dollar and related unpredictability in financing costs.

Oil prices are particularly vulnerable to events such as war, internal strife, or terrorist attacks, especially in the sensitive Middle East region. For example, oil prices spiked in the wake of the Gulf War and the Iraq War of 2003, as well as during the "Arab spring" rebellions across a number of countries in North Africa and the Middle East. In such environments, oil prices trade at a premium to prices implied by supply/demand balance, and this is sometimes dubbed the "fear premium." In contrast, resource nationalism, in the form of higher royalties or outright nationalization of assets, has been decreasing in recent years and many national oil companies are opening up to collaboration with global oil companies due to the scarcity of capital and technological know-how to exploit new reserves.

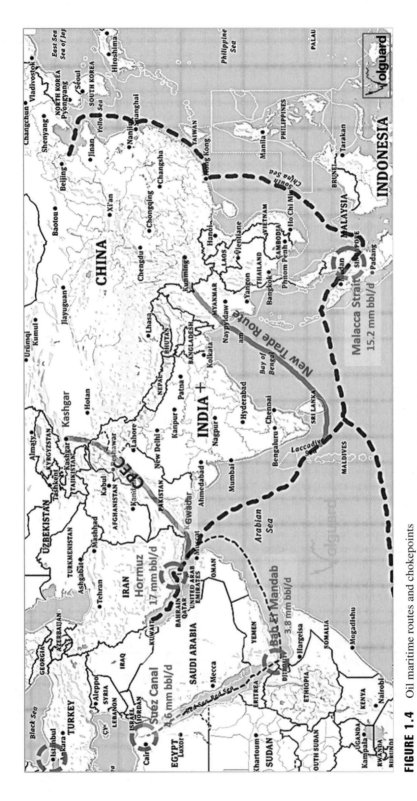

FIGURE 1.4 Oil maritime routes and chokepoints

Data Sources: US Energy Information Administration analysis based on Lloyd's List Intelligence, Eastern Bloc Research, Suez Canal Authority, and UNCTAD, using EIA conversion factors. Estimates are for year 2013.

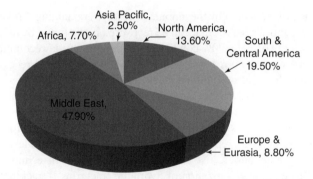

FIGURE 1.5 Distribution of oil reserves by region at the end of 2013; total proved reserves accounted for 1687.9 billion barrels
Source: BP Statistical Review of World Energy 2014.

Long-Term Supply and Demand

To understand the long-term demand and supply in commodity markets, let us take a look at a few of the indicators that are used.

Production and Reserves The supply of crude oil can be gauged by the production of crude oil (measured in millions of barrels per day), the amount of reserves of crude oil, specifically proved reserves (Figure 1.5), and the ratio of reserves to production (Figure 1.6), which gives an estimate of the number of years that the reserves can be expected to last. As expected, when the production of crude oil is high, prices are generally lower, although in general supply growth has tended to lag demand growth, leading to a gradually rising average price over the last two decades.

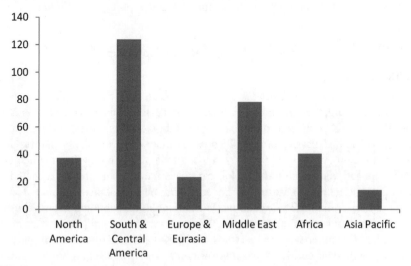

FIGURE 1.6 Reserves-to-production (R/P) ratios by region at the end of 2013
Source: BP Statistical Review of World Energy 2014.

Long-term prices are affected by the amount of reserves remaining. Proved reserves of oil (also called "1P") are those reserves that can be recovered in the future from known reservoirs with reasonable certainty (usually 90% confidence) under present-day economic and operating conditions. Probable reserves correspond to a 50% confidence level of recovery (called "2P" or proved plus probable), and possible reserves are those that have a less likely chance of being recovered (at least a 10% chance) and are called "3P" (proved + probable + possible). Disclosures regarding reserves can be affected by local accounting rules and whether the company reporting the figures is private or public. Since a number of national oil companies are private, the reserve numbers reported by them do not have the same level of scrutiny.

Reserve growth predictions are also affected by developments in technology. For instance, prior to the large-scale commercialization of hydraulic fracturing ("fracking") technology to exploit shale oil reserves and other technological innovations of the last decade, it was widely believed that oil would turn expensive. This was because oil production in the USA had peaked in the early 1970s (known as Hubbert's peak after M. King Hubbert, a US geologist) and the world's production was expected to peak in 1995. However, the introduction of new technologies and the increased viability of developing more difficult-to-extract reserves, such as oil sands, with higher prices of crude oil have combined to allow oil production to continue to grow.

In addition, in recent years there has been a discussion on reviewing the reserves of companies to account for "unburnable reserves" arising from the fact that it would be impossible to utilize some of the reserves if global warming targets are to be met. Similarly, carbon capture and storage (CCS) technologies would need to be developed before all the disclosed hydrocarbon reserves could be tapped. However, it is not yet clear if there is an appreciable impact of this concern on oil prices or the stock prices of energy companies.

Refining and Consumption   Refining capacity is an indicator of the maximum supply of oil products. Demand can be gauged from the consumption of crude oil and the consumption of individual refined products. Refinery throughput or capacity utilization is another measure of the demand for refined products. Data on imports and exports, as in Figure 1.7, can also

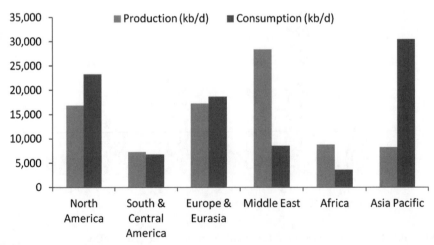

FIGURE 1.7   Oil production and consumption by region
Source: BP Statistical Review of World Energy 2014.

provide clues about the geographical distribution of demand and supply as well as the energy security of individual countries or regions.

Trends in Economic Activity The pace of economic activity is a good barometer of commodity consumption. An acceleration in GDP growth rate leads to higher usage of crude oil and other commodities, leading to higher prices during the uptrend in the economic cycle. Conversely, a contraction in economic output can lead to a sharp fall in commodity prices, as evidenced in the fall of 2008–09, when oil prices dropped from their highs of over 140$/bbl to lows of below 40$/bbl.

Technological Advances Technological advances affect expectations of long-term supply and demand. For example, rising oil prices make it viable to develop more producing assets, thus increasing future reserves and production. However, rising oil prices also spur investment in alternative energy sources and shape future demand as well. For example, the development of hydroelectric, solar, wind, and other forms of energy generation, the growth in the usage of biofuels and compressed natural gas (CNG) for transportation, as well as heightened public awareness and demand for electric-powered vehicles and hybrids are all consequences of higher oil prices. The environmental impact of using oil can also be credited with the development of tougher standards on emissions, reducing energy intensity of new technologies, and increasing investments in alternative energy.

Short-Term Supply and Demand: Supply Chain and Infrastructure

Short-term supply and demand are affected by disruptions in the supply chain of the commodity. For example, the hurricanes Katrina and Rita led to a drop of over 1 million bbl/day in crude oil output from the Gulf of Mexico and refined product capacity was significantly reduced (by a third of national capacity at one point). Maintenance of oil rigs and other equipment can also lead to short-term price dislocations.

Upstream Upstream production capacity and spare capacity affect prices as well. The amount of spare capacity maintained by OPEC, especially Saudi Arabia, has an effect on containing price rises. OPEC is an international organization, which aims to coordinate the petroleum policies of member countries and ensure the stabilization of oil markets. Its members, as of mid-2015, are the states of Algeria, Angola, Ecuador, Iran, Iraq, Kuwait, Libya, Nigeria, Qatar, Saudi Arabia, the United Arab Emirates, and Venezuela. OPEC accounts for over 81% of the world's crude oil reserves as of 2012, and produces about a third of global production, thereby wielding significant influence over oil prices.

Refining Prices of crude oil are also affected by their usability in refineries and refining capacity. As refineries are large installations, which are constructed over a long period of time, refining capacity is finite and inelastic and refineries are typically configured to handle a specific type of crude oil. Thus, price trends for crude oil will be affected by the refining capacity available to process that particular blend of oil. For example, if it is more profitable to refine heavy crude oil in a complex refinery (vs. light crude oil), complex refineries will run at full capacity, reducing the premium for light crude oil. The development of complex refineries in Asia has served to increase the value of heavy, sour crude oils such as Dubai and Saudi Arabian crudes.

The difference in price between crude oil and the products that it can be converted to is called the crack spread or refinery margin. Short-term price movements of crude oil are affected by the margins that refiners can make on processing a particular blend of crude. Quality and yield differences can explain some of the differences in price between different crude oils.

Storage and Transportation   Storage capacity helps to smooth supply and stabilize prices. The USA has a strategic petroleum reserve (SPR), which can be used to manage short-term price spikes due to supply disruptions. However, storage capacity can also explain some short-term price movements. For instance, if storage is full, prices will be depressed and oil producers have to reduce production. Conversely, cheaper storage would provide producers and traders with the option to store oil in order to sell in the future at potentially higher prices.

Transportation infrastructure and capacity helps to connect global prices and can influence the price of one blend of crude oil relative to others. Spreads between similar blends of crude oil can be explained to some extent by wet freight rates. For instance, the spread between Brent Crude Oil and Dubai Crude Oil reflects the relative supply/demand balance in Europe vs. Asia Pacific as well as the cost of shipping between the two delivery locations. Wider spreads can result in traders deploying vessels to deliver crude oil to the more profitable location, thus narrowing the arbitrage (the riskless profit that can be generated after costs). However, regulation can cause this relationship to break down in some cases.

Regulations   Taxation and regulations also play a major role in determining crude oil prices. For example, until recently, crude oil could not be exported from the USA by law, while crude oil can be freely exported from other countries. With the rise in domestic production of crude oil from shale formations in the USA, the local benchmark of WTI Crude Oil has been dislocated from global crude prices over the last few years (Figure 1.8). Traditionally, WTI has traded at a slight premium to global benchmarks like Brent, but the addition of supply from

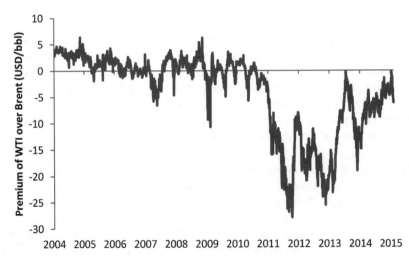

FIGURE 1.8   WTI Crude Oil premium over Brent Crude Oil (front-month prices)
Source: NYMEX, ICE, Bloomberg.

shale oil and Canadian oil sands, coupled with the inability to export crude oil, has caused WTI to trade at a significant discount to international crude oil prices in recent years.

Transportation mix and demand react to taxes on refined products, with customers opting for cheaper fuels such as diesel and electric power when tax rebates are offered. Environmental regulations also impose costs on industries for compliance with norms, requiring continued investment by both car manufacturers and refiners.

Financialization of Commodities

Over the last two decades, with the re-emergence of commodity futures markets, banks and other financial institutions have been participating in the commodity markets as well. As commodity futures are easier to manage than physical commodity inventory, speculators who wish to profit from changes in commodity prices are drawn to the futures markets. In many commodities, the benchmark prices are derived from these derivative markets as opposed to spot markets.

Commodities have shown zero or negative correlation with other asset classes like stocks and bonds over the period from 1959 to 2004. They have also shown significant correlation with inflation, indicating that commodities may be a better hedge against inflation than stocks or bonds. From the early 2000s, this diversification benefit of commodities led to a sharp increase in funds allocated to commodities as an asset class, especially via the commodity index and exchange-traded fund (ETF) route. However, over the last decade, the correlation of commodities with other asset classes has increased. Also, within commodities, non-energy commodities have become increasingly correlated with oil prices. Between 2004 and 2008, correlation between returns on major commodities with crude oil rose from around 0 to 0.5. Volatility also spilled over from oil and other asset classes to non-energy commodities, increasing the volatility of commodity prices as a whole.

Since commodities are denominated and settled mainly in US dollars, commodity prices are also affected by US dollar strength. After the financial crisis, the policies of quantitative easing pursued by the Federal Reserve and other central banks across the world have resulted in a high degree of liquidity for financial assets, which has spilled over into commodities as well, inflating commodity prices as the US dollar weakens. A reversal of these policies would see commodity prices retreating.

Market-Specific Price Drivers

Markets for other energy commodities like natural gas and coal have their own peculiarities. While they correlate well with oil markets in terms of financialization and regulations, supply/demand balances are more often calculated regionally than on a global basis, as these markets are considerably less integrated than global oil markets. A short summary of the factors affecting pricing in the natural gas and coal markets is presented here.

Natural Gas   Natural gas markets are localized and fragmented due to the inability to transport gas cheaply in the absence of pipelines. LNG terminal infrastructure is also sparse in many parts of the world, and this has led to the use of multiple pricing mechanisms and regional benchmarks for natural gas. Traditionally, natural gas contracts have been of a long-term nature, with gas prices linked to prevailing oil prices by a formula – this practice is known as oil indexation or oil price escalation. Thus, natural gas pricing depends not only on long-term supply vs. demand, but also on developments in other markets like crude oil or power generation. Natural gas prices and power prices are closely linked, and both prices are regulated in many countries. However, with the growth in pipeline infrastructure, natural gas is increasingly being transacted based on benchmark prices, adjusted for location basis. The prominent benchmarks for natural gas are Henry Hub Natural Gas in the USA, the National Balancing Point (NBP) in the UK, and Zeebrugge and TTF (Title Transfer Facility) in Continental Europe. While Henry Hub is a physical hub for the pipeline system, NBP and many other European hubs are virtual hubs for trading. Using prices determined from trading at a hub, where supply and demand interact, to set contract prices is known as gas-on-gas competition and is currently the most common pricing mechanism for natural gas. Oil price escalation is still a significant pricing method, especially in the Asia Pacific region where there are no established price benchmarks for natural gas.

Coal   Coal pricing is largely driven by the demand for electricity and the cost of labor and transportation of coal from mines to power plants. Since natural gas is a substitute fuel used for power generation, gas prices also affect the pricing of coal. Additionally, as the mining cost is only a fraction of the total price of coal paid by the final customer, and logistics account for a significant portion of the cost, the freight market also influences coal prices, and traders who deal with logistics are a large part of the coal market. Logistics providers are involved in moving coal from mines to ports, shipping in bulk to destination ports and splitting cargos and delivering them to final customers like power plants and industrial consumers, thus playing a major role in setting physical premiums for delivery. Traders have also served to reduce the credit risk inherent in long-term physical contracts between producers and consumers and provide financing for shipments.

Trading companies have been able to play a major role in coal markets due to the development of liquid coal price benchmarks. The most traded benchmarks of thermal coal include API 2 coal delivered into northwest Europe – Amsterdam Rotterdam Antwerp (ARA), API 4 coal originating from Richards Bay, South Africa, and Newcastle coal from Australia. Increasingly, prices for coal delivered into China have also become important benchmarks as China's appetite for steam coal increases. These price indices are calculated by price providers like Argus, McCloskey, and globalCOAL, and are used in over-the-counter (OTC) financial and physical contracts.

SUMMARY

The US dollar-denominated trade system of energy commodities and the importance of energy security in the modern world have made energy reserves into particularly strategic assets. The vulnerabilities of energy supply chains have been laid bare over the last couple of decades, and emerging powers have been making efforts to mitigate risks through alternative methods of supply and trading. Heightened energy price volatility, combined with the significant energy component in the cost of goods and services, has pressured the finances of consumers and made fuel price risk management imperative.

In this chapter, we have provided an overview of commodities, the main energy commodities, their sources and uses, and the factors affecting the markets for these commodities. We have focused on crude oil and how it is refined into various petroleum products destined for different uses. The price of a refined product is influenced by the supply/demand balance for that product and supply chain-related factors like upstream prices as well as macroeconomic conditions, among others.

In the next chapter, we will take a closer look at the impact of fuel price movements on the financial health of major energy consumers, including airlines, shipping companies, refineries, power producers, and industrial consumers. The commonality of price drivers for crude oil and downstream products translates into a high correlation between the prices of crude oil and products, and this suggests opportunities for the use of traditional hedging mechanisms as well as techniques like proxy hedging in risk management. We will also introduce the rationale for hedging, the basic market structure, and common instruments used for risk management in the fuel markets.

CHAPTER 2

Major Energy Consumers and the Rationale for Fuel Hedging

"We aren't addicted to oil, but our cars are."

—James Woolsey

WTI and Brent Crude Oil are among the most traded commodities in the world. Yet, not one oil trader uses crude oil in his/her car. Extracted crude oil is a mixture of chemicals that are useful for different purposes, ranging from fuel for gasoline or diesel engines to jet fuel for airplanes. Fuel consumers use energy in different forms and their composite demand drives the demand for crude oil. In this chapter, we discuss major fuel-consuming industries such as airlines, shipping, oil refining, and the power-generation industries before elucidating the financial risks faced by these industries. Airline industry metrics are used together with insights from financial statements to emphasize the significance of fuel price-related risks in the context of the overall risks faced by airlines. With reference to the basic principles of modern portfolio theory (MPT), we discuss the concept of hedging in the case of the airline industry to illustrate its potential benefits.

Once the rationale for hedging is established, we present the motivation for the development of the derivatives market and how it complements physical commodity transactions. We then introduce commodity derivatives such as futures and options, which form the building blocks for hedging strategies that will be discussed in subsequent chapters. Before we delve into the details of fuel consumers, we begin with a look at commodity-market participants and their exposures to commodity prices.

ENERGY MARKET PARTICIPANTS

Commodity market participants can be classified on the basis of their exposure to commodity prices. A broad classification of market users would include producers, consumers, refiners, and intermediaries (Figure 2.1). Commodity producers are companies that mine for, drill, or produce commodities and whose revenues depend directly on the price at which the

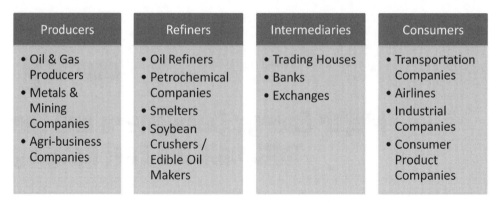

FIGURE 2.1 Commodity market participants

commodities can be sold in the market. Examples of commodity producers include oil and gas producers, metals and mining companies, and agricultural companies (including farmers).

Commodity consumers are industries or companies that transform commodities for end-users or use commodities themselves in order to deliver services to their customers. Examples of commodity consumers include airlines, consumer goods companies, car makers, etc. Nearly every industry uses commodities, especially energy commodities like electricity and petroleum-based fuels.

Refiners or transformers act as both producers and consumers, as they consume a particular commodity and produce another. Examples of transformers include oil refiners, power producers, edible oil makers, etc. Commodity market intermediaries also perform vital functions including transportation, blending, bulk-breaking, financing, and risk management of commodities, in addition to profiting from arbitrages and price movements. Trading companies and financial firms are the main intermediaries in the market. Commodity speculators and investors also form a part of the commodity market landscape, as they provide liquidity to the commodity markets.

We can categorize market participants by their rationale for participating in the market into three major categories: hedgers, speculators, and arbitrageurs. Hedgers transact in commodity markets to manage the price risks that their businesses face due to their exposure to commodities. Speculators provide liquidity to hedgers and trade based on a view of market prices. Arbitrageurs engage in trades to earn a riskless profit, thereby improving market efficiency by profiting from dislocations or mispricing of assets in the market while also contributing to liquidity.

Major participants in the energy markets include producers, traders, refiners, consumers, and financial institutions. We describe these participants and their motivations for dealing in energy markets in this section.

Energy Producers Major energy commodities that are traded globally include crude oil, refined products, coal, natural gas, and power. We consider the example of the oil markets as they are the largest of the energy markets. On the producer side, the largest entities are national oil companies (NOCs), which account for over 75% of global production and 90% of the world's oil reserves. Crude oil is sold by these producers under long-term contracts at official selling prices (OSPs), which may be indexed to market benchmarks. Some of the largest national oil and gas companies are Saudi Aramco (Saudi Arabia), Sinopec (China), China National Petroleum Corporation (China), Gazprom (Russia), Petrobras (Brazil), PDVSA (Venezuela), ADNOC (UAE), and National Iranian Oil Company (Iran). Oil majors and exploration and production (E&P) companies are the other large producers present in the energy markets. Oil majors are multinational companies, which are vertically integrated over the supply chain and engage in all activities including upstream exploration, production, refining, marketing, and distribution. They are among the largest traders in the physical markets and use their existing production, refining, and storage assets to trade profitably in the oil markets. The companies generally regarded as oil majors are Exxon Mobil, Royal Dutch Shell, BP, Chevron, Total, and Conoco Phillips.

Intermediaries The intermediaries in this sector mainly consist of trading houses and financial players. Trading houses trade in the commodity markets and act as an interface between producers and end consumers. In the past, trading houses usually did not have physical assets whose input/output could be traded, but in recent times, independent traders have been expanding by purchasing storage and upstream assets as well. They have also established a large presence in the paper markets for commodities, as banks and other financial entities have been pulling back due to regulatory and capital considerations. Some of the largest trading houses include Vitol Group, Glencore Xstrata plc, Trafigura Beheer BV, Mercuria Energy Group, and Gunvor.

Banks Traditionally, banks have been major players in the hedging market, providing customized OTC derivatives to both producers and consumers, and providing financing for acquisitions, trade, and working capital. In the last decade, banks also ventured into the physical markets by owning warehousing companies, pipelines, and refineries. However, with increased scrutiny and a proposed clampdown on banks' physical market activities under US regulations, and the tighter capital requirements going forward, many banks have been shuttering their commodity trading operations, especially in the physical arena. Banks continue to be the main providers of investment products linked to commodities such as structured notes and indices. In recent times, exchange-traded products like ETFs and exchange-traded notes (ETNs) have gained popularity in terms of helping investors access the commodity markets.

Consumers On the consumption side, the International Energy Agency provides data on the uses of energy by product. Industrial users account for 80% of coal used, while natural gas usage is distributed across industrial use, transport, and other uses including agriculture, commercial and public services, and residential use. Transportation accounted for 63.7% of oil consumption globally, while industrial use accounted for 8.5% of oil consumption in 2012. The residential and commercial sectors are the other major energy users. A breakdown of oil usage by sector is shown in Figure 2.2.

Transportation uses include personal vehicles like cars to commercial vehicles, which is the largest use, followed by air transportation and public vehicles like buses and trains. The shipping sector is also a significant consumer of energy. The fuels used for transportation range from gasoline and gasoil (diesel) for road transport, to jet kerosene for aircraft, and bunker fuel for maritime uses. As per the IEA, all of the net increase in oil demand over the coming years will come from the transport sector in emerging economies.

Residential and commercial usage relates to heating and cooling (air-conditioning), lighting, and electricity usage for appliances, while industrial usage is concentrated among

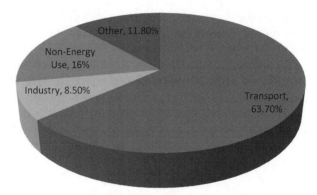

FIGURE 2.2   World oil consumption for 2012 by sector; total consumption amounted to 3652 Mtoe (million tons of oil equivalent)
Source: International Energy Agency, © OECD/IEA 2014, Key World Energy Statistics, IEA Publishing; modified by John Wiley and Sons Ltd. License: www.iea.org/t&c/termsandconditions.

industries like oil refining, chemicals, steel, metals manufacturing, and mining. The petrochemical industry uses products like naphtha and LPG as feedstock. Other energy sources, like coal and natural gas, are heavily used in electricity generation. Among these sectors, only companies or industries with significant scale and price exposure participate in the commodity paper markets. Foremost among these are airlines and shipping companies, as well as refiners and electricity producers and some industrial users.

The major players in the energy market have different motivations, as summarized in Table 2.1.

TABLE 2.1   Commodity market players and their motivations

S. No.	Commodity market player	Physical position	Agenda
1	Producers	Long	Strategic or tactical hedging, financing, asset optimization
2	Refiners	Long/short	Hedging refining margins
3	Trading houses	Long/short/none	Speculative trading, arbitrage, hedging physical cargos
4	Airlines/transportation sector/corporates	Short	Hedging fuel costs
5	Petrochemicals/chemicals	Long/short	Hedging feedstock prices, hedging output where possible
6	Banks	Long/short/none	Hedging client flows, proprietary trades (significantly reduced in recent times), hedging index investments
7	Hedge funds and other investors	Long/short/none	Hedging physical positions, speculative trades

RISKS FACED BY FUEL CONSUMERS – THE CASE OF THE AIRLINE INDUSTRY

Corporations can be active in different industries and sectors but they are all exposed to similar types of risks. Chief among these risks are:

- Industry risk (risk to the business model of the firm, arising either from external factors like competition or changes in demand/supply balances or internal factors).
- Operational risk (risk due to failings in processes or systems or errors made by people).
- Market risk (the risk that market prices of inputs change).
- Credit risk (the risk that a customer or counterparty fails to pay or deliver contracted goods or services).
- Liquidity risk (an inability to purchase inputs at reference prices or an inability to secure financing for operations).
- Legal risk (risk due to uncertainty in rules or legal proceedings).
- Reputational risk (risk of events impacting the firm's reputation).

These risks can be broadly classified into two categories – those related to the specific product market in which the firm operates (operational or enterprise risk) and those related to financial markets (financial risk). In the case of airline companies, the risks listed above are all relevant because airlines are exposed to both financial and operational risks, including those stemming from rising labor and capital costs as well as risks related to the demand for air transport. Moreover, compared with other sectors, the airline industry is highly leveraged and has relatively low margins and returns on equity (ROE).

Airline Industry – Metrics and Operational Risks

In the simplest terms, airline company performance is impacted by the demand for air travel and the cost of providing air transport. The airline industry has a number of performance metrics, which can help identify commercial risks. We take a brief look at some of the most popular metrics used by the industry.

As airlines fly many different routes and planes with different passenger configurations and levels of occupancy, in addition to the variation in airfares paid by passengers, metrics for the industry abstract from this complexity by focusing on the most common attributes of air transport – passengers/seats and distance flown. Metrics based on these attributes are defined as follows.

- Passenger traffic is measured in revenue passenger kilometers (RPK) – defined as one passenger transported for one kilometer. For example, 180 passengers transported for 1000 km would account for 180,000 RPK of passenger traffic:

$$RPK = \sum Passengers * Kilometers$$

- Yield is the average revenue that is generated per passenger kilometer. It is calculated by dividing the total revenue from a flight or set of flights by the total number of passenger kilometers carried:

$$Yield = \frac{\sum Revenue}{\sum RPK}$$

For example, a flight that generates 20,000 USD in revenue for transporting 180 passengers for a distance of 1000 km corresponds to a yield of 0.111 USD per RPK.

■ Airline capacity is measured in terms of available seat kilometers (ASK) – defined as one available seat flown one kilometer. Thus, if a flight operates with 200 seats and travels a distance of 1000 km, this corresponds to 200,000 ASK of capacity:

$$ASK = \sum Available\ Seats * Kilometers$$

■ Airline expenses are classified per unit of capacity to arrive at a unit cost figure that facilitates comparison. The unit cost of an airline is the average operating expense per unit of capacity, also termed CASK (cost per available seat kilometer). Therefore,

$$Unit\ Cost\ or\ CASK = \frac{\sum Operating\ Expense}{\sum ASK}$$

■ Another important metric that is used in the industry is the load factor. This is a measure of capacity utilization for an airline. It is the ratio of revenue-generating traffic carried to the total capacity. That is,

$$Load\ Factor = \frac{\sum RPK}{\sum ASK}$$

■ Trends in RPK, ASK, and load factors for the airline industry are shown in Figure 2.3.

Airline profits are dependent on four metrics according to the equation below:

$$Operating\ Profit = RPK * Yield - ASK * Unit\ Cost$$

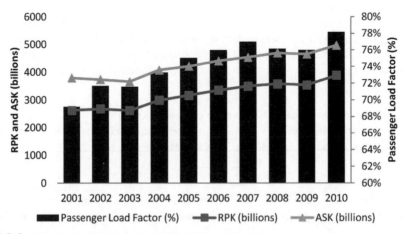

FIGURE 2.3 Trends in airline industry RPK, ASK, and load factors
Source: © International Air Transport Association, 2011. World Air Transport Statistics, 55th Edition, 2011.

In order to increase profits, an airline needs to address the risks affecting the revenue side and the cost of operations. Airlines can increase revenues by raising their RPK, either by attracting more passengers or by adding more flights. Adding flights increases unit costs, while attracting more passengers can be accomplished by lowering fares; however, this impacts revenues by reducing the yield.

Airlines can also increase profits by reducing expenses, either by reducing the ASK flown or by lowering unit costs. Lowering the ASK by lowering the number of flights flown has a negative effect on the RPK that can be generated. Similarly, lowering costs by cutting back on service quality can have a negative effect on the revenue that can be generated, as the market share of the airline would likely drop. Thus, all these factors interact with each other and cannot be viewed in isolation.

Market conditions are critical to determining which measures can be utilized to increase profitability. In cases where demand is inelastic, airlines can increase fares and improve their yields. Underserved markets can allow an airline to improve their RPK by increasing their frequency of flights. Conversely, elastic demand or saturated markets limit the ability of airlines to increase profitability by boosting revenue. Companies in industries where lower-cost alternatives are not present, or those that have more flexibility to manage costs, can profit by switching to a lower-cost model or by managing their costs better. This can be achieved through the lowering of labor costs or by managing other operating expenses, especially fuel costs. Airlines can also pursue business models that reduce unit costs by avoiding long-term capital expenditures. For instance, resorting to leasing vs. buying aircraft can make airlines more nimble in adjusting capacity to market requirements.

The trend in airline profits over the last few years is shown in Figure 2.4. Note that while the industry RPK and ASK have grown steadily over the last decade, profits have been volatile – mainly due to the variability in unit costs. Financial risks have contributed significantly to this volatility, as we will see in the next section.

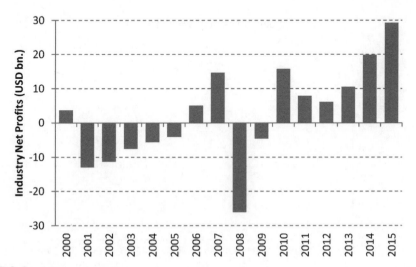

FIGURE 2.4   Industry net profits
Sources: International Air Transport Association, 2014. Annual Review 2014. Tony Tyler, Director General & CEO, IATA. 70th Annual General Meeting, Doha.

Airline Industry – Financial Risks

The airline industry is a very volatile industry, experiencing risks and challenges across the spectrum, ranging from operational and financial risks to risks related to changes in the regulatory and economic landscape, in addition to significant event risks linked to weather, terrorism, and natural disasters (such as volcanic eruptions). Airlines can manage these risks in a variety of ways, both operational and financial. Mature airlines have a codified risk-management strategy and accompanying organizational infrastructure for the implementation and monitoring of such strategy. Common operational risk-management methods include improving the fuel consumption efficiency of aircraft, adjusting the fleet mix, network optimization, and revenue management. Companies are also affected by financial market variables such as interest rates, foreign exchange rates, and commodity prices. We can list the main financial risks as follows:

1. equity risk
2. debt risk
3. foreign exchange risk
4. commodity risk.

Equity Risk   Equity risk for companies is the risk that they are unable to raise capital through the equity markets for funding expansion, acquisitions, restructuring, or other activities of the company. Investor appetite for purchasing a firm's equity depends on the current financial performance of the company and its outlook over the foreseeable future. Sectoral and company performance relative to the market influences demand for new equity issuances. Historically, airlines as a sector has had low returns on invested capital relative to the volatility in airline equity prices, which has been disproportionately high (Figures 2.5 and 2.6). Equity risk consists of company-specific risks as well as market risks, which depend on the expected

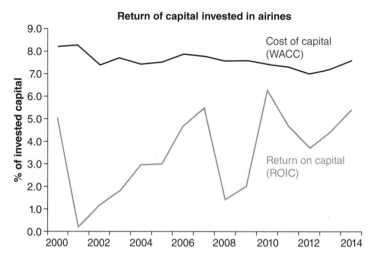

FIGURE 2.5   Return on invested capital vs. weighted average cost of capital for airlines
Source: © International Air Transport Association, 2015. Economic Performance of The Airline Industry. Mid-Year Report, 2014. All Rights Reserved. Available on IATA Economics page.

FIGURE 2.6 Airline stock index performance vs. S&P 500
Data Source: Bloomberg.

performance of the industry in the future and broader economic factors like GDP growth, liquidity, regulations, etc.

Debt Risk Similarly, debt risk is the risk that companies cannot borrow in the debt markets for financing ongoing activities or for long-term investments. Companies can either issue debt in the capital markets or borrow using syndicated loans or traditional loans (Figure 2.7). To incentivize purchases of capital goods like aircraft, export credit agencies (ECAs) provide guarantees for financing made for such purchases. Companies can also make use of leases to acquire capital goods. Airlines in particular are highly capital intensive, having a need for long-term sources of a large quantum of funds for purchasing assets including planes and landing rights, and therefore use significant amounts of debt. They also have short-term financing needs, for purchasing fuel and running operations, which are usually met by the banking sector. Any deterioration in the credit quality of an airline or a paucity of funding can cause disruptions to airline operations and investments.

In addition to securing debt, the price at which debt is raised is also important for corporations. When raising debt with floating-rate interest payments linked to a benchmark

FIGURE 2.7 Types of debt financing utilized by airline companies

interest rate like the London Interbank Offered Rate (LIBOR), corporates are exposed to interest rate risk (i.e., the risk that interest rates may rise). Especially in the case of long-term borrowings, interest rate risk is significant as the tenor of borrowing (typically 5–10 years) usually spans an economic cycle. Overall credit quality is also important, as corporations borrow at a spread over LIBOR. For example, an airline may secure a loan to finance its purchase of aircraft and repay over 10 years at a rate of LIBOR + 300 basis points (3%). This spread of 300 basis points reflects the riskiness of the debt and can be significantly higher when the company, or the industry as a whole, suffers from low profitability and high volatility.

From looking at airline balance sheets, it becomes apparent that flight equipment is the biggest asset for most airlines, especially for older airline companies, which have historically owned most of their fleet. On the liability side, airlines use a significant amount of long-term debt to finance these equipment purchases. In many cases, the long-term debt amount can be comparable to the equity capital of the airline. This is usually the case for airlines with higher growth prospects that need to purchase and finance more aircraft.

For newer airlines, which depend on an asset-light model for expansion, aircraft lease rentals can be a major cost. Essentially, aircraft can be bought outright by the airline from manufacturers or leased from specialized leasing firms that have a large portfolio of aircraft. Aircraft can also be purchased, sold to a leasing company, and leased back over a period – this is called "sale-and-leaseback," which is a common means of financing purchases. Leases can be classified as finance leases or operating leases. Under finance leases, the aircraft lease payments can be capitalized and the aircraft can be purchased by or transferred to the airline at the end of the lease period, while under operating leases, the airline company pays to rent the aircraft and returns it to the lessor at the end of the lease period. Alternatively, the company issues debt or raises funds through the loan market. In either case, firms need to arrange for financing to purchase the aircraft and this involves multiple risks including liquidity risk, credit risk, interest rate risk, and potentially foreign exchange risk (if borrowings are in different currencies).

Foreign Exchange Risk   Foreign exchange (FX) risk is the risk arising from a corporation's exposure to changes in currency exchange rates. This is especially relevant to industries where cash inflows and outflows are denominated in different currencies. The airline industry operates across countries with different currencies, thereby requiring good management of FX exposures. Even if an airline does not operate across borders, it is still required to purchase capital stock like airplanes, which are usually denominated in currencies like the US dollar or Euro (as major airplane manufacturers are concentrated in a few countries). Fuel costs are also typically incurred in US dollars, as commodities traded globally are denominated mainly in US dollars. Companies can manage currency risks by matching their inflows and outflows in various currencies using foreign operations and by hedging any mismatches in cash flows using FX derivatives.

Currency risks can also be managed to some extent by matching revenues against costs incurred in those currencies, but hedging provides an efficient avenue for foreign exchange risk management.

Fuel Price Risk   Commodity price risk is the risk that a movement in commodity prices affects the profitability of the company. Fuel consumers like airlines, where fuel costs form a large percentage of their operating expenses, are significantly exposed to price swings in the commodity markets (Figure 2.8). With the rise in price levels of oil over the last decade, fuel

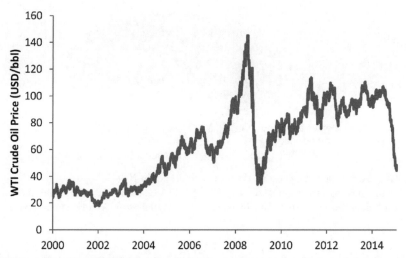

FIGURE 2.8 WTI crude oil front-month futures price
Data Sources: NYMEX, Bloomberg.

costs are either the highest or second highest component of operating costs for firms across the airline industry. Fuel price risk can be managed either through contracting with physical suppliers or by using financial hedges. Increasing operational efficiencies also reduces the exposure to commodity price risk, but does not eliminate it completely.

A large portion of most airlines' revenues accrues from passenger travel, as opposed to cargo, and this makes capacity utilization and routing very important to managing revenue. However, airlines have limited room to adjust fares or levy fuel surcharges in the face of extreme competition in the passenger travel market.

On the operating cost front, fuel expenses and staff costs are the two largest expenses for most airlines. This is true for both budget carriers and full-service airlines, as can be seen from the sample income statements provided in Appendix A at the end of this chapter. Operational measures can be used to reduce staff costs and this is a major part of the business model of budget airlines. Fuel expenses, in contrast, are unpredictable and are the item that an airline has the least amount of control over. Airlines can optimize their operational procedures to realize some fuel efficiencies, but they do not exercise much influence on the price of fuel. Thus, fuel price volatility directly impacts the income variability of airlines. We take a look at a breakdown of costs for airlines in Figure 2.9.

Fuel cost has grown in importance over the last decade, with crude oil prices rising steadily from 2004 to 2008, culminating in a high of over 140 $/bbl in 2008, as seen in Figure 2.10. Airlines in particular have had to calibrate their business models to account for a new regime of higher energy prices. As per the International Air Transport Association (IATA), fuel costs for a sample of 45 major airlines globally constituted 13.6% of operating costs in 2001 and rose to 32.3% in 2008. A recent study of operating statistics of 30 of the largest global airlines revealed that fuel costs account for over a third (35%) of operating expenses. Fuel costs as a percentage of total expenses are higher for Asian airlines and in the USA. This could be due to the fact that jet fuel is highly taxed in Asia and that staff costs are lesser in comparison with European airlines. Staff costs in the USA have been reduced because of court-mandated cost cuts at companies that filed for bankruptcy.

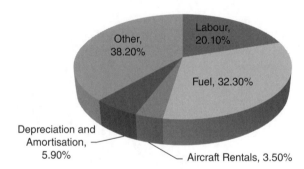

FIGURE 2.9   Airline operating cost shares for major airlines in 2008
Source: International Air Transport Association, 2015. IATA Economics Briefing – Airline Fuel and Labour Cost Share. February 2010. All Rights Reserved. Available on IATA Economics page.

Oil market participants have also experienced extreme volatility as the price of oil dropped from its high in 2008 to levels of about 40 $/bbl by the end of 2008, only to rebound to 100 $/bbl by early 2011. In late 2014, oil prices again collapsed from over 110 $/bbl to 50 $/bbl.

Fuel expenses can be managed in a variety of ways. For most companies, it is easier to manage them directly with their physical supplier by making use of fixed-price physical contracts. For more mature companies, which have sufficient capital and organizational breadth to institute a risk-management program, fuel hedging in the paper markets can be of great use in managing fuel price risks. There is an added dimension of credit risk from contracts or hedging agreements that also needs to be monitored. Airline firms further have some exposure to credit risk on trade receivables, though the short duration of payment terms and bank guarantees help to protect against this risk.

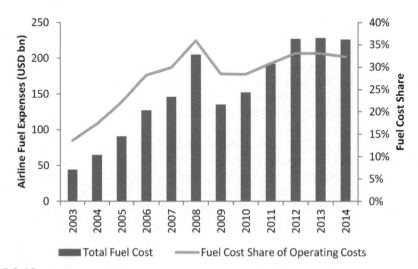

FIGURE 2.10   Fuel cost evolution
Source: IATA, Economic Industry Performance – Forecast Table (IATA Economics), IATA Fact Sheet; Fuel, Jun 2015.

RISKS FACED BY OTHER MAJOR FUEL CONSUMERS

In this section, we take a brief look at other major energy consumers including shipping companies, refineries, and power producers.

Shipping Companies

Risks faced by shipping companies are substantially similar to airlines with interest rate risks, foreign exchange risks, credit risk, liquidity risk, and fuel price risks being significant financial risks for these firms. Additionally, shipping revenue depends on cargo capacity, productivity, and freight rates. Freight rates for certain routes are traded like commodities in the OTC markets and this increases the variability of revenues for shipping companies.

There is no standard cost classification for the shipping industry. One way to classify the costs is shown in Figure 2.11.

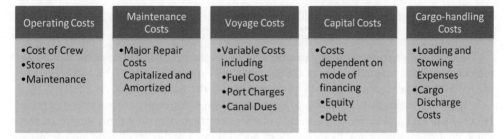

FIGURE 2.11 Cost classification for shipping industry

After capital costs incurred mainly at the beginning of a ship's life, voyage costs and operating costs are the two largest constituents of total cost. Fuel cost accounts for a large fraction of the voyage cost. Total costs, and consequently unit costs, vary based on the size and age of a ship. Unit costs in shipping reduce as the size of the ship increases. As ships age, the total cost decreases due to a drop in capital costs but overall operating, voyage, and maintenance costs are higher than those for new ships.

To emphasize the significance of fuel costs, a new, alternative breakdown of shipping firms' costs shows the following cost elements:

- fuel costs
- terminal costs
- maintenance costs
- vessel costs.

Terminal costs comprise moving and storage costs at terminals (cargo-handling costs), while vessel costs mainly consist of running costs, time chartering, depreciation, and lease rentals (operating cost, capital cost, and voyage cost ex-fuel). Many shipping companies separate out fuel cost information from operating expenses when presented with a classification similar to the one above (see Figure 2.12 for a comparison of the two classification schemes).

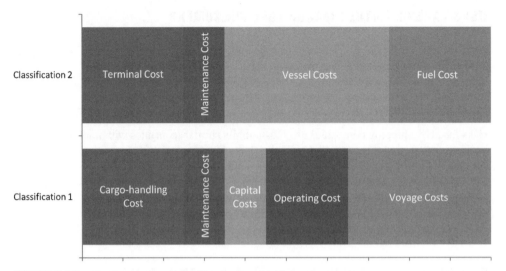

FIGURE 2.12 Two types of cost classification for shipping companies

A survey of shipping company income statements showed that fuel costs for major shipping companies accounted for about 21% of operating expenses in 2013. The cost breakdown for AP Møller Mærsk, the largest shipping company in the world, is shown in Figure 2.13.

Thus, like airline firms, shipping companies are also significantly impacted by fuel prices. However, in addition to the exposure to volatile fuel prices, shipping firms do not exercise much control over revenues. Constituents of both revenues and costs of shipping companies are traded, as freight rates and bunker fuel respectively. The correlation between freight rates and bunker fuel has generally been positive and peaked around 2008, when correlations across assets were high, but has been lower recently. This low correlation implies that a rise in

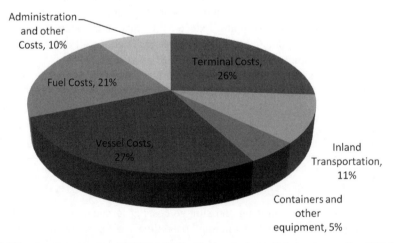

FIGURE 2.13 Breakdown of total EBIT (earnings before interest and taxes) costs for AP Møller Mærsk

Data Source: AP Møller Mærsk A/S. Annual Report, 2013.

bunker prices is not accompanied by an increase in freight rates, thus necessitating hedging of both commodities. However, most large shipping companies do hedge a portion of fuel price risks, but they generally do not engage in strategic hedging of freight rates. Therefore, the market for freight hedging is mainly dominated by traders and freight users. Instead, shipping companies pass on a percentage of fuel costs and other risks using surcharges – including bunker contribution, currency adjustment factors, and emissions control area surcharges. This practice has also become very common in the airline industry. However, their pricing power to impose surcharges has been limited in recent times, and is one of the reasons for an increase in consolidation and the formation of alliances in the industry.

Land Transportation

Rail and road transportation companies are also major users of fuel. Fuels such as diesel, gasoil, or gasoline are used. Thus, the risks faced by these companies with respect to oil price are similar to those faced by airlines and shipping companies. Additionally, these firms typically operate in a fixed-rate environment for fares, implying that fuel price hedging is even more important to guarantee margins, as there is no flexibility to adjust revenues. Commercial service providers like postal organizations or delivery companies have been able to charge surcharges based on fuel prices, but this is typically not the case for passenger transport companies.

Oil Refining, Petrochemicals, and Power Generation

The oil-refining industry is one where firms have limited control over their output prices and are exposed to volatile input costs. The petrochemical industry also faces similar risks. Refiners are exposed to global crude oil prices, while their revenues are derived from local or regional product prices. The business model for an oil refiner, and indeed for any "processors" or "convertors," is represented in Figure 2.14.

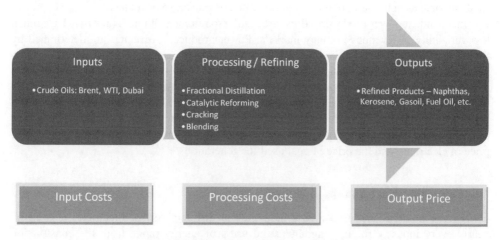

Gross Margin = Output Price – Input Costs

FIGURE 2.14 Business model for a refiner

Oil refining is a very capital-intensive business as the setup time and costs are very high. The fixed costs for refiners include

- staff costs
- maintenance costs and insurance
- capital costs.

The floating costs include

- the cost of crude feedstock
- the cost of chemicals, additives, and catalysts
- energy costs.

Refineries aim to maximize their refining gross margins by optimizing their refineries to produce more valuable products from the same amount of crude oil. They can do so by selecting the appropriate blend of crude oil, using more complex processes to extract more products from the same amount of crude oil, and optimizing the output product mix to maximize profit.

In the course of the refining process, refiners are exposed to specific risks, including the risk of a change in crude oil prices, the risk of changes in product prices, timing risks due to potentially different pricing dates for crude oil and products, in addition to basis risks in terms of the difference in product specifications from those of commercially traded products. They are also exposed to currency risks inherent in the procurement of crude oil at USD-denominated prices and the sale of refined products in local currencies.

Refiners can address risks arising from changes in crude oil and product prices by locking in their margins using instruments called crack spread swaps. These swaps can also be structured to take into account the time lag between the fixing of the purchase price of crude oil and the pricing of the oil products into which it is converted. Inventory values can also be protected against the variability in prices of oil or products stored over and beyond the base level of inventory carried by the business. Price risks related to the inventory of expensive catalysts such as palladium, platinum, or other metals must also be addressed.

Independent power producers (IPPs) are similar to refiners, although they may have much less variability in revenues in many markets. Power producers' revenues are determined by the price at which their output is sold, and this could be fixed or market-determined. However, power producers' inputs – such as coal and natural gas – are subject to fluctuations in price and this impacts the margins earned by these companies. Analogous to the crack spread for refineries, power producers are exposed to the spark spread, which is the difference in price between the power produced and the natural gas used to generate it. Similarly, power producers who use coal are exposed to the dark spread, which is the difference between the price of electricity and the price of coal used for generation.

Industrial Users of Energy Commodities

Energy commodities are used across industries in different forms. Electricity is used by nearly every industry for lighting. Industrial users of energy range from the construction and manufacturing industries to agricultural producers and mining companies. Refining and chemical industries are major users of energy commodities, both as a feedstock as well as for their own consumption. Natural gas is the most commonly used industrial energy commodity. It is widely used in the pulp and paper, food-processing, mining, and metals industries.

As per a survey of the Australian energy industry, energy costs for mining companies account for about 15% of total costs and are a fast-growing component of costs, due to the increasing energy intensity of mining operations. According to research on the energy intensity of the Australian economy, as of 2010, the mining sector was the fastest-growing energy user, growing at an average rate of 6% per annum. Along with the agricultural sector, it was the only other sector to record an increase in energy intensity over the previous two decades. Energy costs for steel manufacturers can be 20% to 40% of the total cost of production. Thus, industrial users also face similar volatility in their margins as transportation companies, because of the variability in fuel prices.

THE CASE FOR HEDGING

In the previous sections, we have looked at the risks impacting energy consumers. In many of these cases, risks arising from adverse commodity price movements dominated other financial risks for these companies. Managing these risks is paramount to maintaining the financial health of a company. Financial hedging of these risks is one of the major ways in which a firm can minimize these risks.

Hedging can be defined as the use of a risk-management strategy to minimize losses arising from an investment or position. It is the use of instruments or techniques to protect against fluctuations in market variables such as commodity prices, foreign exchange rates, securities prices, etc. Hedging can be achieved operationally or financially. For our purposes, we will be dealing with financial hedges as they are more widely applicable.

The Effect of Hedging on Airline Stock Price Volatility

There are many empirical studies on whether hedging is necessary or beneficial to corporations. We will look at some of this evidence in a later chapter. However, at this point, let us consider the effect of hedging on the performance and financial viability of airline companies. We take the case of the US airline industry to illustrate the effect that oil prices have on firm values. We use the WTI crude oil price as the benchmark for fuel prices. In reality, airlines use jet fuel, which is derived from crude oil, but WTI crude oil is much more widely traded than jet fuel and correlates well with it. We first look at the correlation between stock price returns and WTI crude oil returns. The correlation is calculated using a yearly window and charted over the period 1990–2008, as shown in Figure 2.15. We chose this period as the hedging intensity was generally lower than it has been in recent years.

It can be seen that the correlation between returns of stock prices and WTI has largely been negative. In addition, the correlation became significantly more negative over the last few years of the study, when oil prices had risen to high levels. From this negative correlation, we can infer that a portfolio manager, or indeed airline companies, can reduce their risks by adding crude oil positions to their stock exposure in US airlines.

We test this hypothesis by constructing hypothetical portfolios with oil and an airline stock. We create a portfolio of one stock and 40% of the stock's value in crude oil (Figure 2.16). That is, we assume that a hedge ratio of 0.4 is maintained constant by an investor over the term of the analysis, although this would be difficult to achieve in practice as hedges are usually static

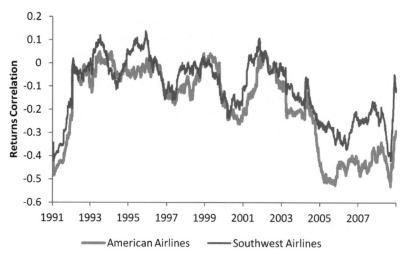

FIGURE 2.15   Correlation between airline stock price returns and WTI crude oil returns, calculated over a yearly window
Data Sources: NYMEX, NYSE, Bloomberg.

and for a fixed notional quantity. Note that this hedge ratio differs from the hedge ratio for an airline, which is the percentage of oil consumption that is hedged. This analysis also discounts the effect that any existing hedging may already have on the firm's share price. Technically, we should also be using a tradable index, like a crude oil excess return index or a total return index, which incorporates the futures roll into the position. This is an important feature of fuel hedging, whereby commodity futures contracts (which have expiry dates) are used to hedge physical exposures, thus necessitating the use of contracts with different expiries (across the forward curve) to manage exposures at different times. However, for simplicity, we disregard

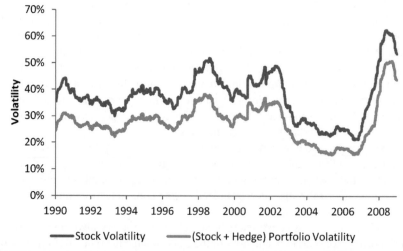

FIGURE 2.16   Historical volatility of Southwest Airlines' stock price and a hypothetical portfolio of the stock and a fuel hedge

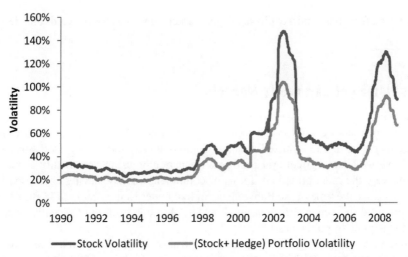

FIGURE 2.17 Historical volatility of American Airlines' stock price before and after hedging

the impact of forward curve shapes for this analysis. We chart the annualized volatility of this portfolio (the standard deviation of daily returns over a one-year window, annualized) against the historical annualized volatility of the stock (Figure 2.17).

It can be seen from the charts that the asset price volatility is significantly reduced after hedging. This lowered volatility can help reduce the financing cost for airlines, as suggested by the Modern Portfolio Theory (MPT). This theory states that investors trade off risk and return, and a rational investor would maximize his return for a particular level of risk (measured by the asset price volatility). Therefore, in addition to stabilizing the cash flows of an airline company, hedging can also reduce financing costs and increase the debt capacity, based on return-variance criteria often used by investors to optimize investment portfolios under the MPT framework (i.e., investors require higher returns for volatile assets).

Moreover, a regression between the stock price level and the correlation between stock and oil returns showed that about 30% to 40% of the variability in correlation could be explained by the stock price level. That is, correlations between oil and stock returns turned more negative as equity prices dropped, suggesting that the negative impact of increasing fuel costs on the stock price becomes even more important in distress scenarios for airline stocks.

COMMODITY DERIVATIVE MARKETS

In the previous chapter, we looked at the drivers for commodity prices in physical markets. However, physical markets are becoming increasingly linked to financial (or paper) markets for commodities. In many cases, benchmark prices for physical transactions are set by the paper market, due to the higher liquidity available in paper markets. In this section, we discuss the functioning of paper markets and the instruments traded in these markets. We will explain how the physical markets are linked to paper markets, and some of the market conventions used in the paper market. To start with, we describe how the commodity markets have evolved over the years, from being purely physical spot markets to venues for forwards and derivatives trading.

A Brief History of Commodity Markets

A commodity market is a place where buyers and sellers gather to trade in commodities. Commodity markets operate on the basis of certain rules and practices, which enable the exchange of goods in an organized manner. Commodities markets have their origins in the trade of livestock and agricultural products via barter or using commodity money. Gold and silver were the most prominent forms of commodity money, having been used in bank transactions since the time of the Babylonians in Iraq under Hammurabi (1754 BC). Gold and silver were used in exchange for commodities or labor and even until recently, money was pegged to the price of gold and silver.

Commodity markets and derivative markets have been intertwined from the outset. According to Aristotle, Thales of Miletus, an early Greek philosopher, had once predicted the weather and the resulting good harvest of olives. Thales profited from this prediction by reserving olive presses in advance of the harvest and renting them at high prices once the forecast materialized, akin to profiting from a derivatives transaction called an option. Commodity markets can be physical or financial. While physical markets have been in vogue for thousands of years, the earliest mention of commodity markets resembling present-day financial markets is of the rice futures market in Osaka, which was subsequently formalized in Dojima (near Osaka) during the late 17th century. Osaka was the rice capital of Japan, with many warehouses and merchants already dealing in rice-backed warehouse receipts (auction bills), as well as loans to warehouses backed by future harvests of rice (prepayment bills). Rice and silver were used interchangeably as currency during that period, and the market was legalized out of the need to maintain the price stability of rice, which was the main asset of the shogunate. The Dojima futures market was formed in 1716, with contracts traded for a specific quantity of standard-grade rice for a particular future maturity date.

In Europe, the Dutch were at the forefront of innovation in the development of markets, with local fairs being used for trade in dairy products and cattle, and local weigh-houses helping to reduce transaction costs. Amsterdam was the location for the listing of the Dutch East India Company, the first joint-stock company, formed in 1602 in order to profit from the spice trade. Trading in commodity futures was intermittent, as evidenced by the tulip mania of the 17th century. Merchants entered into forward contracts to purchase tulip bulbs, while short-selling was not allowed. Tulip mania reached its height in 1636 and collapsed abruptly in the winter of 1636–7, resulting in widespread defaults.

In the USA, forward trading was formalized in the 1840s with the formation of the CBOT for trading in grain. Standardization of forward contracts, which formed the basis for futures, started in 1859. Other exchanges – including the Kansas City Board of Trade, the New York Cotton Exchange, and the Butter and Cheese Exchange of New York (later renamed the New York Mercantile Exchange) – were formed subsequently. With the introduction of the steamship, the telegraph, and transatlantic cables, commodity trading became a global market, taking non-local supply and demand into account for price formation.

Following the Second World War, government intervention in the form of agricultural policies, price supports, central planning, and outright bans on trading in futures contracts led to the regression of commodity exchanges around the world. However, after the collapse of the Bretton Woods system, many financial markets were created in the 1970s and commodity markets were revived, with new markets for oil and energy commodities being created.

In the last two decades, there have been many more innovations in the commodity markets, paralleling the growth of derivatives markets. We will discuss some of these in this chapter and in subsequent chapters.

Commodity Spot Markets and the Need for Standardization

Before we look at derivatives markets, let us examine commodity spot markets and how the need for derivatives markets arose. In the previous chapter, we described the important commodity classes, energy commodities, and the price drivers for spot prices, but we have not considered the mechanism used in spot transactions and the participants in spot markets.

Commodity spot markets typically consist of producers and consumers, who come together at a particular venue to consummate transactions. Additionally, on the consumer side, there is usually a need to tailor the location, quality, and timing of supply to individual consumers and this provides a natural opportunity for traders to address this mismatch.

A typical spot transaction works as follows (see Figure 2.18). A commodity producer sells a certain quantity of the commodity to a consumer or an intermediary (who sells it to the final consumer) and arranges for delivery. A physical contract is negotiated between the producer and the consumer/intermediary. The producer delivers the physical commodities to a designated warehouse or dock, from where the trader can pick up the goods. The trader arranges for payment, often with a letter of credit provided by a bank, and receives the title to the commodities, in the form of a warehouse receipt or a bill of lading. A "bill of lading" is a receipt from a shipping company that undertakes to deliver the underlying goods and is a transferable document. The payment to the producer is generally on a FOB (free on board) basis, meaning that the trader takes on the risks and costs associated with shipping

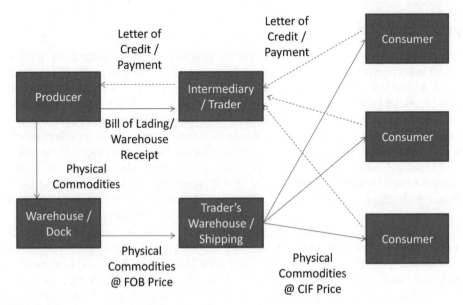

FIGURE 2.18 Stages in a physical commodity transaction

the goods. Usually, the consumer/intermediary arranges for transportation of the goods from the producer's delivery location to the consumer. This involves costs for any storage required, transportation, loading and unloading, insurance, export clearance and customs fees, taxes, etc. Pricing for the end consumer is usually on a cost, insurance, and freight (CIF) basis to defray the costs borne by the trader. FOB and CIF are two common pricing terms, and there could be many ways for commercial pricing terms to be structured in order to transfer one or more risks. The physical contract could cover one shipment of commodities or it could be a long-term transaction involving multiple deliveries.

The risks involved in a physical transaction are of three main types:

1. price risk (especially for long-term transactions)
2. counterparty risk
3. operational risk.

Price risk is present in long-term physical transactions as future realizations of spot price are variable. Counterparty risk is the risk that the counterparty to a transaction will not perform his obligations; i.e., a producer will not deliver commodities of the required grade or a consumer will not make payment. Operational risk involves risk in the completion of the transaction – mainly transportation risk, whether in the cost of transport or any mishaps in the shipment process, as well as payment for goods received. In addition, legal risks and risks in the documentation of contracts must also be considered for physical transactions.

As the commodity market size increased, there was a need to standardize the specifications of commodities traded in order to reduce the costs of verifying the quality and quantity of goods involved. Producers also required financing to grow or extract commodities and needed to secure attractive prices for their output in order to be profitable. Similarly, consumers desired certainty on future prices for commodity purchase. Thus, there was a need for longer-term markets for commodities, which led to the development of forward contracts.

Forward Contracts

In order to mitigate the price risk involved in future spot transactions, producers and consumers can enter into a forward contract. A forward contract is an Over-The-Counter (OTC) instrument that can be used to fix the price for the purchase/sale of commodities at a future date. An OTC contract is one that does not trade at a centralized venue like an exchange, but is traded directly between two counterparties. A forward contract is an agreement between two parties to buy/sell a specified amount of an underlying commodity on a fixed future date for a pre-agreed price. The party who agrees to purchase the commodity at the future date is said to be long the forward contract, while the party who agrees to sell the commodity is said to be short the forward contract. Forward contracts can be settled physically, via delivery of the underlying commodity for the pre-agreed price, or financially, where the counterparties exchange the difference between the prevailing market price and the pre-agreed price.

In the case of physical settlement, the party who is long the forward pays a price K and receives the commodity under the contract. In the case of financial settlement of a forward contract, we can represent the financial payoffs as follows. For the counterparty who is long a forward contract for a maturity of T at a fixed price of K, if the spot price at maturity of the contract is S_T, then the payout to this party is $(S_T - K)$. Conversely, the

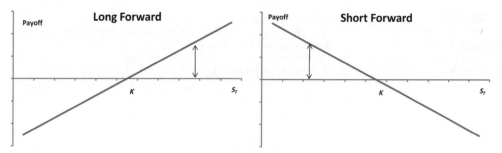

FIGURE 2.19 Payoffs from a long forward position and a short forward position

payoff to the counterparty who is short a forward contract at a fixed price of K for maturity T will be $(K - S_T)$. The payoff varies with S_T, as shown in the payoff diagrams in Figure 2.19.

For the counterparty who is long the forward, the net cost of purchase of the commodity is as follows:

$$\text{Cost of purchase in the spot market} = S_T$$
$$\text{Financial payout from the forward contract} = (S_T - K)$$
$$\text{Net cost of purchase} = S_T - (S_T - K) = K$$

Similarly, for the counterparty who is short the forward, the new realization from sale of the commodity is as follows:

$$\text{Realization from sale in the spot market} = S_T$$
$$\text{Financial payout from the forward contract} = (K - S_T)$$
$$\text{Net realization from the sale} = S_T + (K - S_T) = K$$

Thus, we can see that the party who is long the forward is compensated for a rise in the price of the commodity above the pre-agreed price K, while the party who is short the forward is compensated for a fall in the commodity price below K.

The specifications and amounts of commodities that are traded under these contracts can be customized to the requirements of the counterparties. However, for these instruments to be more liquid, the specifications need to be standardized. Forward contracts also involve counterparty risk, since one of the counterparties can default under the contract and thus, counterparties need to conduct due diligence on each other prior to transacting these contracts.

In order to minimize the counterparty risk associated with forward contracts while standardizing transaction terms, futures contracts were developed.

Futures Contracts

Futures contracts look like forward contracts but for the fact that they are traded on a futures exchange and cleared through a central counterparty (CCP). Futures contracts are agreements made between two parties to buy or sell the underlying asset at a future date for a certain price. The underlying asset for a commodity futures contract is standardized in terms of

TABLE 2.2 Exchanges and major commodities traded

Exchange	Major commodities traded
NYMEX	WTI Crude Oil; Henry Hub Natural Gas; RBOB Gasoline; NY Harbor Ultra Low Sulfur Diesel; Ethanol; Propane and Butane; Platinum, Palladium
CBOT/CME	Corn; Wheat; Soybean, Soybean Oil, Soybean Meal; Sugar; Coffee; Cocoa; Live Cattle; Lean Hogs
COMEX	Gold; Silver; Copper
ICE	Brent Crude; Gasoil; Emissions; Sugar; Coffee; Cocoa; Cotton
LME	Aluminum; Copper; Lead; Nickel; Tin; Zinc; Steel
TOCOM	Gold; Silver; Platinum; Palladium; Rubber
SICOM	Rubber
Bursa Malaysia	Crude Palm Oil
OTC markets cleared through exchanges	Oil Products – Local Benchmarks for Gasoil, Fuel Oil, Gasoline, Jet Kerosene, Naphtha; Thermal Coal, Coking Coal, Iron Ore, Freight

quality, quantity, delivery location, etc. in order to make it easier for more parties to transact in the commodity. The futures exchange also virtually eliminates credit risk by employing a margining and mark-to-market mechanism to credit gains to and debit losses from futures contract holders' accounts on a daily basis. Thus, each counterparty enters into a transaction with the exchange and does not have to evaluate the creditworthiness of the party taking the opposite side of the contract.

Commodities are traded on multiple exchanges around the world. In recent years, the exchanges industry has undergone consolidation. The major US commodity exchanges include the Chicago Mercantile Exchange (CME), the Chicago Board of Trade (CBOT), the New York Mercantile Exchange (NYMEX), and the Commodity Exchange, Inc. (COMEX), all of which are now part of the CME Group. The Intercontinental Exchange, Inc. (ICE) is a network of US and international exchanges, including the New York Board of Trade (NYBOT), the London International Financial Futures Exchange (LIFFE), the International Petroleum Exchange or IPE (now ICE Futures Europe), and the Singapore Mercantile Exchange or SMX (now ICE Futures Singapore). Other major international exchanges are the London Metal Exchange (LME), the Tokyo Commodity Exchange (TOCOM), the Singapore Commodity Exchange (SICOM), Shanghai Futures Exchange, Dubai Mercantile Exchange (DME), etc. Table 2.2 shows the commodities traded at major exchanges.

Every futures contract has specifications such as the underlying asset, the grade of the commodity, contract size, delivery arrangements, delivery periods, price quotation units, price variation allowed on a trading day, etc. We examine the main specifications of a benchmark futures contract, the contract for WTI Crude Oil, in Example 2.1.

WTI Crude Oil refers to light sweet crude oil. The deliverable crudes under the contract can be WTI or other streams of similar crudes, such as North Texas Sweet or Oklahoma Sweet, or international crudes like Brent Blend (UK) or Bonny Light (Nigeria) for which premiums or discounts are paid as mandated under the futures contract specification. The crude oil delivered under this contract needs to conform to quality specifications, such as sulfur content of 0.42% or less and API gravity of not less than 37° for US crudes. Full details on the quality specifications can be found on the exchange website.

EXAMPLE 2.1: SPECIFICATIONS OF NYMEX WTI CRUDE OIL FUTURES CONTRACT

Underlying commodity:	WTI Crude Oil
Contract unit:	1000 barrels
Price quotation:	US dollars and cents per barrel
Minimum fluctuation:	$0.01 per barrel
Delivery:	FOB at any pipeline or storage facility in Cushing, OK
Delivery period:	Between the first calendar day and the last calendar day of the delivery month

Futures contracts are listed by delivery dates. A snapshot of a sample futures contract board can be seen in Table 2.3, with details such as previous settlement price, volume, and open interest for a contract available. The settlement price is a price determined by the exchange, usually at the close of business, and is used for the marking-to-market of futures positions. Open interest is the number of contracts that are outstanding on an exchange at a particular time.

We can draw a forward curve for the commodity price using this data, as shown in Figure 2.20.

Futures curves can be of many different shapes. When futures trade at a premium to spot prices, the forward curve is said to be in contango. When the future price of the commodity trades at a discount to spot, the forward curve is said to be in backwardation. Forward curves also exhibit seasonality and other characteristics that are derived from supply and demand and

TABLE 2.3 Snapshot of WTI Crude Oil futures contract board

Contract month	Last price	Change	Previous settlement price	Estimated volume	Previous day open interest
Jul-15	58.86	−0.27	59.13	496,254	355,370
Aug-15	59.28	−0.28	59.56	160,613	178,535
Sep-15	59.56	−0.33	59.89	100,690	181,815
Oct-15	59.80	−0.33	60.13	39,556	89,955
Nov-15	60.15	−0.33	60.48	31,493	60,867
Dec-15	60.47	−0.39	60.86	74,114	218,171
Jan-16	60.67	−0.52	61.19	11,122	66,164
Feb-16	61.05	−0.41	61.46	5,517	31,741
Mar-16	61.15	−0.54	61.69	8,750	54,782
Apr-16	61.46	−0.45	61.91	1,421	17,863
May-16	61.64	−0.49	62.13	1,169	16,102
Jun-16	61.86	−0.48	62.34	15,229	70,527

Source: Bloomberg, CME Group.

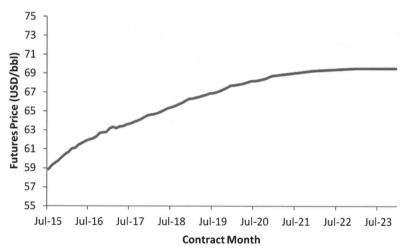

FIGURE 2.20   WTI forward curve

expectations of future supply/demand balance. A few sample forward curves are illustrated in Figures 2.21–2.23. We will discuss forward curves in detail in later chapters.

Futures Transaction Mechanism   An entity (person or company) can take a long position in the future by placing an order with a broker who is authorized to transact on the exchange. For instance, an investor can go long 10 contracts of WTI Crude Oil for delivery in December 2015 by instructing their broker to purchase 10 contracts on the exchange. There is an initial margin required for transacting in futures, and this is placed by the investor with the broker. For example, the margin for transacting in WTI futures could be $2000 per contract (this would vary based on the contract duration, volatility, and other factors). Once the margin is placed with the broker, the broker transacts on the exchange and the client is long 10 futures contracts at, say, $95/barrel.

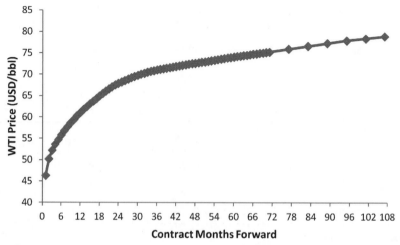

FIGURE 2.21   WTI futures curve in contango (as of January 2009)

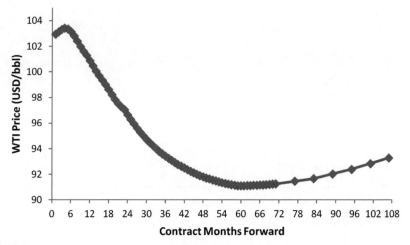

FIGURE 2.22 WTI futures curve in backwardation (as of January 2012)

After the investor enters into a futures position, their position is marked-to-market by debiting or crediting their account on a daily basis. For example, if WTI Crude Oil prices rise to $98/barrel, the investor's account will be credited with $3/barrel or $30,000 (calculated as (98–95) $/bbl*10 contracts*1000 bbl/contract). Alternatively, if the price of crude oil drops, the amount will be deducted from the investor's margin. If the margin in the investor's account drops below a certain amount, called the maintenance margin, the broker will instruct the investor to top up the account to the initial margin. This top-up amount is called the variation margin. If the margin is not topped up, the broker closes the position by liquidating the contract.

Futures contracts can be held to expiry or terminated prior to expiry. The expiry date for a futures contract is the last trading date for that particular contract, which is specified in advance by the exchange. The ability to terminate the futures contract before delivery has allowed the market to grow in size and liquidity by attracting investors, speculators, and arbitrageurs. Only

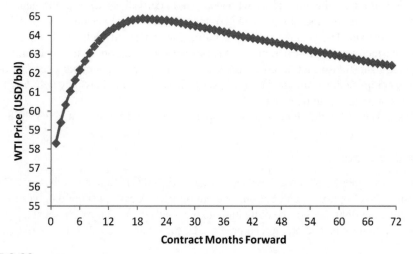

FIGURE 2.23 WTI forward curve with a hump shape (as of January 2007)

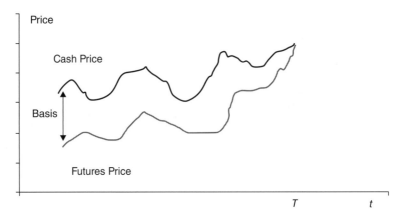

FIGURE 2.24 Convergence of the basis between cash price and futures price

investors who hold contracts on the termination of trading in a contract have to accept/deliver the underlying commodity. Most futures contracts are closed out prior to delivery by entering into the opposite type of trade. For example, the investor in the above example can close out their long position by selling 10 contracts of Dec 2015 WTI Crude Oil.

Futures prices are linked to spot prices by convergence (Figure 2.24). The difference between cash or spot price and futures price is called the "basis," and it represents either a premium or a discount to the futures price at which the spot price trades. As the delivery period for a futures contract approaches, the futures price must converge to the spot price (i.e., the basis must approach zero). This is because, if there is no convergence at expiry, then there would be an arbitrage opportunity (a situation where a riskless profit can be realized). If the futures price is lower than the spot price at expiry, then an arbitrageur can go long the future, accept delivery under the contract, and sell the commodity at the spot price, thus earning a riskless profit. Similarly, if the futures price is higher than the spot price, the arbitrageur can purchase the commodity at the spot price, go short a futures contract, and deliver the commodity under the future and earn the difference.

Traders of physical commodities who also deal in derivatives act as arbitrageurs, closing the gap between futures and spot prices and tightening the link between the spot and derivative markets. Only a small percentage of futures contracts are physically delivered, and arbitrageurs need to consider a number of parameters such as delivery location, cost to deliver, financing cost, storage and transportation costs, grade of the deliverable commodity, etc. in order to profitably complete the arbitrage. We will discuss these costs and how they help link forward prices to spot prices in future chapters.

We summarize the differences between spot, forward and future contracts in Table 2.4.

Option Contracts

An option is another basic derivative contract that is traded OTC and on exchanges. There are two main types of options – call options and put options. A call (put) option gives the holder of the option the right, but not the obligation, to buy (sell) the underlying asset at a pre-agreed price at a certain time. The pre-agreed price under the contract is called the "strike price" or

TABLE 2.4 Comparison between spot contracts, forwards, and futures

Spot contracts	Forwards	Futures
Customized commercial contract between two parties traded OTC	Customized OTC contract between two parties	Standardized contract
Usually traded bilaterally	Traded bilaterally or on an inter-bank/broker market	Traded on an exchange
Illiquid	Illiquid	More liquid than OTC contracts
Price is not transparent and transaction costs are high	Price is less transparent than futures and transaction costs are generally higher than futures	Prices are transparent and transaction costs are low
Flexible arrangements for delivery/settlement	Flexible arrangements for delivery/settlement	Standardized terms for underlying to be delivered as well as delivery procedures
Cash flows occur at maturity	Cash flows occur at maturity	Cash flows occur on daily basis due to mark-to-market
Credit risk present	Credit risk present – can be mitigated using collateralization	Virtually no credit risk present due to margining by clearing house

"exercise price," while the date when the option can be used to buy or sell the underlying asset is the "exercise date" or "expiration date" or "maturity" of the contract.

Options give the holder the right to purchase/sell the underlying asset but they are not obliged to do so, as in the case of forwards and futures. Thus, there is a cost to purchase an option and this is called the option premium. There are variations in terms of when a contract can be exercised and how it is settled. Options that can be exercised only on the expiration date are known as European options, while options that can be exercised on any business day prior to the expiration date are known as American options. Options can be cash-settled, where the option holder receives a payment in the amount of the difference between the prevailing price of the underlying and the strike price, or they can be physically settled, with the option holder receiving or transferring the underlying asset (as is the case with futures).

The payoff for an option can be written as follows. For a call option with a strike price of K, the payout for the call option holder is $\max(0, S_T - K)$, where $\max()$ refers to the function that returns the maximum of the elements contained within brackets. Thus, if the price of the underlying is above the strike price K, the option is exercised and the option holder receives $S_T - K$. This can be thought of as the option holder receiving the underlying commodity at the strike price K and selling it at the market price S_T. However, if the underlying price is at or below the strike price, the option is not exercised and the option holder receives 0.

Similarly, for a put option, the payout to the option holder can be written as $\max(0, K - S_T)$. If the underlying price is below K, the option is exercised and the option holder sells the underlying at the strike price K and earns the difference between the strike price and the prevailing market price S_T. Alternatively, if the prevailing price is higher than the strike price, the option holder can sell at a higher price than possible under the option and hence the option is not exercised.

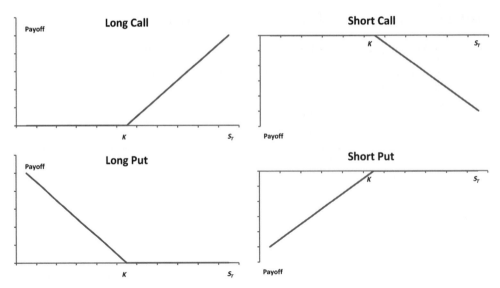

FIGURE 2.25   Payoff diagrams for long call, short call, long put, and short put

Payout diagrams for call options and put options from the long-option and the short-option perspective are shown in Figure 2.25.

The sample terms for an option contract on a WTI future are shown in Example 2.2.

EXAMPLE 2.2: SAMPLE TERMS FOR AN OPTION

Underlying commodity:	WTI Crude Oil Jan 2015 futures contract
Inception date:	1st September 2014
Expiration date:	16th December 2014
Option type:	Call option
Option position:	Long
Strike price:	95 USD/bbl
Settlement:	Futures-based settlement
Option premium:	3 USD/bbl

In the example shown, the settlement is calculated with reference to the settlement price of the WTI Crude Oil front-month futures contract on the expiration date (the Jan 2015 contract). Options traded on exchanges can be cash-settled earlier by taking the opposite position, exercised early if it is allowed under the option, or automatically exercised on the expiration date, with some exceptions depending on rules pertaining to that contract.

In the cases mentioned earlier, settlement is always based on the futures price at a certain time on a certain date (expiration date), or the prevailing futures price when the option is exercised (in the case of early exercise). These are known as bullet settlements, since they depend on the underlying price on a single day for settlement. However, many commodity markets can be illiquid and therefore are more susceptible to market manipulation on a single day. To alleviate this, derivative instruments can be structured so that their settlement price is averaged over several days. These instruments are known as Asian or average-value options and are very common in commodity markets. The payoff under these instruments is calculated by averaging the underlying's settlement price over a preset period (usually a month or a quarter).

Asian options are popular in commodity markets because they reduce the aforementioned risk of market manipulation while also mirroring commodity production and usage trends. Since commodities are mined or utilized on a daily basis, hedging using Asian settlements realizes a price that is closely linked to underlying production or consumption. Price averaging also reduces the premium for an Asian option compared with European or American options.

The premium for a European option is calculated using the Black–Scholes formula, while Asian options are mainly valued using numerical methods. Fischer Black and Myron Scholes developed a formula for the valuation of European options based on parameters including the forward price, strike price of the option, tenor of the option, volatility of the underlying, and interest rates. This has proven to be one of the foundations on which derivative pricing is based. We will discuss the derivation of the Black–Scholes formula and the valuation of options and other derivatives in future chapters.

SUMMARY

Market portfolio theory suggests that investors seek to minimize risks while maximizing expected returns, and it uses the ratio between returns and volatility (the Sharpe ratio) as a criterion to compare assets. The diversification benefits associated with low or negative correlation between assets is also recognized by the MPT, as succinctly put by Jim Rogers, who said that "commodities tend to zig when the equity markets zag." In the case of commodities such as fuel, this effect is especially pronounced for consumers, who are negatively exposed to commodity prices and can benefit from managing this exposure. Therefore, fuel hedging can be viewed as a portfolio-optimization exercise applied at the fuel consumer level, with the objective to achieve stability, enhance equity values, and reduce financing costs.

In this chapter, we have presented a landscape of fuel consumption and hedging activity in addition to taking a deeper look at the cost structure of airlines and shipping companies. The overview of energy market participants helped establish the exposures of various market participants to fuel prices and how consumers, especially those in the transportation sector, form a significant part of these markets. The magnitude of fuel costs for airlines and shipping companies as a fraction of total costs suggests that the viability of these businesses is impacted by two major factors – the elasticity of demand for transportation and a firm's ability to contain fuel costs.

Following the exposition on the need for hedging, we also discussed the evolution of the commodity markets and the basic instruments used for risk management. With this background, we can progress toward examining the use of financial derivatives to mitigate fuel price risks. In future chapters, we will look at commodity derivatives in detail, but we will first consider the establishment and governance of a firm's hedging activities and introduce a framework for hedging programs that provide clear, well-tailored guidelines for fuel risk managers.

APPENDIX A

We present simplified income statements for two airline companies, one a budget carrier in the USA and the other a full-service airline in the Asia-Pacific region. The income statements are presented in Table A.1, with revenues of base 100 to facilitate easy comparison of the components of these financial statements.

TABLE A.1   Income statements of a US budget carrier and an Asia-Pacific full-service airline

US budget carrier	USD	Asia-Pacific full-service airline	USD
Operating Revenue		Operating Revenue	
Passenger	90	Passenger	71
Cargo	5	Cargo	24
Other	5	Other	5
Total	100	Total	100
Operating Expenses		Operating Expenses	
Fuel Expense	30	Fuel Expense	38
Staff Costs	25	Staff Costs	17
Aircraft Lease Rentals	3	Aircraft Lease Rentals	5
Landing, Parking, and Route Fees	6	Landing, Parking, and Route Fees	13
Maintenance Costs	7	Maintenance Costs	8
Depreciation and Amortization	5	Depreciation and Amortization	5
Other Operating Expenses	12	Other Operating Expenses	11
Total	88	Total	97
Other Expenses (Income)		Other Expenses (Income)	
Interest Expense	2	Interest Expense	1
Other (Gains), Losses Net	1	Other (Gains), Losses Net	−1
Total	3	Total	0
Income before Income Taxes	9	Income before Income Taxes	3
Provision for Income Taxes	3	Provision for Income Taxes	1
Net Income	6	Net Income	2
Unrealized Gains and Losses from Derivatives	4	Unrealized Gains and Losses from Derivatives	1
Comprehensive Net Income	10	Comprehensive Net Income	3

CHAPTER 3

Developing Fuel Hedging Strategies

"If you are not willing to risk the unusual, you will have to settle for the ordinary."
—Jim Rohn

Unlike commodity traders and speculators, who expect high returns for the amount of risks that they assume and the liquidity they provide, most fuel consumers are not rewarded for taking on huge fuel price risks. For example, airlines specialize in offering transportation services and investors generally invest in airlines for their expertise in delivering these services. In such cases, airlines' financial results should mainly reflect their core business risk and should not experience large swings due to extraneous factors such as oil price or interest rate changes. This is one of the justifications for the use of hedging and we discuss this, along with other theoretical arguments for hedging, at the beginning of this chapter. We then discuss the important steps in the development of a good hedging program, including the identification of risk factors, risk appetite determination, setting hedging objectives and scope, as well as the implementation and monitoring of the hedge program. The chapter concludes with a sample template for a risk management program and a look at hedging trends in the airline industry.

THE RATIONALE FOR COMMODITY HEDGING

In previous chapters, we dealt with industries that are major energy consumers, focusing on the airline and transportation sectors. We also provided an overview of the commodity markets, price formation in these markets, and the basic instruments traded. However, as yet, we have not discussed the reasons for the popularity of the aforementioned instruments or the way in which they are used by hedgers. To answer these questions, let us first look at the theoretical justification for hedging.

Over the past three decades, there have been many studies on interest rate and foreign exchange risks faced by companies and the hedging behavior of these firms to determine the motives for hedging and the methods used. The rationale for hedging offered by these studies is broadly applicable to fuel hedging as well. There are academic arguments both in favor of and against hedging, but minimizing the variability of income has traditionally been viewed as the main reason for hedging. However, hedging as an extension of financing can also be regarded as a firm value maximizing activity. For example, under an escalating tax schedule, where higher income is taxed at a progressively higher percentage, reducing the volatility of income through hedging can potentially reduce the tax burden on a company.

Hedging may also reduce the costs of financial distress and help conserve capital when credit costs are high. There is an informational dimension to hedging as well, whereby hedging can reduce contracting costs by informing the market of the risk management being undertaken. Thus, hedging provides a signal to investors that management is alert and responsive in managing the external risks facing the firm. Management compensation and incentive structures can also influence the decision to hedge or not to hedge.

As we saw in Chapter 2, fuel cost is often the largest and most volatile component of operating expenses for industries such as airlines. Thus, hedging offers investors predictability on future costs and profits and is rewarded with higher valuations. Empirical research into the impact of hedging on firm values estimated the hedging premium for airlines to be in the range of 5–10%. This hedging premium is especially higher for airline firms that hedge fuel in rising fuel price environments.

Hedging can be exceptionally valuable when a firm is close to bankruptcy (i.e., when its costs spiral and its pricing power is insufficient to ensure a profit from continuing operations). This is apparent in the airline industry, as companies with regular hedging policies have generally been able to handle the higher fuel price environment better. Firms that face significant distress costs benefit from hedging, thus avoiding the problem of underinvestment in positive net present value (NPV) projects, as hedging can provide additional cash flow in distressed situations. This is especially useful when considering investments at a time of high fuel prices, when the cash flows of transportation companies are stressed. Airlines that hedge fuel prices can use the cash flows from hedges to acquire assets like airplanes or distressed airline companies when they are available at a discount.

Hedging has also been shown to reduce the cost of debt. In studies dealing with interest rate and currency hedgers, hedging firms were shown to access financing at lower spreads and have fewer restrictions on capital expenditures in their loan agreements. Similar discounts on credit costs can be obtained when combining airline financing with fuel price hedging, as we will see in a later chapter. Hedging also has a positive effect on debt capacity and is particularly useful for firms with more growth opportunities.

The arguments against hedging are derived mainly from the Modigliani–Miller theory, which states that corporate financing policies do not have an impact on the value of the firm in an idealized setting with no taxes, no transaction costs, and perfect information. According to portfolio theory, investors should not value hedging by the firm as they are able to purchase fuel hedges on their own in the market. No company can make money long term by hedging prices and, if it could, it should be in the fuel price speculation business and not a traditional business. However, this argument does not hold when we introduce imperfections that are common in the real world, such as taxes and information asymmetry, and hedging can be a valuable activity. However, this argument does not hold when we introduce imperfections that are common in the real world, such as taxes, bankruptcy and information asymmetry. Very often, the diversification benefits under market portfolio theories are overestimated as they assume a normal distribution of returns without accounting for bankruptcy risks associated with negative performance. For example, hedges purchased separately by an investor have no impact on the company's cash flow and its survival as opposed to hedges put in place by the firm itself.

FIGURE 3.1   Stages in the development of a risk management program

DEVELOPING A FUEL HEDGING PROGRAM

Developing a risk management strategy requires clarity on the firm's strategic objectives. Once a firm's medium to long-term strategy is identified, management can analyze the risks that might affect the execution of the strategy. A risk management strategy encapsulates management's understanding of risks facing the company, an estimate of their magnitude and effect on the firm's financial health and viability, and a process to measure, manage, and monitor these risks. To maintain its relevance, a risk management strategy needs to be reviewed periodically to identify new threats and gauge its effectiveness in managing previously identified risks. For best results, the risk management strategy of the firm should be formalized in a risk management policy statement that can be accessed by employees, management, and investors in the company. This helps foster a risk management culture and improves transparency on risks for all stakeholders.

As summarized in Figure 3.1, developing a fuel hedging program involves the following major steps:

- identification and assessment of the fuel price-related risks;
- codifying the risk appetite of the firm;
- developing the objectives and scope of the hedge program, including identifying hedge program managers;
- operationalizing the hedge program by selecting underlyings, instruments, quantities, and tenors to hedge;
- managing market risks and unwanted risks arising from hedging;
- monitoring and adjusting the hedge program on a regular basis.

RISK IDENTIFICATION AND ASSESSMENT

The first step in instituting a fuel risk management program is the identification and assessment of fuel price risks. We briefly touched upon some of the risks inherent in commodity trading in Chapter 2. Let us return to this discussion to identify the risks that can be managed with a hedging program.

Types of Risk

In general, the largest sources of risk for companies are business/commercial risk, operational risk, and financial risk. Business risk is industry and company specific and entails the management of any mismatches between demand and supply/capacity, competition, and technological changes. Operational risk is related to the internal workings and processes of the organization and is the risk arising from any shortcomings in processes or inefficiencies in the execution of projects. Financial risk management involves the effective usage of financial instruments and contracts to maximize profit and minimize the chance of insolvency. It involves determining the optimal mix of financing and hedging instruments required to support the company's operations and investment activities. Firms can use a combination of strategic and operational flexibility and financial risk management techniques to reduce risks.

Operational flexibility is not easy to manage due to the long-term nature of the investment in capital stock in these industries, as well as the slower pace of improvements in efficiency and flexibility. For example, airlines that own a large fraction of their fleet cannot change their fleet mix as soon as a more efficient aircraft is available in the market. Airlines that take on debt to purchase aircraft also cannot afford to idle their planes in the face of lower demand. Vertical integration as a strategy can help reduce price risks in some industries. For example, Delta, a large American airline, decided to purchase a refinery in order to hedge their exposure to the differential between jet fuel and crude oil prices. However, this approach is neither universally appropriate nor a cost-effective risk management solution for all commodity consumers.

The major financial risks for a firm are market risk (which includes interest rate risk, currency risk, and commodity risk among others), credit risk, liquidity risk, and operational risk (pertaining to financial transactions), as shown in Figure 3.2. In the following discussion, we confine ourselves to commodity price risks and the associated liquidity and credit risks.

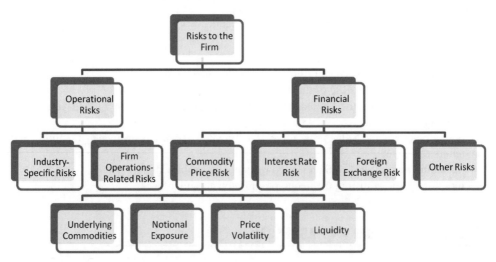

FIGURE 3.2 Types of risk faced by a firm and risk identification

However, an analogous process can be implemented for the management of other types of market risk as well.

Risk Identification

Risk identification begins with determining the commodity prices to which the company is exposed and quantifying the size of the risk associated with commodity procurement. This data can then be used to model the impact of commodity price movements on the profitability of the enterprise. This can be achieved using a simple scenario analysis, where the firm's profit is calculated for various price levels of commodities. The scenario analysis should take into account any correlation between input costs and revenue to arrive at a realistic estimate for commodity price risk. For instance, an oil refiner uses crude oil as an input to the refining process, converting it into refined products like gasoline, diesel, and fuel oil. As the prices of crude oil and refined products are highly correlated, the scenario analysis should reflect the net risk borne by the refiner, which is the spread between the two prices. Similarly, if an airline is able to pass on increases in fuel costs, either completely or partially through surcharges, the net effect of price movements on profits should be considered.

The scenario analysis, or a sensitivity analysis, will help identify whether the changes in the firm's profit from varying commodity prices are material enough to warrant commodity price hedging. It also helps understand the total exposure of a company to a particular commodity price, which can be important for large companies where multiple business units utilize the same commodity.

Forecasting Prices and Conducting Simulations

The scenario analysis used to gauge the impact of fuel price changes on the income statement can be improved by assigning a probability to scenarios used in the analysis. This can help firms get a better, more realistic estimate of the potential losses that can result from exposure to a particular risk. A Monte Carlo simulation of possible price paths can be conducted, using historical parameters for the price distribution or forward-looking parameters derived from the prevailing market for the commodity. From the distribution of price paths, one can derive the distribution of gains or losses arising from fuel price movements. This will yield an estimate for the variability and maximum loss from price movements, providing a guide for the notional and instruments to be used to hedge against this.

Alternatively, if the organization has sufficient expertise, it can develop a forecast for prices over the period where risks are to be hedged. For example, an airline company develops forecasts for revenue growth based on projected GDP growth, increase in demand and capacity, competitor activity, etc. over the normal course of business. This forecast can be used to derive an estimate of the amount of fuel required over the financial year. Similarly, the company can forecast its expected fuel purchase cost by considering the supply-and-demand scenario in the fuel markets. In the absence of in-house forecasting experience, the firm can access market research published by a variety of sources, including hedge providers. Forecasting provides a benchmark level against which the effectiveness of the hedge program can be measured, and most companies do set a target for fuel costs over the accounting year. The easiest guide to future prices for a commodity is the prevailing forward price curve at that point in time, although this may not be an unbiased estimator for future realizations of commodity prices.

ARTICULATING THE FIRM'S RISK APPETITE

In conjunction with identifying the risks faced by the firm, the management also has to make a decision about which risks to hedge and which risks to leave unhedged. A formal method for deciding whether a particular risk needs to be hedged is to codify it in a statement of risk appetite. A risk appetite statement establishes the amount of risk that the organization is willing to take to achieve its objectives. This could be in terms of investment or profit at risk or man-hours dedicated to a particular project. It is closely tied to the strategy of the firm and is derived from a combination of investor expectations for the company and management's comfort in dealing with different types of risk. For example, investors in commodity producers expect the firm's equity prices to vary in tandem with commodity prices and generally do not accord much value to producers hedging prices. Conversely, investors in airline companies generally invest in the core business of transportation and do not want to be exposed to commodity price risk, thus rewarding companies that hedge away these risks.

In addition to selecting the risks that need to be managed, management can prioritize the risks in terms of importance and risk tolerance. Risk tolerance is the amount of variability in revenue or profit introduced by a particular source of risk that a firm is comfortable with being exposed to. For instance, a firm may have a risk tolerance of 5% of profits for risk associated with commodity price movements. If the firm forecasts that commodity price movements could impact profits by a figure higher than the risk tolerance, management needs to take steps to reduce the level of commodity price risk.

A formal statement of risk appetite helps risk managers across the organization have a clear, shared understanding of the risks that need to be addressed and aids in the development of appropriate objectives for hedging programs. This part of the risk management process is a preamble to developing specific hedging objectives and strategies for each type of risk faced by the firm.

SETTING OBJECTIVES FOR FUEL HEDGING AND THE SCOPE OF HEDGING

Once the price risk factors are identified and checked against the firm's risk appetite, it is possible to formulate certain objectives for a fuel hedging program. Typical objectives for hedging include:

- reducing the volatility of earnings and protecting cash flows;
- securing financing for the development or upgrading of assets;
- fixing a maximum for input cost/minimum for revenues;
- achieving a budgeted cost for fuel procurement;
- guaranteeing fixed prices for existing and potential customers;
- maintaining competitive balance or securing an advantage;
- addressing timing mismatches;
- taking advantage of favorable market conditions.

Thus, hedging objectives can be of different types ranging from strategic, such as protecting cash flows and financing development, to operational and opportunistic. Selection of an appropriate goal for the fuel hedging program flows from the risk management policy and risk appetite statements. Ultimately, a commodity hedging program aims to bring more visibility on future performance to company management. It is important to communicate the aims of the hedging program effectively both internally, to stakeholders responsible for the administration of hedging, as well as to outside investors. This will ensure that the hedging program is judged based on its efficacy in achieving stated goals as opposed to some accounting measures such as gain/loss under hedges, which cannot communicate the success or failure of a hedging program appropriately. Thus, it is useful to ensure that there is a direct and demonstrable link between present or future profitability and hedging while formulating the objectives. It is equally important to ensure that the implementation of the hedge program is kept in line with the objectives.

Identifying Risk Managers within the Organization

In addition to determining the objectives of hedging, management needs to identify the individuals responsible for the execution of the strategy and ensure that they have appropriate visibility to undertake holistic hedging. In many organizations, individual business units are responsible for procurement and hedging of input prices. Decentralized hedging allows for business unit reporting to be more informative and can improve a firm's ability to allocate resources more efficiently. However, this can lead to duplication of efforts and could undo natural hedges that are present within the company as a whole. One of the solutions is to ensure that the risk management function is centralized and provided with all necessary information on input costs and sale prices. This is especially useful in the case of financial hedging, since the infrastructure needed to transact, monitor, and manage risk is expensive to maintain. In cases where it is preferable to have physical risk management, individual business units may be better equipped to handle price risk. To avoid unnecessary transactions, management can perform netting internally and hedge residual exposures centrally. For accurate measurement of business unit performance when risk management is centralized, a fair internal transfer pricing mechanism between business units needs to be instituted.

Determining the Scope of the Hedge Program

Prior to implementing the hedge program, the risk tolerance and hedging objective need to be converted into hedging limits that are referenced while managing a particular exposure. The scope of a hedge program may include:

- the variability in prices allowed under the program;
- limits on the percentage of input costs hedged;
- the complexity of instruments used;
- the duration of hedging;
- market/credit risk limits for the hedge portfolio.

As risk management outcomes are undoubtedly influenced by when hedges are entered into and the costs of hedging, the objectives need to allow for some leeway in the implementation of the program.

Some objectives are easy to distill into risk limits. For example, objectives that emphasize a maximum cost or budgeted cost for fuel purchases have an explicit cost threshold, which acts as a limit price for all purchases. Other objectives may have an implied cost threshold for purchases. For example, securing financing for the development of assets may require guaranteeing a rate of return on the project to lenders or investors and, by modeling the cash flows of the project, the hedger can arrive at a maximum purchase price for inputs.

Tactical or opportunistic objectives involve monitoring the market and the industry and making decisions based on expectations of future states. Hedging to maintain competitive balance, or in order to take advantage of market conditions, are examples of opportunistic hedging. These types of hedging require the continuous updating of knowledge on industry developments and commodity market movements, and thus need more leeway to account for uncertainty. Such objectives are best used to supplement more strategic objectives and are better implemented as part of a mature hedging program.

IMPLEMENTATION OF HEDGING

Once the objectives and scope of the program are defined, hedging managers can consider the implementation of hedging, beginning with a decision on the means of hedging.

Selecting the Fuel Cost Management Method

Commodity consumers can manage their fuel cost exposures in three ways. They can either:

1. retain the commodity price risk within the firm;
2. pass on commodity price increases to their customers; or
3. enter into long-term fixed-price contracts with their commodity suppliers to freeze their costs or use hedging mechanisms like derivatives to manage price risk.

Based on price forecasts or simulations, if the firm determines that hedging a particular commodity price is not necessary, it can retain the commodity price risk. For example, if a shipping company believes that oil prices are very high, the company may elect not to hedge their exposures with the expectation that a price drop is imminent. Alternatively, in a scenario where oil prices are not expected to be volatile, a firm may hedge only a portion of its exposures. The retained risk needs to be lower than the risk appetite of the firm.

If a firm is able to manage changes in input prices by passing through costs to customers, then there may not be a need for hedging. The ability to pass costs on to customers depends to a great extent on the elasticity of demand. Raising prices may cause demand destruction, as customers look for cheaper substitutes. Conversely, the firm could also switch the inputs used in its business or improve the efficiency of its operations to reduce the need for hedging. It may also be the case that the firm's competitors engage in hedging, which enables them to either make higher profits or garner market share by passing on any benefits from hedging to their customers. Thus, a firm's decision to hedge or not hedge can be influenced not only by internal assessments of need but also by external factors that impact the demand for its product or services. Hedging decisions require an assessment of the market that the company is operating in and an awareness of the extent of price hedging industry-wide going forward.

Once a need for hedging is identified, firms can decide on using physical hedging or financial hedging. Physical hedging, or the use of long-term procurement contracts, is a useful means of hedging against price increases. However, the prevalence of long-term contracting has reduced over time as commodity prices are amongst the most volatile prices across asset classes, experiencing sustained multi-year upward or downward trends as seen over the last decade. Long-term contracting in such markets involves taking on significant counterparty credit risk and not all firms may be willing or sophisticated enough to do so. Financial contracting, especially with creditworthy counterparties like banks or major trading houses, can be a more transparent and less risky proposition. However, financial hedging does come at a price, with companies paying trading costs (bid/offer spreads and broker fees), funding costs (for margins), operational costs of monitoring and managing the process, as well as the opportunity cost of forgone upside. Companies should also carefully consider the costs of regulatory compliance and the accounting implications of using financial hedges.

We now consider the parameters of a financial hedging program, starting with the underlying to be used for hedging.

Identifying the Underlying to Hedge with and Basis Risk

When a fuel consumer has decided to hedge fuel prices using OTC or exchange-traded markets, it is quite likely that the exact commodity used is not actively traded in the derivative markets. This is because it is only possible to trade commodities after a certain amount of standardization in terms of quantity, quality, delivery location, and other specifications. Thus, identifying an appropriate proxy to hedge input costs with is a very important part of the hedging process.

When hedging a commodity exposure using a different commodity, it is important to ensure that the commodity prices are highly correlated. That is, changes in the price of the commodity used by the company should closely track changes in the price of the proxy used for hedging. Basis is defined as the difference between the prices of the commodity being hedged and the commodity used for hedging. Basis can be of different types, including locational basis (where the commodity being hedged is delivered to a different location from the commodity used to hedge), calendar basis (where the commodity deliverable at a particular time is hedged with the same commodity deliverable at a different time), or quality/grade differential (where one product is hedged with a different grade of the same product). Basis risk arises from changes in the basis between the two commodity prices. Hedging instruments should be chosen to minimize the risk that the basis between the two commodity prices changes.

Let us look at some examples of basis risk. Geographic or locational basis risk is the most common type of basis risk. It arises from the fact that the commodities are available or delivered under exchange rules to one particular location while their use is in a different location. The difference between prices of the commodity in the two locations can largely be explained by transportation costs, taxation, regulations, and handling costs. For example, the price of WTI Crude Oil delivered in Cushing, Oklahoma is different from the price paid for similar-grade crude oil by refiners on the Gulf Coast. Locational basis risk can be managed using basis swaps or by locking in freight rates for transporting the commodity from the delivery location to the place of requirement. The geographical basis is usually stable, but this depends on the availability of transportation and handling facilities. For instance, at the time of writing, natural gas prices across the world are much higher than prices for delivery at Henry Hub in the USA (Figure 3.3). This is because the production of natural gas has expanded dramatically with the tapping of shale gas reserves in the USA, while the export of natural gas requires terminals and pipeline infrastructure that is not readily available. In addition, European gas prices have a strong linkage with crude oil prices. Locational basis can also be influenced by regulations. For example, export restrictions on US crude oil combined with an increase in production from shale formations as well as pipeline bottlenecks at the

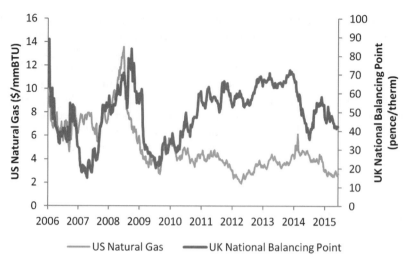

FIGURE 3.3 US Henry Hub Natural Gas vs. UK NBP

delivery location led to the WTI benchmark diverging significantly from global crude oil price benchmarks from late 2010 onwards.

Calendar basis risk is the risk that the contract used to hedge the commodity price risk expires at a different time than the physical price risk. For example, energy consumers use fuel on a daily basis but when they hedge using a futures contract, they are covering their exposure to prices only on the expiry date of the contract. This can be remedied by using other products such as average price swaps, which price on a daily basis. Another example involves the hedging of long-dated purchases of oil products. Many oil product markets have thin liquidity beyond the first few delivery months, and hedging long-dated exposures usually requires traders to use the near-month contracts and roll them as they expire. Thus, calendar basis risk is largely the risk that the shape of the forward curve changes between the contract expiry and the period for which hedging is necessary.

Grade differential or quality basis risk is another common risk taken by consumers while hedging. For example, crude oil producers would generally hedge with WTI Crude Oil, Brent Crude Oil, or Dubai Crude Oil, which are more liquid, even though the crude oil they produce may differ in quality from these benchmarks. Similarly, as the paper markets for many energy products are non-existent or illiquid, consumers choose to hedge with more liquid products. A common example of this is airline companies hedging jet fuel purchases using correlated, liquid benchmarks such as Brent Crude Oil, WTI Crude Oil, gasoil, or heating oil, which have more liquid futures and options markets (Figure 3.4). The underlying used to hedge with should be selected by looking for the highest correlation between price movements of the two products. A regression analysis can be used for this purpose, as explained in the example below.

An airline based in Asia needs to hedge its consumption of jet fuel over the next two years. It can enter into a swap transaction linked to the local benchmark of jet fuel, which is Singapore Jet Kerosene. Jet kerosene is not very liquid beyond the first 3 to 6 months forward, and thus there is a need to find a suitable proxy to hedge longer-term maturities. This is especially true for hedging any options on jet kerosene. The airline can run a regression analysis, where the Singapore Jet Kerosene price returns are regressed against more liquid candidates such as

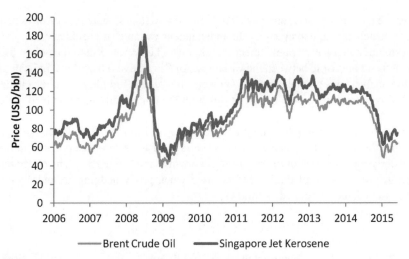

FIGURE 3.4   Brent Crude Oil and Singapore Jet Kerosene prices

Brent Crude Oil and WTI Crude Oil. The regression analysis should typically use at least the same length of time as the duration of the proposed contract, so that longer-term correlations are better approximated.

Using the monthly returns for the underlyings over a 10-year period from July 2005 to June 2015, Brent Crude Oil is found to have a correlation of 0.9 with Singapore Jet Kerosene, while WTI Crude Oil has a correlation of 0.81 with Singapore Jet Kerosene over the same period. A correlation coefficient of over 0.8 indicates a strong relationship between the two prices and is also a necessary condition under some accounting regimes to consider the proxy hedge to be an effective one. The results of a regression analysis between Singapore Jet Kerosene and Brent Crude Oil are shown in the scatter plot in Figure 3.5. The parameter R^2

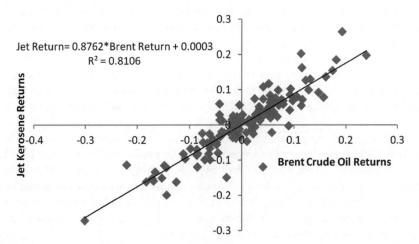

FIGURE 3.5   Regression analysis between monthly returns of Singapore Jet Kerosene and Brent Crude Oil

measures the amount of variation in a dependent variable (the Singapore Jet Kerosene price in this case), which can be explained by the independent variable (it is equivalent to the square of the correlation in a one-variable linear regression). The R^2 value should be high to ensure a good fit of the relationship between the variables. An R^2 value of 0.8 or above indicates that the regression analysis has good explanatory power. The relative liquidity of various underlyings should be considered when their correlations with the commodity to be hedged are close to each other.

When conducting proxy hedging, the size of the position in the proxy hedge underlying differs from the size of the actual exposure. The ratio of the size of the position in the proxy hedge underlying to the size of the exposure is known as the hedge ratio. The hedge ratio used to minimize the variance of the hedged position when proxy hedging an underlying with a different asset can be calculated as follows:

$$\text{Hedge ratio } h = \rho * \sigma_{\text{underlying}} / \sigma_{\text{proxy}}$$

where ρ is the correlation between the two underlyings, $\sigma_{\text{underlying}}$ is the volatility of the underlying commodity to be hedged, and σ_{proxy} is the volatility of the commodity used as the proxy for hedging.

Quantity and Tenor of Hedging

As far as hedge quantities are concerned, having a well-articulated and documented hedging program helps in resolving any uncertainty related to the quantity to be hedged. As stated earlier, the scope of the program can include explicit limits on how much hedging is permitted and how the hedging is performed. Whether clearly stated or not, these figures should tie in with the organization's stated risk appetite. If the firm does not have any risk appetite with respect to higher input prices, the preference would be for risk managers to completely hedge all input prices. If the firm is willing to bear slightly higher risk, the hedging amount can be lowered. Risk managers should note that there is a trade-off between risk-taking and hedging costs, which needs to be considered in the overall financing picture.

Determining the quantity to hedge requires the building of a forecast of the usage of input commodities and expected sensitivity of cash flows to commodity prices. Such forecasts should take into account expected changes in commodity prices (as predicted by the futures market) to arrive at the total expected cost of purchase, which could be one benchmark to use when measuring the performance of the program. Forecasting also needs inputs on future industry conditions and competition and is a subjective process. In relation to hedging, it is important to communicate these expectations well so that risk management can be more proactive.

In cases where hedging is mandated for securing financing, the hedging duration may need to match the project term. For example, a power producer selling power long term at a fixed price needs to ensure that the firm's purchases of inputs such as coal or natural gas are hedged over the duration. The hedging amount in this case would be calculated in such a way as to ensure that the operation remains viable over its life and that investors are suitably compensated. Where hedging is conducted with the aim of ensuring committed prices to customers, there is limited flexibility on hedge duration.

It is the cases where hedging is more opportunistic or discretionary that require more attention to determine hedging tenor and quantity. When hedging is used to lock in favorable prices, market conditions, such as the most attractive hedge tenor in terms of pricing at that particular time, may influence the selection of a particular horizon for a hedge. Hedge notional amounts should be calculated to ensure that the firm is not over-hedged (hedged over 100% of its commodity consumption) at any point in time.

Selection of Instruments for Hedging

The scope of the risk management plan may also explicitly state the types of instruments allowed. In the case of companies that are new to risk management using derivatives, it is advisable to stick to simple instruments at inception. Some of the commonly used instruments are forwards, futures, swaps, and options. Swaps are OTC instruments, which can be a collection of forwards and/or options. More sophisticated risk managers can consider additional exotic products that may suit their organization.

With respect to the simple instruments, there is a straightforward trade-off between costs at inception and ongoing costs. For futures and forwards, there is no cost to enter into a transaction but the hedgers need to maintain margins and are exposed to downside risk (i.e., the risk that prices move against them on the hedge). In the case of bought options, hedgers pay an upfront cost called the option premium and do not have to maintain any margins. Futures and forwards are also transacted at the market price and the hedger is immediately exposed to gains and losses on these transactions, while in the case of options there is no further potential of loss (except for counterparty credit risk). Swap hedges are generally structured to have zero upfront premium but would require usage of credit lines or margins, depending on the hedge counterparty. We discuss hedging structures in great detail in the following chapters.

A rule of thumb for selecting a simple hedge instrument that is based on the level of underlying commodity prices is as follows.

- When prices are low (relative to historical averages or hedger's expectations), hedgers should enter into fixed-price swap contracts. At low prices, swaps can be very efficient for hedging due to the limited downside risk.
- When prices are in line with historical averages or the expectation is that prices will be range-bound, a collar structure (a combination of a bought call option and a sold put option) helps manage commodity price risks better. Collar pricing may also be more attractive when the market expectations for prices, as indicated by the pricing of puts vs. calls, reflects a range-bound view.
- When prices are at high levels, outright purchase of call options may be a safe option for hedgers. Although there is an initial premium outlay required, the potential loss is limited to the premium compared with potential losses on swaps or other zero-cost structures if prices were to drop.

Thus, depending on a firm's capital position and its willingness to pay for protection, risk managers can choose between products. Instruments like options allow for leeway in terms of setting hedging prices (strike prices) and option strategies can be customized to suit hedgers with different levels of expertise. Structured and exotic products can be more useful and manageable for sophisticated counterparties.

In all these cases, back-testing the performance of a strategy can provide management with a degree of comfort on the outcomes of using hedging. This involves simulating the payout of a strategy based on the historical evolution of commodity prices. Especially with regard to more structured hedging products, conducting back-testing can give management insights into the effectiveness of the hedge when faced with similar price movements. However, one must always be mindful of the fact that past performance is not a guarantee of future performance and that underlying structural shifts or regime changes in a commodity market can cause unanticipated moves in prices and term structures. Any knowledge of such potential shifts in commodity price behavior needs to be imputed into the hedge instrument selection process.

Market Risk

Up to this point, we have discussed the market risk management aspects of hedging. Determining the underlying, amount, tenor, and instruments used are all important aspects of the hedging process. Further to initiating hedging transactions, hedgers also need to conduct portfolio monitoring and management activities. We briefly introduce some of the metrics used here. We will discuss the metrics used for portfolio management in detail in later chapters.

With respect to market risks, portfolio risk management includes calculating and managing risk metrics like value at risk (VaR), which is the potential Mark-To-Market (MTM) loss over a given time interval, subject to a defined confidence level. For example, if the one-week VaR for a portfolio at a confidence level of 95% is 1 million USD, then there is a 5% chance that an MTM loss of more than 1 million USD will occur over a one-week period. Other common portfolio metrics used include the sensitivities of a trade or a portfolio to market parameters like spot price, volatility, time to maturity, and interest rates.

In addition to market risk, there are other risks to be considered in the risk management process. Chief among these are credit risk, liquidity risk, operational risk, and legal risk. In the wake of the credit crisis, counterparty credit risk has been a special focus for organizations and we will consider this briefly here.

MANAGEMENT OF THE UNWANTED RISKS OF A PORTFOLIO

In this section, we introduce the types of unwanted risks that arise from hedging and the considerations involved in managing them.

Credit Risk

Credit risk is the potential loss that may occur due to the non-performance of a counterparty under a financial contract. Credit risk is present in loans and bonds as well as in derivative transactions that are uncollateralized. In a derivative transaction, if a hedger has a positive mark-to-market (MTM) on a transaction, they are exposed to the risk of the counterparty defaulting. Increasingly, counterparty credit risk also influences the decision regarding the instruments and parties that an organization can transact with. Exchange transactions or OTC transactions conducted through brokers or clearing counterparties are usually collateralized, meaning that margins are maintained with a central party and there is virtually no chance of default. OTC transactions that are uncollateralized pose significant credit risk to the hedger and, therefore, risk managers should guard against excessive concentration of credit risk with a few counterparties. Risk managers should also monitor the credit markets for any signs of distress among their trading partners.

In a later chapter, we will discuss how credit risk is generally managed, using margining methods or a credit support annex (CSA) for OTC transactions. The CSA forms a part of the master agreement between the counterparties to a transaction and sets out the collateral mechanism for OTC trades. Credit risk can also be mitigated using the credit derivatives markets, by means of instruments like credit default swaps (CDS).

Liquidity Risk

Liquidity risk is the risk that an instrument cannot be traded easily, resulting in financial loss. Alternatively, it is the risk that the transaction cost of trading and the time to execution increases. Liquidity risk is a function of the market that the instrument trades in and the complexity of the instrument. For example, exchange-traded commodities are generally able to attract more liquidity than commodities traded OTC. Simple instruments like futures and options are more liquid than exotic structures. Simple instruments can easily be transacted with and transferred between multiple counterparties, while complex instruments may only be offered by select parties such as banks or trading houses. Therefore, unwinding complex transactions may be more difficult due to the lack of a secondary market. Liquidity risk is manifested in the form of the bid/offer spread for a security, the impact cost of a trade (the impact of a trade on market price, which is related to market depth – the amount of a security that can be bought or sold at different prices or the depth of the order book), and the time taken to execute a particular notional amount.

With respect to hedge portfolio management, we are mainly concerned with market liquidity, as opposed to funding liquidity. The two are closely related though, as market liquidity issues can impact a firm's liquidity position by preventing it from raising cash through the disposal of assets. Similarly, funding liquidity problems can cause deterioration in a hedger's credit profile, leading to market liquidity risk arising from counterparties' unwillingness to deal with them.

Operational Risk

Operational risk is the potential for loss arising from inadequate processes and controls, errors committed by personnel, failed systems, fraud, or external events. It encompasses a broad variety of risks not covered under market risk or credit risk. In the context of managing a commodity hedging program, the main risks include:

- improper use of hedging (selecting products not allowed by the risk management policy, using products that do not hedge risks as expected under the program, etc.);
- errors in execution and reporting of hedges (caused by miscommunication with hedge providers, improper booking of trades in a risk management system, etc.);
- systems failures and business disruption (incorrect implementation of valuation models, failure of risk management infrastructure leading to loss on existing or anticipated transactions);
- fraud (committed by internal staff or those at an external counterparty).

Operational risk can have a knock-on effect on the credit risk of a corporation, as large frauds or operational issues can impact the financial health and reputation of the firm.

Legal and Reputational Risk

Over the last few years, legal and regulatory compliance issues have taken center stage at many financial firms. Following the credit crisis, many firms have been rocked by scandals, including the breaching of sanctions, price rigging, and other market manipulation activities. In this environment, legal and reputational risk demands special attention in the risk management process.

Legal risk is the risk of loss due to potential legal restitution or settlements paid out under disputes, or fines imposed by regulators or the courts. It can also be the risk borne by the company through exposure to changing laws or a failure to accurately document and enforce contracts. Legal risk is classified as an operational risk under Basel II regulations for banks, but it has become very important over the last few years.

A firm can be exposed to reputational risk if it is found to trade with counterparties that would lower its standing in the market. Dealing with trading counterparties who have been sanctioned or are embroiled in lawsuits, or those who have a bad reputation in credit markets, can lead to repercussions on the firm. For example, the Office of Foreign Assets Control (OFAC) at the US Department of the Treasury has a mandate to enforce US sanctions and has jurisdiction over USD-denominated transactions. If a counterparty is subject to US sanctions, then dealing with them, especially through USD-denominated transactions that are cleared in New York, exposes a firm to legal fines imposed by OFAC and others as well as reputational risk. In addition to the reputational impact of dealing with such counterparties, firms may be exposed to liquidity and credit risks arising from the unwillingness of other parties to deal with them. Especially on the environmental and human rights fronts, firms are pressured by the investment community and lenders to conduct due diligence and deal responsibly with counterparties.

MONITORING AND CALIBRATION OF THE HEDGING PROGRAM

The hedging program needs to be reviewed on a regular basis to ensure that it does not deviate from its stated goals and remains in compliance with the stated risk appetite. Effective monitoring of the risks faced by a company requires good technical and organizational infrastructure for information sharing and cooperation between various business units to manage risks both financially and operationally. Developing a risk culture within the organization is important to ensure existing and new risks are identified and appropriately quantified. In addition, the effectiveness of the instruments used should be documented prior to and following the expiration of a hedge.

The hedge program should be reviewed whenever there is a material change in overall conditions. For instance, hedging conducted for financing of development projects might become unnecessary once the debt servicing is completed. Hedging that might have been essential to protect capital may not be necessary once the capital position of the firm is stronger. Similarly, changes in the competitive landscape and the trend in commodity prices should also trigger a review of hedging policy.

TEMPLATE FOR A RISK MANAGEMENT POLICY

Now that we have examined the steps involved in developing a risk management strategy and the risks to be managed, we can formally codify the risk management policy of the organization. A risk management policy statement should have the following major parts.

- The purpose of the risk management policy and the risk tolerance of the firm.
- An inventory of risks faced by the firm, especially those that will be managed under the policy.
- The objectives of the risk management strategy.
- Identification of managers responsible for execution and oversight of the risk management process.
- The scope of the risk management strategy, in terms of quantity, tenor, types of risk managed, and risk limits.
- The instruments to be used and the counterparties for dealing, duly approved by management.
- Risk reporting and compliance procedures, along with a schedule for periodic review of the hedge program.

The risk management policy should conform to any regulatory requirements for the documentation of such policies. Management should also obtain an opinion on the accounting treatment of proposed hedges in order to avoid conflicts with the stated objective of hedging. An abridged sample version of a risk management policy statement for an airline company is shown in Table 3.1.

THE AIRLINE INDUSTRY – TRENDS IN FUEL RISK MANAGEMENT

Airline fuel hedging has assumed prominence over the last decade with the sustained rise in the general level of oil prices, punctuated by bouts of extreme volatility. Fuel price has become the largest contributor to operating expenses for most airlines. This has been reinforced with the growth of the low-cost carriers (LCCs), where the business model is dependent on lowering operating costs. Fuel price is one part of the operating cost structure that cannot be controlled easily. The increase in fuel price volatility is a compelling reason for airlines to hedge fuel prices.

Magnitude of Fuel Price Risk

We chose a sample of 30 of the largest airlines across the Americas, Europe, and the Asia Pacific region to describe the trends in airline hedging. The broad trend in fuel costs as a percentage of operating expenses has been upward (Figure 3.6). The figures arrived at from the sample are in line with industry-wide figures referenced earlier.

Fuel costs as a percentage of operating costs are higher for airlines in the Asia Pacific region. This may be due to the fact that staff costs are generally lower than in other parts of the world. In the sample, fuel costs as a percentage of total costs are lower for European airlines.

TABLE 3.1   Risk management policy sample

Fuel risk management policy for Albatross Airlines	
Purpose of risk management policy	To support the execution of management's strategy for the long-term growth of Albatross Airlines. The risk management policy will specify the policies and procedures governing the management of the airline's risks.
Risks faced by the firm	Commodity price risk linked to jet fuel prices.
Objectives of risk management	To reduce the volatility of cash flows by hedging fuel prices. Achieving a lower price for fuel procurement compared with monthly purchase of jet fuel by combining strategic hedging with tactical execution.
Management of hedging program	Risk Management Oversight Committee, consisting of CEO, CFO, and Company Secretary, to oversee hedging program. Hedging program execution to rest with Fuel Risk Management Team, consisting of CFO, Company Secretary, Hedging Manager, Fuel Market Analyst, and Credit Analyst.
Scope of risk management strategy	i. The Risk Management Team to have authority to hedge up to 50% of projected annual consumption, with individual monthly hedges not exceeding 100% of monthly forecast consumption.
	ii. In case an annual hedge ratio of higher than 50% is recommended, the Risk Management Oversight Committee's approval is required.
	iii. Hedging can be conducted for a tenor of 24 months from the date of execution.
	iv. The Risk Management Team to ensure no more than 50% of overall hedges are placed with a single counterparty.
	v. Negative MTM exceeding 10 mm USD on any hedge to be escalated to Oversight Committee. Overall negative MTM of 25 mm USD to trigger portfolio review.
Instruments to be used for hedging	WTI and Brent Crude Oil swaps, futures, and options Jet Fuel swaps and options WTI, Brent, or Jet Fuel zero-cost collars or three-ways WTI or Brent extendible swaps
Risk reporting and compliance procedures	Monthly report of hedging positions to be submitted to Oversight Committee. Any operational breaches to be escalated immediately. Portfolio review based on MTM as per scope above. Quarterly review of hedging strategy by Oversight Committee. Annual review of risk management policy to be conducted.

In terms of disclosures regarding the quantity of hedging and the manner of hedging, the quality of information available varies significantly. This is due to the lack of standardization in the level of disclosures required, which provides some leeway for management in terms of disclosure requirements. Many US and European airlines disclose details related to hedging, including the types of instruments used, the tenor of hedging, the percentage of future requirements hedged, etc. Fuel cost data is readily available in financial statements. Airlines also disclose the types of instruments and underlyings that they use to hedge fuel costs. However,

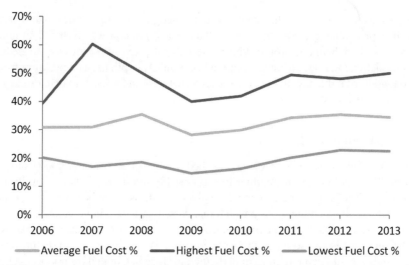

FIGURE 3.6 Fuel cost as a percentage of operating costs for major airlines

many airlines do not disclose the parameters of their hedging policies, including the limits on the hedge ratio for a particular year, the average hedged price for future purchases, and so on. Arguably, some of these details may not be disclosed in order to protect information on their market positions, but the lack of transparency on hedging limits or a formal policy can undermine investors' confidence in the effectiveness of a firm's hedging.

Underlyings and Hedging Instruments

In terms of the underlying commodities that are used for hedging, airlines have been using many benchmarks including WTI and Brent crude oils, gasoil, diesel, gasoline, and jet kerosene. In recent years, airlines have moved away from using WTI crude oil due to the lack of hedge effectiveness caused by the divergence of WTI prices from Brent and other global oil prices.

Airlines generally use average-price or "Asian" swaps and options for hedging. These instruments have become popular in commodities markets as they reduce the risk of manipulation of prices, which is a legitimate concern in illiquid markets. Compared with bullet forwards or options, the potential for manipulation of prices is much lower for monthly average price swaps. Extendible swaps or swaptions were also popular in the early years of the oil price rise. From 2005 onwards, the degree of customization in payoffs grew significantly, beginning with extendible and Bermudan extendible structures and culminating in 2007/8 with target redemption swaps and their variants. However, as these transactions were mostly OTC, information on structured hedging activities is difficult to gather from publicly available sources.

Based on annual reports of the firms in our sample, the preferred instruments for price hedging include swaps, call options, and collars, in addition to crack spread swaps for hedging the basis risk between underlyings. These instruments have been consistently used over the last decade, while the use of more exotic instruments like extendibles and target redemptions has decreased. This may be due to the decrease in hedging activity in the Asia Pacific region, where exotic transactions were more popular, as well as the reluctance of airlines to enter into these trades, which were much maligned in the aftermath of the crash in oil prices.

However, disclosures related to the exact payouts of hedges are largely unavailable. Although some airlines provide aggregate statistics on the average price at which their fuel purchases are hedged, or their hedging profile with respect to oil price, it is not easy to deduce the kind of transactions that an airline has entered into unless explicitly stated. Moreover, most airlines only describe the payout (swap, collar, etc.) at best and neglect to disclose any exotic enhancements to these strategies.

Quantity and Tenor of Hedging

For our sample of airlines, we observed that the hedge ratio for airlines increased from 2006–8, dropped in 2009, and has been trending lower, possibly due to the lower volatility in 2013 (see Figure 3.7). The hedging percentage is relatively stable as a number of airlines, especially in Europe, adhere to a hedging policy which mandates that a certain percentage of fuel costs should be hedged in advance. Large European airlines maintain the highest hedge ratios, while data on hedge ratios is sparse for Asia Pacific airlines. This may be due to the prevalence of surcharges in the Asia Pacific region. In particular, airlines in China have not been allowed to significantly hedge fuel prices after 2008 and are compensated for oil price increases with a fuel surcharge schedule that is determined by the civil aviation authority. The actual percentage of fuel costs that are hedged by an airline would be understated as surcharges are excluded from our calculations of hedge ratios.

The tenor of hedging, as measured by either the duration of outstanding hedges or explicit limits in the hedging policy of an airline, is also a good measure of the appetite for risk management at airlines. Prior to the 2008 crisis, many airlines engaged in hedging over tenors of 2 to 5 years, with hedging for 2 to 3-year tenors being the most common. However, after the 2008 crisis, many airlines discontinued hedging either temporarily or completely shut down their hedging programs. This is especially true of airlines in the Asia Pacific region, which drastically curtailed hedging fuel costs after large MTM losses on their derivative portfolios in 2008/9. Airlines have also been affected by the reduction in the number of available hedge counterparties, as many banks have retreated from the commodities market. As of 2013, most

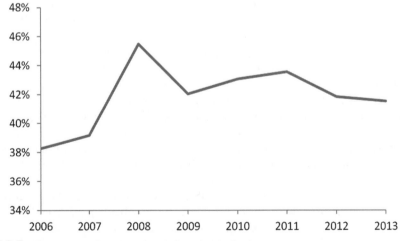

FIGURE 3.7   Percentage of next year's requirements hedged

airlines that disclosed their hedging practices used derivatives with tenors not exceeding 1 to 2 years.

Recent Developments

In the first half of 2014, a number of airlines reduced their hedging exposures due to the low volatility of oil prices. This was especially true of US airline companies, some of which reverted to being unhedged. This has helped US carriers benefit more from the oil price fall in late 2014 compared with European carriers, which have higher hedge ratios as they mostly follow consistent hedging strategies that require certain percentages of consumption to be hedged in advance. Similarly, Asian airlines, which have generally hedged less than airlines in other regions, would see the benefit of lower fuel prices immediately. The downward trend in oil prices through 2015 has also benefited airlines who curtailed their hedging activity over the year.

SUMMARY

We began this chapter with a discussion of the theoretical justification for hedging and the benefits for fuel hedgers, including:

- increased visibility on cash flows to treasurers;
- reduced cost of capital, borrowing costs, and the costs of financial distress;
- minimizing the negative effects of a convex tax schedule;
- positive signaling to investors of active risk management.

However, entering into commodity hedging transactions involves multiple unwanted risks. Airlines are exposed to market risks and liquidity risks in the execution of their hedges, which depend on the market depth and volatility of prices. Jet fuel markets can be non-existent or illiquid beyond six months to a year forward, and volatility can quickly switch between regimes of low and high volatility. Basis risk can be present between financial hedges and the costs of underlying physical consumption. Firms are also exposed to the creditworthiness of their hedge counterparty (credit risk) and this is of increasing importance, especially after the default of Lehman Brothers during the credit crisis. Credit risk management of financial contracts can involve exchange clearing, necessitating the placement of potentially large margins at clearing houses. Alternatively, airlines can manage credit risk on a bilateral basis with their hedge providers by requiring collateral to be posted by their counterparty when their trades are profitable.

We have discussed the important steps in the development of a hedging program, starting with risk identification, assessment, and risk appetite setting to fixing the objectives and scope of the risk management program, implementing hedging, and continuously monitoring and managing both wanted and unwanted risks. It is important to have a clearly documented hedging policy so that employees and risk managers are cognizant of the risks that need to be managed and the process to be used to manage such risks.

We will look at how a hedge can be designed and implemented in the following chapters.

CHAPTER 4

Shipping and Airlines – Basics of Fuel Hedging

"The connection between what is habitually believed to be a cause and what is habitually believed to be an effect is not necessary, according to us."

—Al-Ghazali

Occasionalism denies any link of efficient causation between events, but a speculator would endeavor to detect patterns with the aim of profiting from the consequences of events. A hedger, in contrast, is not interested in realizing high profits as much as ensuring that heavy losses are avoided. Derivative instruments allow both parties to translate these views into financial contracts. In this chapter, we discuss how basic derivatives are used by fuel hedgers to limit the range of possible fuel costs. We also look at how some of these instruments are valued based on a probabilistic approach. Prior to providing a quantitative derivation of the Black–Scholes–Merton model and Black's model, we show how these frameworks are used to price derivative instruments such as options and measure the sensitivities of derivative prices to changing market parameters. We supplement the discussion of these vanilla instruments with a look at variations such as average-price or Asian swaps and options, which are widely used in commodity markets.

SPOT–FORWARD RELATIONSHIPS

In our earlier discussion on forward curves, we briefly mentioned the various shapes that forward curves can take. Forward prices can be higher or lower than spot prices and can exhibit features such as seasonality. However, forward prices must be linked to spot prices as the prices converge at the maturity of the forward contract. Thus, forward prices should be derivable from spot prices based on the cash-and-carry relationship, with any differences, other than those arising from storage or transportation costs, being exploited by arbitrageurs. In this section, we attempt to quantify the relationship between forward prices and spot prices.

Theories on the Shape of Forward Curves

Before we derive the mathematical relationship between spot and forward prices, let us look at some of the theories that were developed to explain their relationship.

One of the early approaches to explain the backwardation seen in the futures prices of many commodities was the theory of normal backwardation. Longer-dated futures contracts are less liquid than shorter-dated futures. Commodity producers were the predominant users of longer-dated contracts, while commodity consumers usually only hedged their short-term needs. Thus, there was a mismatch between supply and demand for long-term futures contracts. In order to address this mismatch, commodity producers would have to give up some of the value that they could potentially receive from selling their goods in order to induce counterparties to deal with them. This discount, which producers give to investors to bear the risk of long-term commodity prices, may lead to futures prices being in backwardation in some cases. However, with the emergence of many different participants with diverging motivations in the commodity markets and the overall increase in liquidity over the last two decades, it is hard to explain forward curve shapes using only the relative demand for hedging from producers. Figure 4.1 illustrates the main forward curve shapes seen in the oil market.

Another theory that was developed to model forward curve shapes uses inventories as the underlying explanatory variable. Spot prices are inversely related to inventories at that point in time (Figure 4.2). In cases where the inventory of a commodity is high, spot prices will be low and vice versa. If inventories are expected to drop over time, the price of the commodity can be predicted to rise from current levels. This would result in futures prices being higher than the spot price, resulting in an upward-sloping or contango shape for the forward curve. Alternatively, if inventories are currently low and the supply/demand balance is expected to improve over time, futures prices would be lower than the spot price of the commodity, resulting in a backwardated shape of the futures curve.

Forward curve shapes can also be said to depend not only on current inventories but also on the total reserves for a commodity. This is especially relevant for commodities such as oil and gas, where the total reserves are limited. Depletion of reserves implies that long-term prices would be higher than spot prices, while new discoveries and technological innovations that increase the percentage of oil recoverable from existing reserves put downside pressure on long-term prices.

We now look at developing a quantitative relationship between spot and futures prices under the assumption of no arbitrage.

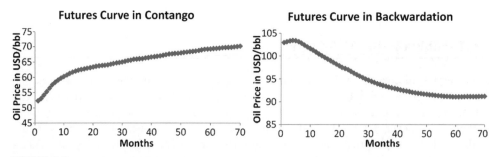

FIGURE 4.1   Oil forward curve shapes
Data Sources: NYMEX, Bloomberg.

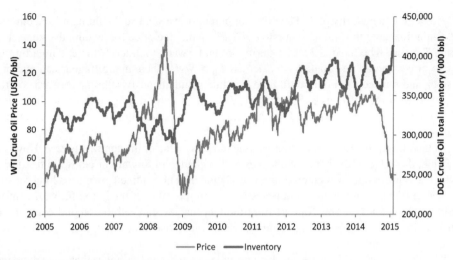

FIGURE 4.2 WTI Crude Oil price vs. inventories
Data Sources: NYMEX, US Department of Energy, Bloomberg.

Spot–Forward Relationships for Investment Assets

We begin by setting out the notation that we will use throughout this chapter and in the following chapters as well. The main variables that we deal with are as follows.

S_t: spot price of the underlying at time t

F_t: forward price of the underlying at time t

T: time to the delivery date/maturity of a forward or other derivative contract

r: risk-free rate of interest, using continuous compounding, for an investment that matures on the delivery date of the forward/future

Continuously compounded interest rates are commonly used in pricing derivatives. For an investment of A dollars, which is compounded m times per annum for n years at a rate of $R\%$ p.a., the final value of the investment is $A(1 + \frac{R}{m})^{mn}$. When we take the limit of this value as m tends to infinity, we arrive at the continuously compounded value of Ae^{Rn}.

We deal with investment assets initially as they are more tractable than commodities. Investment assets refer to stocks, bonds, or even some commodities such as gold or silver, which are primarily held for investment purposes. Investment assets can be bought and sold with ease and generally do not have significant costs linked to storage. Investment assets are also interchangeable with money and easily tradable, with no attendant benefits that can be accrued from holding them, unlike commodities that can be used for other purposes. We make some simplifying assumptions for the purpose of our analysis. The main assumptions are that transaction costs for trading in derivatives or spot markets are minimal and the tax treatment of profits arising from these trades is similar. As mentioned, the overarching assumption is that any arbitrage opportunities that arise in these markets can be closed by market participants.

The no-arbitrage argument allows us to determine the link between spot and forward prices for investment assets. Let us consider a stock with current price S_0 and a current forward price of F_0 for a time to maturity of T. The price for purchasing a stock and holding it for a duration of T while financing the purchase at rate r is $S_0 e^{rT}$, while the price for owning the same stock at time T can also be fixed at F_0 by entering into a forward contract. If there is no arbitrage, the two prices should be equal: $F_0 = S_0 e^{rT}$. If $F_0 > S_0 e^{rT}$, then an arbitrageur can purchase the stock and finance its purchase till time T, while simultaneously selling a forward contract at F_0, and earn the difference. Similarly, if $F_0 < S_0 e^{rT}$, an arbitrageur can short the stock and receive interest on the proceeds of the sale while also entering into a forward contract to purchase stock at F_0.

At the inception of a forward contract, the intrinsic value of the contract is zero. However, over time, the value of the contract changes with a change in forward price. If the fixed price at which a long contract was entered into was F_0 and the current fixed price for a long forward contract with the same maturity and terms is K, then the value of the initial forward contract would be $(F_0 - K)e^{-rT}$. This follows from the fact that we can sell the second contract and realize a difference of $(F_0 - K)$ at maturity, which when discounted by the interest rate gives the value of this portfolio.

We can generalize this to assets which provide income, such as stocks that issue dividends or bonds that pay coupons. We take the case of a dividend-paying stock, which pays a dividend at rate q. For ease of handling, we assume that it is a continuously earned dividend. If there were no dividend, we would expect the stock price S_0 to grow to $S_0 e^{rT}$ in time T. However, the dividend yield over the period would diminish the final price by e^{-qT}; that is, the final price for the stock at time T is $S_0 e^{(r-q)T}$. This is equivalent to saying that an arbitrageur would only need to invest $S_0 e^{-qT}$ at time 0 against a sold forward contract with maturity T. Dividends earned during the course of the transaction would be reinvested into purchasing stock and are financed at a rate r and, for no arbitrage, the following relationship holds:

$$F_0 = S_0 e^{(r-q)T}$$

Futures prices are identical to uncollaterized forward prices under the assumption that interest rates (on futures margins) remain constant over the tenor of the forward/future or are uncorrelated to the price. However, in practice, liquidity and transaction costs, credit costs and taxation of these contracts create differences between the values of forwards and futures. We will ignore these differences in our discussions and use the terms "forwards" and "futures" interchangeably.

Spot–Forward Relationships for Commodities

In the introductory chapters, we have seen how commodity forward curves can have different shapes. As interest rates are non-negative in general, the equation derived above mainly results in upward-sloping forward curves. These are common across stocks, bonds, and some commodities like gold and silver. However, the vast majority of commodities' forward curves cannot be explained based on this relationship.

Unlike investment assets, most commodities are mainly held for the purpose of consumption. Holding commodities requires the payment of storage costs, which can be significant for commodities like crude oil. At the same time, commodities do not provide their owners with income. However, holding commodities does provide companies with the ability to use them in the course of their business and minimize disruptions caused by market price movements. For instance, having physical inventories of crude oil allows a refinery to operate regardless of any supply disruptions or price spikes that may occur in the market for crude oil. It also allows them to react faster to increases in the demand for oil products. These benefits are not provided by a futures contract. Benefit that accrues only to owners of physical commodities and not to holders of financial contracts is known as the convenience yield.

Both storage costs and convenience yield can be expressed as a proportion of the spot price. We assume that storage costs are continuously accrued at the rate c and the convenience yield rate is denoted y. The difference between yield and costs would be the net return from holding the commodity, analogous to the dividend yield of an asset. Hence, the following relationship between futures and spot prices holds for commodities:

$$F_0 = S_0 e^{(r-(y-c))T} = S_0 e^{(r+c-y)T}$$

Therefore, when the convenience yield from holding a commodity is higher than the cost of carry (the sum of the storage and financing costs), the futures curve will be in backwardation. Arbitrage opportunities exist when the futures price is higher than the price implied by the cost of carry. An investor can sell the commodity forward, finance its purchase and storage costs up to maturity, and deliver the commodity under the futures contract; this is known as cash-and-carry arbitrage. Note that this relationship only holds for storable commodities and does not apply to commodities such as electricity. Similarly, reverse cash-and-carry arbitrage is also possible in cases where the commodity can be shorted or sold. However, companies that hold commodities for convenience would not generally enter into such transactions.

Spot and Futures Volatility

Similar to the manner in which spot and futures prices are different for different maturities, the volatility of spot and futures contracts also differs by maturity. We introduce the concept of volatility at this point, as it is important to understanding the valuation of options. The square root of the variance of returns is the standard deviation of price returns and is termed "volatility." If we denote returns as r_i, which are calculated as $r_i = \ln(\frac{S_i}{S_{i-1}})$, the standard deviation of returns or volatility σ is calculated as

$$\sigma = \sqrt{\frac{1}{(n-1)} \sum_{i=1}^{n} (r_i - \mu)^2}$$

where μ is the mean of returns r_i and n is the number of observations of the returns of the stock or futures contract:

$$\mu = \frac{1}{n} \sum_{i=1}^{n} r_i$$

Volatility can be calculated using a historical series of prices (backward looking) or based on market expectations of price movements (forward looking), and is expressed on an annualized basis. Annualizing is accomplished by multiplying daily volatility by the square root of the number of business days in a calendar year (roughly 250):

$$\sigma_{annualized} = \sigma_{daily} * \sqrt{250}$$

Commodity futures contracts have different volatilities and longer-dated futures contracts generally have lower volatilities than short-dated futures. There are several theories that attempt to explain this phenomenon.

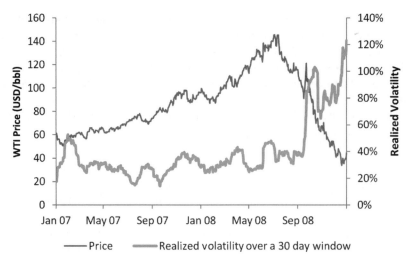

FIGURE 4.3 WTI Crude Oil price vs. volatility
Data Sources: NYMEX, Bloomberg.

Akin to the relationship between prices and inventories, the volatility level of prices also depends on the inventories available. The presence of inventories can serve to dampen any price shocks that may arise from a sudden increase in demand or a drop in supply. Maintaining inventories can help firms to tide over temporary market disruptions and reduce the variability in their business. Thus, both prices and volatilities are negatively dependent on inventories and are positively correlated with each other, and this relationship is known as the inverse leverage effect. This contrasts with the case of investment assets such as equities, where volatility is negatively correlated with prices. Intuitively, inventory levels also impact spot prices more than futures prices, since there is no time to address any imbalances in spot supply and demand without the market price adjusting itself, while future volatility would depend on the expectation of future inventory levels, which can normalize over time. However, price and volatility levels need not be positively correlated if factors other than inventories impact price formation. Oil price and volatility movements during the credit crisis in 2008 deviated from those predicted by the inverse leverage effect (Figure 4.3).

The phenomenon of futures volatility being a decreasing function of futures contract tenor is referred to as the Samuelson effect. The Samuelson hypothesis states that the volatility of futures prices increases as they approach expiration. This is because delivering or receiving commodities under futures contracts introduces sources of volatility linked to the physical supply chain of commodities. It can also be viewed as describing the elasticity of commodity markets to incoming information. New information affects the prices of near-dated futures contracts more, as there is less time for supply and demand to balance (spot markets are inelastic), while longer-dated futures contracts react less to this information.

OPTIONS

We briefly introduced options in an earlier chapter. We now revisit the basics of options and clarify the relationship between options and futures prices.

Call and Put Options

A call option is a derivative contract that gives the owner the right, but not the obligation, to purchase the underlying asset at a fixed price. Similarly, a put option is a derivative that gives the owner the right, but not the obligation, to sell the underlying asset at a fixed price. The main parameters of an option are as follows.

- Underlying asset: a commodity, equity, bond, futures contract, or any other asset.
- Option type: either a call or a put option (vanilla options).
- Option position: either long or short.
- Option inception date: the date that the option contract is entered into.
- Option exercise date (tenor): the date when the option can be exercised.
- Strike price: the fixed price at which the option owner can buy/sell the underlying asset.
- Option premium: the initial price to be paid to purchase the option.

Additional parameters include the settlement style, which could be cash or physical settlement, and the option exercise dates, which can be European, American, or Bermudan. Cash settlement means that upon option exercise, the option owner receives the difference between the prevailing price of the underlying and the strike price in cash (only when the price is higher than the strike price in the case of call options and vice versa for put options), while physical settlement implies that the physical asset is purchased or sold upon exercise. Option exercise could be at expiry (European style) or at any time prior to a fixed date (American style). If an option can be exercised only on a set of predetermined dates, the exercise style is known as Bermudan (between European and American).

The payout diagrams for call and put options are revisited here in Figure 4.4. An option is exercised when it is profitable for the owner of the option to exercise it, that is, when the option is in-the-money (ITM). Conversely, when the option is out-of-the-money (OTM), it is not profitable to exercise the option. When the price of the underlying is equal to the strike price, the option is said to be at-the-money (ATM). Usually, options are struck ATM or OTM at inception.

Note that the payouts described here are the payouts received upon exercise and do not include the premium paid at inception. The inclusion of the premium within the payoff diagrams does not affect the exercise decision, that is, options continue to be exercised irrespective of the actual premium paid. Figure 4.5 shows the net profit after accounting for the premium payment.

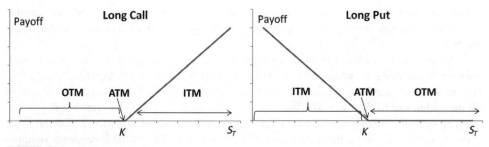

FIGURE 4.4 Call and put option payouts

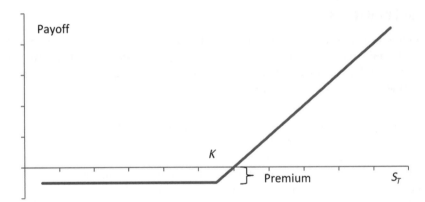

FIGURE 4.5   Net payout (including premium) for a call option

Option exercise can be at the discretion of the option holder or automatic, if the option is profitable to exercise for the holder. The concept of moneyness of the option (whether it is ITM or OTM) can be related to the value of the option. The intrinsic value of an option is the payout from the option if it is exercised immediately. In the case of American options, where early exercise is possible, the value of the option must be greater than or equal to the intrinsic value, because the option holder can receive the intrinsic value by exercising it immediately. The additional value of the option over and above the intrinsic value is called the time value of the option. Thus, an option's value can be split into intrinsic value and time value.

Call options are popular instruments among consumers, who use them to hedge against rises in prices of input commodities. They are also useful for investors to express a bullish view on the prices of assets. Similarly, put options are used by commodity producers or investors to protect the value of their output or investments. However, on their own, they are quite limited in terms of the view that they can monetize; they can also be quite expensive, depending on market conditions and contract-specific terms. In order to limit the premium outlay required to enter into an option structure, option buyers can pursue a variety of strategies, ranging from capping their payouts to selling options to finance the purchase of other options. We will discuss the various option strategies that are popular in the market after a brief discussion of option valuation.

Put–Call Parity

We can see that the payout from a forward can be replicated using call and put options. To establish the relationship between forwards and options, let us consider the following portfolios.

The first portfolio consists of a stock purchased at a price S_0 and a put option, with maturity T and strike K, which costs P. Thus, the cost of setting up this portfolio is $S_0 + P$. The value of this portfolio at time T is the stock price at time T (S_T) added to the payout of the put option $\max(0, K - S_T)$, which equates to $\max(S_T, K - S_T + S_T) = \max(S_T, K)$.

The second portfolio consists of a call option with the same maturity T and the same strike K, costing C, and a bond that pays K at maturity T. The initial investment required to set up this portfolio is $C + Ke^{-rt}$, where Ke^{-rt} is the investment required to pay out K

TABLE 4.1 Portfolios considered to illustrate put–call parity

	Portfolio 1	Portfolio 2
Initial cost	$S_0 + P$	$C + Ke^{-rt}$
Final value	$\max(S_T, K)$	$\max(K, S_T)$

at time T, assuming a constant interest rate of r. The value of this portfolio at maturity is $K + \max(0, S_T - K) = \max(K, S_T)$.

Thus, the values of the two portfolios are equal at time T, as summarized in Table 4.1. By the principle of no arbitrage, the initial value of the two portfolios also must be equal. Otherwise, investors can make a riskless profit by purchasing the cheaper portfolio and selling the more expensive one. Thus, equating the initial values, we get the following expression:

$$S_0 + P = C + Ke^{-rT}$$

The prices of put and call options are related by this expression, which simply states that holding a stock and a put option on the stock is equivalent to purchasing a call option and investing in a bond that pays out the strike price at maturity. This relationship is known as "put–call parity." Thus, by valuing only one of either a call or a put option, we can get the value of the other option using this relationship.

In the case of commodities, options are generally written on futures contracts and not spot prices. Investors hold forward or futures positions and not spot positions and, therefore, the put–call parity relationship is simplified as follows:

$$F_0 e^{-rT} + P = C + Ke^{-rT},$$

or

$$C - P = (F_0 - K)e^{-rT}$$

where the discounted futures price replaces the stock price in the corresponding equation for put–call parity for stock options.

Option-Based Hedging for a Shipping Company

To motivate the discussion on hedging, we take the case of a shipping company that has not engaged in hedging previously. The shipping company consumes bunker fuel and is exposed to changes in fuel price. The current practice at the shipping company is to purchase fuel just prior to use, at which point the price is fixed. The management of the company would like to explore the potential for hedging their future purchases of fuel.

The shipping company consumes bunker fuel, which is a type of fuel oil that is used on vessels. The company is expected to consume about 1 million metric tons of bunker fuel annually. The company's board has approved a policy to hedge up to 50% of their consumption over the next financial year. The firm would like to use WTI Crude Oil as a proxy to hedge against fuel price increases, due to its liquidity and the ease of transacting in futures. Assuming a conversion ratio of 6.35 barrels/metric ton for fuel oil, the total hedging volume on WTI Crude Oil would be $1,000,000 * 6.35 * 50\% = 3,175,000$ barrels, assuming one-for-one hedging in terms of volume. In practice, the hedge ratio would be adjusted to account for the imperfect correlation and the volatility difference between WTI and bunker fuel. We assume that hedges are conducted in tranches of 100,000 barrels each. Hedging transactions are entered into with a hedge provider, like an investment bank, trading house, or brokerage for exchange-traded instruments. While many of these trades can be executed on an exchange, we will use OTC transactions in our examples as they allow for flexibility in contract terms.

If we look at a scenario where the objective of the firm is to fix a maximum price for their fuel consumption, there are a number of strategies that the firm could employ to achieve this. If the firm is willing to set aside a budget for hedging, the objective of hedging can be achieved by the purchase of call options on fuel price. We consider the case where the firm purchases call options that are OTM. This would be appropriate when a firm is willing to absorb some changes in fuel price up to a particular point; that is, where there is reasonable risk tolerance. An option purchase transaction would be structured as in Example 4.1.

Thus, by entering into this option transaction, the shipping company has fixed the maximum price for the purchase of 100,000 barrels of fuel at 72.50 USD/bbl (inclusive of the option premium paid).

Transactions in the OTC market are documented using term sheets and confirmations, which reference an International Swaps and Derivatives Association (ISDA) Master Agreement and attached schedules. The ISDA Master Agreement is a standard agreement used by the derivatives industry and is negotiated between the two counterparties prior to entering into derivative transactions. It provides the general terms applicable to all transactions that are executed between the two parties – including netting of transactions, termination of transactions, credit support, etc. The ISDA provides the definitions for commonly used terms in the documentation of derivative transactions.

Term sheets or confirmations may also be accompanied by scenario analysis, sensitivity analysis, best-case/worst-case analysis, and/or an illustration of how payoffs are calculated under the transaction. This additional information may or may not be presented based on the complexity of the product being transacted, the sophistication of the counterparties involved, and any regulations or guidelines mandating the provision of such information.

IMPLIED VOLATILITY AND THE BLACK–SCHOLES MODEL

In an earlier section, we looked at the definition of volatility and how historical volatility is calculated. Options are instruments whose value depends on the market's prediction for future volatility. Implied volatility is the value of the volatility of the underlying, which, when input into an option pricing formula, returns the market price of the option. While historical volatility can be calculated based on historical prices for an underlying, implied volatility is a subjective parameter, dependent on the market price for an option and the pricing formula used. Implied volatility, as its name states, is the volatility derived from market prices of options based on an accepted pricing model. The model that traders use to derive implied volatility from market prices is called the Black–Scholes model for option prices.

Here, we briefly introduce the Black–Scholes model for pricing options written on stock prices. This is followed by a discussion of Black's model for pricing options on futures, which is appropriate for commodity markets. We then state the sensitivity metrics, known as the Greeks, which are used to manage option portfolio risks.

EXAMPLE 4.1: SAMPLE TERMS FOR AN OPTION PURCHASE TRANSACTION

Transaction terms

Party A:	Hedge Provider
Party B:	Shipping Company
Trade Date:	2 March, 2015
Effective Date:	15 June, 2015
Termination Date:	15 June, 2015
Commodity:	OIL-WTI-NYMEX
Total Notional Quantity:	100,000 barrels
Notional Quantity per Calculation Period:	100,000 barrels/month
Calculation Period:	Effective Date
Settlement Dates:	5 Business Days following the end of the Calculation Period, subject to adjustment in accordance with the Modified Following Business Day convention
Business Days:	New York
Premium:	2.50 USD/bbl
Premium Payer:	Party B
Premium Payment Date:	9 March, 2015

Floating amount details
Cap

Floating-Price Payer:	Party A
Cap Price:	70 USD/bbl
Floating Price:	Commodity Reference Price
Commodity Reference Price:	"OIL-WTI-NYMEX" means that the price for a Pricing Date will be that day's Specified Price per barrel of West Texas Intermediate light sweet crude oil on the NYMEX of the Futures Contract for the Delivery Date, stated in US dollars, as made public by the NYMEX on that Pricing Date
Specified Price:	Official Settlement Price
Delivery Date:	First Nearby Month
Pricing Dates:	Each Commodity Business Day during the relevant Calculation Period
Calculation Agent:	Party A
Documentation:	Confirmation under ISDA Master Agreement

The Black–Scholes–Merton Model

In the 1970s, Fischer Black, Myron Scholes, and Robert Merton advanced the field of derivative pricing with important results applicable to the pricing of options. Since then, the universe of derivatives priced and traded has grown enormously, permeating all asset classes. We present the Black–Scholes model for pricing European options on a non-dividend-paying stock here.

The Black–Scholes model is used to arrive at the price of European options under certain assumptions that include no arbitrage, constant interest rates and volatility, short-selling being allowed, and no taxes or transaction costs. The stock price is also assumed to be lognormally distributed. A full list of the assumptions is provided later in the chapter, where we discuss the derivation of the Black–Scholes formula. The Black–Scholes price for a call option, C, depends on the following parameters:

S_0: the spot price of the stock

K: the strike price of the call option

T: the time to maturity of the option

σ: the volatility of the stock price

r: the risk-free interest rate

The Black–Scholes price for the European call option on a non-dividend-paying stock is

$$C = S_0 N(d_1) - Ke^{-rT}N(d_2)$$

where

$$d_1 = \frac{\ln(S_0/K) + (r + \sigma^2/2)T}{\sigma\sqrt{T}}$$

$$d_2 = \frac{\ln(S_0/K) + (r - \sigma^2/2)T}{\sigma\sqrt{T}} = d_1 - \sigma\sqrt{T}$$

Here, $N(x)$ is the cumulative distribution function for the standard normal distribution. $N(x)$ represents the probability that a variable with the standard normal distribution $N(0, 1)$ is less than x.

From put–call parity, the value of a European put option at the same strike is calculated as

$$P = Ke^{-rT}N(-d_2) - S_0 N(-d_1)$$

The value of volatility σ is not observable in the market and is inferred from the prices of options. Thus, in practice, traders use the volatility derived from market prices of options to value other options.

For a dividend-paying stock with a dividend yield of q, the corresponding expressions for the price c of a European call option and the price p of a European put option are as follows:

$$c = S_0 e^{-qT}N(d_1) - Ke^{-rT}N(d_2)$$
$$p = Ke^{-rT}N(-d_2) - S_0 e^{-qT}N(-d_1)$$

where

$$d_1 = \frac{\ln(S_0/K) + (r - q + \sigma^2/2)T}{\sigma\sqrt{T}}$$

$$d_2 = \frac{\ln(S_0/K) + (r - q - \sigma^2/2)T}{\sigma\sqrt{T}} = d_1 - \sigma\sqrt{T}$$

Black's Model for Pricing Options on Futures Contracts

We now consider options on futures contracts, which are especially popular in the fixed-income and commodities markets. Futures options are options on futures contracts where the underlying futures contract is delivered upon exercise of the option, as opposed to the underlying stock in the case of stock options. For example, a futures call option – when exercised – gives the holder of the option the difference between the strike price and the futures price, in addition to a long position in the futures contract. Similarly, a put option gives the holder a short position in the underlying futures contract and the difference between the strike price and the futures price as a cash amount upon exercise. Futures options are popular because the futures contracts themselves are more liquid and easily tradable compared with the spot price in the case of commodities and other assets like interest rates.

Fischer Black extended the Black–Scholes–Merton model to account for the valuation of futures options. The assumption here is that futures prices are lognormally distributed, like stock prices are assumed to be in order to derive the Black–Scholes–Merton equation. With this assumption and replacing the initial spot price with the futures price, we get the Black's model as follows. The price c of a European call option and the price p of a European put option are

$$c = e^{-rT}[F_0 N(d_1) - KN(d_2)]$$
$$p = e^{-rT}[KN(-d_2) - F_0 N(-d_1)]$$

where

$$d_1 = \frac{\ln(F_0/K) + (\sigma^2/2)T}{\sigma\sqrt{T}}$$

$$d_2 = \frac{\ln(F_0/K) - (\sigma^2/2)T}{\sigma\sqrt{T}} = d_1 - \sigma\sqrt{T}$$

Here, F_0 is the initial value of the futures price and σ is the volatility of the futures price.

THE GREEKS

The Greeks are a set of metrics that describe the sensitivity of option prices to underlying parameters such as spot price, volatility, interest rates, and time to maturity. Estimating the Greeks will help in devising risk management strategies for individual options as well as portfolios of derivatives.

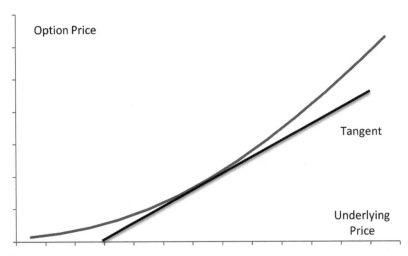

FIGURE 4.6   Delta is the slope of the tangent to the option price

Delta

The delta (Δ) of an option is the ratio of the change in the price of the option to the change in the price of the underlying. It is the rate of change of the option's price with the change in the underlying price. Thus, the delta for a call option is

$$\Delta = \frac{\partial c}{\partial S}$$

For example, if the delta of a call option on a stock is 0.4, then in order to hedge that sold call option, the option seller needs to purchase 0.4 stocks for every option sold. Assuming the call option allows the owner to purchase 100 shares, the hedger needs to purchase $0.4 * 100 = 40$ shares in order to hedge the call option. When the option price is charted against the spot price, for a particular value of the option price, Δ represents the slope of the tangent to the option price at that point (Figure 4.6).

When the derivative position is offset by the purchase of shares, the delta of the portfolio is zero and it is said to be a delta-neutral portfolio. As can be seen from the function for the call option price, the delta of the portfolio can change depending on the level of the stock and, thus, the portfolio needs to be rebalanced frequently. This rebalancing of a portfolio is known as dynamic hedging.

From the equation for the value of a call option on a non-dividend-paying stock, we can see that the delta of a call option is

$$\Delta(\text{call}) = \frac{\partial c}{\partial S} = N(d_1)$$

Similarly, the delta of a put option on a non-dividend-paying stock is

$$\Delta(\text{put}) = \frac{\partial p}{\partial S} = N(d_1) - 1 = -N(-d_1)$$

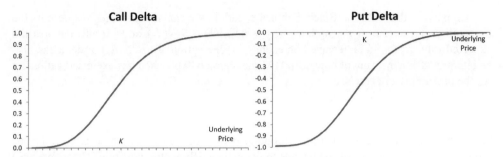

FIGURE 4.7 Call option and put option delta vs. strike

For a dividend-paying stock, the equivalent expressions are

$$\Delta(\text{call}) = \frac{\partial c}{\partial S} = e^{-qT}N(d_1),$$

and

$$\Delta(\text{put}) = \frac{\partial p}{\partial S} = e^{-qT}(N(d_1) - 1)$$

where d_1 is as defined earlier for a dividend-paying stock.

The variation of delta with stock price for call and put options is displayed in Figure 4.7.

Intuitive Interpretation of the Black–Scholes Equation   After defining the delta of an option as above, we can revisit the Black–Scholes equation as follows. The price of a call option as per Black–Scholes is

$$C = S_0 N(d_1) - Ke^{-rT}N(d_2)$$

Upon exercise of a call option, the option holder pays the fixed strike price K in order to receive the stock underlying the option. The option is only exercised when the stock price is higher than the strike price K and, thus, the present value of the cash outflow when the option is exercised, after discounting, is

$$Ke^{-rT}p(S_T > K)$$

Similarly, upon exercise of the call option, the option holder receives the stocks underlying the option. The present value of the stocks received is dependent on both the probability of exercise and the expected value of the stock conditional on exercise, appropriately discounted. The present value of the stocks received on exercise is

$$E(S_T \mid S_T > K) * e^{-rT} * p(S_T > K)$$

where $E(S_T \mid S_T > K)$ denotes the expected value of S_T in scenarios where the option is exercised.

Thus, the value of the call option can be described as the present value of stocks received upon exercise less the discounted value of the strike price paid in order to exercise the option:

$$c = E(S_T \mid S_T > K) * e^{-rT} * p(S_T > K) - Ke^{-rT}p(S_T > K)$$

Comparing this with the Black–Scholes equation, we can see that $N(d_2)$ represents the probability of exercise of the option $(p(S_T > K))$, while $S_0N(d_1)$ or $S_0\Delta$(call) denotes the expected value of the stock received on exercise of the option. Thus, $N(d_1)$ or delta can also be interpreted as a measure of how deep ITM the option will be when it is exercised, adjusting for the probability of exercise.

Gamma

As we have seen above, the delta of an option is not constant across stock prices and this requires dynamic adjustments to be made to maintain a risk-neutral portfolio. The gamma (Γ) of an option is the rate of change of the option's delta with respect to the price of the underlying stock. That is,

$$\Gamma = \frac{\partial^2 c}{\partial S^2}$$

It is the second derivative of the option price with respect to the stock price. Thus, gamma represents the curvature of the option price function at a particular stock price.

The gamma of a call option and a put option are the same and, for a non-dividend-paying stock, are given by

$$\Gamma = \frac{\partial^2 c}{\partial S^2} = \frac{\partial^2 p}{\partial S^2} = \frac{N'(d_1)}{S_0\sigma\sqrt{T}}$$

where

$$N'(x) = \frac{1}{\sqrt{2\pi}}e^{-x^2/2}$$

For a dividend-paying stock, the value is

$$\Gamma = \frac{e^{-qT}N'(d_1)}{S_0\sigma\sqrt{T}}$$

where d_1 is as defined earlier for a dividend-paying stock.

Unlike delta hedging, where positions in the underlying asset can be used to offset the delta of the derivative, gamma hedging requires trading in other derivatives to maintain gamma neutrality. Thus, gamma is more relevant when discussing portfolios of options, where appropriate derivative instruments can be used to offset the gamma of the entire portfolio. The variation of gamma with stock price is plotted in Figure 4.8.

Theta

The theta (Θ) or "time decay" of an option is the rate of change of the option price with respect to time, with all other parameters remaining constant. For European options on a non-dividend-paying stock, the expressions for theta for call options and put options, respectively, are

$$\Theta(\text{call}) = -\frac{S_0N'(d_1)\sigma}{2\sqrt{T}} - rKe^{-rt}N(d_2) = -Ke^{-rt}\left[\frac{N'(d_2)\sigma}{2\sqrt{T}} + rN(d_2)\right]$$

$$\Theta(\text{put}) = -\frac{S_0N'(d_1)\sigma}{2\sqrt{T}} + rKe^{-rt}N(-d_2) = -Ke^{-rt}\left[\frac{N'(d_2)\sigma}{2\sqrt{T}} - rN(-d_2)\right]$$

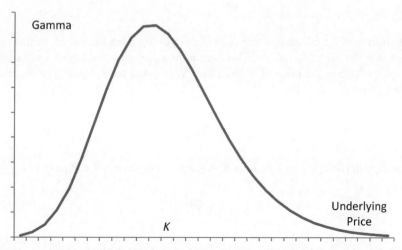

FIGURE 4.8   Option gamma vs. underlying price

For a dividend-paying stock, with d_1 and d_2 as defined earlier for dividend-paying stocks, the equivalent expressions are

$$\Theta(\text{call}) = -\frac{S_0 N'(d_1)\sigma e^{-qt}}{2\sqrt{T}} + qS_0 N(d_1)e^{-qt} - rKe^{-rt}N(d_2)$$

$$\Theta(\text{put}) = -\frac{S_0 N'(d_1)\sigma e^{-qt}}{2\sqrt{T}} - qS_0 N(-d_1)e^{-qt} + rKe^{-rt}N(-d_2)$$

The variation of theta for a European call option is displayed in Figure 4.9.

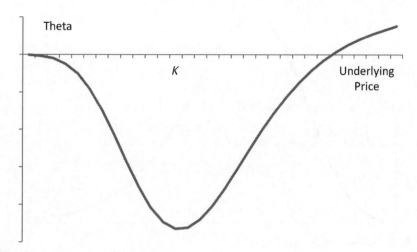

FIGURE 4.9   Theta vs. underlying price

Vega

For the derivation of the Black–Scholes price of an option, we have assumed that the volatility is constant over the life of the option. However, in practice, the volatility of a stock price can change and this affects the price of a derivative. Vega (v) is the sensitivity of the derivative price to volatility:

$$v = \frac{\partial c}{\partial \sigma}$$

For an option (call/put) on a non-dividend-paying stock, vega is calculated as

$$v = S_0 \sqrt{T} N'(d_1)$$

For an option (call/put) on a dividend-paying stock, vega is given by

$$v = S_0 \sqrt{T} N'(d_1) e^{-qT}$$

where d_1 is calculated as per the Black–Scholes formula for dividend-paying stocks.

The vega of an option with reference to the underlying price is shown in Figure 4.10.

Rho

Again, as per the derivation of the Black–Scholes–Merton formula, interest rates are constant for all maturities. However, this is not the case in practice as interest rates are dependent on maturity and can also change over the life of the derivative. The interest rate sensitivity of a derivative or a portfolio of derivatives is represented by rho (ρ). The interest rate sensitivities

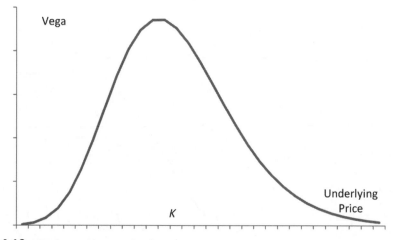

FIGURE 4.10   Option vega vs. stock price

of European call and put options are given by

$$\rho(\text{call}) = KTe^{-rT}N(d_2)$$
$$\rho(\text{put}) = -KTe^{-rT}N(-d_2)$$

These are the most important Greeks that are tracked by derivative traders. They are especially useful in handling portfolios of derivatives as they aid in the simplification of the exposures under the portfolio into underlying risks and help identify appropriate instruments to hedge with. In addition, there can be many second-order Greeks, which are more important to portfolios exposed to multiple correlated underlyings or containing complex instruments.

Higher-Order Greeks

Some of the higher-order Greeks, other than gamma, which traders can use are as follows. The Greeks have been calculated for a call option.

- Vanna is the change in delta with change in volatility $= \frac{\partial^2 c}{\partial \sigma \partial S} = -e^{-qt}N'(d_1)\frac{d_2}{\sigma}$.
- Volga is the change in vega with change in volatility $= \frac{\partial^2 c}{\partial \sigma^2} = e^{-qt}S_0\sqrt{T}N'(d_1)\frac{d_1 d_2}{\sigma}$.
- Charm is the change in delta with time, also called delta bleed $= \frac{\partial^2 c}{\partial t \partial S} = -qe^{-qt}N(d_1) + e^{-qt}N'(d_1)\frac{(2(r-q)T - d_2\sigma\sqrt{T})}{2\sigma T\sqrt{T}}$.
- Speed is the change in gamma with respect to spot, or the third derivative of option price with respect to spot price $= \frac{\partial^3 c}{\partial S^3} = -e^{-qt}\frac{N'(d_1)}{S^2\sigma\sqrt{T}}(\frac{d_1}{\sigma\sqrt{T}} + 1) = -\frac{\Gamma}{S}(\frac{d_1}{\sigma\sqrt{T}} + 1)$.
- Color is the change in gamma with respect to change in time, also called gamma decay $= \frac{\partial^3 c}{\partial S^2 \partial T} = -e^{-qt}\frac{N'(d_1)}{2S\sigma T\sqrt{T}}(2qT + 1 + \frac{d_1(2(r-q)T - d_2\sigma\sqrt{T})}{\sigma\sqrt{T}})$.
- For multi-asset options, cross-gamma measures the rate of change of delta of one underlying with respect to the other underlying $= \frac{\partial^2 c}{\partial S \partial S'}$.

While dynamic hedging requires continuous trading of the derivative and cash instruments to maintain risk-neutral portfolios, transaction costs and the infrastructure required to achieve continuous trading limit the frequency of hedging in practice. Aggregating portfolio risks using Greeks helps to reduce the amount of trading required by matching offsetting risks present in the portfolio. In practice, risks are also managed in the order of their magnitudes with priority generally being given to delta hedging, followed by gamma and vega hedging.

Black's Model Option Greeks

From Black's model, we can restate the Greeks for options on futures as below. These are more useful for commodities, as options are usually written on futures prices rather than spot prices.

Greek	Call	Put
Delta (Δ)	$e^{-rt}N(d_1)$	$e^{-rt}(N(d_1) - 1)$
Gamma (Γ)	$\dfrac{e^{-rT}N'(d_1)}{F_0\sigma\sqrt{T}}$	$\dfrac{e^{-rT}N'(d_1)}{F_0\sigma\sqrt{T}}$
Theta (Θ)	$-\dfrac{F_0N'(d_1)\sigma e^{-rt}}{2\sqrt{T}} + rF_0N(d_1)e^{-rt}$ $- rKe^{-rt}N(d_2)$	$-\dfrac{F_0N'(d_1)\sigma e^{-rt}}{2\sqrt{T}} - rF_0N(-d_1)e^{-rt}$ $+ rKe^{-rt}N(-d_2)$
Vega (v)	$F_0\sqrt{T}N'(d_1)e^{-rT}$	$F_0\sqrt{T}N'(d_1)e^{-rT}$
Rho (ρ)	$KTe^{-rT}N(d_2)$	$-KTe^{-rT}N(-d_2)$

Now that we have discussed pricing options on futures contracts, we can revisit the case of the shipping company. Again, the company can contact an options market-maker to purchase a call option or enter into any other strategy that it deems appropriate. These European options will be able to offer protection against purchase price movements for a particular delivery date. However, most companies purchase and consume fuel on a daily basis and hedging based on a single day's price may open up the possibility that the price hedged is not reflective of actual fuel costs over a period of time. This can occur in the commodity markets due to limited liquidity and the presence of only a few counterparties at a point in time, which is the reason that many counterparties prefer to average prices over an interval.

In this context, we now discuss Asian swaps and options, which are the instruments of choice in the OTC commodities markets.

ASIAN SWAPS AND OPTIONS

Asian or average-price swaps and options are the instruments of choice for OTC hedgers. "Asianing" (averaging) reduces the potential for manipulation of price fixings in commodity markets, arising from the paucity of transactions and the concentration of market power in a limited number of banks and trading houses. Averaging also helps mimic the price exposure of commodity hedgers, who produce or consume commodities on a daily basis, and helps reduce any disconnect between their physical business and financial realizations (revenues or costs) that can arise from timing mismatches. Finally, averaging smooths the impact of price movements on a hedger's position, which can be valuable in volatile markets where liquidity is scarce. This smoothing makes average-price options cheaper than the corresponding futures options.

Average-price instruments are transacted in the same way as traditional instruments like forwards or futures. Swaps and average-price options (APOs) can be traded and/or cleared on exchanges for most commodities. Exchange-traded APOs are generally cash-settled, with the customer receiving the difference between the calculated average price and the strike price of the APO when the option is exercised. Averaging is usually carried out over a calendar monthly period. The usual reference contract for calculating the average price is the front-month futures contract for that particular date. Thus, when a contract expires in the middle of a calendar month, the next contract is used to determine the remaining fixings for that calendar month.

For example, assume that a firm has entered into an Asian swap to purchase 10,000 barrels of WTI Crude Oil at a price of 75 USD/bbl for the month of June 2015. If the expiry of the WTI July futures contract (which would be the front-month contract at the start of June) is 22 June 2015, then the daily settlement price used from the start of the month up to 22 June would be the price of the July futures contract and for the remaining days of the month, the August 2015 futures contract would be used.

The hedging of Asian swaps takes this averaging methodology into account. Thus, in order to accurately hedge an Asian swap, two futures contracts need to be used with their notional amounts in proportion to the number of business days in the calendar month that each future contract is used to calculate the average. Thus, in the previous example, if the number of business days prior to and including the expiry date (22 June 2015) is 16 and the total number of business days in June 2015 is 22, then hedging an average-price swap for June 2015 will require the hedge provider to purchase (16/22*monthly notional amount) in July WTI futures and (6/22*monthly notional amount) in August WTI futures. Similarly, in order to realize the average price, the hedge provider would have to price out the swap by selling the equivalent daily notional amount (1/22*monthly notional amount) of the front-month futures contract at the official settlement price (closing price) on each trading day. In practice, for longer-dated swaps, hedge providers "cover the delta" (make their portfolio delta-neutral) by purchasing or selling the most liquid futures contract (usually the front-month future) first and then addressing the time-spread positions created. This works in most commodity markets where longer-dated futures are highly correlated with shorter-dated contracts. Time spreads are also quite liquid, especially in OTC markets, thus presenting a cheaper way to hedge Asian swaps.

Asian Swap-Based Hedging for a Shipping Company

In the case of the shipping company discussed earlier, if the company is unable to pass on fuel price increases to its customers, it may want to fix the price of fuel. This can be accomplished using a commodity fixed-price swap. An appropriate underlying to consider for hedging bunker fuel is high sulfur fuel oil (HSFO), which is used as a bunker fuel. We use Singapore High Sulfur Fuel Oil 380 centistoke (CST) as the benchmark for hedging and assume that the company hedges in monthly tranches of 20,000 metric tons per month.

A sample term sheet for a swap transaction is shown in Example 4.2 . With this transaction, the shipping company is able to hedge the monthly average price for Singapore HSFO 380 CST over a period of six months.

OPTION STRUCTURES

We can now develop structures based on European and Asian swaps and options. This section highlights the popular option strategies used by consumers for hedging.

Call Spreads and Put Spreads

One of the common strategies to reduce the cost of an option strategy is to cap the upside offered by the option. Call spreads involve the purchase of a call option and the sale of a

EXAMPLE 4.2: SAMPLE TERMS FOR A COMMODITY SWAP

Transaction terms

Party A:	Hedge Provider
Party B:	Shipping Company
Trade Date:	2 March, 2015
Effective Date:	1 April, 2015
Termination Date:	30 September, 2015
Commodity:	Singapore High Sulfur Fuel Oil 380 CST
Total Notional Quantity:	120,000 Metric Tons
Notional Quantity per Calculation Period:	20,000 Metric Tons/month
Calculation Periods:	Monthly periods, from and including the Effective Date to and including the Termination Date, for a total of six Calculation Periods
Settlement Dates:	5 Business Days following the end of each Calculation Period, subject to adjustment in accordance with the Modified Following Business Day convention
Settlement Business Days:	Singapore, New York

Fixed amount details

Fixed-Price Payer:	Party B
Fixed Price:	310 USD/MT

Floating amount details

Floating-Price Payer:	Party A
Floating Price:	For a particular Calculation Period, the unweighted arithmetic average of the Commodity Reference Price for each Pricing Date over the Calculation Period
Commodity Reference Price:	"FUEL OIL-380 CST SINGAPORE (CARGOES)-PLATTS ASIA-PACIFIC" means that the price for a Pricing Date will be that day's Specified Price per metric ton of fuel oil with a viscosity of up to 380 centistoke, stated in US dollars, published under the heading "Singapore: HSFO 380 CST" in the issue of Platts Asia-Pacific that reports prices effective on that Pricing Date
Specified Price:	Mean of Platts Singapore
Pricing Dates:	Each Commodity Business Day during the relevant Calculation Period
Calculation Agent:	Party A
Documentation:	Confirmation under ISDA Master Agreement

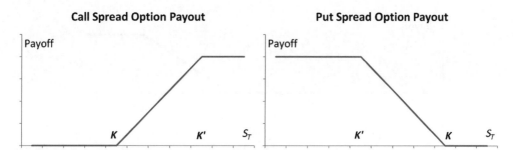

FIGURE 4.11   Payouts for call spread and put spread options

call option at a higher strike (K') than the strike of the option purchased (K). Similarly, put spreads are constructed by buying a put option and selling a put option at a lower strike than the strike of the bought put option. The payouts from the call spread and the put spread are shown in Figure 4.11. This strategy is popular in many markets due to the reduced cost and lower potential exposure to sellers of these options in OTC markets. They are also useful in cases where prices are expected to rise above (drop below) the bought option strike levels but not significantly higher (lower).

Collars, Three-Ways, and Calendar Spread Options

A collar trade for a consumer or investor who believes that prices will rise involves the purchase of a call option and the sale of a put option to finance the purchase of the call. That is, the consumer takes on the risk of prices falling below the put strike price while getting protection from prices rising above the call strike price. The payout for the collar trade is shown in Figure 4.12.

Collar structures are usually set up to have no premium outflow at the inception of the structure. These are commonly referred to as zero-cost collars or more accurately, zero-premium collars.

Another payout that involves the purchase and sale of options is the three-way strategy (Figure 4.13). The objective of this strategy is to reduce the cost of setting up the collar

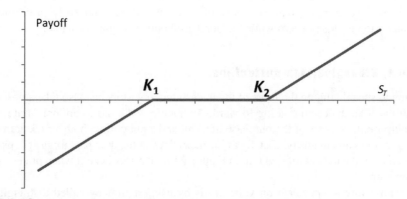

FIGURE 4.12   Collar structure payoff

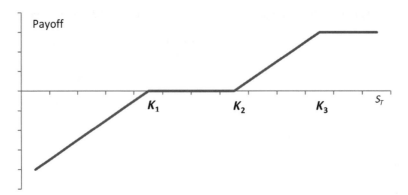

FIGURE 4.13   Payoff profile for a three-ways

transaction by capping the potential upside under the trade. For instance, consumers can purchase a call spread option (instead of a call option under the collar) and sell a put option to finance its purchase. In cases where the structure is meant to have zero cost at inception, the strikes for the bought call and/or the sold put can be enhanced in comparison with the collar structure.

Instead of selling an option for the same maturity, investors can also sell options with different maturities to finance the purchase of other options. For instance, an investor can finance the purchase of a call option for a certain maturity T by selling a call option for maturity T', where $T > T'$. In this case, the investor is wagering that prices will rise above the call strike price at time T while staying below the option strike price at time T'. This type of option is known as a calendar-spread option or a time-spread option. In practice, time-spread options are usually closed out upon maturity of the shorter-dated option in order to avoid holding a naked option (an option held without any offsetting position, like another option or a stock) and to reduce margins. When the strategy is implemented for an investment asset like a stock, it can be viewed as a position on the volatility of the asset. With regard to commodities, they are more frequently used by speculators as opposed to commodity consumers and can be used to speculate on changes in forward curve shapes.

The value of a calendar-spread option at the time of expiry of the shorter-dated option is shown in Figure 4.14. The time-spread option pays out when the price of the underlying is close to the strike at time T'. When the price of the asset is close to the strike price, the value of the sold option is close to zero while the purchased option is quite valuable.

Straddles, Strangles, and Butterflies

In addition to speculating on the price of the underlying, investors can also take a position on the volatility of an underlying going forward. A straddle is the most common strategy used for this purpose. It consists of the purchase of a call and a put option, both struck at the same strike and for the same maturity. Usually the strike is fixed at the then prevailing spot price. As can be seen from the net payoff diagram in Figure 4.15, investors benefit when prices move in either direction.

A cheaper way to speculate on volatility is by using a strategy called a strangle (Figure 4.16). A strangle is similar to a straddle but for the fact that the call and put option strikes

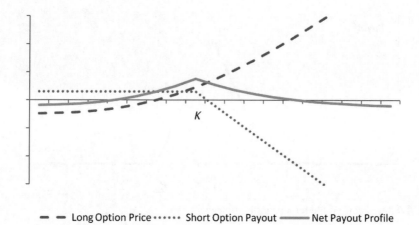

— — Long Option Price ····· Short Option Payout ———— Net Payout Profile

FIGURE 4.14   Calendar spread payout at shorted-dated option's expiry

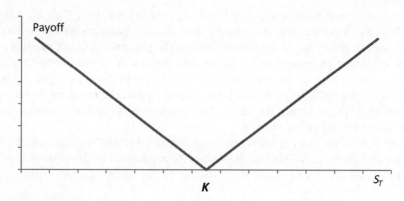

FIGURE 4.15   Straddle payout

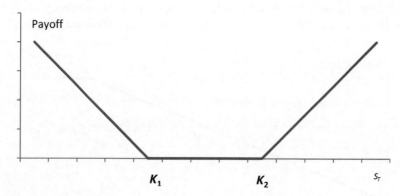

FIGURE 4.16   Strangle payout

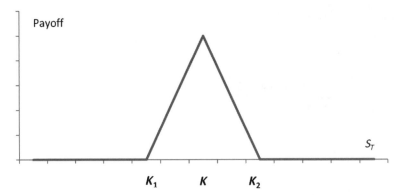

FIGURE 4.17 Payoff profile for a butterfly strategy

are different. The strikes are both OTM at inception, reducing the premium outlay required to pursue this strategy.

Investors may also want to wager that volatility will not rise going forward. In order to do this, they can short a straddle or a strangle. However, in practice, shorting (selling) these structures requires the usage of large credit lines or the placement of high margins as these structures are almost guaranteed to result in a cash outflow at the maturity of the trade. A cheaper way to monetize a view on volatility is by using a butterfly strategy. The butterfly strategy ensures that investors get paid if prices stay in a particular range, while not resulting in any outflows if prices breach the range. The only loss possible in this case is the initial premium required to set up the strategy.

The butterfly strategy's payout is shown in Figure 4.17. The strategy can be executed using either put options or call options. It involves the purchase of a call option at a low strike, the sale of two call options ATM, and the purchase of a call option at a high strike.

Capped Forwards

Finally, hedgers or investors can also combine swaps or forwards with options to achieve lower costs or enhanced payouts. One of the simplest strategies involves combining a long forward position with a sold call. This is called a covered call or a capped forward (Figure 4.18). This

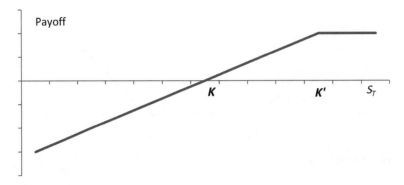

FIGURE 4.18 Capped forward payoff

caps the gains of the investor while providing additional income from the sale of an option or, equivalently, it enhances the strike of the forward. Conversely, we can also have a floored forward, where the investor purchases a put option to limit their downside on the bought forward.

Capped Swap Usage for a Shipping Company

Let us assume that the shipping company discussed earlier can pass on some of the costs of higher fuel to its customers. Indeed, it has become common practice over the past few years for shipping companies to levy a bunker adjustment factor or bunker surcharge when fuel prices rise. This obviates the need for companies to hedge against extreme spikes in fuel prices. However, shipping companies may be adversely affected if they impose surcharges too early or charge too much as opposed to their competition. In such cases, these firms can enter into swap transactions that protect them against any fuel price increases while giving up some upside on the hedge to reflect their ability to charge customers for fuel. This is achieved by means of a capped swap, that is, a swap with a sold call option (or cap). The premium from the sold option is used to improve the strike of the swap.

The term sheet for this transaction can be constructed using the terms for the two strategies discussed earlier. For this case, we illustrate potential payouts using a scenario analysis as follows (Tables 4.2 and 4.3). We assume that the shipping company is able to buy a swap at a strike of 300 USD/MT by selling a cap with a strike of 330 USD/MT. This translates into a tolerance for rising prices of 10%, above which the company is able to levy surcharges to cover further rises in fuel cost.

The net fuel price paid in the first case is offset by surcharges that limit the price paid to 300 USD/MT (the swap price). Using this strategy, the shipping company can fix its fuel spend at an attractive level, compared with prevailing costs, by mitigating the effect of fuel price movements while monetizing the ability to pass on costs to customers in extreme price scenarios.

TABLE 4.2   Scenario 1 – rising prices

Month	Fuel oil price (USD/MT)	Capped swap payout (USD/MT)	Net fuel price (USD/MT)
1	300	0	300
2	305	5	300
3	315	15	300
4	328	28	300
5	341	30	311
6	360	30	330
7	357	30	327
8	372	30	342
9	390	30	360
10	411	30	381
11	419	30	389
12	436	30	406

TABLE 4.3   Scenario 2 – falling prices

Month	Fuel oil price (USD/MT)	Capped swap payout (USD/MT)	Net fuel price (USD/MT)
1	295	−5	300
2	301	1	300
3	292	−8	300
4	283	−17	300
5	279	−21	300
6	271	−29	300
7	254	−46	300
8	246	−54	300
9	249	−51	300
10	239	−61	300
11	242	−58	300
12	235	−65	300

DERIVATIVES PRICING

We now discuss the derivation of the Black–Scholes formula, beginning with an introduction to stochastic processes.

Stochastic Processes for Asset Prices – An Introduction

Unlike forwards or futures, which have linear payouts, options are non-linear products where payouts are dependent on an exercise decision triggered by the underlying's price at the time of exercise. The non-linear payout from an option cannot be replicated using a physical position, unlike in the case of forwards or futures, which are related to spot prices by convergence. Thus, no-arbitrage arguments alone are not sufficient to determine the value of an option. Option pricing requires an understanding of the behavior of prices. Specifically, the probability distribution of prices is needed to value an option, and certain assumptions and approximations related to the distribution are required.

Asset prices move randomly over time and in random steps. Any variable (not necessarily price) that changes in value over time in a random fashion is said to follow a stochastic process. Stochastic processes can be considered over a time interval where the variable changes only at fixed points in time (a discrete-time process) or changes at any random point in time (a continuous-time process). Although the actual points in time where prices change can be determined, we approximate these price changes with continuous-time processes as they are mathematically tractable. Similarly, we also prefer to use continuous variables, where changes in the variable are random within a certain range (determined by its distribution) unlike price movements in real life, which are actually in discrete steps.

Brownian Motion and Wiener Processes

One of the earliest stochastic processes observed was the Brownian motion. In 1827, Robert Brown observed the motion of pollen particles in water through a microscope and noted that the movements of these particles were erratic and unpredictable. It was later postulated that the random motion was due to the particles' collisions with molecules of water, helping to confirm the existence of atoms and molecules. Brownian motion was later described mathematically as a Wiener process. A Wiener process has the following properties.

1. If W_i is used to represent the Wiener process, $W_0 = 0$.
2. The Wiener process has independent and identically distributed (i.i.d.) increments.
3. The increment in the process ΔW over a short time period Δt is normally distributed as follows:

$$\Delta W \sim N(0, \Delta t)$$

where $N(0, \Delta t)$ is the standard normal distribution with mean 0 and variance Δt.

The increment ΔW is arrived at by sampling from the standard normal distribution $N(0, 1)$ and multiplying the value by the square root of the time interval, i.e. $\Delta W = N(0, 1)\sqrt{\Delta t}$.

By virtue of having independent increments, a Wiener process has the property that the future value of the process depends solely on the present value and not on past values. This is known as the Markov property, and the processes that exhibit this feature are called Markov processes. Asset prices are generally assumed to follow Markov processes as efficient markets impute all available information into the asset price and any further increments occur upon the arrival of new information.

A generalized Wiener process allows for a drift in the value of the variable, in addition to the random changes that follow a Wiener process. A generalized Wiener process for a variable x can be expressed as

$$\Delta x = \mu \Delta t + \sigma \Delta W$$

where μ and σ are constants. This process has a drift of μ per unit time and a standard deviation of σ. As we prefer to deal with variables in continuous time, we use the notation dx to indicate a small change in x as the time interval Δt tends to 0. Thus, the equivalent continuous-time representation of a generalized Wiener process is

$$dx = \mu dt + \sigma dW$$

Thus, we can consider the drift μ to be the average appreciation in absolute terms for the price of an asset and σ to be the standard deviation of asset prices. However, this cannot be considered to be a realistic formulation of the process for an asset price as the appreciation is independent of the prevailing price level. A more appropriate formulation for a price process would liken the drift term to the average return expected by investors in the asset, which leads us to the geometric Brownian motion process. If we consider a stock price S, the model for the price process is

$$\frac{dS}{S} = \mu dt + \sigma dW,$$

or

$$dS = \mu S dt + \sigma S dW$$

Thus, in this price process, μS is the expected appreciation in the stock price over the interval dt and μ is the expected rate of return.

An Itô process is a special case of a Wiener process where the drift and standard deviation are functions of time and the variable itself. It can be represented as

$$dx = \mu(x, t)dt + \sigma(x, t)dW$$

where $\mu(x, t)$ and $\sigma(x, t)$ are functions of x and t. This process has a drift of $\mu(x, t)$ per unit time and a standard deviation of $\sigma(x, t)$, which can change with the variable x and with time.

Itô's Lemma

Itô's lemma is an important mathematical result in the area of stochastic differential equations. As the value of an option or any other derivative is dependent on the underlying's price and the time to maturity of the option, the stochastic process of the underlying price is of interest in determining the evolution of the derivative's value. We state Itô's lemma as follows.

Assume that a variable x follows an Itô process as follows:

$$dx = \mu(x, t)dt + \sigma(x, t)dW$$

Itô's lemma states that for any twice-differentiable function F of x and t follows the process

$$dF = \left(\frac{\partial F}{\partial t} + \mu \frac{\partial F}{\partial x} + \frac{1}{2}\sigma^2 \frac{\partial^2 F}{\partial x^2} \right) dt + \sigma \frac{\partial F}{\partial x} dW$$

which is also an Itô process with a drift of $(\frac{\partial F}{\partial t} + \mu \frac{\partial F}{\partial x} + \frac{1}{2}\sigma^2 \frac{\partial^2 F}{\partial x^2})$ and a variance of $\sigma^2 (\frac{\partial F}{\partial x})^2$.

The proof of this lemma is beyond the scope of this book, but it can be viewed as an extension of the Taylor-series expansion in differential calculus.

For the geometric Brownian motion process

$$dS = \mu S dt + \sigma S dW$$

applying Itô's lemma for a function F of x and t gives the process of F as

$$dF = \left(\frac{\partial F}{\partial t} + \mu S \frac{\partial F}{\partial S} + \frac{1}{2}\sigma^2 S^2 \frac{\partial^2 F}{\partial S^2} \right) dt + \sigma S \frac{\partial F}{\partial S} dW$$

If we apply Itô's lemma to the function $F = \ln S$, the process followed by F can be derived as follows:

$$\frac{\partial F}{\partial t} = 0, \quad \frac{\partial F}{\partial S} = \frac{1}{S}, \quad \frac{\partial^2 F}{\partial S^2} = -\frac{1}{S^2}$$

Therefore

$$dF = \left(\mu - \frac{1}{2}\sigma^2 \right) dt + \sigma dW$$

This implies that $\ln S$ is normally distributed with a constant drift rate of $(\mu - \frac{1}{2}\sigma^2)$ and a constant variance rate of σ^2:

$$\ln S(t) \sim N\left(\left(\mu - \frac{1}{2}\sigma^2 \right) t, \sigma \sqrt{t} \right)$$

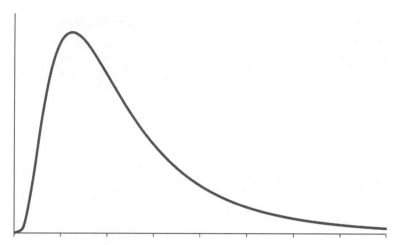

FIGURE 4.19   Lognormal distribution

In other words, S is lognormally distributed. Thus, a stock price that follows a geometric Brownian motion process is lognormally distributed (Figure 4.19).

This result forms the basis for the derivation of the Black–Scholes–Merton formula used in valuing vanilla options, which we now consider.

Option Pricing Using the Black–Scholes–Merton Formula

The Black–Scholes model establishes the price for a European option based on certain assumptions about the market. We list the assumptions here.

1. There are no arbitrage opportunities present in the market.
2. The stock price follows the geometric Brownian motion process

$$dS = \mu S dt + \sigma S dW$$

3. Interest rates are constant and the same for all maturities.
4. The stock does not pay any dividend during the life of the option.
5. There are no taxes or transaction costs.
6. Short selling of stocks is permitted without any penalty and stock borrowing is at the short-term interest rate.
7. Trading of fractions of a stock is also allowed and trading in securities is continuous.

The derivation of the Black–Scholes result is based on the creation of a risk-free portfolio consisting of the derivative and the underlying stock in a certain proportion. By eliminating the Wiener process, which is the source of riskiness, the portfolio can be made risk-free. Since no arbitrage is present in the market, such a risk-free portfolio should yield the same as the risk-free rate, a constant. Let us choose a call option C as the derivative that we wish to value. The process followed by C is

$$dC = \left(\frac{\partial C}{\partial t} + \mu S \frac{\partial C}{\partial S} + \frac{1}{2} \sigma^2 S^2 \frac{\partial^2 C}{\partial S^2} \right) dt + \sigma S \frac{\partial C}{\partial S} dW$$

Consider a portfolio that is long a call option C and short $\frac{\partial C}{\partial S}$ amount of stocks. The value of the portfolio would be

$$V = C - \frac{\partial C}{\partial S} S$$

The change in the value of the portfolio over a small time interval dt is

$$dV = dC - \frac{\partial C}{\partial S} dS$$

Substituting the processes for dC and dS into the equation gives

$$dV = \left(\frac{\partial C}{\partial t} + \frac{1}{2}\sigma^2 S^2 \frac{\partial^2 C}{\partial S^2} \right) dt$$

Thus, the Brownian motion process dW is eliminated and the portfolio is instantaneously risk-free. Therefore, the change in the value of the portfolio should be the same as an equivalent investment in a risk-free bond at the risk-free interest rate r. Hence,

$$dV = Vrdt$$

Equating the two expressions gives

$$\left(\frac{\partial C}{\partial t} + \frac{1}{2}\sigma^2 S^2 \frac{\partial^2 C}{\partial S^2} \right) dt = Vrdt$$

Substituting the value of V in terms of C and S, we arrive at

$$\left(\frac{\partial C}{\partial t} + \frac{1}{2}\sigma^2 S^2 \frac{\partial^2 C}{\partial S^2} \right) dt = \left(C - \frac{\partial C}{\partial S} S \right) rdt$$

which simplifies to

$$\frac{\partial C}{\partial t} + rS\frac{\partial C}{\partial S} + \frac{1}{2}\sigma^2 S^2 \frac{\partial^2 C}{\partial S^2} = rC$$

This is the Black–Scholes–Merton differential equation. The equation can be solved, resulting in values that depend on the boundary conditions prescribed. In this case, the boundary condition is the terminal value of the derivative C, which is $\max(0, S - K)$ at time T.

The Black–Scholes price for the European call option on a non-dividend-paying stock is

$$C = S_0 N(d_1) - Ke^{-rT} N(d_2)$$

where

$$d_1 = \frac{\ln(S_0/K) + (r + \sigma^2/2)T}{\sigma\sqrt{T}}$$

$$d_2 = \frac{\ln(S_0/K) + (r - \sigma^2/2)T}{\sigma\sqrt{T}} = d_1 - \sigma\sqrt{T}$$

Normal Distribution

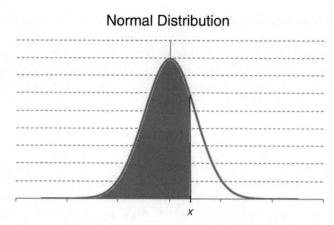

FIGURE 4.20 Normal distribution and cumulative probability distribution (shaded area)

Here, $N(x)$ is the cumulative distribution function for the standard normal distribution. $N(x)$ represents the probability that a variable with the standard normal distribution $N(0, 1)$ is less than x. It is the shaded area in Figure 4.20.

From put–call parity, we can derive the price of the European put option at the same strike as

$$P = Ke^{-rT}N(-d_2) - S_0 N(-d_1)$$

Thus, we have arrived at the valuation of European call options on a non-dividend-paying stock. For dividend-paying stocks, the stock price can be adjusted lower by the amount of dividends expected to be accrued over the life of the option to reuse the above formulae. In the case of a stock with a dividend yield of q, the price c of a European call option and the price p of a European put option are as follows:

$$c = S_0 e^{-qT}N(d_1) - Ke^{-rT}N(d_2)$$
$$p = Ke^{-rT}N(-d_2) - S_0 e^{-qT}N(-d_1)$$

where

$$d_1 = \frac{\ln(S_0/K) + (r - q + \sigma^2/2)T}{\sigma\sqrt{T}}$$

$$d_2 = \frac{\ln(S_0/K) + (r - q - \sigma^2/2)T}{\sigma\sqrt{T}} = d_1 - \sigma\sqrt{T}$$

The Black's formula for the valuation of options on futures follows from these results. We now discuss some of the approaches that have been used to arrive at the value of Asian options.

Asian Option Pricing

Asian swaps and options form the basic building block of most strategies employed by hedgers in the commodity markets. When it comes to the pricing and hedging of Asian options, the approach is not as straightforward as using Black's formula. While individual futures prices can be assumed to be lognormally distributed, the arithmetic average of lognormally distributed prices is not lognormal and is not amenable to closed-form solutions as under the Black–Scholes model. Numerical methods such as Monte Carlo simulation, which we shall describe shortly, need to be used to arrive at approximate option prices. However, there are certain assumptions that can be made in order to estimate the price of Asian options without using numerical techniques.

One of the earliest methods for valuing an Asian option was proposed by Kemna and Vorst, who used the fact that the geometric average of lognormally distributed variables is also lognormally distributed in order to establish a lower bound on arithmetic average option prices. As the geometric average of variables is always less than or equal to the arithmetic average, pricing a geometric average call option gives a lower bound on the value of an Asian call option. It is also established that the price of an Asian option, using a single underlying and prior to the averaging period, is bounded above by the price of a European option. Thus, by calculating the values of a geometric average price option and a European option, we can arrive at a range for the value of an Asian option. For a lognormally distributed geometric mean of variables, it is possible to arrive at the value of the average price option by adjusting the asset's growth rate from r to $(r - \frac{\sigma^2}{6})/2$ and scaling the volatility to $\frac{\sigma}{\sqrt{3}}$. We arrive at the following expression for a call option on the geometric average price:

$$G_c = e^{-rT}\left(S_0 e^{\frac{1}{2}\left(r-\frac{1}{6}\sigma^2\right)T}N(d_1) - KN(d_2)\right)$$

where

$$d_1 = \frac{\ln(S_0/K) + \frac{1}{2}(r + \sigma^2/6)T}{\sigma\sqrt{\frac{1}{3}T}} \quad \text{and} \quad d_2 = d_1 - \sigma\sqrt{\frac{1}{3}T}$$

This provides a lower bound for arithmetic average option prices. By combining this methodology with a Monte Carlo approach, Kemna and Vorst were able to arrive at the value of Asian options.

When the averaging period is smaller than the tenor of the option, as in the case of monthly Asian options common in commodities, the volatility calculated above needs to be adjusted. The variance of the option is the sum of the variance over the period prior to averaging and the variance over the averaging period (scaled, as above). This variance, while being higher than the variance in the case when averaging starts at the inception of the option, is still lower than the variance of a vanilla European option with the same tenor. This makes Asian options cheaper than European options and more attractive for hedgers.

Kemna and Vorst used the analytic expression for geometric average options to help reduce the variance in the results obtained from a Monte Carlo simulation. Monte Carlo simulation is a mathematical technique that is used to understand the behavior and potential outcomes of stochastic processes by creating multiple potential paths for the stochastic variables involved. It is a methodical approach to what-if analysis involving the computation of a result or outcome from many scenarios generated by random sampling of one or more variables. In this instance, Monte Carlo simulation refers to the creation of multiple sample price paths taking into account the distribution of the underlying price variable in order to value derivatives linked to the underlying. Monte Carlo simulation is a useful technique in the valuation of options, especially path-dependent options such as Asian options, where analytical formulae for the price of the derivative are not available. Monte Carlo simulation is a computationally intensive approach to option valuation, but this has become less of a concern due to the easy availability of cheap processing power.

Monte Carlo simulation involves the following steps.

1. Identifying the sources of uncertainty that affect the derivative's value (underlyings, prices, volatilities, correlations, interest rates, etc.), selecting the most important ones, and making assumptions regarding the other variables.
2. Sampling from the distribution of the underlying variable, say price, to create a price path over the life of the derivative. The distribution is chosen based on the assumptions made in the earlier step.
3. Calculating the payoff from the derivative for a particular price path.
4. Repeating this process of creating sample paths (iterations) and calculating the resultant payoffs for a sufficiently large number of paths. The number of paths chosen will depend on the computational resources available and the desired accuracy (in terms of variability of the expected payoff).
5. Calculating the average of discounted payoffs over all the price paths generated as well as the standard deviation of the estimate or equivalently, the distribution of the payoff.

Monte Carlo simulations are the preferred method for valuing derivatives or portfolios exposed to multiple risks that could be correlated.

In order to reduce the need for applying numerical procedures, several authors have proposed methods to arrive at closed-form approximations for Asian option prices. One technique to estimate the value of an Asian option is to use an approximation for the distribution of prices. Turnbull and Wakeman approximate the distribution of the arithmetic average of lognormal variables by a lognormal distribution and match the first four moments of the approximate and actual distributions (using an Edgeworth expansion). Levy simplifies this approach and takes only the first two moments of the distribution (using a Wilkinson approximation) and argues that the accuracy of the lognormal assumption affords acceptable accuracy in the approximation. Both of these approximations perform well for lower levels of volatility (below 20%) and short maturities. They perform better for options that resemble European options, that is, forward-starting options where the averaging period is small compared with the option tenor. The Levy approximation becomes less accurate at volatilities higher than 20% and when the options are deep ITM.

Asian option behavior also changes when the averaging has already started, and some of the observations that will be used to calculate the final average are already known. This reduces the variance of the terminal distribution of the average, thus lowering the option price as the option becomes equivalent to an option on a lower notional with a shifted strike. The averaging has the effect of shifting the effective strike of the option, as described below.

The expression for the payout of an average-rate call option with a strike of K is

$$(\max(A(t, T) - K, 0)$$

where $A(t, T)$ denotes the average of prices between t and T.

At time t_1, where $t < t_1 < T$, the prices between t and t_1 are known and hence the average price $A(t, t_1)$ in this time interval is known. The payoff for the average-rate option can thus be written as

$$\max\left(\frac{A(t,t_1)(t_1-t) + A(t_1,T)(T-t_1)}{(T-t)} - K, 0\right)$$

where the average is calculated by weighting the known and unknown averages by the fraction of time over which they are observed.

This is the same as

$$\frac{(T-t_1)}{(T-t)}\max(A(t_1,T) - K', 0)$$

where

$$K' = \frac{(T-t)}{(T-t_1)}K - \frac{(t_1-t)}{(T-t_1)}A(t,t_1)$$

Thus the effective strike changes from K to K' during the averaging period. In some cases, the effective strike price of the option can become negative, meaning that the option is always exercised. In such cases, the Asian option could be more valuable than the corresponding European option.

A number of other approaches have been proposed for the valuation of Asian options, and there exists an extensive literature on this subject. Some other prominent methods proposed in this regard are

a. partial differential equation (PDE) approaches
b. binomial tree methods
c. transform approaches including Laplace transforms and fast Fourier transforms.

SUMMARY

Over the course of this chapter, while navigating the basics of fuel hedging derivatives, we have come across valuation challenges that we attempted to overcome with efficient markets and no-arbitrage arguments. We began with a discussion of theories that helped us grasp the relationship between spot and forward prices for different assets. Before we could arrive at a viable pricing framework for basic derivatives like options, we had to deal with the complexity of stochastic calculus, Itô's lemma, and the derivation of the Black–Scholes formula. Once on comfortable ground with regard to the valuation of options, we could turn to calculating the option's Greeks and attempting to extend our findings to Asian options.

However, this is only the beginning of our discussion on derivative pricing, and the assumptions that we have made have considerably simplified our journey to this point. For example, we have not only presumed that all available information is already accounted for, but also that information keeps arriving at a constant rate (homoskedasticity or constant variance/volatility). In our view, the major breakthrough of the Black–Scholes formula has been to achieve a consensus among market participants about using one framework to simplify option price negotiation by clearly defining the underlying parameter – implied volatility.

In the following chapters, we will look at the limitations of the Black–Scholes framework and some of the peculiarities of the commodity market, which will have a bearing on the valuation of the derivatives we have considered in this chapter. We will also introduce exotic hedging structures that have proven to be popular in the commodity markets.

CHAPTER 5

Advanced Hedging and Forward Curve Dynamics

"There are two types of people in this world: Those who can extrapolate from incomplete data."

In the quest for more optimized and sophisticated risk-taking, investor demand provided the impetus for the development of targeted derivatives products and these products were later introduced in the commodities space as tailored hedging solutions. The growth in the demand for these advanced products was facilitated by the development of valuation capabilities that were far superior to the Black–Scholes formula, providing more flexibility in modeling observed behaviors of market prices in order to value new payouts accurately. In this chapter, we introduce some of these advanced hedging structures and highlight the special considerations in the valuation of these derivatives. We begin with a recap of swap and vanilla option-based structures along with a discussion of the rationale for options usage in fuel hedging. The volatility surface is described and its relevance to the pricing and risk management of multi-option structures is demonstrated. We introduce the concept of early-expiry options and take a closer look at the construction of an instantaneous volatility surface and its role in the pricing of common structures like swaptions. Finally, we cover some important term-structure models that are used to account for the peculiarities of crude oil price movements.

SWAP AND VANILLA OPTION-BASED STRUCTURES

In this first section, we revisit some basic fuel hedging strategies that employ forwards and vanilla options and provide a hedger's rationale for using options.

Fuel consumers may choose to hedge their future price exposure by buying and selling vanilla options in line with their exposure and market view. However, though these structures might look simple from an economic perspective, there is a need to fully understand how different parts of the same structure interact in order to ensure fair pricing prior to execution and accurate valuation, risk metrics, and risk mitigation strategies post-execution.

Zero-Cost Structures and the Usage of Options

From time to time, airlines and shipping companies might resort to purchasing options in order to hedge their fuel exposure or to mitigate downside risks arising from an existing derivatives transaction. Such purchases would require the use of the airline's cash to pay for the option premium. Therefore, it is important to have a clear idea about the option price and the amount of risk that the purchased option will be able to mitigate. In this respect, option prices for standard options that are normally traded on exchanges are easily available. Option prices themselves depend on the perceived volatility of the futures price. Hence, it is equally important to keep track of implied volatilities and understand the main drivers of their evolution over time.

Purchasing call options on fuel price might be the most efficient strategy to protect against rising prices. However, the high volatility of energy prices makes these options very expensive and the purchase of such options can significantly impact the cash flow of a company, potentially hurting its competitiveness. Fuel hedgers are usually very reluctant to spend cash upfront or enter into negative-carry trades. They usually prefer zero-cost structures (where the cost of entering into the transaction is zero) such as pure swaps, zero-cost option combinations, or exotic structures. With respect to hedging, options have traditionally been used for two main purposes.

1. *Capping the downside under the derivative*
   For a consumer, fixing the fuel purchase price using forwards implies that the consumer forgoes all potential benefits arising from any potential drop in fuel price. In the case of an airline, this forgone opportunity can impact their competitiveness if other airlines do not hedge and decide to pass on all or part of the benefit of lower fuel prices to their customers. Using options to ensure that losses under the derivatives are capped at a predetermined level helps protect fuel consumers against the side-effects of zero-cost hedges. In later chapters, we will discuss the impact of a sharp drop in fuel price on the cash management of a company in cases where the derivatives hedges are collateralized, meaning that MTM losses require the posting of collateral.

2. *Enhancing (lowering) the purchase price*
   Some fuel hedgers are more concerned about ensuring a lower purchase price and don't mind forgoing any potential benefit from the price dropping below their target price. They sometimes resort to selling put options struck at or below their target price to enhance the economics of zero-cost hedging structures. Others use options to express their range-bound view of the market price; that is, if they expect the fuel price would not rise above a certain level. In such cases, they would sell a call option struck at or above the upper limit of their price forecast.

Leveraged Swaps

A combination of a swap with a sold option or strip of options is referred to as a "leveraged swap." For example, under a leveraged swap, the fuel consumer undertakes to

- buy a notional N at a fixed price X, if the floating price is higher than the fixed price X and
- sell a higher notional M (e.g., $2*N$) at the fixed price X, if the floating price is lower than the fixed price X.

The floating price here refers to the price of the underlying commodity. A sample of the terms and conditions for a leveraged swap, as would be drafted by a hedge provider, is shown in Example 5.1 and the payoff is shown in Figure 5.1.

EXAMPLE 5.1: SAMPLE TERMS FOR A LEVERAGED SWAP

Counterparties:	Client & Bank (Hedge Provider)
WTI Price:	NYMEX WTI Crude Oil front-month futures contract (monthly average)
Effective Date:	Start of calendar month after Trade Date
Final Expiry Date:	Effective Date + 2 years
Termination Date:	Final Expiry Date + 2 weeks
Notional Quantity:	50,000 barrels per month
Calculation Periods:	Monthly calendar periods starting from Effective Date, to Final Expiry Date
Payment Dates:	2 weeks after the end of each Calculation Period
Fixed Price:	50 USD/bbl
Settlement Amounts:	For each Calculation Period, on respective Payment Date: If WTI Price < Fixed Price, Client pays **2 * Notional Quantity * [Fixed Price − WTI Price]** If WTI Price > Fixed Price, Client receives **Notional Quantity * [WTI Price − Fixed Price]**

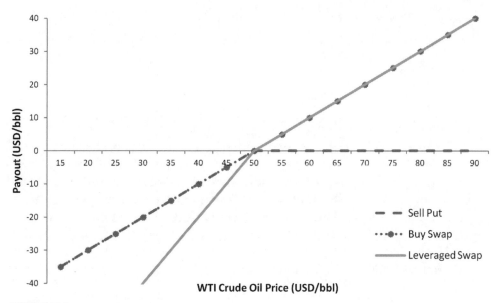

FIGURE 5.1 Payoff from a leveraged swap

The structure above can be summarized as follows:

Buy leveraged swap at X = Buy swap at X + Sell put struck at X

The leveraged swap price X is much lower than the prevailing vanilla swap price and the aggregate difference is equivalent to the undiscounted put option premium.

It is important to differentiate between the concept of the hedged amount and the "Notional Quantity" mentioned in the terms and conditions. This structure implies that the consumer's downside under the leveraged swap is based on twice the Notional Quantity. It is important to take this into account when entering into subsequent transactions in order to keep the aggregate notional on the downside of the entire hedge portfolio lower than the expected total fuel consumption (to avoid over-hedging).

Capped Swaps

In the case of the capped swap discussed in the previous chapter, instead of selling a put to enhance the swap price, as seen in the case of a leveraged swap, the fuel hedger sells a call option struck at a level corresponding to his/her range-bound view (see Example 5.2). The aggregate difference between the prevailing swap price and the fixed price under the capped swap is equivalent to the undiscounted call option premium.

EXAMPLE 5.2: SAMPLE TERMS FOR A CAPPED SWAP

Counterparties:	Client & Bank
WTI Price:	NYMEX WTI Crude Oil front-month futures contract (monthly average)
Effective Date:	Start of calendar month after Trade Date
Final Expiry Date:	Effective Date + 2 years
Termination Date:	Final Expiry Date + 2 weeks
Notional Quantity:	50,000 barrels per month
Calculation Periods:	Monthly calendar periods starting from Effective Date, to Final Expiry Date
Payment Dates:	2 weeks after end of each Calculation Period
Fixed Price:	55 USD/bbl
Cap Price:	80 USD/bbl
Settlement Amounts:	For each Calculation Period, on respective Payment Date: If WTI Price < Fixed Price, Client pays **Notional Quantity * [Fixed Price – WTI Price]** If Cap Price > WTI Price > Fixed Price, Client receives **Notional Quantity * [WTI Price – Fixed Price]** If WTI Price > Cap Price, Client receives **Notional Quantity * [Cap Price – Fixed Price]**

The structure above can be summarized as follows:

Buy capped swap at X = Buy swap at X + Sell call struck at Y

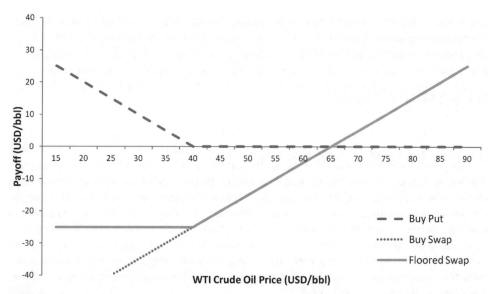

FIGURE 5.2 Payoff from a floored swap

Floored Swaps

Under a floored swap, the fuel hedger limits his downside under the swap by buying a put option (Figure 5.2). The structure is still zero-cost; that is, there is no cash paid at inception. An abbreviated set of sample terms for a floored swap is shown in Example 5.3, with the settlement amount calculations highlighted.

EXAMPLE 5.3: ABBREVIATED TERMS FOR A FLOORED SWAP

Fixed Price: 65 USD/bbl
Floor Price: 40 USD/bbl
Settlement Amounts: For each Calculation Period, on respective Payment Date:
  If Floor Price < WTI Price < Fixed Price, Client pays
  Notional Quantity * [Fixed Price – WTI Price]
  If WTI Price < Floor Price, Client pays
  Notional Quantity * [Fixed Price – Floor Price]
  If WTI Price > Fixed Price, Client receives
  Notional Quantity * [WTI Price – Fixed Price]

The structure above can be summarized as follows:

$$\text{Buy floored swap at } X = \text{Buy swap at } X + \text{Buy put struck at } Y$$

The floored swap price X is higher than the prevailing swap price and the aggregate difference is equivalent to the undiscounted put option premium.

We have discussed some of the simple structures that can be created using a combination of swaps and bought or sold options. Before we consider structures involving multiple options, we provide a discussion of the volatility surface.

THE VOLATILITY SURFACE

Most market professionals are attracted by the hypothesis that prices have lognormal distributions due to the simplicity of representation and computational ease in derivative pricing. However, statistical tests have shown that this hypothesis is invalid and that the energy price returns distribution exhibits skewness and highly pronounced kurtosis. Options markets reflect this by quoting prices for different strikes that are often inconsistent with the lognormal distribution. Predictably, when the Black–Scholes framework is applied, the implied volatilities arrived at from these prices are different. To avoid looking for an entirely new framework, practitioners have retained the Black–Scholes pricing model while replacing a volatility term structure with a volatility surface. Volatility surfaces represent a composite volatility term structure where implied volatilities of options are quoted for both various tenors and different strikes (Figure 5.3).

For each futures contract, the relevant standard European options are used to derive the implied volatilities for various strikes. This helps determine the smile and the skew for each contract. When volatility is plotted against the strike of an option, if the volatility curve is downward sloping, as is commonly seen in equities, it is called a volatility skew chart. The volatility for options with lower strike prices is higher in this case. A volatility curve where the

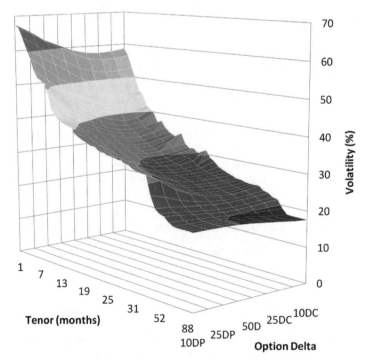

FIGURE 5.3   The volatility surface

OTM option volatilities are higher than the ATM volatility is referred to as a volatility smile. The volatility surface is built by combining this data for all contracts, thereby constructing term structures of implied volatilities for various strikes.

The shape of the volatility surface is very important for traders, as it provides valuable information about the market's view of price risk. For instance, a higher implied volatility for lower strikes indicates that market participants are concerned about a potential drop in price. Furthermore, a high volatility for a certain tenor might indicate a lack of consensus or certainty with respect to the price level for that particular tenor. In the context of derivatives pricing and risk management, the volatility surface is of paramount importance during the life of a commodity derivative, be it at the time of pricing and execution, during the calculation of the Greeks and price risk hedging, dynamic hedge rebalancing, unwinding or restructuring of existing transactions. Therefore, it is worthwhile making the effort to understand the shape of the volatility surface in order to determine the right implied volatility to be used for pricing instead of using a one-volatility-fits-all approach. Failing to do so not only allows sophisticated hedge counterparties to take advantage of this information asymmetry but also leads to incorrect valuation and risk management of the trade portfolio.

The shape of the implied volatility surface is dictated by supply and demand for options at different strikes. To aid in option pricing, market participants tend to consider this options market demand in conjunction with their knowledge of the underlying physical markets. For instance, demand for options at a certain strike is linked to factors such as the marginal cost of production of a commodity. Many market participants tend to attribute a low value to put options at strikes below the minimum marginal cost of production. This view is based on the assumption that producers would cease to produce commodities when the selling price is below their marginal cost of production. However, this assumption has been proven to be inaccurate in a number of instances, where commodity producers kept producing even during periods when the price was below the cost of production. This may be due to the need to honor contractual commitments or to avoid shutdown costs and keep businesses going with the expectation that prices will recover. There could also be cases where a producer may have derivative hedges in place that ensure a minimum selling price and thus would be well positioned to cover their costs. This kind of hedging is very common and often required by mining project financiers. Therefore, when considering options struck near the cost of production of a commodity, one must take into account the amount of hedging coverage that all producers have in place.

Another factor that affects volatility surfaces and the supply and demand for particular strikes is the dynamic hedging of structured products and exotics. Dynamic hedging of such products may result in trading activity that can sometimes be misinterpreted by participants as arising from fundamental physical market activity. Option markets, being primarily financial markets, draw a variety of counterparties whose motivations may not be connected to the underlying physical market dynamics. Thus, while being closely connected to the dynamics of underlying physical markets, option markets have developed their own peculiarities. Misunderstanding the hedging and risk management techniques practiced in these markets can cause market participants to draw inaccurate conclusions about producer behavior.

MULTI-OPTION STRUCTURES

The knowledge of the volatility surface is particularly critical to the pricing of structures involving multiple options, which must be treated as a bundle to ensure accurate valuation.

Zero-Cost Collar

A fuel consumer may consider buying a call option to protect against rising fuel prices. If the consumer is prepared to limit his potential benefit from falling fuel prices, he can also consider selling a put option in order to finance the purchase of the call, thereby creating a hedge structure with no initial cost (Example 5.4). Fuel consumers can tolerate a certain level of fluctuation in their fuel costs, as they can either absorb them or pass them on to their customers. Collars are an appropriate structure for this type of consumer as they guarantee a range for their net fuel purchase price between the put and the call strikes.

EXAMPLE 5.4: SETTLEMENT TERMS FOR A COLLAR

Call Price:	78 USD/bbl
Put Price:	50 USD/bbl
Settlement Amounts:	For each Calculation Period, on respective Payment Date:
	If WTI Price < Put Price, Client pays
	Notional Quantity * [Put Price – WTI Price]
	If WTI Price > Call Price, Client receives
	Notional Quantity * [WTI Price – Call Price]

By entering into this collar structure, the fuel consumer ensures that his/her net fuel cost will fluctuate within a range determined by the collar strikes.

Three-Ways

Fuel consumers often enhance the economics of a collar by selling an OTM call option. The resulting structure is called a "three-ways" (Example 5.5).

EXAMPLE 5.5: SETTLEMENT TERMS FOR A THREE-WAYS

Call Price:	78 USD/bbl
Put Price:	48 USD/bbl
Cap Price:	93 USD/bbl
Settlement Amounts:	For each Calculation Period, on respective Payment Date:
	If WTI Price < Put Price, Client pays
	Notional Quantity * [Put Price – WTI Price]
	If Cap Price > WTI Price > Call Price, Client receives
	Notional Quantity * [WTI Price – Call Price]
	If WTI Price > Cap Price, Client receives
	Notional Quantity * [Cap Price – Call Price]

By using this structure, fuel consumers lower the strike prices of their sold put options while giving up some upside potential.

Risk Reversals and their Hedging

Collars are also referred to as risk reversals, and their pricing is very sensitive to the implied volatility skew. The difference between the implied volatilities on calls and puts reflects the imbalance in supply and demand for these options and can provide valuable information on market sentiment. A relatively higher implied volatility on calls versus puts can be a sign that hedgers are more concerned about rising prices than about falling prices.

Traders also use risk reversals as a means of taking positions on volatility skew. For instance, if a trader thinks that the market implied volatility on calls is too high versus the implied volatility on puts, he/she can consider selling a call to buy a put and delta-hedge these options to immunize his/her position against price changes (Figure 5.4). This leaves the trader with a pure position on the implied volatility differential.

For trading desks, risk reversals can be tricky in terms of risk management. After delta-hedging the position, Greeks such as the vega, gamma, and theta for each option can net off against those of the other option. It is very common that the strikes of the risk reversal are chosen such that the put and the call have similar Greeks, so that many of these Greeks cancel each other. Nevertheless, as the futures price starts moving, the residual Greeks start changing. As the price moves, the gamma, vega, and theta of the option whose strike is closer to the price increase while those of the option with the more distant strike decrease. If the forward price moves closer or above the call strike, the risk becomes similar to that of a put spread, which is far from being gamma, vega, and theta-neutral. On the contrary, when the forward price moves closer or below the put strike, the structure becomes similar to a call spread, which is also not gamma, vega, and theta-neutral.

Furthermore, when the overall implied volatility level rises, the deltas of the OTM put and the OTM call increase in absolute terms and the delta changes add up, making the overall position far from delta-neutral.

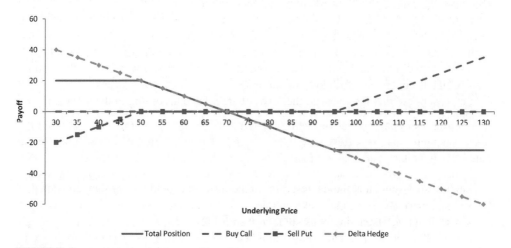

FIGURE 5.4 Delta-hedged risk reversal position

While the vega, gamma, and theta of a call option can be netted against those of a put option, the vannas, in contrast, are of opposite sign and are additive in a risk-reversal structure:

$$\text{vanna} = \frac{\partial \text{vega}}{\partial S} = \frac{\partial \text{delta}}{\partial \sigma} = \frac{\partial^2 V}{\partial S \partial \sigma}$$

Vanna is an important Greek when it comes to monitoring a risk reversal. It is the second partial derivative of the option, once to the underlying price and once to the volatility. It is also equivalent to the sensitivity of the option's vega to changes in price or the sensitivity of the option's delta to changes in volatility. Vanna can help a trader anticipate the evolution of his/her residual risks and keep them under control.

EARLY-EXPIRY OPTIONS AND INSTANTANEOUS VOLATILITY TERM STRUCTURES

As discussed earlier, crude oil market participants tend to buy or sell exchange-traded standard options, which expire around three days before the expiry of the underlying futures contract. In case the option is exercised, the option holder has time to avoid physical delivery. The volatility smile implied from these exchange-traded standard options is referred to as the standard volatility smile for that particular futures contract. However, there are situations where a market participant may want to trade an option that expires much earlier than the underlying futures contract. These are called early-expiry options and their pricing requires an understanding of instantaneous volatility term structures, which we now introduce.

The Samuelson Effect and the Storage Theory

An observation of the pattern of historical volatility of energy futures contracts shows that the volatility of a futures contract tends to increase as it approaches expiry. The increase in volatility is more pronounced during the last 6 to 12 months of the life of a contract. This phenomenon is referred to as the Samuelson effect.

Unlike other asset classes, such as equity or foreign exchange (FX), cash-and-carry arbitrages are not always practical in the commodities space. As such, a linear spot–forward relationship does not always hold. A strong spot–forward linear relationship would imply high correlation between the long end and the short end of the forward curve and similar volatility levels, which is not the case for most commodities.

Let us suppose that the spot and the forward are related according to the storage theory as follows:

$$F_{t_0,T} = S_{t_0}\, e^{\int_{t_0}^{T} (r_t - c_t)dt}$$

Let us also assume that the interest rate and convenience yield are constant and equal to R and C, respectively.

The daily log-return of the futures price F is as follows:

$$\ln\left(\frac{F_{t+1,T}}{F_{t,T}}\right) = \ln\left(\frac{S_{t+1}}{S_t}\right) - \int_{t}^{t+1} (R - C)dt$$

The formula above shows how the difference between the returns on holding the physical good and holding the future is equal to the cost of carry (which could be positive or negative depending on the convenience yield and interest rates). Thus, we can deduce that when interest rates and convenience yields are constant, the volatility of any futures contract is equal to that of the spot price. In other words:

$$\text{stdev}\left(\ln\left(\frac{F_{t+1,T}}{F_{t,T}}\right)\right) = \text{stdev}\left(\ln\left(\frac{S_{t+1}}{S_t}\right)\right)$$

When storage is possible and readily available, the Samuelson effect is less pronounced, as big swings and shocks in one part of the curve get propagated to the rest of the term structure. Cash-and-carry trades as well as repo trades (sale and repurchase) help maintain a relationship between different parts of the term structure. The Samuelson effect is usually more pronounced in markets where storage is difficult or costly. The inability to store commodities and deliver them over time in a predictable manner prevents shocks to the spot price from propagating throughout the forward curve.

Commodities that are easily stored and preserved tend to behave like currencies, with term structures dictated mainly by interest rates and repo rates. It is for this reason that precious metals (gold, silver, platinum, palladium, etc.) are modeled and traded like currencies.

Implied Volatility of Energy Futures Contracts

The energy futures options market is a great source of information about the market expectation of the volatility of futures contracts. The options market is used to derive the expected level of volatility implied by options prices. The Black–Scholes model has long been used to reverse-engineer implied volatility from option prices. In some OTC options markets like FX options, Black–Scholes implied volatility is quoted directly as opposed to the prices of the options themselves.

However, in the energy markets, this approach of using the Black–Scholes model to derive implied volatilities is conceptually inappropriate due to the Samuelson effect, which violates the Black–Scholes formula's underlying assumption of homoskedasticity (constant volatility), as can be seen from Figure 5.5. That said, Black–Scholes implied volatilities are still used by practitioners for ease of communication between traders and other market participants.

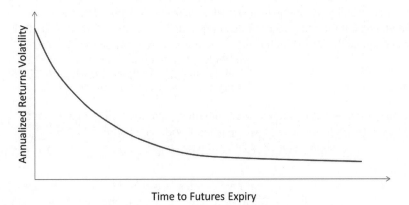

FIGURE 5.5   Backwardation in historical volatility of commodities

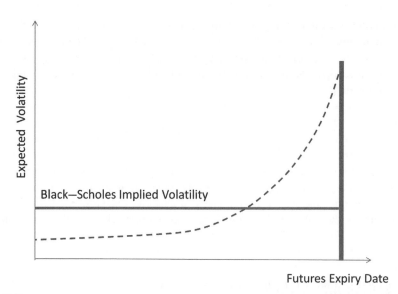

FIGURE 5.6 Black–Scholes implied volatility compared with the evolution of commodity futures volatility

Exchange-traded options are only available for a limited number of expiries, which usually fall about three days before the expiration of the relevant futures contract (for major energy commodities). Therefore, the exchange-traded options are used to derive the Black–Scholes implied volatility of options expiring just prior to the futures expiration.

However, pricing an early-expiring option using Black–Scholes volatilities leads to an overestimation of the price of the option. This is because early-expiry options have a tenor during which volatility is low relative to the volatility during the months just prior to the futures contract expiry (Figure 5.6). This means that such options should have a lower implied volatility than that implied by the exchange-traded options.

Early-Expiry Profile Construction

In order to price early-expiring options (options with tenors shorter than exchange-traded options), the concept of the early-expiry profile is introduced to account for the manner in which a futures contract's volatility evolves as it approaches expiry. The construction of such an early-expiry profile needs to be carefully optimized to minimize the likelihood of creating arbitrage opportunities and it is critical to calibrate the early-expiry profile to the market. Some of the considerations in calibrating volatility early-expiry profiles are as follows.

1. The term structure of the Black-Scholes (BS) volatilities of monthly contracts provides a guide to how implied volatility varies over time. The shape of the early-expiry profile will be motivated, to a certain extent, by the shape of the term structure of B–S volatilities (Figure 5.7).

    This term structure of implied volatilities is consistent with the backwardation in historical volatilities discussed earlier. Under the assumption that the term structure of

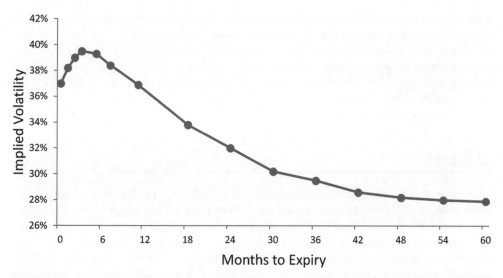

FIGURE 5.7 Sample Black–Scholes implied volatility term structure for WTI Crude Oil

B–S volatility is stable over time, the volatility of the nearby contract provides an indication about the expected volatility of a futures contract one month before its expiry.

2. To ensure that there is no arbitrage in pricing standard options, the early-expiry volatilities should agree with the B–S implied volatility for the relevant futures contract. One way to achieve this is to ensure that the terminal variance of the futures contract is equal to the square of the B–S implied volatility multiplied by the time to maturity. The terminal variance is calculated as the sum of the daily variances of the futures contract. Thus, for no arbitrage, the relationship between the B–S implied volatility and the daily volatilities should be as follows:

$$\sigma_{\text{implied}}^2 T = \int_0^T \sigma_F^2(\tau)\, d\tau$$

or

$$\sigma_{\text{implied}}^2 = \frac{1}{T} \int_0^T \sigma_F^2(\tau)\, d\tau$$

We can describe this approach graphically, as in Figure 5.8.

The gray area is equal to $\sigma_{\text{implied}}^2 T$, whereas the hatched area is equal to $\int_0^T \sigma_F^2(\tau)\, d\tau$. These two areas need to be equal to minimize arbitrage opportunities. Figure 5.9 summarizes the process of developing an early-expiry profile.

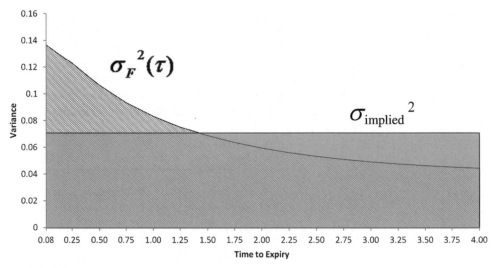

FIGURE 5.8   Black–Scholes implied variance and terminal variance

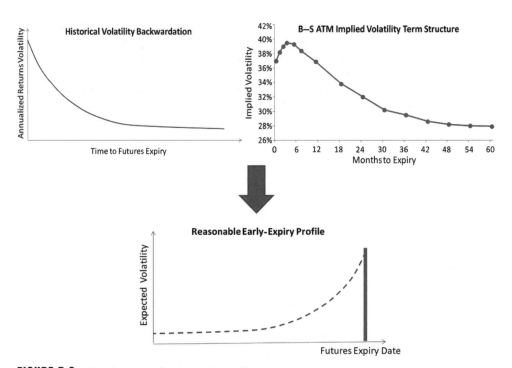

FIGURE 5.9   Development of early-expiry profile

Other structures where the early-expiry profile of instantaneous volatility is critical to valuation include swaptions and extendibles. Early-expiry options are a particular case of swaptions, which are a popular instrument in the commodity markets.

COMMODITY SWAPTIONS AND EXTENDIBLE SWAPS

A swaption is an option on a swap. The underlying swap can be any kind of swap including interest rate swaps or, in our case, commodity swaps. The holder of a European swaption has the right, but not the obligation, to enter into a commodity swap at a predetermined fixed price on a predetermined exercise date. There are two types of swaptions: payer swaptions and receiver swaptions.

In a payer swaption (option to pay fixed), the holder has the right to enter into a commodity swap as the payer of the fixed price and receiver of the floating price. The writer of the payer swaption has the obligation to receive fixed price if the swaption is exercised. The payer swaption is a call option on a pay-fixed swap.

In a receiver swaption (option to receive fixed), the holder has the right to enter into a commodity swap as the receiver of the fixed price and payer of the floating price. The writer of the receiver swaption has the obligation to pay fixed price if the swaption is exercised. The receiver swaption is a call option on a receive-fixed swap.

Usage of Commodity Swaptions and the Reasons for their Popularity

Before discussing the case of commodity swaptions, we briefly look at how the swaptions market evolved in other asset classes before being replicated in the commodities market. In the interest rates market, interest rate swaptions were implicit in traded assets such as callable bonds. Callable bonds are bonds that can be redeemed by the issuer of the bond prior to the stated maturity. These bonds are popular as they provide issuers with an option to take advantage of a drop in interest rates by terminating high-cost liabilities and replacing them with bonds at a lower interest rate. Investors also benefit from holding these bonds as they have higher yields than corresponding non-callable bonds. In the case of a newly issued callable bond, the issuing company will find itself long optionality on interest rates and it might consider monetizing this optionality by selling an interest rate swaption.

In the commodities markets, swaptions are usually packaged together with a vanilla swap in structures called extendibles. An extendible swap is a swap that gives a party the option to extend the tenor of the swap beyond the original tenor. In the case of a fuel hedger, the hedge provider might offer a 6-month swap, extendible for another consecutive 6-month period. The fuel hedger (fixed-price payer) has a guaranteed hedge for the initial 6 months but has the obligation to extend the transaction for an additional 6 months if the hedge provider (fixed-price receiver) opts to exercise his/her right to extend.

Instead of receiving an upfront premium for the sale of the extension option, fuel hedgers often get an enhanced (lower) swap price. The aggregate difference between the prevailing swap price and the enhanced price for the guaranteed period is equivalent to the undiscounted swaption premium. Spreading the premium over the tenor of the swap helps reduce the credit risk for the hedge provider (the bank) and the associated credit costs. We will revisit credit costs in Chapter 7. Example 5.6 contains some sample terms for an extendible swap.

EXAMPLE 5.6: SAMPLE TERMS AND CONDITIONS FOR AN EXTENDIBLE SWAP

Counterparties:	Client & Bank
WTI Price:	NYMEX WTI Crude Oil front-month futures contract (monthly average)
Effective Date:	Start of calendar month after Trade Date
Expiry Date:	Effective Date + 6 months
Termination Date:	Expiry Date + 2 weeks (subject to the Extendible Terms)
Notional Quantity:	50,000 barrels per month
Calculation Periods:	Monthly calendar periods starting from the Effective Date to the Final Expiry Date
Payment Dates:	2 weeks after end of each Calculation Period
Extendible Terms:	The Bank has the right to extend the trade for an additional 6 months by giving notice to the Client on or before the Extendible Date
Extendible Date:	2 business days prior to the Expiry Date
Fixed Price:	47 USD/bbl
Settlement Amounts:	For each Calculation Period, on respective Payment Date: If WTI Price < Fixed Price, Client pays **Notional Quantity * [Fixed Price – WTI Price]** If WTI Price > Fixed Price, Client receives **Notional Quantity * [WTI Price – Fixed Price]**

The structure above can be summarized as follows:

Extendible swap = Buy swap at X + Sell receiver extendible at Y (in this case, $Y = X$)

In the example described in the terms and conditions in Example 5.6, the consumer enjoys a guaranteed hedge at an attractive level for the first 6 months but takes the risk of being extended into another 6 months at an unfavorable level. A rational hedge provider (the bank in this case) would only exercise the extendible option when the prevailing swap level is below the fixed price. In contrast, if fuel prices are high at the end of the first 6 months, the client would be in dire need of a hedge but the swap would not be extended.

As in the case of interest rate swaptions, trading desks often find themselves in a situation where most clients are net sellers of swaptions but on the other side, they have many other counterparties looking to buy monthly options. The trading desks face the technical challenge of hedging a long swaption position by selling monthly options.

Swaption vs. a Basket of Options

To understand the pricing and valuation of a swaption, it is important to formulate its payout correctly. A swaption is a call option on a swap. Therefore, its payout upon exercise is based on the present value (PV) of the underlying swap at the time of exercise. The PV of the underlying swap of a payer swaption can be written as follows:

$$PV_{swap}(t) = \sum_{n=1}^{N} [F_n(t) - X] w(n, t)$$

where $w(n, t)$ is a weighting factor for the futures contract F_n taking into account the discounted fraction of the total swap volume in month n and X is the fixed price of the swap.

The payout of the swaption is

$$FV_{swaption} = \max[PV_{swap}(T_{exp}), 0]$$

This same payout could be written as

$$FV_{swaption} = \max[Basket - Strike, 0]$$

where

$$Basket = \sum_{n=1}^{N} F_n(t) w(n, t)$$

and

$$Strike = \sum_{n=1}^{N} Xw(n, t)$$

Assuming constant (or uncorrelated) interest rates, the payer swaption can be valued as a call option with a basket as underlying. The following equivalences help recapitulate the above analysis:

Receiver swaption $\approx$ Call on receive fix swap $\approx$ Put on futures basket

Payer swaption $\approx$ Call on pay fix swap $\approx$ Call on futures basket

The main challenge in pricing swaptions lies in determining the volatility of the basket (i.e., the swaption underlying). The volatilities of futures contracts F_n and the correlations between their monthly returns are used to obtain the volatility of the weighted average by matching moments.

To develop an intuition with regard to the pricing and the risk assessment of swaptions, let us compare the two structures (Table 5.1).

First Observation The price of a swaption (option on basket) should always be lower than the sum of the early-expiring put options (basket of options):

$$\max\left[0, \sum_{n=1}^{N} W_n(K - F_n(t))\right] \leq \sum_{n=1}^{N} W_n \max[0, K - F_n(t)]$$

TABLE 5.1 Swaption and a basket of options to be compared

Swaption as option on basket	Basket of options
Receiver swaption (option to receive fixed) expiring at the end of December Underlying: 6-month WTI swap (Jan to Jun) Total Volume: $6N$	6 European put options, early expiring at the end of December with the following underlyings Option 1: Jan WTI monthly average Option 2: Feb WTI monthly average Option 3: Mar WTI monthly average Option 4: Apr WTI monthly average Option 5: May WTI monthly average Option 6: Jun WTI monthly average Volume for each option: N

The payout of the swaption is equal to the payout of the basket of options when *all* the options are ITM or *all* the options are OTM. However, if there are monthly options that are ITM and others OTM, the swaption payout is strictly lower than the payout of the basket of options. Figure 5.10 provides a scenario that illustrates this point for the receiver swaption.

For this reason, a swaption is a cheaper hedge than independent monthly options. To lower the hedging costs, consumers should consider buying payer swaptions for their long-term needs instead of APOs, which are more expensive.

At the inception of the trade, the forward curve was in backwardation and well above the fixed price of the swaption's underlying swap. But after a significant sell-off, the forward

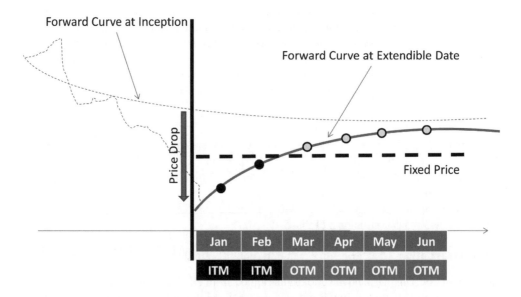

FIGURE 5.10 Moneyness of individual monthly options

curve switched to contango with a fast-moving front and a more stable back end. At expiry, the January and February early-expiring put options are ITM whereas the other options remain OTM. In this particular situation, the basket of put options yields a profit whereas the receiver swaption is OTM.

As explained earlier, trading desks hedge their long swaption positions by selling European options. However, the challenge here is to find the right combination of options to dynamically replicate the swaption. For both fuel hedgers and hedge providers, the inequality above provides a basic check to recognize abnormal pricings. If a hedger receives quotes that show a swaption premium higher than the aggregate premium of the basket of options, he can point out the anomaly to his hedge provider or try to profit from this arbitrage opportunity, as will be explained later.

Second Observation   Very often, swaptions are traded with expiries longer than 6 months or 1 year. The forward curve in these cases is usually flat over the window of the underlying swap (Figure 5.11). This means that the swaption pricing is based on forward points that are almost equal. Therefore, under the assumption that these forward points are highly correlated, the pricing will mainly be driven by the terminal variance for each forward point. Considering the high correlation between the forwards within the swap window, if the volatilities of these forwards were equal, then the swaption price would be very close to that obtained from any of the early-expiring European options.

Unfortunately, the backwardation of the implied volatility term structure and the Samuelson effect suggest that, over the life of the swaptions, the forwards move at different volatilities and these volatilities change at different rates. Close to the expiry of the swaption, the January forward's volatility increases at a higher rate than for the other months and this increases the gap between its instantaneous volatility and that of the following months (Figure 5.12). If we use the analogy of volatility being equivalent to the speed of a car, the Samuelson effect could be thought of as the acceleration experienced.

In this example, during the life of the swaption, the highest instantaneous volatility is that of the January contract and the lowest instantaneous volatility is that of the June contract. In other words, the January contract is expected to achieve the highest terminal variance during the life of the swaption and the June contract is expected to achieve the lowest terminal variance.

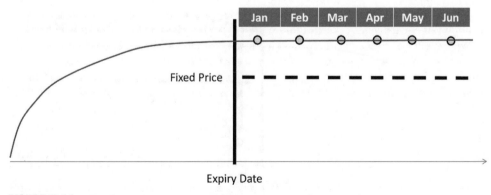

FIGURE 5.11   Flat forward curve over underlying swap tenor for a swaption

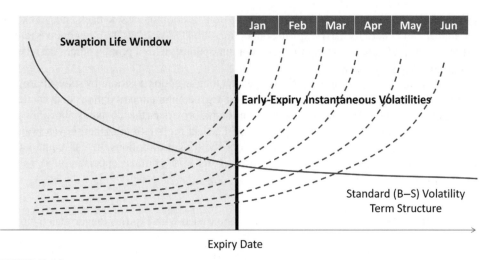

FIGURE 5.12 Early-expiry instantaneous volatilities at swaption exercise date

Therefore, provided that the relevant forward in the window is flat, the swaption price should be higher than that obtained using the early-expiry put option referencing the month of June:

$$E\left(\max\left[0, \sum_{n=1}^{6} W_n(K - F_n(T_{\exp}))\right]\right) \geq \left(\sum_{n=1}^{6} W_n\right)E(\max[0, K - F_6(T_{\exp})])$$

This is because it is rational to expect that, for a flat and highly correlated forward curve, if the slowest-moving forward point (future) manages to move below the strike K (ITM for the put), then the faster-moving points are expected to move even lower (Figure 5.13).

In this case, if a hedger receives quotes that show a swaption being cheaper than the early-expiry option referencing the last forward point, he can point out the anomaly to his hedge provider or try to profit from this opportunity as explained below.

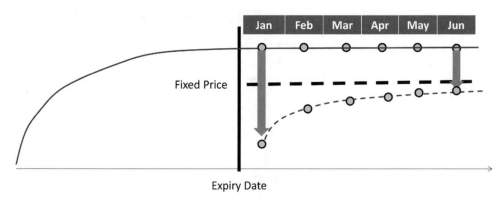

FIGURE 5.13 Forward curve movement for a correlated curve assuming flat curve at inception

Mispricing swaptions and early-expiry options can give rise to arbitrage opportunities. For example, if a basket of early-expiring options is offered in aggregate at or lower than the swaption's bid, then a risk-free arbitrage strategy would be to sell the swaption and buy the basket of early-expiring options. In contrast, in the case of a flat forward-curve window, if the receiver swaption is offered cheaper than the early-expiry option referencing the last forward point, then a good strategy would be to buy the swaption and sell the early-expiry put option referencing the last forward point in the swap window.

All the products discussed up to now require a good understanding of the dynamics of the forwards term structure for traders to risk-manage the structures efficiently. We now proceed to a discussion of commodity term structures and the models used to account for their movements.

UNDERSTANDING COMMODITY FUTURES TERM STRUCTURES

In order to understand the risks associated with crude oil futures, it is important to examine not only their evolution over time but also how they behave across maturities. The term structure of oil futures prices summarizes how futures behave in relation to the spot price. Hedgers need to consider the shape and the dynamic of the term structure before entering into a hedge transaction and should monitor it during the life of the hedge.

In the previous chapter, we briefly introduced the concepts of contango and backwardation and the various theories used to describe forward curve shapes. It is worthwhile delving deeper into some traditional theories that attempt to explain the dynamics of the futures price term structure. Chief among these theories are the normal backwardation theory (the Keynesian theory) and the theory of storage. In the following discussion, we will use the terms "futures market" and "futures curve" interchangeably.

The Normal Backwardation or Keynesian Theory

The Keynesian theory of normal backwardation is based on the assumption that speculators require a risk premium to enter into oil futures contracts. In other words, speculators consider commodity futures as risky and require a price discount to compensate for the risk that they are assuming. In the absence of any risk premium, the futures price should be equal to the unbiased expectation of the future spot price. However, under the risk premium hypothesis, when speculators are rewarded for taking the risk, the futures price becomes a biased expectation of the future spot price.

Let us consider the situation where all corporate hedgers have the same view of the market. They would not hedge with each other but would instead look for speculators who are willing to take on that risk. In this situation, the futures price will be lower than the expected future spot price. While Keynes assumes in his normal backwardation theory that the commodities market is dominated by hedgers who hold long positions in the underlying physical commodity and are net short in futures, we can also consider market situations where hedgers are net long futures. In this case, the futures price will be higher than the expected future spot price and such markets are considered to be in normal contango.

It is important to clearly distinguish between contango and normal contango, and between backwardation and normal backwardation. Contango refers to a market where the futures price is higher than the spot price, whereas normal contango refers to a market in which the current futures price is higher than the expected spot price in the future. Similarly, backwardation refers to a market where the futures price is lower than the spot price, whereas normal backwardation refers to a market in which the current futures price is lower than the expected spot price in the future (at the expiry of the futures contract).

To illustrate the presence of risk premia in futures prices, we take the case of the WTI futures curve. Between 2005 and 2006, the WTI futures term structure switched from back-wardation to contango due to increased hedging activity from airlines. The bulk of this hedging was done within a 24-month window, resulting in the shape of the term structure characterized by a hump at around the 18-month tenor.

During the backwardation period, speculators enjoyed positive premiums by holding futures contracts and rolling them as they expired (via commodity indices such as the GSCI). Rolling refers to the practice of selling a nearby futures contract and simultaneously purchasing a longer-dated futures contract. In a backwardated market, rolling futures contracts involve the sale of a futures contract at a high price and the purchase of another futures contract at a lower price, and this can amplify the returns from price movements in the future. These rolling gains can be explained by the risk premium associated with normal backwardation. However, these strategies proved unsuccessful after the term structure shape reverted to contango. Rolling the contracts incurred substantial costs, which, in this case, can be explained by the risk premium associated with normal contango.

The Theory of Storage

Under the theory of storage, commodities can either be consumed or stored for later use. According to this theory, the futures price depends mainly on the spot price and the cost associated with owning and storing the physical commodity (cost of carry). These costs include the cost of storage as well as the cost of financing the purchase of the physical good. As financing costs are positive and storage costs are usually high for commodities other than precious metals, futures prices can be expected to be higher than spot prices.

While this relationship helps explain term structures that are in contango, it fails to account for backwardated forward curves. To address this shortcoming of the theory, the concept of convenience yield was introduced. Market participants believe that they benefit from holding the physical commodity and this benefit is represented by the convenience yield. These benefits are revealed by the extent of backwardation seen during periods of scarcity of a commodity.

Convenience Yield   The convenience yield commonly refers to the benefits of owning the physical commodity vs. holding a futures contract. In practice, the convenience yield includes storage costs and can therefore be positive or negative:

$$\text{Convenience yield} = \text{Benefit of owning the commodity} - \text{Cost of carry}$$

The new spot–forward relationship can be represented as follows:

$$F_{t_0,T} = S_{t_0}\, e^{\int_{t_0}^{T} (r_t - c_t)dt}$$

where S_t: spot price at time t
   $F_{t,T}$: price at time t of a futures contract expiring at T
   r_t: short-term interest rate, which is the annualized interest rate at which an entity can borrow money for an infinitesimally short period of time around time t
   c_t: convenience yield determined by satisfying the arbitrage-free condition

In the real world, the convenience yield is not constant but varies over time, which renders the modeling of the spot and forward prices much more complex. It can be seen that as the convenience yield increases, the futures price drops relative to the spot price. During periods of scarcity, futures prices generally trade at a discount to the spot price, reflecting a high convenience yield for owning the physical commodity. Thus, the convenience yield can be said to be positively correlated with the spot price. However, the futures price term structure not only mirrors inventory levels but also reflects the expected changes in convenience yield. Thus, backwardation in futures curves may exist even when inventories are high, and this is usually the case when a change in the supply/demand balance is expected (e.g., in the case of war or extreme weather events).

Furthermore, a close analysis of the basis between the price of the physical commodity and that of the futures contract shows a clear asymmetry depending on whether the market is in contango or backwardation. This is due to the fact that when the market is in contango, the basis is capped by the cost of carry that includes the cost of storage, which is not the case when the curve is in backwardation. The presence of active arbitrageurs can help keep forward prices from exceeding spot prices by more than the cost of carry, but is less effective in preventing it from falling significantly below the spot price. This asymmetrical behavior has implications for the dynamic of the convenience yield, leading us to view the convenience yield as an option. In other words, in comparison with holding futures contracts, the holder of the physical good is long the fat tail of the distribution associated with extreme backwardation (a shortage "black swan"). This asymmetrical behavior will be discussed further when we deal with price and volatility term structures.

In summary, under the storage theory, oil futures prices correspond to the spot price adjusted to account for the incurred cost of carry and the benefits associated with owning the physical good that are forgone by holding a futures contract instead.

TERM-STRUCTURE MODELS

To effectively value commodity derivatives and manage associated risks, trading desks use different term-structure models depending on the complexity of the transacted derivatives and the sophistication required. While it is tempting to borrow common models that are used to price equity, FX, or interest-rate derivatives, such an approach would be inefficient and potentially dangerous for risk managers in the commodity derivatives arena. In this section, three popular pricing models are presented along with a discussion of the intuition behind each of these approaches.

Most derivatives pricing models assume continuous market trading, no frictions in terms of transaction costs or taxes, and equal costs for lending or borrowing underlying securities. Commodities pricing models also make use of similar assumptions. However, with regard to market completeness (i.e., the ability to duplicate commodity derivatives using a combination of other assets in a dynamic hedging portfolio), commodity markets are not perfectly complete and arbitrage opportunities exist. This occasionally allows for the coexistence of different prices of risk.

Schwartz's One-Factor Model

Schwartz's one-factor model is perhaps the most well-known commodity model that incorporates mean reversion. In this model, the spot price fluctuates around a long-term mean and regresses to this mean according to a speed of adjustment. The behavior of the spot price is characterized by its volatility, its propensity to return to a long-run mean, and the ability to move away from it.

In the real world, mean reversion represents the behavior of physical market participants. For example, producers tend to lower their production of a commodity when the spot price is below the long-term average and increase their production when it is higher than the long-term average. Consumers, in contrast, exhibit the opposite behavior by purchasing less when prices are high and building inventories when prices are low. The price mean reversion is the result of the combination of these behaviors.

The process for the spot price of a commodity under this mean-reverting model is as follows:

$$dS = S\beta\left(\alpha - \ln(S)\right)dt + \sigma S dz$$

where S: spot price

      dz: a Wiener process associated with the Brownian motion of the spot price

      β: speed of adjustment of the spot price

      α: logarithm of the long-term mean price

      σ: volatility of the spot price

In light of the previous discussion relating to the asymmetrical behavior of the basis between the spot price and the futures price, it is clear that Schwartz's one-factor model does not account for this asymmetry. It does not reflect the asymmetry of the convenience yield in contango and backwardation. In contango markets, the spread between the spot price and the futures price is capped by the cost of carry and is limited by the availability of storage. In backwardation, however, the spread between the spot price and the forward price has no constraints and can be large. This can be attributed to the difficulty of shorting physical commodities.

Schwartz's Two-Factor Model

Schwartz's two-factor model relies on both the spot price and the convenience yield to explain the behavior of the futures price. Both spot price and convenience yield are treated as stochastic variables, as follows:

$$dS = S\left(\mu - C\right)dt + \sigma_S S dz_S$$

$$dC = \beta\left(\alpha - C\right)dt + \sigma_C dz_C$$

where S: spot price

      C: convenience yield

      μ: spot price drift

      α: long-term mean of the convenience yield

      β: adjustment speed of the convenience yield

In this model, the spot price dynamic is a function of the convenience yield as it is taken into account in the calculation of the net drift of the spot price. The convenience yield is also supposed to be mean reverting. This is in line with the behavior of the physical market operators discussed previously. Moreover, there is a positive correlation between the convenience yield and the spot price. This is modeled by introducing a correlation between the two Brownian motions as below:

$$[dz_S dz_C] = \rho dt$$

This can also be expressed as

$$\text{cov}\left(z_S z_C\right) = \rho t$$

A major weakness of Schwartz's two-factor model is the independence of the volatility of the spot price and the convenience yield. It is observed in the energy market that the volatility of the spot price is correlated with the level of backwardation. As the backwardation increases, indicating that the commodity is scarce, the volatility of spot prices increases. This dependence between spot price volatility and convenience yield is not reflected in Schwartz's two-factor model.

Gabillon's Model

The most important contribution introduced by Gabillon is the use of the long-term price as a second factor. The intuition behind this choice is that the spot price is impacted by two different categories of events: those that have short-term effects and those that have long-term effects. Factors that have long-term effects would include, for example, the introduction of new technologies, expected inflation, or discoveries of new reserves.

Gabillon's model uses the spot price and the long-term price as stochastic variables to describe the term-structure dynamics. Gabillon's model assumes that the spot price S follows a Gaussian process that mean-reverts to a lognormal long-term price L as follows:

$$\frac{dS}{S} = \beta \left(\ln \left(\frac{L}{S} \right) \right) dt + \sigma_S dz_S$$

$$\frac{dL}{L} = \mu dt + \sigma_L dz_L$$

$$[dz_S dz_L] = \rho dt$$

where S: spot price

          L: long-term price (base price)

          β: a measure of the speed of adjustment of the price to the long-term price L assuming that the ratio between S and L influences the term structures of the prices and volatilities; this also captures the decreasing term structure of volatility and the Samuelson effect

          σ_S: short-term volatility

          σ_L: long-term volatility (base volatility)

          ρ: correlation between long-term and short-term prices

Gabillon's model has gained popularity among commodity derivatives professionals compared with the Schwartz model due to the fact that the convenience yield, which is central to the Schwartz model, is unobservable in practice.

The Gabillon model has a simplified closed-form solution for futures prices, based on the final condition related to the convergence of spot price to futures price at expiry of the future:

$$F = A(\tau)\, S^{B(\tau)} L^{1-B(\tau)}$$

$$B(\tau) = e^{-\beta\tau}$$

$$A(\tau) = e^{\frac{v}{4\beta}(B(\tau)-B(\tau)^2)}$$

$$v = \sigma_S^2 + \sigma_L^2 - 2\rho\sigma_S\sigma_L$$

where τ is the time to expiry of the future.

When the future is very close to expiry, τ tends to zero ($\tau \to 0$). When $\tau \to 0$, $B \to 1$ and $A \to 1$, which implies that $F \to S$ (i.e., the spot price converges to the futures price).

When the time to expiry τ is very long, $B \to 0$ and $A \to 1$, which implies that $F \to L$ (i.e., the long-dated futures price is close to the long-term price L).

Thus, when the futures contract reaches expiry, the futures price converges toward the spot price and when the futures contract is long-dated, the futures price is closer to the long-term price L. The formula above allows us to reproduce different term structures, which are entirely parameterized by a limited number of parameters: S, L, ρ, σ_S, σ_L, and β.

Gabillon's Stochastic Equation for Futures

When futures prices are used in the pricing of commodity derivatives, the Gabillon stochastic equation for a futures contract can be formulated as follows:

$$\frac{dF}{F} = \alpha\, [\, \sigma_S e^{\lambda\tau} dz_S + \sigma_L (1 - e^{\lambda\tau})\, dz_L\,]$$

$$E[dz_S dz_L] = \rho dt$$

where λ is the mean reversion, which measures the steepness of the volatility term structure.

The above formula can be used to derive the instantaneous volatility of the futures contract at any point before expiry.

σ_S is typically higher than σ_L. This explains how the price term-structure dynamics is characterized by a fast-moving front end and a more stable back-end (Figure 5.14).

A high correlation between the spot and the base price implies that all the points of the term structure move in the same direction. However, the speed at which the spot and long-term prices change can be very different. Thus, even with a perfect correlation between the two variables, the forward curve can switch from backwardation to contango and vice versa, mainly due to the difference between spot volatility and the long-term price volatility.

The spot price and the long-term price movements can occasionally be uncorrelated or negatively correlated, resulting in parts of the forward curve moving in opposite directions. This can be experienced, for example, when a significant notional of time-spread transactions is executed in the market.

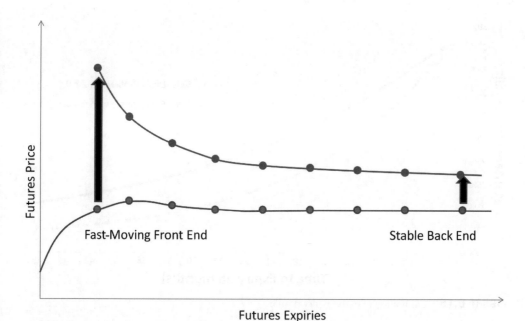

Futures Price

Fast-Moving Front End　　　　Stable Back End

Futures Expiries

FIGURE 5.14　Price term-structure dynamics

Early-Expiry Profile Using Gabillon's Model

Gabillon's stochastic equation for futures implies an early-expiry profile that should be in line with market observations.

Instantaneous volatilities inferred from the Gabillon stochastic equation can be formulated as follows:

$$\sigma_F^2(\tau) = (\sigma_S e^{-\lambda\tau})^2 + (\sigma_L(1 - e^{-\lambda\tau}))^2 + 2\rho\sigma_S\sigma_L e^{-\lambda\tau}(1 - e^{-\lambda\tau})$$

This allows us to plot a futures early-expiry profile (i.e., the instantaneous volatility as a function of the time to expiry). It is worth noting that, according to the Gabillon model, all the futures contracts have a common early-expiry profile.

With short-term volatility of 38%, long-term volatility of 20%, and correlation of 95%, the early-expiry profile can be calibrated using the parameter λ as shown in Figure 5.15.

In practice, a volatility normalization factor is applied so that the early-expiry volatilities are scaled to give the correct vanilla option implied volatility for each futures contract.

Importance of Early-Expiry Profile for Exotic Products

The term structure of volatility has a direct impact on the shape and dynamic of the forward curve, as the short end is fast moving while the back end is more stable. An appropriate choice of the early-expiry profile (EEP) is critical from a trading desk's perspective, as any mismatch between the realized volatility and the implied volatility can result in mispricing and theta leakage (due to imperfect hedging strategies).

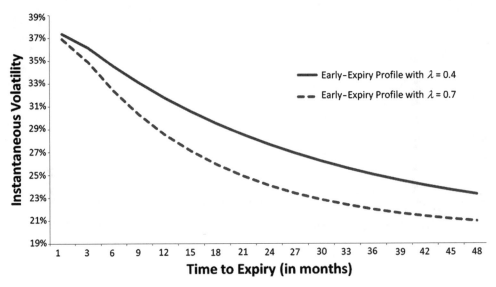

FIGURE 5.15   Calibration of early-expiry profile

Pricing models that ignore the Samuelson effect and assume constant volatility, that is equal to B–S implied volatility, often lead to mispricing of payouts that contain triggers or conditions that apply much earlier than the expiry of the underlying contracts. The closer these triggers are to the expiry of the contract, the smaller is the discrepancy between the two pricing methods (constant B–S implied volatility vs. EEP).

The hedging structures that are very sensitive to the shape of the EEP include barrier options, swaptions, extendible structures, target redemption features, Bermudan extendibles, auto-callable structures, as well as time-spread options.

SUMMARY

Vanilla products such as futures and standard options are the sources of market data, which is usually summarized in forward curves and volatility surfaces. However, this data is not sufficient to price non-standard products without additional assumptions and extrapolations. Financial engineers are constantly looking for parameterizations of the historical behavior of forward curves and volatility surfaces in order to predict their future dynamics. Over time, new parameters have been added to account for new behaviors, making these pricing models increasingly complex. In this chapter, we have covered a few popular term-structure models that aim to replicate phenomena such as the historically observed mean reversion, the Samuelson effect, and the convenience yield (as per storage theory). We also noted how the implementation of such dynamics is calibrated to match the observable prices of standard products. In the following chapters, we will explain how the dynamics of the volatility surface impact the valuation and risk management of exotic hedging products. We will also discuss the behavior of these products under stress scenarios such as the market movements and events that unfolded during the credit crisis of 2008.

CHAPTER 6

Exotic Hedging and Volatility Dynamics

"You can fool some people sometimes but you can't fool all the people all the time."
—Bob Marley

Exotic derivatives transactions usually place quantitative market-makers at an advantage over clients with limited valuation capabilities, but even these sophisticated traders often incur losses when their dynamic hedging goes wrong. Upon executing an exotic transaction, the trader faces other parties on the vanilla derivatives constituting the replicating portfolio, the construction of which is completely reliant on the accuracy of the assumed market dynamics. Sometimes the market outsmarts the trader by proving that certain assumptions are unnecessary or insufficient.

In the previous chapter, we introduced advanced hedging structures, which are composed of combinations of vanilla products. We also discussed the early-expiry type of options that are embedded in structures like swaptions and extendible swaps. During the last decade, fuel hedging has evolved toward the use of more sophisticated hedging strategies, reflecting the maturation of the commodities derivatives market, increased liquidity, the accumulated knowledge related to hedging, and improvements in pricing and risk management capabilities. The trend toward exotic commodity derivatives was embraced by both commodities hedgers and hedge providers. Chief among the factors that make exotic structures attractive for hedgers is the flexibility to tailor payouts to accommodate the complex real-world constraints that most fuel consumers face. The high cost of hedging using vanilla structures has also encouraged hedgers to consider sophisticated ways to enhance hedge economics and take advantage of any optionality inherent in their business model.

The use of exotics in fuel hedging has not been without risks for hedgers. During the financial crisis of 2008, the sudden disappearance of market liquidity was accompanied by a sharp rise in fuel price volatility and a drop in fuel prices. The extreme market conditions at that time constituted a stress test for the exotic hedging structures that were very popular from 2006 onwards. Many fuel hedgers in Asia were party to leveraged exotic structures and suffered significant losses that went relatively unnoticed by the media as the world's focus was absorbed by the colossal losses emanating from credit derivatives. The few fuel hedgers who fared better did so as they had competent fuel-hedging desks and hands-on senior management, who were alert to the regime change in global fuel markets and quickly restructured those exotic hedges that were no longer optimal under the new market order.

In this chapter, we will take a closer look at some of the most popular exotic structures, the rationale for using these derivatives, and the attendant risks for both the corporate hedger and structured products dealing desks. The impact of volatility surface dynamics will be discussed in depth. With reference to these exotic structures, volatility models and their appropriateness will be compared in order to better understand the intricacies from a pricing and dynamic risk management perspective, while providing the intuition behind the structuring of commodity exotics. But before addressing modeling aspects, let us begin with a discussion of variants of the extendible swap structure discussed in the previous chapter.

EXTENDIBLE OPTION STRUCTURES

In the previous chapter, we introduced extendible swaps and looked at how they are used as an attractive alternative to plain vanilla swaps in order to achieve enhanced economics for zero-cost hedging structures. We also looked at the impact of the forward curve dynamics on the valuation and risk management of these structures. Swaptions can be seen as a particular case of a wider family of extendible structures. Extendible structures can be defined as bilateral transactions that give one counterparty the right, but not the obligation, to extend an existing hedging structure or enter into a new hedging structure. In the case of swaptions, the underlying hedging structure is a vanilla swap but we can now extend our definition to include hedging structures that include a combination of options.

Extendible Collar

An extendible collar is an instrument that applies the extendible approach to enhance the strikes available in a collar hedging structure. Sample terms for an extendible-collar transaction are illustrated in Example 6.1. Note that these are leveraged structures, as can be deduced from the settlement calculations.

EXAMPLE 6.1: SAMPLE TERMS FOR A LEVERAGED EXTENDIBLE COLLAR

Counterparties:	Client & Bank
WTI Price:	NYMEX WTI Crude Oil front-month futures contract (monthly average)
Effective Date:	Start of calendar month after Trade Date
Expiry Date:	Effective Date + 1 year
Termination Date:	Expiry Date + 2 weeks, subject to Extendible Terms
Notional Quantity:	50,000 barrels per month
Calculation Periods:	Monthly calendar periods starting from Effective Date up to Final Expiry Date
Payment Dates:	2 weeks after the end of each Calculation Period

Extendible Terms: On the Extendible Date, the Bank has the right to extend the trade for an additional 6 months by giving notice to the Client

Extendible Dates: Expiry Date
Put Price: 50 USD/bbl
Call Price: 68 USD/bbl
Settlement Amounts: Subject to Extendible Terms, for each Calculation Period, on the respective Payment Date:

If WTI Price < Put Price, Client pays
1.5 * Notional Quantity * [Put Price – WTI Price]
If WTI Price > Call Price, Client receives
Notional Quantity * [WTI Price – Call Price]

In this extendible collar, the hedger buys call options for the notional quantity and sells 1.5 times the notional quantity of put options. This is in addition to selling the right to extend the transaction for an additional 6 months.

Extendible Three-Ways

Similarly, sample terms for an extendible three-ways transaction are as shown in Example 6.2.

EXAMPLE 6.2: SAMPLE TERMS FOR A LEVERAGED EXTENDIBLE THREE-WAYS

Counterparties: Client & Bank
WTI Price: NYMEX WTI Crude Oil front-month futures contract (monthly average)
Effective Date: Start of calendar month after Trade Date
Expiry Date: Effective Date + 1 year
Termination Date: Expiry Date + 2 weeks, subject to Extendible Terms
Notional Quantity: 50,000 barrels per month
Calculation Periods: Monthly calendar periods starting from Effective Date up to Final Expiry Date
Payment Dates: 2 weeks after end of each Calculation Period
Extendible Terms: On the Extendible Date, the Bank has the right to extend the trade for an additional 6 months by giving notice to the Client
Extendible Dates: Expiry Date
Put Price: 50 USD/bbl
Call Price: 62 USD/bbl
Cap Price: 77 USD/bbl

Settlement Amounts: Subject to Extendible Terms, for each Calculation
                             Period, on the respective Payment Date:

                             If WTI Price < Put Price, Client pays
                             1.5 * Notional Quantity * [Put Price – WTI Price]
                             If Cap Price > WTI Price > Call Price, Client receives
                             Notional Quantity * [WTI Price – Call Price]
                             If Cap Price < WTI Price, Client receives
                             Notional Quantity * [Cap Price – Call Price]

In both the transactions described, the client enjoys attractive hedging levels during the first year (i.e., the guaranteed period). The value of the enhancement of the economics of the hedge during the guaranteed period is equivalent to the premium of the extendible option (see Figure 6.1):

PV(enhanced guaranteed collar) – PV(zero-cost collar) = PV(extendible option)

Before moving further into the discussion, we describe how cancellable structures can be viewed as extendibles. Extendible and cancellable structures are economically similar transactions and only differ in the semantics of their terms. Using the example of the extendible collar above, we can develop the terms for an equivalent cancellable collar.

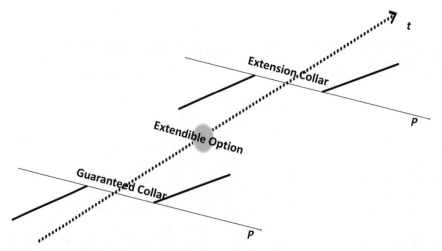

FIGURE 6.1   Guaranteed and extendible portions of an extendible collar

Cancellable – Extendible Parity

The extendible collar described above can be decomposed as follows:

12-month guaranteed consumer collar + option to enter into 6-month consumer collar

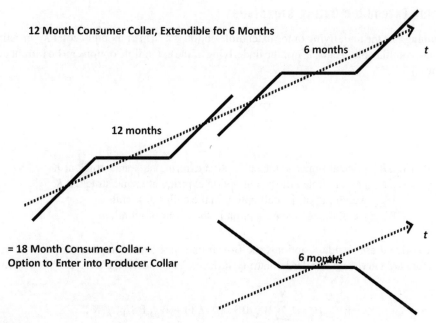

12 Month Consumer Collar, Extendible for 6 Months

6 months

t

12 months

= **18 Month Consumer Collar +**
Option to Enter into Producer Collar

6 months

t

FIGURE 6.2 Extendible option as option to enter into offsetting structure

This is equivalent to the following cancellable collar:

18-month guaranteed consumer collar + option to terminate the trade after 12 months

The option to terminate the trade after 12 months is equivalent to the option to enter into a 6-month offsetting collar (Figure 6.2). Note that the option indicated here is owned by the hedge counterparty (the bank). The option to extend can also be considered as follows:

6m collar extendible option = 6m collar + option on offsetting 6m collar
 ↑ ↑
 underlying option on offsetting
 transaction transaction

Therefore, in the case of a consumer collar:

Consumer collar extendible option = Consumer collar + Option to enter into producer collar

In light of the above decomposition of extendible option structures, an extendible structure can also be priced as the sum of the underlying structure for the full tenor (including the extendible period) and the cancellable option, which can be expressed as the option to enter into the offsetting transaction. In the case of the extendible collar, the offsetting structure is the corresponding producer collar. We will use this result in the pricing of Bermudan extendible structures later.

Pricing Extendible Option Structures

Assuming that the underlying of the extendible option is a strip of monthly collars consisting of standard vanilla options, the PV of the underlying of the extendible option can be formulated as follows:

$$\text{PV}_{\text{ext}}(t) = \sum_{n=1}^{N} W_{c,n} C(t_n, K1) - W_{p,n} P(t_n, K2)$$

where $C(t_n, K)$: price at time t of the call option expiring at t_n and struck at K

$P(t_n, K)$: price at time t of the put option expiring at t_n and struck at K

$W_{c,n}$: weighting of the call option in the collar of month n

$W_{p,n}$: weighting of the put option in the collar of month n

To price these standard options, the B–S framework can be applied to available market data (forward curve and standard volatility surface). The underlying's PV can be written as

$$\text{PV}_{\text{ext}}(t) = \sum_{n=1}^{N} W_{c,n} \text{BS\_c}(t_n, K1) - W_{p,n} \text{BS\_p}(t_n, K2)$$

The extendible is only exercised when PV_{ext}(extendible date) is positive. Assuming interest rates are constant or uncorrelated to fuel price, the undiscounted price of the collar extendible is the risk-neutral expectation of the payout:

$$P = E[\max(0, \text{PV}_{\text{ext}}(\text{extendible date}))]$$

$$= E[\max(0, \sum_{n=1}^{N} W_{c,n} \text{BS\_c}(t_n, K1) - W_{p,n} \text{BS\_p}(t_n, K2))]$$

On the extendible date, the payout of the extendible option is a function of the forward points $F_n(t)$ and the implied volatility surface, which contains the implied volatilities $\sigma_n(t, K1)$ and $\sigma_n(t, K2)$ for the collar strikes. The price of the extendible has to take into account all the dynamics of the forward curve and the volatility surface.

To gain a good intuition about the impact of market dynamics on the pricing of collar extendibles, let us consider a simplified case consisting of an extendible on a single monthly collar instead of a strip of collars. We consider an extendible option expiring on the extendible date with underlying collar expiring on the collar expiry date (Figure 6.3). Similar to swaptions, an extendible collar is also sensitive to the forward dynamics, as we discussed in the previous chapter.

As the forward curve does not move in a parallel fashion, the payout and the exercise decision of an extendible are based on the relevant forward point, which is less volatile than the front month. In the case of a swaption, the terminal variance of the forward up to the extendible date is the most important factor in the pricing. Similarly, the behavior of the value of a collar with vega close to zero is similar to that of a swap. In that case, the value of the extendible is driven by the volatility of the forward from pricing date to extendible date.

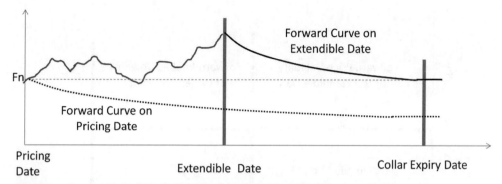

FIGURE 6.3 Extendible collar timeline and forward curve dynamics

Extendibles and the Samuelson Effect The Samuelson effect has been discussed in Chapter 5 to stress the impact of the early-expiry profile on the pricing of swaptions. The early-expiry profile can also have a bearing on the valuation of other exotic products, and this is often overlooked by commodity traders and structurers. Insufficient insight into the effect of the early-expiry profile can lead to mispricing and inappropriate risk management. For example, fuel hedgers usually ask for quotes from different commodity trading houses and compare prices. Prices can differ significantly if some traders submit prices calculated using quick and unsophisticated methods. Blindly trusting a black-box pricing tool without having an adequate understanding of its working can also lead to price differences that are large enough to be arbitraged by other sophisticated participants and fuel hedgers.

In the above example, the underlying of the extendible can be expressed as follows:

$$W_c\text{BS\_c}(t_{\text{collar}}, K1) - W_p\text{BS\_p}(t_{\text{collar}}, K2)$$

The collar above can be negative or positive vega depending on the leverage and moneyness of the strikes based on the current forward price. Assuming that the underlying collar above has a positive vega at the prevailing forward prices, let us examine the impact of the Samuelson effect on the pricing of the extendible (Figure 6.4).

In the case of swaptions, the pricing is highly dependent on the volatility of the forward up to the swaption exercise date. Similarly, for collar extendibles, the PV of the collar also moves in a manner commensurate with its delta. In cases where the collar strikes are very close to each other, the MTM of the collar behaves like a swap. In this type of situation, the extendible price depends on the terminal variance of the forward up to the extendible date, with an average volatility of

$$\sigma_{\text{initial}}^2 = \frac{1}{(\text{Extendible Date} - \text{Pricing date})} \int_{\text{Pricing date}}^{\text{Extendible Date}} \sigma_F^2(\tau)d\tau$$

During the period up to the extendible date, the forward moves, on average, by the volatility defined above. This initial volatility is very important in determining the moneyness of the collar options at the extendible date. It impacts the distribution of the forward at the extendible date, which is a key factor in the pricing of the collar.

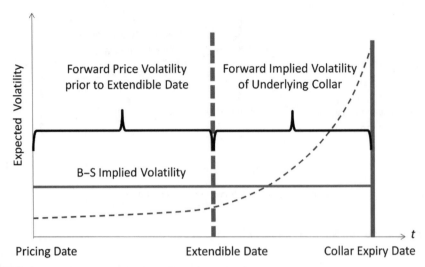

FIGURE 6.4   Extendible collar volatilities

Once the forward is fixed at the extendible date, the PV of the collar is mainly driven by the terminal variance from the extendible date to the collar expiry date. We calculate the expected implied volatility for the collar at the extendible date as follows:

$$\sigma^2_{\text{implied}} = \frac{1}{(\text{Collar expiry date} - \text{Extendible Date})} \int_{\text{Extendible Date}}^{\text{Collar expiry date}} \sigma^2_F(\tau) d\tau$$

The shape of the early-expiry profile suggests that the corresponding forward implied volatility is higher than the B–S volatility. This means that, for a collar with positive vega, even if the hedge is zero-cost on pricing date, the extendible can be ITM forward, as the forward value of the collar is positive due to the higher expected volatility close to expiry. That is,

$$[W_c C(t_{\text{collar}}, K1) - W_p P(t_{\text{collar}}, K2)]_{\text{on extendible date}}$$
$$> [W_c C(t_{\text{collar}}, K1) - W_p P(t_{\text{collar}}, K2)]_{\text{on pricing date}}$$

A positive vega position in a zero-cost structure is often accompanied by negative carry and this is compensated by the benefit of also being positive gamma. The positive gamma implies favorable changes in the delta of the structure as the price moves. The B–S framework expects that, on average, the expected revenue from delta-hedging the position should cover the negative carry. But if the price volatility is lower than the B–S volatility, the revenues from rebalancing the long gamma position might not be sufficient to cover the negative carry.

Due to the Samuelson effect, long-dated futures contracts are less volatile, making the gamma rebalancing strategy less profitable at the beginning of the tenor. This shortfall is compensated as the volatility spikes above the B–S implied volatility close to expiry. For extendibles on zero-cost option structures with positive vega, this translates into extendibles being ITM forward. In other words, the collar can be zero-cost spot (when priced as of the pricing date) but is positive-MTM forward (when priced as of the extendible date) because of the higher expected volatility close to expiry.

Like other corporate hedgers, airlines and shipping companies prefer structures with favorable economic terms at inception and abhor negative-carry situations. As there is no free lunch with the hedge providers, these structures usually come with a long-volatility (positive-vega) position for the hedge provider. In other words, the corporate hedger gets enhanced hedging terms by selling optionality. Consider, for example, a zero-cost leveraged collar where the notional of the put is twice that of the call. The hedge provider is long volatility and any extendible on such a collar (one with positive vega) is likely to be ITM forward (when priced as of the extendible date).

Extendibles and Forward Skew Dynamics   In the case of an unleveraged collar extendible, if the strikes are significantly close to each other, the delta of the underlying collar is close to that of a plain swap and the price is very sensitive to the terminal variance of the forward point up to the extendible date. On the contrary, when the strikes are sufficiently distant from each other, the underlying unleveraged collar has a delta that can be significantly lower than that of the plain swap, especially when the put and call options are OTM. In these situations, the forward volatility dynamics become an important factor in the pricing of the collar extendible.

In the example in Figure 6.5, the implied volatilities of the put and the call options expiring on the collar expiry are quoted on the pricing date as σ(pricing date, $K1$) and σ(pricing date, $K2$). The volatility surface on the pricing date implies a risk reversal close to zero, but as we reach the extendible expiry, the ATM volatility increases and the risk reversal (σ(extendible expiry, $K1$) – σ(extendible expiry, $K2$)) also becomes significant. This change in the shape of the volatility surface impacts the payout and needs to be accounted for in the pricing and risk management of extendible options.

As we move from the pricing date to the collar expiry, the price moves according to a transition density (the distribution of the price returns). This transition density is characterized by the implied volatility smile on the pricing date. It is this transition density that determines the price of the vanilla options as of the pricing date. Similarly, the transition density from the

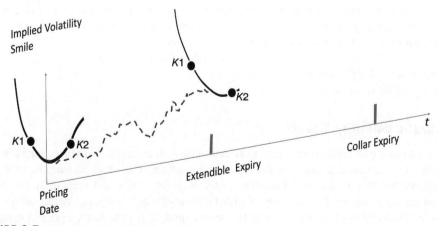

FIGURE 6.5   Forward skew/smile dynamics

extendible expiry to the collar expiry is characterized by the forward smile (which can depend on the forward price). In other words, the volatility smile observed on the pricing date reflects market participants' view, on the pricing date, of the price distribution at the collar expiry (as implied by the options prices they quote for different strikes). But as market participants' view of the price distribution changes over time, the smile that is observed at the extendible expiry (forward smile) will reflect the price distribution implied by the options market at that point in time.

Non-arbitrageable pricing requires a tight calibration of the model parameters to fit the volatility surface at the pricing date. Nevertheless, a reasonable pricing of the extendible requires assumptions about the forward skew of the underlying contract at the extendible expiry, especially since the volatility surface evolves as the price moves. In other words, the question is whether the volatility surface remains constant as the price moves or changes shape as market participants react to market conditions.

In our example, the payout of the collar is very sensitive to the risk reversal at the extendible expiry. More importantly, the correlation between the risk reversal and the forward price can have a big impact on the distribution of the payout of the extendible, thereby affecting its price and risk metrics. It is therefore paramount to understand whether the risk reversal is positively or negatively correlated with the forward price.

VOLATILITY MODELS

Black–Scholes-based models assume constant volatility and derive an option premium from the expected cost of delta-hedging under the constant-volatility assumption. However, options traders often find themselves obliged to do vega hedging to immunize the trading book from changes in volatility levels. This clearly contradicts the initial assumption of homoskedasticity of returns. Moreover, the cost of vega hedging is not reflected in the option premium. Therefore, traders seek out models that take into account volatility smile, volatility changes, and the dynamics of future volatility.

The volatility surface reflects behavioral factors such as the fear of a crash, shortages, technical price supports and resistances, risk reversals due to trading of zero-cost structures, and market expectations of the price distribution. Other fundamental factors include market frictions, non-continuous trading, and the correlation between the price and volatility. More sophisticated pricing models use techniques to fit these inputs to the volatility surface to account for its dynamics. The most famous approaches are

a. stochastic volatility models
b. local volatility models.

Stochastic Volatility Models

Exotic options models that are based on B–S assumptions frequently lead to inaccurate pricing and risk metrics, thus necessitating the use of more advanced models. Stochastic volatility models attempt to provide an explanation of the volatility smile and the highly fat-tailed distributions that characterize mixtures of distributions with different standard deviations.

It has been discussed previously that B–S-based models assume that the price is the only source of randomness. The random behavior of the price was assumed to be lognormal, with volatility as a constant parameter. Under the stochastic volatility framework, volatility is also considered as a source of randomness. Under the B–S framework, a derivative with value V is instantaneously hedged using a replicating portfolio made up of the underlying asset only. However, under the stochastic volatility framework, there is a need for a portfolio made up of the underlying asset S and another asset with value V' that is sensitive to volatility. The resulting portfolio is

$$V - \Delta S - \Psi V'$$

Δ and Ψ are the amounts of S and V' necessary to make the portfolio instantaneously risk-free. This implies the following conditions for

$$\text{Delta neutrality:} \quad \frac{\partial V}{\partial S} - \Delta - \Psi \frac{\partial V'}{\partial S} = 0$$

$$\text{Vega neutrality:} \quad \frac{\partial V}{\partial \sigma} - \Psi \frac{\partial V'}{\partial \sigma} = 0$$

Stochastic volatility models often assume a mean-reverting stochastic variance v and square-root diffusion (from the term $\sqrt{v}$):

$$dv = \beta(\alpha - v)dt + \omega\sqrt{v}dz_v$$

where v: instantaneous variance
α: long-term mean of variance
β: speed of adjustment of the variance to the mean
ω: volatility of variance, usually referred to as Vol of Vol

When the spot price follows a geometric Brownian motion as follows:

$$dS = S\mu dt + \sqrt{v}S dz_s$$

the two Brownian motions are correlated with correlation

$$E[dz_S dz_v] = \rho dt$$

The mean reversion of volatility is well supported by historical volatility patterns. For example, the historical volatility of oil prices has remained within a certain range for decades. If the volatility were not mean reverting, current volatility levels could have been much higher. The correlation between the variance and the spot price is a parameter used to reproduce the volatility smile. This correlation is also called the leverage parameter, which is typically negative, implying that the dynamics correlate a down move in the price with an up move in the volatility (leverage effect).

The mean-reverting process of the variance needs to be specified in a way that ensures the variance is positive. From a theoretical point of view, the Brownian paths followed by this process are continuous. This means that the variance cannot get negative before being equal to zero. Once the variance is equal to zero, the diffusion stops and the strictly positive parameters α and β help bring back the variance to positive levels. To avoid situations where the variance reaches zero, α and β need to be sufficiently large, as per the Feller condition, stated as follows:

$$\beta\alpha > \frac{\omega^2}{2}$$

If Feller's condition is respected, the upward drift is sufficient ($\beta\alpha$ is large enough) for the simulated variance to never exactly reach zero.

In the real world, processes are not simulated continuously. Numerical models use discretization, which needs to be small enough to avoid cases of simulated negative variance. We will return to the discussion on volatility models when we discuss local volatility later in the chapter.

BARRIER OPTION-BASED STRUCTURES

Barrier options are exotic derivatives that are very similar to standard vanilla options except that they can be terminated or activated conditional on the price reaching a certain level. This trigger feature makes them an important building block for structured products. The most popular barrier options are the knock-out options and knock-in options.

Knock-Out Options and Knock-In Options

A knock-out (KO) option can be American or European in terms of settlement convention or barrier observation. European settlement (fixed settlement dates) is generally more popular while American style barrier observations are preferred. Their payouts are similar to those of vanilla puts and calls except that the option early-terminates if the price reaches a predetermined price level (barrier). There are many types of KO options: up-and-out calls, down-and-out calls, up-and-out puts and down-and-out puts.

The barrier of an up-and-out call is normally above the strike; otherwise the option would be worthless (Figure 6.6). Similarly, the barrier of a down-and-out put is normally below the strike level (Figure 6.7).

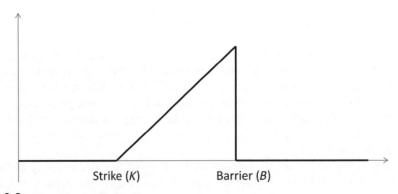

FIGURE 6.6   Up-and-out call payoff

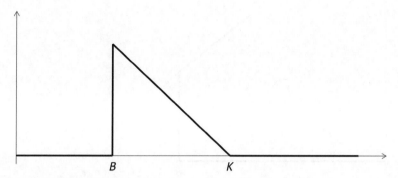

FIGURE 6.7   Down-and-out put payoff

Knock-in (KI) options are similar to vanilla puts and calls, except that the option is only active if the price reaches a predetermined price level (barrier). In other words, the payout of the corresponding vanilla option is only paid if the price hits a predetermined price level (the barrier). KI option types include: up-and-in calls, down-and-in calls, up-and-in puts and down-and-in puts.

In an up-and-in call, the barrier is normally above the strike (Figure 6.8); otherwise the option would be equivalent to a vanilla call. Similarly, the barrier of a down-and-in put is normally below the strike level (Figure 6.9).

The payouts above are drawn based on the price at expiry. In reality, the payout is a function of both the price at expiry and the maximum price or the minimum price. The dotted line in the two figures indicates the possibility of payouts even if the price at expiry is below the barrier if the barrier has been hit earlier.

Fuel hedgers resort to purchasing barrier options as a cheap alternative to vanilla options. If the hedger has a range-bound view of the market, he/she can buy a KO call, which is a cheaper alternative to vanilla calls. On the contrary, if he/she is concerned about incurring immediate losses when he/she sells puts to finance the purchase of call options, the hedger

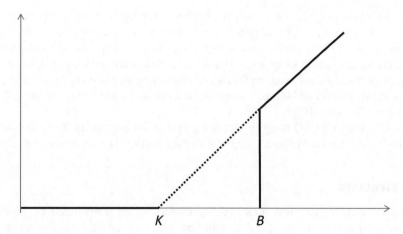

FIGURE 6.8   Up-and-in call payoff

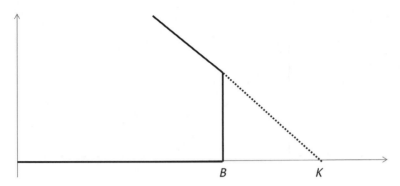

FIGURE 6.9   Down-and-in put payoff

could opt to sell a KI put, which provides him/her with a cushion. Losses under the put would only be incurred should the price drop below the barrier level.

Other barrier option-based hedging structures include KO swaps, airbags, knock-in knockouts (KIKOs), and accumulators.

Relationship between KI and KO Options

KI and KO options are tightly linked through the underlying option. When both barrier options are taken together, the barrier effect gets offset in the combined position. In other words, the combination of a KI option and a KO option with the same strike and barrier is equivalent to the underlying vanilla option:

$$\text{KO call} + \text{KI call} = \text{call}$$
$$\text{KO put} + \text{KI put} = \text{put}$$

Knock-Out Swaps

A fuel hedger with a range-bound view of the market can choose to hedge using an up-and-out swap instead of a vanilla swap and benefit from an attractive hedging price. If the barrier is never breached, the KO swap has the same payout as a vanilla swap. The KO swap fixed price is lower than the prevailing swap price. The difference between the prevailing swap and the KO swap price is equivalent to the undiscounted price of an up-and-in call minus the price of an up-and-in put. The up-and-out KO swap can be replicated using an up-and-out call and an up-and-out put (Figure 6.10).

A major criticism of KO swaps is that in the case of a sharp rise in fuel price, the hedge terminates leaving the fuel hedger unhedged at a time when he/she is in dire need of the hedge.

Airbag Structure

Fuel hedgers often try to adapt their hedging choices as the market moves, in an effort to add value by timing the market and adjusting their risk profile. Airbags are zero-cost structures that allow the hedger to benefit from a cushion should the price drop below the

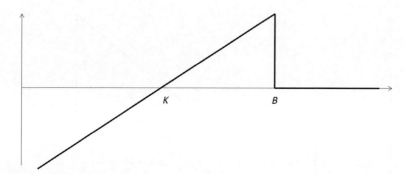

FIGURE 6.10   Knock-out swap payoff

swap price, as long as the barrier *B* is not breached. The airbag structure in Figure 6.11 can be replicated by:

- a call option struck at fixed price – a KI put struck at fixed price OR
- a swap at fixed price + a KO put.

The fixed price of a zero-cost airbag swap is higher than the prevailing swap price. The difference in swap level is used to finance the purchase of the KO put.

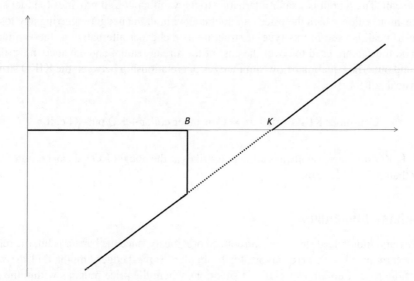

FIGURE 6.11   Airbag structure payoff

KIKOs and Combinations of KI and KO Options

KIKO options are derivatives that have two barriers, a KI barrier and a KO barrier. These derivatives pay out if the KI barrier is hit and the KO barrier is not hit. The KO barrier still remains active even if the KI barrier is hit.

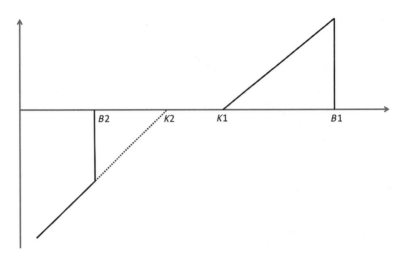

FIGURE 6.12 Airbag KIKO collar structure payoff

A popular combination of KI and KO options is the airbag KIKO structure, which combines the airbag feature and the range-bound KO call hedge as in Figure 6.12. The structure is similar to a collar hedge except that the put and the call of the collar are replaced by a KI put and a KO call. The KI put is a safer alternative to the vanilla put as it provides the fuel hedger with a cushion within which the price can fluctuate without the hedger incurring any losses.

The KO call is used in this type of structure as a cheaper alternative to the vanilla call. Savings on the call are used to cover the cost of the airbag feature and enhance the strikes of the call and put. The equation below summarizes the relationship between the KIKO structure and classical collars:

$$\text{Consumer KIKO structure} = \text{Consumer collar} + \text{KO put–KI call}$$

The KIKO structure usually has attractive strikes as the bought KO put can be significantly cheaper than the sold KI call.

Accumulator Structures

In the barrier option-based structures introduced previously, once the barrier is hit, the relevant option is terminated with zero payout to the holder. Some hedgers might find the binary nature of the payout unfair, especially in situations where the price remains within the range for the majority of the tenor of the option but knocks out just before expiry due to a sharp price move. To mitigate this effect, accumulators were introduced in order to spread the payout calculation across the tenor of the trade, instead of only at the end of the tenor, as in Figure 6.13.

For example, in an accumulator swap, the payout is similar to that of a vanilla swap but with daily payouts subject to the KO event not occurring. As the name "accumulator" suggests, the payouts are accumulated daily as long as no KO has occurred and the aggregate of accumulated daily payouts is paid on the payment date.

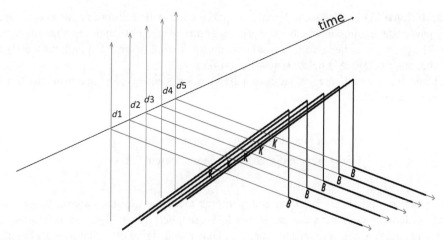

FIGURE 6.13   Accumulator swap structure payoff

Accumulators are replicated using a strip of KO options expiring on different days but paid on the same date.

European or Asian-Style Barrier Options

Fuel prices are very volatile compared with other asset classes such as FX or interest rates. Fuel hedgers wishing to use barrier options are often concerned about sudden price spikes that increase the likelihood of KO events. To mitigate this risk, they prefer to base both the payout amount and the KO event on the price at expiry. In other words, the barrier is only observed at expiry. This significantly reduces the likelihood of the barrier event occurring as the KO is no longer based on the maximum (or minimum) price reached during the tenor of the option.

Another common practice involves calculating the barrier event based on the monthly average of the price. Daily prices of crude oil can be very volatile and sudden spikes in oil price can cause barriers to trigger. The main issue in such scenarios is that the daily volume can be a very small fraction of the total volume of the whole transaction. Hence, concerns over manipulation of daily prices during windows of low liquidity arise when the cost of market manipulation is relatively low compared with the payouts when barriers are triggered.

To address these concerns, hedging transactions often calculate the barriers on the monthly arithmetic average of daily closing prices. The averaging effect minimizes the impact of a short-term spike and makes price manipulation a costly maneuver.

Barrier Payouts and Non-linearity – Digital Options and Replication

Unlike vanilla products, barrier structures are not linear as they have a binary character. For example, in an up-and-out call, the payout at expiry can immediately drop from as high as (barrier – strike) to zero once the price touches the barrier level. This non-linear behavior is a challenge for financial engineers when pricing barriers and managing associated risks. A discussion of European digital payouts gives a flavor of the issues to be tackled when dealing with barriers and binary payouts.

Digital Options   Digital call and digital put options are usually European options that have a binary payout depending on whether the price at expiry is greater than or less than the digital strike. The payout is either zero or a fixed amount (the digital height). Digital puts (calls) are ITM when the final price is below (above) the strike.

The undiscounted theoretical value of a digital price is easily calculated using the Black–Scholes formula as $N(d_2)$:

$$\text{Undiscounted digital call} = \text{Digital height} * N(d_2)$$
$$\text{Undiscounted digital put} = \text{Digital height} * N(-d_2)$$

In practice, digitals are rarely priced using the theoretical formula above. Risk-neutral pricing of derivatives reflects the profit and loss generated by the dynamic replication (or dynamic hedging) of the derivative in question. Dynamic hedging of digital payouts based on the theoretical B–S framework becomes extremely challenging as the price approaches the barrier closer to expiry. Over-hedging replication is introduced to address this issue.

Over-hedging Replication   When pricing derivatives, financial engineers assume that markets are dynamically complete (any derivative can be replicated using marketable assets). The risk-neutral price is then defined at the profit and loss of such dynamic replication. However, an inherent assumption of this method is the availability of sufficient securities and the ability to trade them continuously. In the real world, the volume of these tradable assets is not unlimited, trading is not continuous, and transaction costs exist. This leads to imperfect replication that leaves residual risks, which are usually factored into the price of such derivatives.

In the case of digital payouts, as the price gets close to the barrier and the digital option approaches expiry, the delta of the digital becomes extremely high. Delta-hedging becomes risky and is a costly exercise when market liquidity becomes a constraint.

We take the example of a $1,000,000 WTI digital with strike at 100$/bbl and implied volatility of around 20%. The B–S theoretical value of the delta of the digital a year before expiry and one day before expiry are shown in Figure 6.14.

On the day before expiry, the delta can vary by over 140,000 bbl for a 1$/bbl change in price. The dynamic hedge of such a risk profile becomes a tricky and costly exercise in view of the market liquidity.

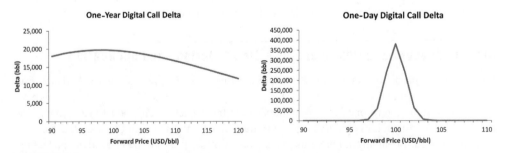

FIGURE 6.14   Digital call deltas one year before expiry and one day before expiry

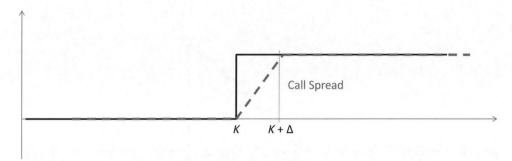

FIGURE 6.15   Long digital call over-hedge using a call spread

A solution to alleviate this issue consists of over-hedging the digital payout using a call spread. When traders bid for digitals, they usually price them as a call spread with strikes at strike K and $K + \Delta$, as in Figure 6.15. The notional of the call spread is equal to $\frac{\text{Digital height}}{\Delta}$.

But when they sell these digitals, they would typically use a call spread struck at $K - \Delta$ and K, as shown in Figure 6.16.

The call spread is a conservative over-hedge in both cases and the spread Δ can be chosen to be wide enough to smooth the risk profile. The delta of the call spread in such cases would never be greater than the maximum delta, $\frac{\text{Digital height}}{\Delta}$. The choice of the spread takes into account many factors, including the expected daily liquidity of the underlying over the tenor of the trade and portfolio risk limits.

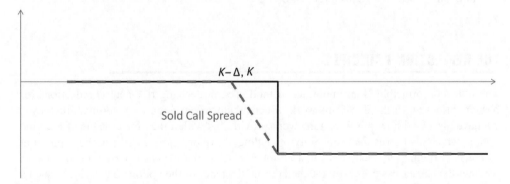

FIGURE 6.16   Short digital call over-hedge using a call spread

Replicating At-Expiry Barrier Options   European (at-expiry) barrier options are also priced and hedged using the same mechanism. For example, a KO call (with barrier observed at expiry) can easily be replicated using a call spread and a digital call, as shown in Figure 6.17.

- Long European up-and-out call = Long call spread – Digital call
  The replication is done by going long a call struck at K, short $\left(\frac{B-K}{\Delta}\right)$ calls struck at $B - \Delta$, and long $\left(\frac{B-K}{\Delta} - 1\right)$ calls struck at B.

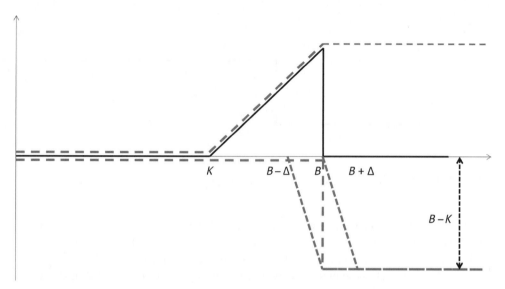

FIGURE 6.17   Replicating European barrier options with vanillas and digitals

- Short European up-and-out call = Short call spread + Digital call
  The replication is done by going short a call struck at K, long ($\frac{B-K}{\Delta} + 1$) calls struck at B, and short ($\frac{B-K}{\Delta}$) calls struck at $B + \Delta$.

THE REFLECTION PRINCIPLE

The reflection principle is an important method used in deriving risk-neutral valuations for barrier options under the B–S framework, which assumes constant price volatility. Previously, we have discussed how the B–S framework provides us with a theoretical value of a digital option, which also gives the probability of settling above or below a strike at the expiry. Let us consider digital payouts based on a no-touch barrier (the payout is binary depending on whether the barrier has ever been touched during the tenor of the option). The price of such a payout depends on the probability of hitting the barrier.

Figure 6.18 illustrates the reflection principle. After touching the barrier at point M, the dashed path has the same probability of realization as the solid path. In other words, the Brownian motion means that for each path hitting the barrier at M and settling below the barrier at expiry, there is an equally probable path hitting the barrier at M and settling above the barrier at expiry. This implies that the probability of touching the barrier is twice the probability of settling above the barrier. This principle simplifies the valuation of anytime barrier options significantly. The price of a one-touch barrier binary is twice the price of a European digital.

It is important to note that the observation above means that the probability of hitting a barrier only depends on the price distribution at expiry. Such an important simplification stems from the assumptions of the B–S framework, namely homoskedasticity and market efficiency

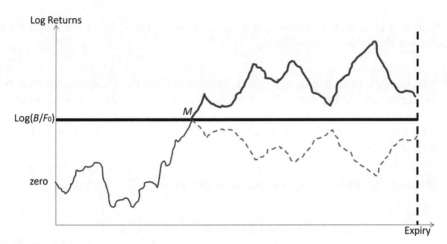

FIGURE 6.18 Illustration of the reflection principle

(i.e., the changes in the log returns are constant across the tenor and the probability of a down move is equal to the probability of an up move).

Barrier Options Under the Black–Scholes Framework

In the case of barrier calls and puts, the payout at expiry is a function of both the intrinsic value at expiry and the barrier trigger event. The pricing of such payouts will depend on the distribution of the payout at expiry as well as the probability of the occurrence of a barrier event conditional on the price at expiry.

To come up with an easy way to formulate the pricing of barrier options under the Black–Scholes framework, a solution would be to find a static replication of the barrier options using vanilla options. The barrier option behaves like a vanilla option except that it is worth zero if the price touches the barrier. For example, the price of a KO option is lower than that of the vanilla option $V(F, t)$ and we can write the KO option as

$$\text{KO\_option}(F, t) = V(F, t) - H(F, t)$$

If the barrier is never breached, $H(F, t)$ needs to expire worthless as the value of the KO option at expiry is equal to the vanilla option. But if the barrier is touched, its value should be equal to that of the vanilla option; i.e., $H(B, t) = V(B, t)$. $H(F, t)$ should also satisfy the Black–Scholes equation. For this purpose, we will use the reflection principle for derivatives on futures contracts.

The reflection principle states that if $V(F, t)$ is a solution to the B–S equation, then $FV(\frac{B^2}{F}, t)$ is also a solution. This transformation helps generate new solutions from existing ones. F and $\frac{B^2}{F}$ are on opposite sides of the barrier B and coincide when $F = B$.

Let's consider the example of an up-and-out put with strike K and barrier B, which is higher than K:

$$\text{KO\_put}(F, K, t) = \text{Put}(F, K, t) - H(F, t)$$

In light of the reflection principle, choosing $H(F, t) = \frac{F}{B}\text{Put}(\frac{B^2}{F}, K, t)$ will satisfy the B–S equation but also achieves the following:

- If the barrier is never breached, F remains lower than B and $\text{Put}(\frac{B^2}{F}, K, t)$ expires worthless. This helps achieve $\text{KO\_put}(F, K, t) = \text{Put}(F, K, t)$ at expiry, if the barrier has never been breached.
- If the futures price touches the barrier, $H(B, t) = \frac{B}{B}\text{Put}(\frac{B^2}{B}, K, t) = \text{Put}(B, K, t)$. This helps achieve $\text{KO\_put}(B, K, t) = 0$.

Therefore, the price of an up-and-out put (UOP) under the B–S framework is

$$\text{UOP}(F, K, t) = \text{Put}(F, K, t) - \frac{F}{B}\text{Put}\left(\frac{B^2}{F}, K, t\right)$$

Similarly, we can derive the value of a down-and-out call (DOC) with barrier B lower than K as follows:

$$\text{DOC}(F, K, t) = \text{Call}(F, K, t) - \frac{F}{B}\text{Call}\left(\frac{B^2}{F}, K, t\right)$$

The valuation of a UOP and a DOC is relatively simple because when the KO occurs, the underlying vanilla option has no intrinsic value. For up-and-out calls (UOCs) or down-and-out puts (DOPs), the replication is trickier.

For a UOC, we should first define the payout at expiry using vanilla options and then apply the reflection principle to the vanilla payout in order to offset the vanilla payout, if the price reaches the barrier, and satisfy the vanilla payout at expiry, if the barrier hasn't been breached.

At expiry, the payout of the UOC can be written as

$$\text{UOC}(F, K, B, T) = \text{Call}(F, K, T) - \text{Call}(F, B, T) - (B - K)\text{DC}(F, B, T)$$

where DC denotes the digital call.

We define the vanilla payout as

$$V(F, K, B, t) = \text{Call}(F, K, t) - \text{Call}(F, B, t) - (B - K)\text{DC}(F, B, t)$$

We apply the reflection principle to the payout above by subtracting the following:

$$H(F, t) = \frac{F}{B}\left\{\text{Call}\left(\frac{B^2}{F}, K, t\right) - \text{Call}\left(\frac{B^2}{F}, B, t\right) - (B - K)\text{DC}\left(\frac{B^2}{F}, B, t\right)\right\}$$

We can verify that if F never breaches the barrier, $H(F, t)$ has no intrinsic value and expires worthless. We can also see that as F approaches B, $H(F, t)$ gets closer to $V(F, K, B, t)$.

We can conclude that

$$\mathrm{UOC}(F, K, B, t) = \mathrm{Call}(F, K, t) - \mathrm{Call}(F, B, t) - (B - K)\mathrm{DC}(F, B, t)$$
$$- \frac{F}{B}\left\{ \mathrm{Call}\left(\frac{B^2}{F}, K, t\right) - \mathrm{Call}\left(\frac{B^2}{F}, B, t\right) - (B - K)\mathrm{DC}\left(\frac{B^2}{F}, B, t\right)\right\}$$

The price of a DOP can be obtained in a similar manner.

Put–Call Symmetry

Most derivatives professionals are familiar with put–call parity, but the put–call symmetry relationship is not used very often. It is a simple relationship that not only helps simplify the payout of barrier options under the B–S framework, but also gives a straightforward idea about the static hedge of barrier options:

$$F\,\mathrm{Call}\left(\frac{B^2}{F}, K\right) = K\,\mathrm{Put}\left(F, \frac{B^2}{K}\right)$$

$$F\,\mathrm{Put}\left(\frac{B^2}{F}, K\right) = K\,\mathrm{Call}\left(F, \frac{B^2}{K}\right)$$

The demonstration is quite easy. At expiry:

$$F\,\mathrm{Call}\left(\frac{B^2}{F}, K\right) = \max(B^2 - KF, 0) = K\max\left(\frac{B^2}{K} - F, 0\right)$$

Put–call symmetry helps simplify the payouts above tremendously. For example,

$$\mathrm{UOP}(F, K) = \mathrm{Put}(F, K) - \frac{K}{B}\mathrm{Call}\left(F, \frac{B^2}{K}\right)$$

$$\mathrm{DOC}(F, K) = \mathrm{Call}(F, K) - \frac{K}{B}\mathrm{Put}\left(F, \frac{B^2}{K}\right)$$

$$\mathrm{UOC}(F, K, B) = \mathrm{Call}(F, K) - \mathrm{Call}(F, B) - (B - K)\mathrm{DC}(F, B)$$
$$- \left\{\frac{K}{B}\mathrm{Put}\left(F, \frac{B^2}{K}\right) - \mathrm{Put}(F, B) - (B - K)\frac{F}{B}\mathrm{DP}(F, B)\right\}$$

These simplified static replications not only allow for easy pricing of the barrier options but also provide a clear breakdown of the replicating portfolio using basic European vanilla options.

MTM Analysis of Barrier Options Under the Black–Scholes Framework

Even though barrier options resemble vanilla options when they are not knocked out, their MTM behaves differently as market conditions move. To get a better idea about the behavior of barrier option MTM, let us consider the example of a UOC option on a 1-year WTI futures

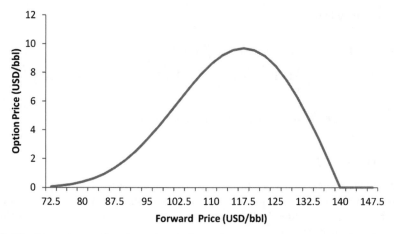

FIGURE 6.19 Up-and-out call option price vs. forward

contract, expiring in 1 year, with the strike at $100/bbl and a KO barrier at $140/bbl. Implied volatility is assumed to be constant (20%) and the interest rate is fixed at 1% p.a.

Using the closed-form equation detailed previously, the MTM is calculated for different forward prices and plotted in Figure 6.19 to understand the relationship between the price of the UOC and the forward price.

Compared with a vanilla call, the price of a KO call is seen to be close to that of the vanilla call option when the futures price is far from the barrier, as shown in Figure 6.20. The delta of the UOC is also very close to that of the vanilla call but as the spot price gets closer to the barrier, the prices of the KO call and the vanilla call start to diverge and the delta of the KO call starts to decrease and becomes negative.

Moreover, unlike vanilla options, the UOC price is not an increasing function of volatility. The vega of a barrier option depends on the volatility level. As volatility levels increase, the KO option holder becomes short volatility, as seen in Figure 6.21.

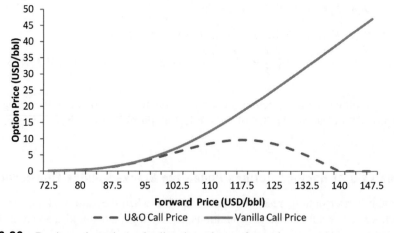

FIGURE 6.20 Barrier option price and call option price vs. forward

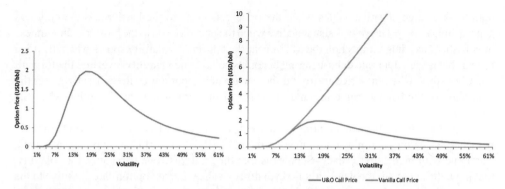

FIGURE 6.21 Barrier option and call option price vs. volatility

Being long a UOC does not necessarily mean being long vega. As the price gets close to the barrier, the vega gets negative. Vanna is an important Greek in the case of barrier options. A common mistake in quoting barrier options is when a market-maker assumes that option price is an increasing function of volatility, leading him/her to occasionally quote a bid price higher than the offer price. In a simple barrier structure, the mistake is quite obvious for the market-maker, but when the traded structure is more complex or includes more features, such pricing mistakes might go detected.

Pricing and Risk Management of Barriers with Real-World Constraints

In general, most traded exotic payouts are priced using numerical methods such as Monte Carlo simulations, trees, or partial differential equation (PDE) resolution methods. Deriving a closed formula to price and manage the risk of exotics is not an easy task and when pressed to do so, financial engineers and quants often resort to approximations and simplification of the issue at hand. Typically, these simplifications include assumptions about the behavior of the market and conditions that are very far from those observed in the real world.

When we priced the barrier options earlier, the B–S framework was used and this came with the assumption of constant volatility. In reality, volatility is seen to be random and risks stemming from this randomness need to be compensated for. Valuing the barrier options under the B–S framework does not include the premium required to account for randomness in volatility. Moreover, the framework does not account for transaction costs and assumes that trading is continuous. With these two facts in mind, continuous dynamic hedging becomes very costly and almost impractical for many exotic payouts. In the case of barriers, traders rebalance their hedging portfolio less frequently to save on transaction costs and usually resort to over-hedging techniques to minimize the frequency of rebalancing. Traders cannot dissociate pricing from the way they manage the risk of structured products. In the real world, the price quoted by traders will take into account the cost of over-hedging and the frequency of dynamic hedging of the position.

Let us consider the case of barrier options. When added to a vanilla option, the barrier KO feature changes the pricing and the risk profile significantly. As seen previously, the hedging of a UOC can be challenging because the intrinsic value of the option can suddenly switch to zero if the barrier gets hit. It has been discussed earlier that the gamma of the barrier option takes large negative values when the price gets close to the barrier and the option is approaching expiry. The vega is also negative when the price is close to the barrier. Randomness in volatility has a huge impact on the MTM near the barrier. If volatility spikes when the price is near the barrier, dynamic delta-hedging becomes costly. The volatility level and the forward volatility smile when the price is around the barrier are important as they directly affect the likelihood of the barrier triggering and the value of the terminated vanilla option when the barrier is hit.

While it has always been tempting for market participants to look for a shortcut to quickly price barrier options assuming constant volatility like in the B–S world, this approach is flawed. The issue with models like Black–Scholes is that they only use one parameter for volatility, making it difficult to fit the whole implied volatility surface. Barrier options are sensitive to the implied volatility both at the strike and at the barrier. One can think of using a combination of the two implied volatilities in order to price the KO option, but this too does not work because the option price is not a monotonic function of volatility (as seen earlier). Even when the barrier options market is liquid and price information is available, it is not possible to derive implied volatility for barrier options as is the case for vanilla options.

The monotonic character of the vanilla call price as a function of implied volatility makes it possible to derive implied volatilities from the market price of such options. This is not the case for barrier options. In the UOC example discussed earlier, if the option price is too high, the closed formula does not have any solution. But when it is low, we can get two solutions σ_1 and σ_2, as shown in Figure 6.22. If we choose σ_1 as "implied volatility," the vega is positive but if we choose σ_2, the vega is negative. The same problem is observed with the delta (because of the vanna profile of KO options). So, these two solutions are not equivalent and using any one of them to hedge the position might lead to taking on additional risks.

Under the B–S framework, we managed to find a price and a static replication of the barrier option using a portfolio of European options as

$$\text{KO\_call}(F, K, t) = \text{Call}(F, K, t) - H(F, t)$$

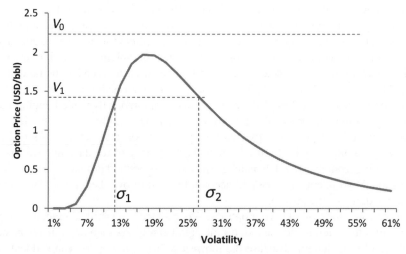

FIGURE 6.22 Multiple B–S implied volatilities for barrier options

The rationale is to hold a portfolio of options that have the payout of the vanilla option at expiry but would have zero value if the price reached the barrier. With such a portfolio of options, once the barrier is hit, the trader will have to unwind the whole portfolio immediately. Ideally, the unwinding of the replication portfolio should be at zero cost: $\text{Call}(B, K, t) - H(B, t) = 0$. But in the real world, volatility is not constant and an implied volatility surface that is not flat might necessitate some unwind costs. Therefore, the price of the barrier option should take into account these unwind costs. From a pricing perspective, traders should choose the static replicating portfolio that would minimize the unwind cost in case of knock-out.

The unwind cost at the barrier is very sensitive to the forward smile. In other words, the value of $\text{Call}(F, K, t) - H(F, t)$ is a function of the implied volatility smile. So, the unwind cost will depend on the expected smile, conditional on the price being close to the barrier. Just like extendible options-based structures, barrier options depend on the conditional transition densities that describe, at different points of time and for different price levels, the market participants' view of the price distribution at expiry.

Barrier Options on a Nearby Futures Contract

Very often, barrier options are linked to the nearby contract or front-month arithmetic average. This leads to situations where the barrier is observed based on the front month while the option's payoff is based on a longer-dated contract. In addition to the issues discussed earlier with regard to the volatility surface and the forward skew dynamics, this type of option has an additional complexity related to the forward curve dynamics.

For a UOC, the fast-moving front contract increases the chance of knock-out, while the stability of the back-end contract implies that when the front contract touches the barrier, the underlying vanilla option might still be relatively cheap (compared with a vanilla option whose payout is based on the front contract). The digital risk for the trading desk (in case of a knock-out) is lower than (barrier – strike), as illustrated in Figure 6.23. For the UOC holder, basing the knock-out on the front contract increases the likelihood of the KO substantially.

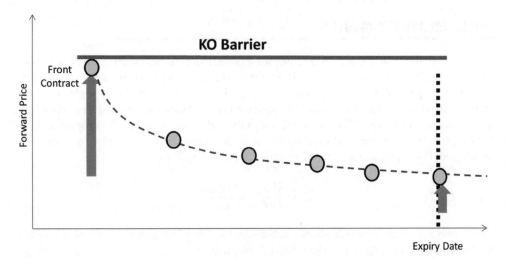

FIGURE 6.23 Forward curve dynamic impact on UOC options where barrier monitoring is on front-month contract

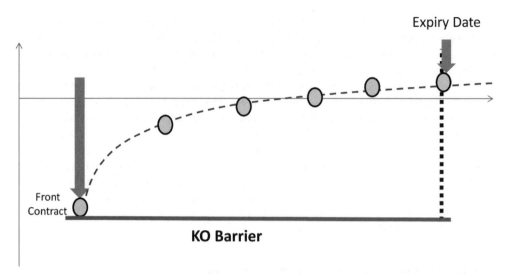

FIGURE 6.24 Forward curve dynamic impact on DOC options where barrier monitoring is on front-month contract

For the DOC, the fast-moving front increases the likelihood of knock-out while the option is ITM, as seen in Figure 6.24.

Intuitively, such barrier options behave as if they are based on two highly correlated underlyings – the long-dated contract for the payout and the rolling front contract for the knock-out. The terminal variance of the long-dated contract is dictated by the market B–S implied volatility, but the rolling contract has a terminal variance equivalent, on average, to the volatility of the front contract, which is generally the most volatile contract of the forward curve.

We now revisit volatility models as we discuss local volatility formulations.

LOCAL VOLATILITY MODELS

As discussed in Chapter 5, there is a consensus among traders to use the Black–Scholes model to quote vanilla options even though it is not the correct model to value and hedge derivatives. This also suggests that the replication portfolio given by the B–S model under the non-arbitrage condition is also inaccurate. Therefore, it is important to understand how this affects the Greeks of a derivative. The use of the volatility surface to overcome the shortcomings of the B–S framework means that the calculation of the Greeks of the derivatives also needs to be adapted. For example, the delta of an option should be written as

$$\Delta = \frac{\partial V_{B\_S}}{\partial F} + \frac{\partial V}{\partial \sigma}\frac{\partial \sigma}{\partial F}$$

This means that there is an incremental risk due to the relationship between the volatility and the forward price (as implied by the volatility surface).

Due to the complexity of the stochastic volatility model and the difficulties trading desks face in calibrating the model's parameters to the market volatility surface, many practitioners

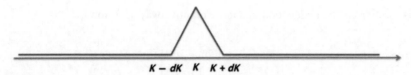

FIGURE 6.25 Risk-neutral density calculated using a butterfly

sought out easier ways to model volatility without significant detriment to the accuracy of the pricing. Local volatility models were introduced to describe volatility as a deterministic function of the price. Local volatilities can be seen as the expectation of the stochastic volatility, conditional on the price being at a certain level.

The intuition behind the local volatility model starts with the relationship between the options price and the risk-neutral density of the futures price. Under the assumption that the futures price risk-neutral density is a known function $D(p)$, the undiscounted price of a call option with strike K and expiry T can be expressed as follows:

$$C = \int_K^\infty D(F, T)(F - K)dF$$

This helps calculate the risk-neutral density as

$$D(K, T) = \frac{\partial^2 C}{\partial K^2}$$

This is equivalent to calculating a butterfly, as shown in Figure 6.25, with dK being infinitesimally small.

In other words, with sufficient market data, we can use call prices to construct the price distribution. This density is in line with the volatility surface and can then be used to price derivatives that only depend on the terminal distribution.

A standard Brownian motion for a futures contract can be expressed as

$$\frac{dF}{F} = \sigma(F, t)dz$$

The diffusion of the Brownian motion should produce the same price distribution implied by the options market (the risk-neutral density, as explained earlier). As the Brownian motion equation is mainly driven by the choice of the function $\sigma(F, t)$, we need to choose a deterministic volatility function for the Brownian motion to achieve the exact terminal distribution of the price. The local volatility model (as proposed by Dupire) defines a unique local volatility function $\sigma(F, t)$ that serves this purpose:

$$\sigma^2(K, T) = \frac{2 \frac{\partial C}{\partial T}}{K^2 \frac{\partial^2 C}{\partial K^2}}$$

This formula can be understood in a more intuitive way as follows:

$\frac{\partial C}{\partial T}$ is a calendar spread of a call for an infinitesimal time window

$\frac{\partial^2 C}{\partial K^2}$ is a butterfly spread (with very tight spread between strikes)

The implied volatilities read from the volatility surface can be seen as an average of the local volatility over any price path that starts at the initial forward price on the start date and terminates at the strike K on the expiration date. This also helps explain why, when the price moves, the local volatility moves faster than the implied volatility, which is an average of local volatility. This behavior of the local volatility has an influence on the behavior of the forward skew as the price moves. The resulting forward skew dynamics is also similar to that suggested by the leverage effect observed in the equity market (volatilities rise when stocks drop) but this might not always be true in the commodities market, which frequently displays the inverse leverage effect (volatilities rise when commodity prices increase).

Another risk management issue with local volatility models is the commingling of delta and vega hedges. In other words, when the volatility is a deterministic function of the price, the delta calculation already captures some changes in volatility. Similarly, vega calculations include the effect of changes in price.

BERMUDAN EXTENDIBLE STRUCTURES

Bermudan extendible structures are similar to the one-time extendible structures introduced previously, except for the fact that they give the extendible option owner multiple extendibility

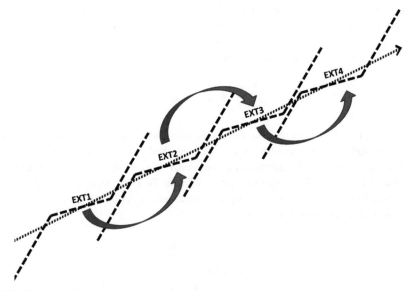

FIGURE 6.26 Multiple extendible options in a Bermudan extendible collar

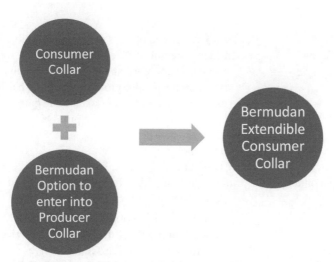

FIGURE 6.27 Decomposition of Bermudan extendible collar into a collar and a Bermudan option to enter the opposite collar

rights, exercisable on a periodic basis. The owner has the opportunity to reassess the profitability of the trade on a periodic basis, giving him/her the chance to exit the transaction if he/she deems it no longer favorable. If the Bermudan extendible owner does not exercise his/her right to extend the trade for a particular period, the trade terminates and subsequent extendible rights are forfeited.

In the example shown in Figure 6.26, the Bermudan extendible collar can be extended on four predetermined dates. Each time the transaction is extended, the counterparties are locked into the underlying trade for an additional extendible period until the next extendible date. As previously discussed, this extendible structure can also be expressed as a cancellable trade (Figure 6.27). The Bermudan cancellation option is similar to an American option to enter into the offsetting trade, except that it can only be exercised on a specific set of dates.

Sample terms for a Bermudan extendible collar are shown in Example 6.3.

EXAMPLE 6.3: SAMPLE TERMS FOR A BERMUDAN EXTENDIBLE COLLAR

Counterparties:	Client & Bank
WTI Price:	NYMEX WTI Crude Oil front-month futures contract (monthly average)
Effective Date:	Start of calendar month after Trade Date
Expiry Date:	Effective Date + 1 year
Termination Date:	Expiry Date + 2 weeks, subject to Extendible Terms
Notional Quantity:	50,000 barrels per month
Calculation Periods:	Monthly calendar periods starting from the Effective Date to the Final Expiry Date

Payment Dates:	2 weeks after end of each Calculation Period
Extendible Terms:	On each Extendible Date, the Bank has the right to extend the trade for an additional 3 months by giving notice to the Client, provided the trade has been extended on all previous extendible dates
Extendible Dates:	Quarterly, starting from the Expiry Date, for four quarterly periods
Put Price:	50 USD/bbl
Call Price:	67 USD/bbl
Settlement Amounts:	Subject to Extendible Terms, for each Calculation Period, on the respective Payment Date:

If WTI Price < Put Price, Client pays
Notional Quantity * [Put Price – WTI Price]
If WTI Price > Call Price, Client receives
Notional Quantity * [WTI Price – Call Price]

In general, Bermudan options are more expensive than European options but cheaper than American options. In Example 6.3, there are four extendibility dates giving the holder the option to reassess the economics of the underlying trade. However, the extendible rights are interlinked and the right to extend is lost if the transaction has not been extended previously. This also allows us to draw the conclusion that the value of a Bermudan extendible is lower than the sum of the four independent extendibles (Figure 6.28). This reflects the

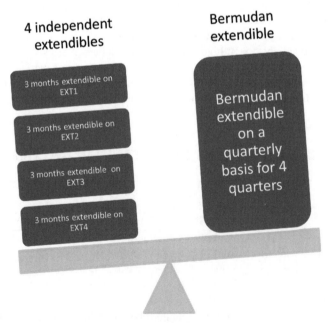

FIGURE 6.28 Comparison between values of a quarterly Bermudan extendible and four independent extendibles

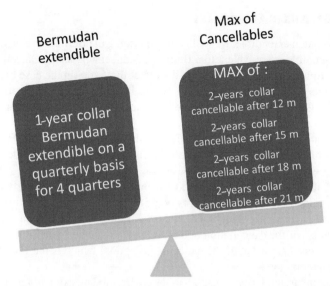

FIGURE 6.29 Comparison between values of a quarterly Bermudan extendible and the most valuable cancellable transaction

fact that the Bermudan extendible is more restrictive than holding four independent one-time extendibles.

In contrast, the Bermudan extendible offers more flexibility in choosing the time to get out of the trade compared with a trade with only one cancellation opportunity (Figure 6.29). In other words, the Bermudan extendible is more valuable than the most valuable of the one-time cancellable trades, which are as follows:

- 2-year collar cancellable at the end of month 12;
- 2-year collar cancellable at the end of month 15;
- 2-year collar cancellable at the end of month 18;
- 2-year collar cancellable at the end of month 21.

The holder of the Bermudan extendible needs to use some criteria based on which the decision to extend the trade can be made. If these criteria are known beforehand, he/she can then place a value on the Bermudan extendible based on the exercise criteria. The Bermudan option seller might disagree with the valuation of the buyer, especially if he/she thinks that the assumed exercise criterion is sub-optimal.

The optimal extendible strategy for Bermudan extendibles can be non-trivial and requires sophisticated analysis of the transaction. For example, there are situations where the underlying transaction is underwater for the extendible holder but the optimal strategy might be to extend the trade. In this case, the option holder has to endure negative cash flow if the time value of the optionality of the future extendible options is significantly high. The negative cash flow might be viewed as the cost of maintaining the right to benefit from the extendible optionality.

Valuation of Bermudan Extendibles

To value the Bermudan extendible, we will focus on pricing the Bermudan cancellation option. A Bermudan extendible is equivalent to a Bermudan cancellable as the cancellation option is nothing but a Bermudan option to enter into the offsetting trade. In the case of the Bermudan extendible consumer collar, the cancellation option is a Bermudan option to enter into the producer collar. PDEs and Monte Carlo methods are used for the valuation of Bermudan extendibles.

Pricing derivatives using a PDE is usually done in a backward fashion. The pricing starts from the payout of the derivative and as we move backwards in time, the derivative's value is calculated for each generated price F based on the discounting of the subsequent cash flows generated along the path. In the case of a Bermudan option, the derivative's value is the value of the trade if continued, which is why it is often referred to as the "continuation value." The exercise decision is then based on the continuation value, which is compared with the value of exercise of the cancellation option, referred to as the "exit value." The exit value in this case is the intrinsic value of the cancellation option, which is the PV of the producer collar for the remaining tenor.

The most popular numerical method to price Bermudan extendibles is Monte Carlo simulation, complemented by the approach proposed by Longstaff and Schwartz to apply optimal exercise strategies.

Longstaff–Schwartz Method and Exercise Boundaries

Monte Carlo simulations are forward-looking numerical methods that are not designed to value Bermudan payouts without knowledge of the optimal exercise strategy. As discussed previously, the exercise strategy needs to take into account the "continuation value," which is the value of continuing the trade, and compare it with the value of exiting the transaction, the "exit value." Longstaff and Schwartz introduced backward valuation into the Monte Carlo method by expressing the continuation value as a function of the current price (or swap price). With such a function at hand, it is easy to run Monte Carlo simulations and make exercise decisions based on the continuation value calculated as a function of the simulated price on the extendible date.

Continuation Value Function   To understand the method used to define the continuation value function, let us consider a derivative V (such as a call option). The price of the derivative can be seen as the average of all discounted simulated payouts. Let us now consider the case where we can simulate a cloud of possible payouts for many starting prices. We can try to use regression analysis to find a function that best fits the cloud. The value of the option as a function of the price can be approximated using the curve that best fits the cloud of discounted payouts, as shown in Figure 6.30. Ideally, for each price P, the regressed value is close to the average of the payouts generated from price P.

The Longstaff–Schwartz method uses a similar approach to define the continuation value function (a polynomial function for example) by regressing the payout at time point $T+1$ to the price at time T. To take into account the discounting effects, the payouts are discounted to time point T before running the regression. The Longstaff–Schwartz methodology is illustrated in Figure 6.31.

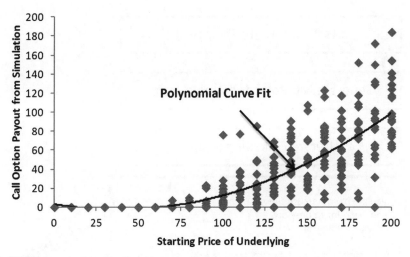

FIGURE 6.30 Simulation of call option price (strike = 100) based on various starting prices

Exercise Boundaries We discussed how the continuation value can be approximated by a function of the market price at a certain simulation step. The decision to exercise is based on observable market data and follows certain criteria. These criteria are usually defined as conditions on the observable market data being within a specified range. For example, an exercise strategy can be defined according to an exercise boundary and the extendible option is only exercised if the price is below/above the exercise boundary. But the strategy can be based on other variables, such as the swap price or the value of a combination of options (for example, the Black–Scholes price of appropriately selected vanilla options). In such cases, the continuation value needs to be regressed accordingly.

It is important to bear in mind that it is almost impossible to prove that an exercise strategy is the optimal one. Using a sub-optimal exercise strategy to bid for a Bermudan extendible is a conservative approach. The Longstaff–Schwartz method has been proven to give very good exercise boundaries, which however remain sub-optimal in view of the simplifications made and the limited number of market parameters considered in the exercise criterion (it typically does not include all the forward curve and volatility surface data). Traders are more than happy to bid for Bermudan extendible structures, but often shy away when asked to offer them. The reason behind this is that sub-optimal exercise boundaries give conservative bids but aggressive offers.

Hedgers' Sub-optimal Exercise Some trading desks might sell Bermudan extendibles to non-sophisticated clients, hoping that they will exercise the Bermudan options in a sub-optimal way relative to the sophisticated strategy used by the desk. When such an option is exercised too early or when the optimal exercise date is missed, the option seller realizes an instantaneous gain with reference to his valuation model. Corporate hedgers seldom buy Bermudan extendible options but when they do, they can lack the appropriate tools to value them and exercise them optimally. At times, the exercise decision is driven by business factors

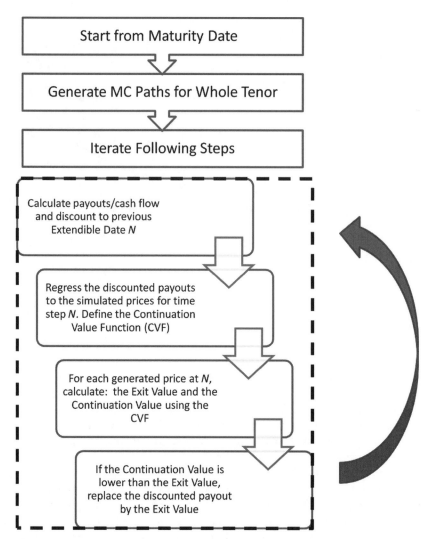

FIGURE 6.31   Longstaff–Schwartz methodology

that include those not related to the economics of the trade itself. For example, a corporate has a project that is contingent on external factors and it enters into a cancellable structure to hedge the commodity costs of the project. If the project is abandoned, the hedger may choose to cancel the structure because the hedge is no longer necessary. Another scenario may be one where a corporate hedger enters into an extendible transaction, where it would need to commit cash to extend the transaction or is likely to endure negative carry (cash outflow) immediately after extending the transaction. If the liquidity of the hedger is constrained, the hedger may decide not to extend the trade. This approach disregards the value of the extendible option, which is dependent only on market parameters. In such cases, the option holder should unwind the transaction to recover the value of the option instead of letting it expire worthless.

Extendible vs. Auto-callable Transactions

Auto-callable structures are transactions that terminate if the price reaches predefined levels on specific dates. They are very similar to barrier structures except that the knock-out is only observed on specific dates and the barrier is usually different for each knock-out date.

The pricing of Bermudan extendible/cancellable structures is very dependent on the choice of the exercise boundary. The Longstaff–Schwartz method helps define the exercise boundary or exercise frontier, which gives, for each extendible date, the price limit beyond which the transaction should be terminated. This exercise boundary is defined as the cancellable strike for each extendible date. Once the exercise boundary is fixed, the pricing of the extendible structure is the same as the pricing of the auto-callable structure. One can price the extendible structure as an auto-callable and look for the combination of auto-callable barriers $\{B_{t_i}\}$ across different extendible dates that maximizes the value of the cancellable option. This manual method to price extendible structures is much simpler and can produce results that are very close to those given by Longstaff–Schwartz. This method is sometimes automated by parameterizing the auto-callable strikes (using a polynomial function $B(t_i)$), running the Monte Carlo simulations, calculating the auto-callable value for each parameterization, and then choosing the parameterization that gives the highest auto-callable value.

For the extendible option holder, the auto-callable is an interesting over-hedge for the extendible because he/she can always change the parameters of the auto-callable strikes when market conditions change, giving him/her additional optionality. In other words, if an extendible structure is booked in a risk management system by the traders as an auto-callable, the valuation is conservative. From time to time, the trader can recalculate the optimal auto-callable strikes and when a more optimal strike combination is found, the trading book would show an instantaneous profit.

Revenues generated from re-optimization of an over-hedge are not shared with the option seller (usually the corporate hedger), which is unfortunate for the corporate hedger who only receives a premium at inception corresponding to the over-hedged structure (the auto-callable) parameterized at inception. This is very common in the commodities market because many market participants are not familiar with the way such transactions are valued and hedged. To recoup some of this premium given over to counterparties, at the expense of additional complexity in documentation, corporate hedgers can opt for auto-callable structures over Bermudan extendibles.

To address this, a corporate hedger should transform the pricing complexity into a documentation issue. Structured products traders and structures often use static over-hedging structures to quote complex payouts instead of seeking legal palliatives that can be fast and cheap. This behavior is understandable as there is a reluctance to reveal the secrets of the trade to clients. In such situations, the hedger would legally commit to an extendible while he/she is only compensated initially for an auto-callable. This is the same as when digitals are priced as call spreads. In such cases, the hedger is better off trading the call spread itself. Unfortunately, many hedgers take the easy route of preferring transactions that come packaged as an extendible, with more concise terminology, compared with documentation as an auto-callable.

Bermudan Extendibles and the Forward Skew

The importance of the forward-skew dynamics has been stressed while discussing the valuation and risk management of one-time extendibles. In the case of Bermudan extendibles, the issue is much more complex as the path dependency of the payout is much stronger. In the case of a one-time extendible, we were only concerned about the forward skew at the extendible date and were interested in the correlation between the forward skew and the price. The skew conditional on price level at the extendible date has a direct impact on the payout (the PV of the risk reversal) at the extendible date.

In the case of a Bermudan extendible, the payout at an extendible date is not only dependent on the skew but also on the forward skew at subsequent extendible dates. This is because the payout also includes the expected value of subsequent extendible options. We are looking not just for a forward skew conditional on price on a certain date, but the forward skew conditional on a path. For example, the price of a Bermudan extendible collar is dependent on the forward skew (risk reversal) conditional on the price of that date and on the structure being extended on all previous extendible dates.

As far as volatility models are concerned, both local volatility and stochastic volatility approaches have advantages as well as shortcomings. It is important to be mindful of the limitations of each model and maintain flexibility in adopting a conservative approach depending on the structure at hand. The most common pitfall is that many traders and quants assume that the mere fact of calibrating a model to the observable products in the market is an indicator of the quality and accuracy of the pricing.

Bluntly speaking, calibrating a model to the market-observable vanilla products guarantees two outcomes.

1. The ability to price combinations of vanilla payouts free of arbitrage.
2. Preserving the job of a quant, as the imperfections of a calibrated model are hard to pinpoint.

To illustrate this, let us consider the way models are calibrated to futures and options, which are mostly European payouts. When it comes to path-dependent products, discrepancies arise depending on the model's assumptions and approach. Tweaking models to match volatility surfaces or other constraints sometimes introduces unrealistic path dependencies that can significantly impact the pricing and risk management of such payouts. For example, local volatility models are very accurate when structures are not sensitive to forward skew dynamics. However, they are unreliable in predicting the dynamics of the volatility surface, giving wrong predictions of the forward skew. The forward skew predicted by local volatility models tends to be very flat. When prices rise or fall, the predicted forward skew may move in the opposite direction to the behavior observed in the market. This not only leads to mispricing, but also to bad hedging of exotic payouts.

Stochastic volatility models, in contrast, produce a forward skew similar in shape to the skew observed at inception. However, unlike the local volatility model, stochastic volatility models might not always be "arbitrage-free." The mere assumption of considering volatility as a stochastic variable can introduce "incompleteness" due to the absence of volatility instruments such as volatility swaps, and a structure might not be replicable without trading both volatility/options and the underlying futures.

To understand the correlation between the forward skew and the price, we will discuss leverage and inverse leverage in the commodities market and their importance in the pricing and risk management of exotic fuel hedging.

The Inverse Leverage Effect in Commodities Markets

In equity markets, "leverage effect" refers to the negative correlation between the implied volatility and stock prices. This is mainly due to the market's aversion to equity prices going down. When stock prices start dropping, panic spreads among investors who look for ways to exit or hedge their downside. This risk aversion impacts put option prices, which translates into higher implied volatilities as prices drop. This behavior is typically reversed in the commodities market and is referred to as the "inverse leverage effect." Commodity markets have been driven by physical hedgers who are more concerned about situations of shortage of the physical good. This effect can also be linked to the asymmetry observed in convenience yields.

In Chapter 5, the notion of convenience yield as an option was briefly discussed by drawing the link between high spot price volatility and the convenience yield. We also mentioned that the convenience yield can be seen as the premium paid for the optionality inherent in holding the physical asset compared with holding paper contracts. Most consumers are naturally short the physical underlying, which means that they are short the related optionality and would pay a premium for that. This premium translates into convenience yield, which is also linked to price volatility. Commodity price, convenience yield, and volatility can be expected to generally be positively correlated.

Let us look at how leverage and inverse leverage are mathematically modeled, using constant elasticity of variance (CEV) to give us an intuition on how these behaviors can be replicated by adding a parameter to the Brownian motion process.

Constant Elasticity of Variance Model   For futures contracts, the CEV equation can be written as follows:

$$dF_t = \sigma F_t^{\gamma} dZ$$

The choice of the parameter γ can produce leverage or inverse leverage effects depending on the value given. The same equation can be written as

$$\frac{dF_t}{F_t} = \sigma F_t^{\gamma-1} dZ$$

This clearly shows that if γ is lower than 1, the resulting volatility of the futures contract is negatively correlated to the futures price (leverage effect). However, if γ is greater than 1, the CEV gives the inverse leverage effect.

The Oil Market and the Feedback Effect   The "feedback effect" refers to the phenomenon where the causality of the correlation between price and volatility can be reversed (changes in volatility can also cause changes in price). This can be explained by the behavior of investors and asset managers and their reaction to market volatility. Market portfolio theory (MPT) and methods based on historical mean/variance analysis have become the norm for most investment managers and are widely taught at business schools and on finance programs. As a marketing tool, such simplistic, backward-looking frameworks have been employed by many financial product marketers to market investments. The application of such frameworks means that assets that show low historical returns and high volatility are systematically taken out of investment portfolios and replaced by assets with higher Sharpe ratios (higher historical returns compared with their volatility). In other words, when the volatility increases, investors would require proportionally higher returns and will remove investments that have a lower Sharpe ratio from their portfolios. The feedback effect shows that the causality under the "leverage effect" can be reversed.

During the last decade, there were periods when oil markets showed a behavior consistent with the leverage effect. One explanation for this was the increased investor interest in oil-linked products and how commodities have been marketed as a new asset class. Commodity indices, especially those with high weightings of crude oil, became popular and such indices were included in investment portfolios. This resulted in crude oil prices being subjected to the same feedback effect arising from portfolio management techniques.

We now discuss target redemption structures, which, along with extendibles, have been among the most popular exotic structures in the commodities markets.

TARGET REDEMPTION STRUCTURES

The term "target redemption" does not designate a specific hedging structure but rather is a feature that is added to conventional hedging structures such as swaps, collars, three-ways, or any combination of options. This concept has been borrowed from the investment products space and adapted to the corporate hedging world. The target redemption feature consists of capping the aggregate positive payments made to one counterparty at a predetermined cap. Once the accumulated positive payments to the designated counterparty reach the target, the whole transaction is terminated. Sample terms for a target redemption collar are described in Example 6.4.

EXAMPLE 6.4: SAMPLE TERMS FOR A TARGET REDEMPTION COLLAR

Counterparties:	Client & Bank
WTI Price:	NYMEX WTI Crude Oil front-month futures contract (monthly average)
Effective Date:	Start of calendar month after Trade Date
Final Expiry Date:	Effective Date + 2 years
Termination Date:	Final Expiry Date + 2 weeks, subject to Knock-Out
Notional Quantity:	10,000 barrels per month
Calculation Periods:	Monthly calendar periods starting from the Effective Date, to the Final Expiry Date
Payment Dates:	2 weeks after end of each Calculation Period
Put Price:	50 USD/bbl
Call Price:	60 USD/bbl

Settlement Amounts:	Subject to Knock-Out condition, for each Calculation Period, on the respective Payment Date:
	If WTI Price < Put Price, Client pays Bank **Notional Quantity * [Put Price – WTI Price]** If WTI Price > Call Price, Bank pays Client **Notional Quantity * [WTI Price – Call Price]**
Knock-Out:	Knock-Out occurs when the total positive payments to the Client reach the Target Profit (30 USD per barrel)

The target redemption feature is usually added to a transaction consisting of a strip of derivatives. In the example above, the target redemption is added to a strip of monthly collars. The target redemption feature is based on the payouts of the call option and once the accumulated payout from the calls reaches 30$/bbl, the whole structure is early-terminated.

The terms and conditions above are incomplete because they do not provide details about the last payment made when the target redemption knocks out. There are, in fact, two types of target redemptions, based on the method of calculating the last payment.

1. "Full" target redemptions, meaning that if the knock-out occurs, the last payment is paid in full based on the calculated payout of the underlying derivative. In the case of the collar above, the last payment is the payout of the call option.
2. "Exact" target redemptions, where, if the knock-out occurs, the last payment will be adjusted in such a manner that the aggregate of the positive payments is exactly equal to the target, thereby not exceeding it.

Corporate hedgers usually use target redemptions with the objective of entering into zero-cost structures with levels better than the market price for corresponding vanilla structures. This implies that the target cap is usually applied to the hedger. From the bank's perspective, payments under the target redemption transaction are capped but the bank's upside is not. This payout asymmetry translates into optionality and the premium is given to the hedger in the form of enhanced fixed price or strikes.

Such transactions have been portrayed in the news as zero-sum game situations where the bank is supposedly better off when the market goes against the corporate hedger, in which case the payments to be made under the target redemption would be substantial. This type of analysis indicates a flagrant misunderstanding of derivatives trading. On the contrary, exotics trading desks view these transactions as win/win strategies for both parties. Traders typically dynamically hedge these positions and resort to selling put options to immunize their books against changes in implied volatility and forward price changes. On average, a perfectly dynamically hedged target redemption would not generate profit from changes in market prices even if the corporate hedger incurs losses. Bank trading desks are actually under pressure when a customer's MTM is negative, due to the increased credit exposure and related credit hedging and funding costs. Trading desks are more interested in margins made at inception (on trading date) and are actually happy to see target redemption transactions knocking out as this frees up credit lines for new transactions with the client. This situation is very similar to accumulators, which have been very profitable for exotics trading desks as knock-outs imply more margins due to recurring transactions.

That being said, corporate hedgers should be aware of the risks inherent in leveraged transactions such as target redemptions and structures that include knock-out features. As discussed in the case of accumulators and KIKO structures, one issue with the use of this type of structure in the hedging space is that the hedge might knock out and disappear when it is needed the most. The other issue is the leverage inherent in asymmetric payouts.

Target Redemptions and the 2008 Debacle

The bull run in oil prices during the last decade was driven by market sentiment, with leading market voices raving about the "super-cycle" in commodities, thereby attracting investors to tap into the crude oil-linked products market. This led to rising prices, pressuring airlines to enter into hedging transactions to manage their costs. This fear/greed behavior was spurred on by market analysts from some major banks discussing the possibility of prices of 200 $/barrel for WTI in case there was a major supply disruption. As the debate was mainly focused on further rises in the price of oil, many airlines rushed into hedging transactions without seriously considering scenarios of falling prices.

Asymmetric payouts such as target redemptions were excessively used by hedging departments due to the highly attractive terms and the good performance of previous transactions during the trending market of 2007–8. Corporate hedgers did not concern themselves too much about the long-term prospects of target redemption transactions as they expected them to knock out within 1 to 4 months. Some corporate hedgers had a very short-term view about the market and requested target levels small enough that the trade would knock out within 2 to 3 months if oil prices stayed unchanged. When a hedger enters into a target redemption collar that has a call option which is 10 USD/bbl ITM, a target redemption cap set at 30 USD/bbl implies a knock-out within 3 months, if the market price remains unchanged. The trending market made these structures even more attractive as the knock-out was accelerated, adding to hedgers' complacency.

By the second half of 2008, the WTI price started plunging, reaching levels as low as 34 USD/bbl by December 2008. At the beginning of the sell-off, most hedgers expected the market to revert back up, but as the downward trend started taking shape, some airlines who were more familiar with derivatives decided to start restructuring these trades while the MTM sensitivity was still manageable. This proved to be a very wise decision. Other airlines, who decided to wait and watch, were adversely affected by the acceleration in MTM losses, due to the significant gamma of these trades when the spot price falls below the call strike and the knock-out becomes less likely (i.e., the fact that the MTM of target redemptions is highly convex as prices drop).

As daily MTM losses increased, many corporate clients who had a Credit Support Annex (CSA) with their hedging banks had to post significant margins, which impacted their cash management. Hedgers who managed to restructure their target redemption transactions were less affected as they managed to change their risk profile before the gamma effect kicked in. A few hedgers even unwound those trades before incurring big losses.

The situation worsened as the credit crisis deepened with the default of Lehman Brothers, which was a counterparty to fuel hedges including target redemptions. While the crude oil price was plunging, hedgers restructuring their portfolios were in dire need of cooperative and responsive hedging banks. However, clients of the defaulting bank could not easily restructure their hedges and had to deal directly with creditors much later during the liquidation of the banks' trade portfolios.

In the aftermath of the crisis, a number of fuel hedgers who had entered into exotics and target redemption transactions, and incurred losses, resisted payment of dues under these transactions and accused hedge providers of mis-selling these derivatives. The main arguments put forth by these hedgers included characterization of these transactions as speculative, as not being true hedges, and as being beyond the authority or the capacity of those individuals who dealt with the banks on behalf of the hedger. In a number of cases, notably that of Ceylon Petroleum Corporation, these arguments were overturned by the courts.

The 2008 debacle spurred discussions on transaction structuring and pushed banks and corporate hedgers alike to devise new guidelines with regard to the appropriateness of hedging transactions and ways to mitigate legal as well as counterparty risks. One of the recommendations was regarding the use of leverage in hedging transactions.

Defining Leverage

The term "leverage" is heavily used when it comes to discussing risks but when it comes to devising guidelines, compliance departments as well as regulators find it difficult to put together a clear and practical definition. For example, in the case of commodity hedging, many corporate hedgers and banks define leverage based on the volumes of options bought or sold. For example, in the case of a collar, if the notional of the put option is twice that of the call option, the structure is described as twice leveraged. Many hedging guidelines use such definitions to limit the leverage of hedging transactions. Such definitions of leverage can be very misleading, giving a false sense of comfort.

The notional of the underlying options is not an indicator of leverage on its own. For example, in the case of a 1-year × 1-year extendible swap, the notional can be the same on the downside and the upside but the extension is similar in MTM dynamics to selling a put option, as the swap will only get extended if the swap price drops below the swaption strike. When the extendible swap is deep underwater for the client, it behaves almost like a 1-year leveraged swap. Thus, the notional amount, taken on its own, is a flawed way to define leverage; the tenor optionality and asymmetry in payouts should also be considered in determining leverage.

All derivative instruments are leveraged as they offer the potential for outsized gains or losses with limited initial investment. Futures are leveraged instruments to the extent that the margin required to transact in futures is a fraction of the notional amount. Options, by definition, are leveraged instruments as they allow for gains calculated on the scale of a notional quantity that is far higher than the premium invested and are a clear example of payoff asymmetry. In the case of target redemptions, the asymmetry of the payout is very significant. In the example discussed previously, the maximum payout for the client was 30$/bbl, which could be reached within 3 months if the call is over 10$/bbl ITM. However, the client is short a strip of 24 monthly KO puts. For the sake of simplicity, let us consider a trade where the client receives a premium equivalent to monthly notional times $30 per barrel and sells 24 monthly puts. This trade is equivalent to selling the 24 monthly KO puts for $1.25/bbl. From the client's perspective, this trade is superior and more favorable than the target redemption. From this analysis, we conclude that when entering the collar target redemption (TAR), the corporate client is selling, at best, 24 monthly KO puts for $1.25/bbl. His/her best-case scenario makes this a leveraged transaction.

It is true that when the total notional of the put is spread over a longer tenor, monthly losses are better managed from a cash-flow perspective. However, banks have increasingly been insisting on signing CSAs to collateralize derivative transactions. When a CSA is in place, market movements translate into huge MTM swings for leveraged transactions (and short options), which require the posting of significant margins. The longer the tenor of the hedge, the harder it is to cover margin posting out of available cash. In these situations, hedgers would have to borrow money to cover for hedge losses on their long-term operations.

Target Redemption Pricing and Risk Management

Target redemptions are typically priced using Monte Carlo simulations as the target redemption is based on forward-looking accumulation. For each simulated path, the payout of the underlying transaction is calculated until the termination date or the accumulated amount reaches the target redemption cap.

The target redemption (TAR) can be decomposed into a long "TAR knock-out" call spread and a short "TAR knock-out" put. It is important to note here that the knock-out of the put is based on the payout of the call. Target redemption parameters are typically structured in such a way that the KO probability is maximized. The maximization of the KO probability is accompanied by an increase in leverage. Over 2007–8, many TARs were structured in such a way that the model probability of knock-out was between 85% and 90%. To do so, the tenor of the TAR was sometimes extended to 2 or 3 years and the notional on the put side was leveraged up to two times.

To make the TAR zero-cost, the value of the TAR KO call needs to be equal to the KO put. Ignoring the discounting effect, the value of the undiscounted KO call is within the following range:

$$\text{Prob(KO)}^*\text{Target cap} < \text{TAR KO call} < \text{Target cap}$$

For example, if KO probability = 90% and target cap = $30, the value of the undiscounted TAR KO call is within the range [$27, $30] per barrel.

It is more difficult to find a range for the value of the TAR KO put. The most obvious boundary for its value is

$$\text{TAR KO put} < \text{Put}$$

This boundary can be made tighter by adding a barrier on the upside at call strike + target cap. In other words, if the monthly price reaches call strike + target cap, the TAR KO put would also have knocked out:

$$\text{TAR KO put} < \text{KO}_{\text{call strike+cap}} \text{ put}$$

As the price drops, the likelihood of knock-out of the puts decreases, making the TAR gradually resemble a strip of sold puts. This increased survival probability of the put adds to the gamma when the price gets closer to the put strike, making the Greeks of the TAR change in an accelerated fashion. To give an example, let us imagine that when the price drops by 4$/bbl, the survival probability of a put moves from 10% to 20%. The effect is close to that of doubling the notional of a put option. The 4$/bbl drop in price not only gets us closer to the put strike but also has a "leverage" effect.

TAR pricing is very sensitive to the shape of the forward curve. A significantly backwardated forward curve enhances the moneyness of the long-dated puts compared with the spot price, and also gives a higher probability of knocking out early as the spot price is trading high. This makes the TAR terms look very attractive.

The Mean-Reversion Trap

Some say "The trend is your friend." We say, "Friendship is give and take."

In the commodities markets, mean reversion takes care of giving back what was taken. Oil prices have been volatile during the last decade, moving by over 100 $/bbl within months, but participants' behavior remained unchanged. It is important to look back and analyze how the attractiveness of TARs was exaggerated by the trend.

In Chapter 5, we discussed the Samuelson effect and the dynamics of the forward curve. It has been established that mean-reverting markets such as fuel oils have term structures with a fast-moving front end and a more stable back end. This was clearly witnessed during the bull run between 2007 and June 2008. As fuel prices moved higher, the backwardation intensified, boosting the economics of hedging structures when evaluated based on the front-month price. As the front-month price was trending higher, TAR structures kept knocking out and hedgers rushed to renew their TAR structures. They were encouraged by the historical success of the TAR strategy, the bullish views given by most oil price analysts, and the sense of comfort arising from the high probability of TARs knocking out in the near future (Figure 6.32).

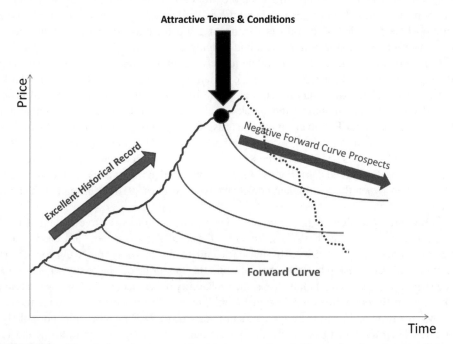

FIGURE 6.32 Historical performance and pricing perspectives influence the attractiveness of hedging instruments

The higher the price got, the steeper was the backwardation and this helped achieve attractive zero-cost TAR structures with strikes much lower than the prevailing spot price. On top of that, the higher front end implied a fast knock-out of the structure if the price trended higher or remained range-bound.

This effect witnessed back in 2008 could be compared with the positive rolling premium inherent in normal backwardation, in which case the lower forward prices are not suggestive of negative prospects but signal significant producer hedging activity, as explained in Chapter 5. However, backwardation does not necessarily mean normal backwardation. It is possible to have a normal contango with a backwardated term structure. The backwardation witnessed in 2008 was actually accompanied by increasing consumer hedging activity, making the normal backwardation hypothesis less likely. In contrast, there was a very strong demand from speculators who usually go long the front end. This suggests that the strong backwardation then was more driven by investor demand than by producer hedging. Thus, the rolling premium was not supported by fundamentals and was not likely to persist and, on the contrary, the prices were set to revert to the mean. The attractive terms and conditions of the TAR hedges were a form of compensation for entering into a trade with negative forward curve prospects. As the trend continued, the backwardation intensified, hedge structures became more attractive, and the resulting spiral exaggerated the impact of mean reversion.

Target Redemption and Trading Risks

From trading desks' perspective, the dynamic hedging of target redemptions poses serious challenges similar to those in barrier options. When a target redemption knocks out, all put options vanish. The discontinuity effect is more pronounced when the accumulated payout is close to the cap and the spot price is around the call strike. In this scenario, the trader is in a situation where the value of the puts is significant and if the knock-out happens, he needs to unwind his short put options (on the dynamic hedging portfolio).

The digital risk in this case is equivalent to the value of the strip of put options. The height of the digital (digital risk) is a function of the remaining tenor of the TAR, implied volatility, and the forward skew (the volatility surface at the time of knock-out). Traders will usually over-hedge this risk by smoothing the knock-out effect, as seen in the case of digital options, or by shifting the target KO level. In other words, the payout of the call option is based on a target cap as specified in the trade terms (30$/bbl) but the KO of the put is based on a lower target (i.e., the KO put is hedged as if the KO happens when the accumulated payout reaches a value lower than the agreed cap). For example, the over-hedge might consist of assuming that the KO happens when the accumulated positive payout reaches 29$/bbl (instead of the agreed 30$/bbl).

During the dynamic hedging of target redemptions, the forward curve dynamics have a huge impact, especially as the KO is driven by the front end of the forward curve and the knock-out digital height is driven by the back end of the forward curve. On top of these challenges, the relationship between the skew and the spot price can be costly when it comes to vega hedging. As the front month drops, the probability of KO decreases, making the trading book longer on the put options and the trader would sell puts to neutralize the incremental vega. But when the front end rises, the book gets short vega as the TAR puts become more likely to knock out. The trader then buys back some of the puts. The trader can opt to hedge the vega by trading ATM options but that exposes him/her to skew risks. He/she can opt to perfectly execute dynamic hedging by trading puts at the same strikes as the puts sold initially. Such a strategy can produce a profit or a loss depending on the correlation between the skew and the spot price, a measure of which is $\frac{\partial \text{Skew}}{\partial \text{Spot}}$. In other words, if the implied volatility of the relevant puts drops when the spot price increases, the dynamic hedging of the vega leads to buying volatility low (when the price rises) and selling it high (when the price drops). If, however, the implied volatility of the relevant puts increases with spot price, the dynamic hedging will be costly and such costs need to be taken into account when pricing TAR transactions.

Another issue when pricing target redemptions is the choice of the volatility model. The path dependency and the sensitivity of the payout to the conditional distribution at the time of knock-out suggests that stochastic volatility models are a good choice. However, because the knock-out might happen at a very early stage in the trade, it is very important to closely fit the volatility surface for very short-term tenors. Stochastic volatility models can give poor fitting of the volatility surface for the short-term smile because the stochastic volatility diffuses and its initial change might not be enough to reflect a steep smile, which would require the use of a very high Vol-of-Vol (volatility-of-volatility) parameter.

STICKY STRIKE AND STICKY DELTA

The relationship between implied volatility and the spot price, as well as the changes in the shape of the volatility surface, were discussed previously with reference to the local volatility and the stochastic volatility surface. This relationship was discussed from a pricing perspective with regard to the forward skew and its impact on the value of extendibles, barrier options, and target redemptions. However, the relationship also impacts the calculation of Greeks, and any discrepancies between the actual mark-to-market change and what can be implied by the Greeks exposes trading books to significant residual risks. Financial markets practitioners mainly use two methods to describe how the volatility surface evolves as the price changes – the sticky strike and the sticky delta approaches.

Sticky Strike Approach

This model is the easier model and involves keeping the implied volatility of an option constant as the price moves. For this reason, the sticky strike model is sometimes referred to as the "lazy trader" model to describe the complacency inherent in this approach. In other words, the sticky strike approach assumes no correlation between an option's implied volatility and the price level. In the case of negative skew, this approach is consistent with the greedy behavior observed in a upwardly trending market, where it is reflected in how ATM put options are sold cheaply without much worry about the market dropping.

The implications of this model are as follows.

- ATM volatility moves in accordance with the skew or smile of the volatility surface.
- As $dV/dS = 0$ (i.e., implied volatility is not sensitive to changes in price), vanilla option deltas will be equal to those derived using the Black–Scholes model:

$$\frac{dV}{dS} = 0 \Rightarrow \Delta_{\text{sticky strike}} = \Delta_{\text{Black–Scholes}}$$

Sticky Delta or Sticky Moneyness

In this approach, traders tend to keep ATM volatilities unchanged as the price moves. In general, assuming that the volatility surface is "sticky delta" means that as the underlying price moves, the value of options with a fixed delta is independent of the price level. In cases of negative skew, this implies a need to raise volatility across all strikes to keep ATM volatilities at the same level. This implies the following.

- The ATM volatility is independent of the price level.
- Fixed-strike volatility movement is the opposite of that implied by the skew/smile. For example, given a negative skew, a particular strike's volatility increases with the price.
- As $dV/dS > 0$ (because of negative skew), vanilla options' delta will be higher than that derived using the Black–Scholes model:

$$\frac{dV}{dS} > 0 \Rightarrow \Delta_{\text{sticky delta}} > \Delta_{\text{Black–Scholes}}$$

The concepts of "sticky strike" and "sticky moneyness" are a good example of how risk management and MTM sensitivities depend on the valuation model adopted. Local volatility models and stochastic volatility models were previously introduced and we noted that the local volatility model assumes that local volatility is a deterministic function of price. This assumed a rigid relationship between volatility and price, which has a significant impact on risk management as the vega, delta, and gamma calculations are inaccurate. For example, when a sensitivity calculation is done with regard to the price (delta), such sensitivity calculation also captures part of the sensitivity to the volatility (vega). This is because the model automatically changes the volatility if there is a change in price. The issue is the same for vega calculations. In contrast, stochastic volatility models allow for a less rigid relationship between volatility and price and can be calibrated to produce realistic Greeks and MTM sensitivities.

Gamma/Theta Ratio

Let us put ourselves in the shoes of an exotic trader who just traded a TAR on a collar with the terms summarized in Example 6.5.

EXAMPLE 6.5: COLLAR TARGET REDEMPTION TERMS

Tenor:	24 months
Call Strike:	58$/bbl
Put Strike:	50$/bbl
Target:	20$/bbl
Monthly Volume:	100,000 bbl/month
Current Spot Price:	72$/bbl

If the price remains higher than 68$/bbl, the trader would pay a total of $2,000,000 within 2 months and the trade terminates. This means that the trader needs to find a way to recover this premium using an appropriate dynamic hedging portfolio. The dynamic hedging portfolio includes short puts with tenors up to 24 months. The notional of each put in the replicating portfolio reflects the probability of knocking out earlier. The zero-cost pricing of the target redemption indicates that the revenue from hedging with the puts is equal to $2,000,000 on average. The issue here is that the trader is short long-tenor puts while the TAR trade might knock out within 2 months and he/she needs to recover the money paid out.

At the inception of the trade, the trader sells enough options to hedge his vega profile. If the price remains the same, the knock-out probability will start increasing with time and the trader will be buying back the puts. By the time the knock-out happens, he would have bought back all the puts that he had sold. According to this strategy, the only way to recover the $2,000,000 paid to the counterparty is from the profit of selling the options at a high price and buying them back later after they have decayed for 2 months. The trader might make some money on the roll of the forward curve if the spot price remains the same after the first month for a backwardated curve (as he/she is long futures to hedge the TAR), but we focus here on the vega and the premiums made from selling and buying optionality.

The difference in tenor between long-tenor puts and the expected knock-out time discussed above leads very often to cases where the vega hedge does not necessarily ensure gamma neutrality. The negative theta of the short options helps recover part of the payment made by the trading desk and any residual positive gamma is also a source of additional revenues through delta rebalancing.

Owning options is accompanied by being positive gamma and negative theta. The theta can be seen as the price of having gamma. Generally, positive gamma positions generate profits through gamma trading (delta rebalancing). If realized volatility is high enough, the profit made from gamma trading can cover or exceed theta (the cost of holding the option). The option seller, in contrast, is positive theta and hopes that the realized volatility is low, so that the cost of his dynamic hedging of the option (gamma trading) does not exceed the premium received.

One question that often arises with regard to owning gamma is about the choice of strike of the option. An option that is OTM will have lower theta and lower gamma than one that is ATM. So, one might opt to own a higher notional of options that are OTM to reach the equivalent amount of gamma that would be achieved with ATM options. The issue to consider here is the cost of this strategy.

Traders typically use the gamma/theta ratio to express the cost of gamma. In other words, how much theta is needed to own a unit of gamma. The theta of an option is a function of the implied volatility and, in cases of steep skew, OTM put options can be very costly compared with ATM options. In the case of structured hedging solutions, traders should keep track of their gamma/theta ratio when they are long gamma to make sure they are not suddenly paying a high price for holding gamma, especially when the shape of the volatility surface changes. To illustrate the importance of this ratio, let us consider the case of a collar in which the trader is long the put and short the call. If the skew is very steep in such a way that the implied volatility of the put is much higher than that of the call, there can be situations (when the price is close to the call strike) in which the trader can find himself negative gamma and negative theta at the same time. In the case of the target redemption, any residual gamma needs to be analyzed in this way to make sure that the gamma from the long put options in the TAR does not get too expensive as the shape of the volatility surface changes.

Another issue with regard to vega-hedging is related to the early-expiring optionality. In the simple case of an early-expiring option, a trader has only one proxy to hedge his vega with, and that is to trade the standard vanilla option. In this case, by holding a long position in the early-expiring option and a short position in the standard vanilla option, the trader can be neutral vega. However, as time passes, the residual gamma starts spiking as the early-expiring option approaches expiry. The increase in gamma from the early-expiring option is not matched by that of the standard option because of the difference in tenors. Any knock-out or exercise frontier that is indexed on a long-dated futures contract will give rise to similar residual gamma that is difficult to neutralize by vega-hedging.

SUMMARY

Exotic transactions require a lot of attention in terms of valuation and risk management. In this chapter, we have covered the most popular exotic hedging structures in the commodities space and set out the intuition behind their structuring, valuation, and risk management. After going through this chapter, readers will be familiar with the challenges posed by these products from a market risk perspective. The breakneck pace of development of these products between 2005 and 2008 was mainly driven by demand, and the ability of front-office traders to respond to such demand, but less attention was paid to middle-office and back-office functions at that time – even as they struggled to accommodate product innovations using outdated capabilities and ad-hoc solutions. For example, most of the focus was on market risks emanating from new products and insufficient resources were dedicated to developing capabilities to efficiently monitor and mitigate credit risks associated with these products. However, after the events of 2008, tremendous efforts have been made to raise the effectiveness of control functions and align front-office staff incentives with overall risks. In the next chapter, we will look at some of the developments in credit exposure measurement, monitoring, and mitigation that have come to the fore in recent years. We will also address collateralization and the cost of credit and funding, which are important inputs in the valuation of commodity derivatives.

CHAPTER 7

Fuel Hedging and Counterparty Risk

"It's impossible that the improbable will never happen."

—Emil J. Gumbel

I n the previous chapters, we have discussed how fuel hedging derivatives are used to mitigate fuel price risks and reduce cash flow volatility for fuel consumers. Hedgers attempt to make certain losses impossible by entering into offsetting positions but there are always residual unwanted risks when an offsetting position is not a perfect hedge, making unwanted outcomes a possibility. Counterparty default risk, residual market risks, liquidity and funding matters are all examples of such unwanted risks. In this chapter, we will introduce some of these risks and discuss them from both the hedger's and the hedge provider's perspective. Counterparty risks will be discussed in greater detail, including credit risk measurement methods as well as the monitoring and management of credit exposures.

THE IMPORTANCE OF VALUATION AND TRANSACTION MONITORING

Fuel hedgers and hedge providers alike need to keep a close eye on their trade portfolio as market conditions change. For example, both hedgers and hedge-provider desks need to ensure proper reporting of trade valuations and mark them to market accurately. Banks typically commit to sending periodic valuations of hedge portfolios to their clients, but this should not lead to complacency on the part of the fuel hedgers by relying solely on these valuation reports. Ideally, hedgers should have their own capabilities to independently value their transaction portfolios. Such valuation tools do not have to be as accurate as those used by traders within banks, but they should be good enough to capture the main drivers of the pricing and detect any significant mispricing. This approach also helps build know-how within the hedging department. The mishaps of late 2008 revealed that many hedgers were completely dependent on their banks for proposing hedging structures, valuations, and even scenario analysis and restructuring solutions. Experience with the behavior of hedgers has shown that most corporate clients typically wait until they are required to make a significant payment or post collateral against a transaction before they start asking questions about the MTM behavior of a trade. For example, in 2008, many corporate clients were surprised by the MTM sensitivity of their trades to a drop in oil price and only started getting concerned about the non-linear price exposure when asked to post large collateral amounts on their collateralized transactions. The best advice for corporate hedgers is: "If you can't price it, don't trade it!"

Corporate clients should not be intimidated by the complexity of derivative transactions and the approach that traders use to value them. The pricing models discussed in this book might use mathematical formulae that are complex, but corporate hedgers do not have to build these models from scratch. There are tools available that provide reasonably accurate pricing for most of the structures currently traded in the market. The officer in charge of hedging only needs to develop a good intuition of how these models work. Unlike in disciplines such as mathematics and physics, there are no absolute truths when it comes to valuing structured derivatives; only relative valuation. This means that in order to value something illiquid, the best way is to use the market price of something liquid that gives the same (or approximately the same) payout.

The same rule applies to hedge providers. Trading desks need to be even more vigilant in monitoring their trade portfolio and ensuring the proper management of market risks, operational risks, liquidity risks, and counterparty risks.

MARKET RISK MANAGEMENT

In the previous chapters, we discussed, in great detail, how market risks are statically or dynamically hedged using replicating portfolios of standard derivatives. We also stressed how the costs and revenues from the hedging of market risk determine the price of the derivative. For trading desks, combinations of vanilla derivatives pose lesser issues than exotic hedging structures. Liquid vanilla derivatives can be hedged at the inception of the trade on a back-to-back basis (executing the same derivative with another market-maker), leaving no market risks on the trading book. In contrast, illiquid hedging structures such as exotics might require frequent rebalancing of the replicating portfolio.

When a fuel hedger manages his price risk by entering into a hedging derivative, the risk is transferred to the hedge provider, who then becomes exposed to market risk. Very often, the fuel hedger requires a tailored hedging solution that cannot be constructed simply by using standard derivatives. Such a transaction creates market risk for the hedge provider that cannot be statically mitigated but requires frequent attention throughout the life of the trade, as illustrated in Figure 7.1.

Unlike FX or equity traders, commodity desks need to have market risk management tools that provide bucketed sensitivities to each futures contract's price and volatility smile. A delta profile will give the sensitivity of the trade portfolio to each futures contract. Similarly, the vega profile gives the sensitivities of the portfolio's MTM to the changes in the volatility of each futures contract. To neutralize the overall vega and delta, traders should ideally keep delta and vega in every bucket close to zero. If they fail to do so, the residual exposure will be similar to that of futures time spreads or options time spreads. Therefore, traders are required to trade standard options and futures very frequently to keep these risk profiles under control. In practice, traders will tolerate some residual time-spread risks, but make sure the aggregate vega and delta are close to zero.

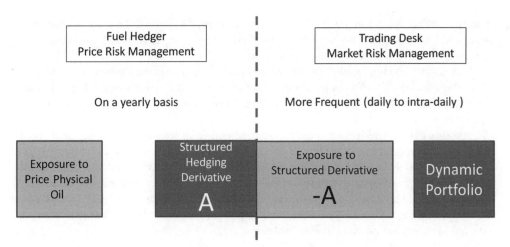

FIGURE 7.1   Portfolio risk management frequency for hedgers and hedge providers

Desks should also keep a close eye on their exposure to the shape of the volatility surface. They need to have a clear map of strikes and barriers and reduce residual option spreads as they hedge their vega to minimize the impact of risk reversals in the hedging book. Additionally, they should recalculate their model parameters and correlations frequently to make sure that the underlying models remain well calibrated.

Corporate hedgers should also keep track of the market risks to a certain extent so that they can have a clear idea about the expected MTM swings as market conditions change. This can help hedgers decide when to restructure or exit existing transactions. A sensitivity or scenario analysis is ideally suited for this purpose.

Fuel Hedgers: Lottery Tickets and Spring Cleaning

Fuel hedgers should not wait for springtime to clean their hedging books but should rather watch for the right market conditions to revisit existing transactions and request hedge providers to restructure existing trades. Complacency with regard to lottery tickets is a common mistake made by fuel hedgers. A lottery ticket refers to a very OTM option. The premiums of such options are very small or close to zero, but holding them can be very profitable in the case of a black swan event. Thus, trading desks are always keen to own such options to take advantage of extreme market events. Being long deep OTM options might appear redundant but, as in the case of engineering, redundancy improves stability and is a source of convexity that improves outcomes. In contrast, when fuel hedgers are short lottery tickets, they get exposed to long-tail events without being appropriately compensated appropriately.

For example, fuel hedgers who entered into hedging derivatives transactions in the last quarter of 2007 managed to lock in great hedging levels for 1 to 2 years. In these hedging structures, they were short put options struck between 60 and 70$/bbl. Subsequently, the oil price rose as high as 140$/bbl over the following 6 months. As the price of oil was rising, the sold put options became very cheap or almost worthless, but many hedgers neglected to remove them or did not think about restructuring them as part of their subsequent transactions. Unfortunately, many of these hedgers were caught by surprise when the oil price dropped sharply in late 2008. Accompanied by the surge in implied volatility, the price decline made these sold lottery tickets very valuable, contributing to the negative MTMs of hedgers and increasing the associated margining requirement.

The same reasoning applies to barrier options. As explained in Chapter 6, as the price drops, the value of a UOC becomes closer to that of the vanilla call. However, it is surprisingly rare that hedgers request a restructuring of KO calls into vanilla calls when the market drops significantly.

Another case where hedgers could have benefited from restructuring at minimal cost is that of the TAR transactions entered into during the latter half of 2008. As the oil price dropped to a level of 40$/bbl, the value of these TARs became very close to that of the short vanilla put. This was a great opportunity for fuel hedgers to request a restructuring of these target redemptions at a very low cost by removing the target cap, or, at the very least, increasing it. By doing so, hedgers would have been well positioned to benefit from a faster recovery of their MTMs as the oil market climbed back up in 2009.

Value at Risk

In addition to the valuation of trades in the hedging portfolio and monitoring its sensitivity to changes in market conditions, it is important to use a standardized framework to quantify the level of risk undertaken by the company. The statistical technique of VaR has traditionally been used by market participants to measure and ensure that market risk exposures are kept within limits to avoid intolerable losses.

VaR is a statistical measure that is expressed using three values: the amount of the potential loss, the probability of incurring this loss, and the time frame. For example, a 5% 1-week VaR of $10 million means that there is a probability of 5% that the firm will lose over $10 million in a 1-week time period. It also means that we can expect, with a confidence level of 95%, that over a 1-week timeframe, the potential loss would not exceed $10 million. Stated differently, keeping a 5% 1-week VaR at $10 million implies that a loss of $10 million should be expected once every 20 weeks.

There are a few methods to calculate the VaR, including the following.

- The historical method, which uses statistical techniques to analyze losses based on past performance.
- The variance method, which uses statistical analysis of returns, assuming that they are normally distributed based on the average return and the standard deviation.
- Monte Carlo simulations.

For simple hedging portfolios of trades with monotonic payouts, the VaR calculation can be as simple as valuing the whole portfolio while assuming a price movement of a certain number (X) of standard deviations (σ), depending on the confidence interval used. However, for more complex portfolios, especially those comprising exotic payouts, Monte Carlo remains the most practical numerical method. It involves simulating a significant number of scenarios and generating a distribution of the MTM for the relevant timeframe, based on a model developed to predict the future evolution of prices.

LIQUIDITY RISK

There are two main types of liquidity risk. Market liquidity risk refers to situations where a market participant is unable to trade a certain asset because of the absence of counterparties willing to assume the other side of the trade. Funding liquidity risk is another form of liquidity risk that is related to the ability to meet liabilities as they fall due. Funding liquidity risk is associated with situations of unexpected cash outflow that can be accompanied by a credit downgrade, constraining the firm's ability to get access to funding. It is important to understand that market and funding liquidity risks are interrelated by the fact that it is difficult to find trading counterparties when market participants face funding problems, as it constrains their ability to invest or hold leveraged positions. This effect is compounded by the fact that the ability to raise funds is also dependent on the quality of the collateral. Lenders will usually apply a haircut and charge higher interest rates for financing assets if the collateral is considered illiquid.

From a market risk perspective, liquidity risk needs to be taken very seriously before entering into hedging transactions. For trading desks, the ability to dynamically replicate the risks of the underlying contract depends on the ability to trade the basic instruments in a timely fashion and at minimal cost. Market liquidity can have a large impact on the ability to manage risks. For this reason, traders resort to smoothing their risk profiles to make sure that risk metrics are capped at a comfortable level based on historical liquidity. This was illustrated previously with the case of digitals or barriers and the use of call spreads to replicate binary payouts.

Furthermore, as market liquidity risk has a compounding effect on market risk, VaR calculations need to take liquidity into account as well. When risk metrics breach certain limits, traders are forced to rebalance their books to get back within approved risk ranges. However, in the case of liquidity shortage, immediately unwinding existing positions becomes more difficult. VaR calculations usually account for this by assuming a longer timeframe, reflecting the risk of having to hold the position while it is being unwound. For example, if a transaction may require between 1 and 4 days to unwind, then the daily VaR could be calculated based on a 3-day VaR, reflecting a cushion over the weighted-average timeframe for liquidation. Lack of liquidity comes with a cost that is reflected in the widening of bid/offer spreads and an increase in funding costs due to cash shortage.

Unlike market risk that can be managed using derivatives and other instruments, liquidity risks are much more difficult to mitigate. There are techniques that might be effective in transferring such risk to counterparties who are more tolerant to a specific liquidity risk. One example is to include an option in the transaction contract that allows the firm to put the whole trade at prevailing MTM. Such a clause allows the firm to dispose of a trade without having to incur unwinding costs. Such trades will be at less favorable levels for a hedger at inception, as the counterparty is assuming the liquidity risk at the time of unwind. Other techniques involve the use of return swaps that aim to replicate the payout of an asset without having to hold it. Nevertheless, these techniques remain limited by the difficulty in effectively documenting such clauses and the need to convince the other counterparty to assume the risk in return for some economic incentive.

COUNTERPARTY RISK

Prior to the 2008 debacle, fuel hedgers and hedge providers paid little attention to counterparty risk and simply monitored counterparty risk exposures without actively managing these risks or stress testing the mitigants that they had in place. The spectacular fall in oil price during the second half of 2008 was a stress test for most hedge providers, who had to hold their breath as their clients in the airline and shipping businesses struggled to keep up with rising liabilities under their fuel hedge contracts. In contrast, the collapse of Lehman Brothers was a wake-up call for hedgers to start paying attention to the credit quality of their hedge providers, their diversification in terms of counterparties, and the treatment of the collateralization of hedging derivatives. To understand the techniques used in monitoring and mitigating counterparty risk, we will first explore the most popular statistical methods used by market participants to measure counterparty risk before looking at credit hedging instruments and counterparty risk mitigation techniques.

Credit Risk and Counterparty Risk

To understand counterparty risk, exposures are typically contrasted with bonds or loans. When an investor invests his/her cash in a bond or loan, his/her credit exposure corresponds to the risk of losing his/her principal. In the case of a derivative, instead of committing a principal amount, the counterparties enter into a bilateral contract that references a specific notional. The notional of the derivative is only used as a reference to determine the cash flows to be exchanged. In contrast to a loan or bond, where the exposure is predetermined, derivatives pose a challenge in terms of determining the credit exposure. When two counterparties enter into a fair derivative transaction, the MTM of the deal is close to zero at inception for both counterparties. Subsequently, as time passes and market conditions change, the value of the transaction becomes positive or negative. The counterparty who makes an MTM gain on the transaction faces counterparty risk as he/she stands to lose his/her MTM gain should the other counterparty default. Unlike a holder's exposure to a bond, which is equal to the principal, the future exposure under a derivative is uncertain and can be positive or negative.

Let us take the example of a 1-year WTI swap with periodic settlements. We can use a Monte Carlo approach to simulate future MTM paths based on modeled risk factors and assumptions. It can be noted from Figure 7.2 that all MTM paths start at zero and end at zero after all scheduled cash exchanges have taken place.

All these paths are impacted by the volatility of the underlying, which can push the MTM away from zero, and the remaining notional, which drops toward zero with periodic settlements as we approach maturity.

When fuel price increases, the hedge provider makes an MTM loss and does not need to be concerned about counterparty risk, but the hedger should be concerned about counterparty risk as he/she stands to lose his/her MTM gain in case of a default of the hedge provider. Similarly, the hedge provider is only concerned about counterparty risk when there is a mark-to-market gain.

Based on these observations, we can use statistical methods to measure the expected and potential credit exposures of a trade at different points in time. To understand the future exposure at different points in time, we take multiple slices of time and look at the statistics of the simulated MTM. For each slice of time T, the MTMs at time T from all the simulated paths are used to construct the distribution of the future MTM at time T, as shown in Figure 7.3.

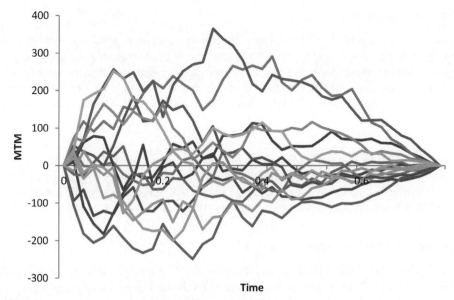

FIGURE 7.2 Monte Carlo simulation of future MTM paths

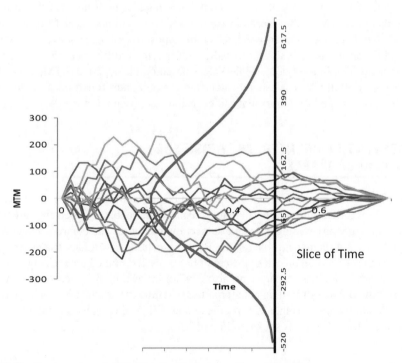

FIGURE 7.3 Construction of the MTM distribution at a slice of time T

Expected Exposure

Counterparty risk can be defined as a form of credit risk with an exposure determined by the MTM gain made on a derivative. In other words, credit exposures are calculated based on the positive MTM of existing transactions. By excluding the negative mark-to-market, we can calculate the expected credit exposure for any target date in the future. We define the expected exposure (EE) as the probability-weighted average of the positive MTM on a future target date:

$$EE(t) = E[\max(0, MTM(t))]$$

where $MTM(t)$ is the mark-to-market on the future date t based on simulated paths.

This is also equivalent to the undiscounted value of a call option on the MTM, struck at zero, indicating that only gains expose a party to credit risk. It is also equivalent to a put option on the MTM from the other counterparty's perspective.

Potential Future Exposure

The EE gives a good idea about the credit exposure on an average basis but there is a risk that the exposure will diverge from this average to levels that can be significantly higher. The extent of this gap is driven by the variability of the MTM. To account for this, potential future exposure (PFE) is used as an additional credit exposure measure and is equal to the credit exposure on a specific future date, based on a specified confidence interval. For instance, a 2-year PFE of $10 million with a 95% confidence interval indicates that the firm is 95% confident that the MTM of the transaction in 2 years' time will not exceed $10 million. This also means that there is a 5% chance that the credit exposure will reach or exceed $10 million.

The PFE concept is very similar to VaR, with two main differences. Firstly, the PFE is based on the positive MTM (gain), while VaR is based on the negative MTM, as can be seen in Figure 7.4. Secondly, VaR is usually calculated for very short timeframes (up to 10 days), but the PFE is calculated for tenors that can be as long as 5 years or more.

MEASUREMENT OF COUNTERPARTY RISK FOR A PORTFOLIO OF TRADES

OTC transactions are increasingly cleared through central counterparties (CCPs), but a large proportion of OTC transactions are still managed on a bilateral basis. When entering into OTC transactions, commodity trading desks are subject to procedures and controls that aim to keep counterparty risk within manageable ranges. Before executing new trades, traders are required to check that they are not in breach of the credit limits, as determined for each counterparty by the credit department. Credit departments also monitor the evolution of credit exposure metrics and the creditworthiness of trading counterparties. Credit exposure metrics for a counterparty are typically summarized using a PFE profile and an EE profile, which give the PFE and the EE at various slices of time, as shown in Figure 7.5.

Peak PFE

Traders and credit risk managers use PFE profiles to monitor exposures and make decisions with regard to new trades and restructuring transactions. Credit lines are typically linked to

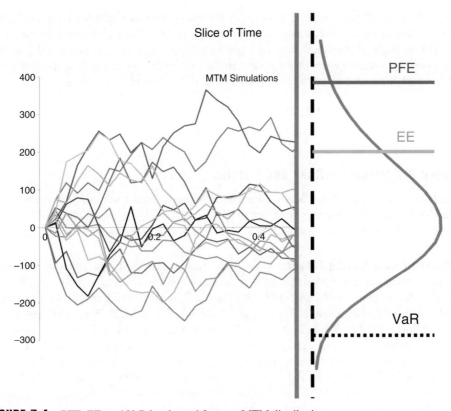

FIGURE 7.4   PFE, EE, and VaR levels read from an MTM distribution

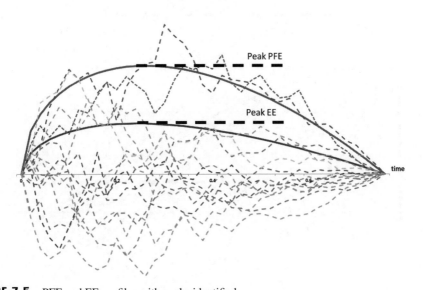

FIGURE 7.5   PFE and EE profiles with peaks identified

the peak PFE, which is the highest PFE across the remaining tenor. In other words, the peak PFE of a portfolio of trades with a particular counterparty should be maintained below a credit limit. For example, if the credit limit of a particular counterparty is set at $50 million, the trader is only allowed to enter into a trade with this particular counterparty if the new trade does not push the peak PFE of the total portfolio of trades beyond $50 million:

$$\text{Peak PFE} = \max[\text{PFE}(t)]_{0<t<\text{maturity}}$$
$$\text{Peak EE} = \max[\text{EE}(t)]_{0<t<\text{maturity}}$$

Common PFE Misconceptions and Pitfalls

Though the concept of PFE has been in use for many years, credit risk managers and hedging professionals can still encounter issues when they fail to anticipate the evolution of PFE and peak PFE over time. We discuss some of the common errors in the usage of PFE statistics here.

Credit Limit as a Moving Target   Very often, traders and credit risk managers make the mistake of considering the peak PFE as a static maximum for the PFE of the trade portfolio during the life of these trades and fail to think about it as an evolving maximum that varies as volatilities and prices change. For example, ensuring that the peak PFE at inception of a trade is below a limit of $50 million is not a guarantee that the PFE will never move above the limit. The peak PFE is only valid at the time of its calculation and once market conditions change, this peak keeps changing. Before entering into new trades, desks generally calculate PFE profiles for the new trades and aggregate them with the existing trade portfolio's PFE to verify that the resulting peak PFE is within the credit limits set for that particular counterparty. But on the very next morning, if prices move downwards (for a consumer's hedge portfolio), the PFE and EE profiles shift in a way that can breach the credit limits almost immediately after the trade is executed, as illustrated in Figure 7.6.

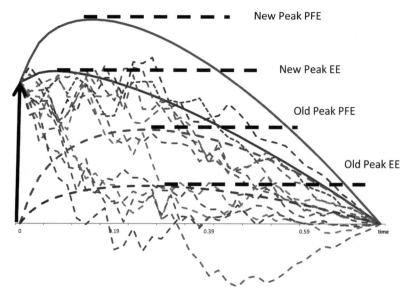

FIGURE 7.6   Change in peak PFE and EE profiles with a change in MTM

The peak PFE is an important credit exposure risk measure, which is not static, unless proper PFE-capping derivatives techniques are used. The issue with most credit risk management departments is that they place limits on the peak PFE calculated when the new trade is executed but completely lose control of the exposure after execution, unless proper credit hedging is in place. Later on, when the peak PFE of the trade portfolio increases, credit limits for the counterparty are adjusted to allow for more business. There have been situations where the peak PFE of a portfolio of trades exceeded the market capitalization of the counterparty, which signals poor management of credit exposures.

Addition of Peak PFEs and Incremental PFE   PFE profiles are usually calculated before approving the execution of a new trade with any counterparty. Very often, commodity trading desks and credit teams run Monte Carlo simulations to calculate the PFE of the new trade and refer to internal systems to get the current peak PFE of the existing portfolio. One common mistake is to assume that the peak PFE of the new portfolio, including the new trade, is the sum of the portfolio's peak PFE and the peak PFE of the new trade. The peak PFEs should not add up in this way unless the PFE profiles peak at exactly the same time. In general, the peak PFE of the portfolio of trades is lower than the sum of the peak PFEs of individual trades:

$$\text{Peak PFE (trade A + trade B)} \leq \text{Peak PFE (trade A)} + \text{Peak PFE (trade B)}$$

Figure 7.7 illustrates how the timing of the peak of each trade is important. Failing to account for the impact of the timing of the peak does not allow a risk manager to penalize deals that lead to concentrated exposure at a certain point of time and does not differentiate between deals that diversify the exposure in terms of timing and those that exaggerate it.

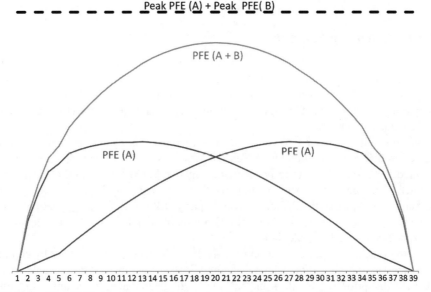

FIGURE 7.7   Peak PFE of a new portfolio vs. sum of peak PFEs of portfolio constituents

Furthermore, the example above assumes perfect correlation between the MTMs of trade A and trade B. In general, trade MTMs can be uncorrelated because of the underlying or the trade payouts. For example, the MTMs of trades referencing different commodities are not perfectly correlated. The same is true of trades that reference different futures contracts. The PFE profile of a portfolio of a trade referencing a short-dated futures contract and another trade referencing a long-dated futures contract will be slightly lower than the sum of the PFE profiles. Even when the trades reference the same underlying, there can be a diversification in terms of payouts that can cancel each other. It is a mistake to ignore the netting effect (when it is applicable under ISDA) and calculate the PFE of new trades independently:

$$\text{PFE (trade A + trade B)} \leq \text{PFE (trade A)} + \text{PFE (trade B)}$$

A trade should not be considered based on its standalone PFE, but risk managers should have the necessary tools to generate an incremental PFE profile that corresponds to the difference in PFE between the initial portfolio and the portfolio after executing the new trade.

CREDIT EXPOSURE OPTIMIZATION TECHNIQUES

Counterparty risks can be mitigated fully or partially by limiting the credit exposures in a static manner. Techniques to manage exposures vary in effectiveness, sophistication, and cost. For this reason, it is important to begin with the cheaper and speedier actions that are practical and then work on optimizing them by adding more sophisticated techniques. For example, legal documentation loopholes can be easier to fix, especially those linked to bilateral netting and credit support annexes.

Bilateral Netting Agreements

The netting of payments or liabilities is a very common mechanism used to help reduce settlement and credit exposures in the OTC derivatives market. There are two main types of netting agreements: the payments netting agreement and the close-out netting agreement. Two counterparties can agree to net by signing a master agreement that specifies the type of netting and the contracts to include.

Payments netting agreements help reduce settlement risk by netting cash flows to be exchanged in the same currency on a given day, whereas close-out netting agreements help reduce credit exposures by netting positive and negative MTMs in the case of a termination event, such as the default of one counterparty. In the absence of close-out netting, there is a risk that the creditors of the defaulting counterparty will resort to cherry-picking and only ask to be paid on the amounts owed to them. Close-out netting has tremendous impact on the credit exposure and EE/PFE calculations.

Nevertheless, netting agreements carry legal risks that need to be handled by competent financial markets lawyers. For example, netting agreements are not enforceable in many jurisdictions that prioritize creditors and consider netting agreements to be unfair to them.

Credit Support Annexes

To standardize the legal documentation of OTC hedging derivatives, market participants wishing to enter into bilateral trades typically sign an ISDA (International Swaps and Derivatives Association) Master Agreement that becomes part of any derivative executed by the two parties and provides clarity with regard to terminology, settlements, and the treatment of collateral. The Credit Support Annex (CSA) is a legal document, which is typically executed together with the ISDA Master Agreement. It helps define the rules under which collateral for OTC derivatives is transferred between counterparties to mitigate credit exposures due to positive MTM.

The most important terms and conditions pertaining to the CSA are the following.

- The threshold amount, which is the value of MTM beyond which collateral must be posted. When the MTM exceeds the threshold amount, the counterparty with negative MTM has to post collateral with value equivalent to the difference between the MTM and the threshold. For example, if the threshold amount is $10 million and the MTM reaches $11 million, $1 million worth of collateral needs to be posted.
- Eligible collateral. Counterparties typically negotiate the type of assets that are acceptable as collateral. In general, cash and government bonds are used but parties can opt to include other securities and agree upon haircuts to be applied in order to account for the liquidity and the volatility of the collateral.
- Frequency. Collateral posting can be required on a daily or weekly basis or as negotiated between the two parties. A lower collateral posting frequency increases operational efficiency but reduces the effectiveness of the credit support as counterparties are exposed to the gap risk associated with a jump in MTM and a default of the OTM counterparty between collateral posting dates. This gap risk is higher when collateral is posted less frequently.

The CSA helps cap the credit exposure and is considered a good way to manage credit risks. However, this credit risk mitigation method raises other issues with regard to liquidity squeezes and the funding of collateralization.

CSA Negotiations – Key Considerations

Like any negotiation, executing a CSA with a financial counterparty like a bank is never an easy exercise. The challenge has less to do with negotiating power and is mainly due to a gap in legal and financial sophistication. Corporate clients seldom use an external counsel to help them negotiate agreements with banks and even when this is the case, clients need to understand the impact of the CSA on their business in order to inform external counsel of their requirements.

Before executing a CSA, fuel hedgers should take the time to analyze its pros and cons and negotiate the CSA terms in line with their objectives and constraints. The following are some issues that need to be carefully considered.

Hedging Cost Saving   Banks typically charge for expected credit exposures depending on the creditworthiness of the counterparty. When a CSA is in place, the EE is reduced and this translates into cheaper hedging costs for the fuel hedger. However, this saving needs to be evaluated against other factors inherent in the CSAs.

Funding Liquidity Issues   Airlines and shipping companies should keep in mind that CSAs increase their funding needs when the MTM of their hedges becomes negative. The magnitude of the potential funding needs is driven by the tenor of the hedge, the leverage, the notional, and the volatility of the underlying. For example, airlines typically hedge their fuel costs for up to 2 years, which implies that the MTM of the hedge moves with a sensitivity based on the total volume for 24 months. When a CSA is in place, the fuel hedger is required to post margins equivalent to MTM losses for a hedge that corresponds to 24 months of business. This creates a cash management issue as the revenues that match the savings on fuel cost are not available immediately. The threshold and frequency of the CSA should be well negotiated as per the firm's ability to raise funds.

Moreover, airlines or shipping companies often conduct scenario analysis of their hedging derivatives and these are usually provided by the hedge providers/banks with the term sheets of transactions. Such scenario analysis typically shows the monthly payments to be made by each party under the derivative based on hypothetical scenarios which can be misleading as it gives the fuel hedger a false sense of comfort with regard to the amount of cash needed to meet the monthly payments under adverse scenarios. In fact, when a CSA is in place, the fuel hedger is required to post collateral that will be the aggregate of the PV of all expected monthly losses. In 2008, many airlines had to post significant amounts of collateral, which put a lot of pressure on their cash management functions, especially as funding became scarce. This issue was intensified by the correlation between the liquidity crunch and asset depreciation. The treasury department of these airlines should have conducted scenario analysis of the funding needs under the CSAs.

Gap Risks and Derivatives Greeks   CSA frequency is used to limit the gap risk, which reflects the potential increase of the MTM between two scheduled collateral posting dates. However, the frequency alone is not enough to control the gap risk. The potential MTM move is also driven by the sensitivity of the MTM to market changes. Therefore, it is important to manage the gap risk by also taking into account the Greeks of the trade portfolio. The gap risk should reflect the potential MTM move during the period between collateral calls in addition to the time required to put the counterparty in default, liquidate the existing collateral, and close the trades.

Collateral Re-hypothecation Risks   Financial institutions generally use collateral re-hypothecation to minimize their funding costs. For example, collateral can be used in a repo to get access to cheap funding. The reuse of collateral in such a way seems optimal for the financial system, as it enhances liquidity and reduces transaction costs while the collateral pledger maintains the economic ownership of the collateral. However, re-hypothecation of collateral makes collateral ownership less transparent and, in the case of a default, establishing ownership becomes much more complicated.

For instance, on Monday, September 15, 2008, the CEO of an Asian airline called in panic, seeking advice and requesting to meet urgently as the airline had tens of millions of dollars pledged with Lehman Brothers under a CSA. The airline tried contacting Lehman Brothers but no one was answering the phone, as many of the bank's employees might have had other pressing concerns at the time. During the month preceding Lehman's filing for bankruptcy, oil prices experienced a significant drop that led to huge negative MTMs on the airline's fuel hedges. Many airlines had to post collateral as required by the CSAs in place. The issue in such a situation was that the secured party (Lehman Brothers in this case) might have reused or pledged the collateral before going bankrupt. If the market went back up, the value of the pledged collateral might exceed the MTM liability. In that case, the airline might become an unsecured creditor for the excess.

The lesson to be learnt from this is to make sure that CSAs are well drafted, taking into account such extreme scenarios. For example, the re-hypothecation risk could have been mitigated by barring collateral re-hypothecation or by adding a credit rating trigger allowing re-hypothecation only if the rating of the secured counterparty is higher than a minimum level, below which the latter would have to reacquire the collateral and keep it in its custodian's possession. Moreover, when trading with a bank, it is preferable for the fuel hedger to be facing an entity in a jurisdiction that has better customer protection.

Unilateral vs. Bilateral CSA Many airlines and shipping companies have unilateral collateralization agreements with banks under which only the fuel hedger is required to post collateral. But CSAs can be bilateral, requiring both parties to post collateral. Bilateral CSAs can be symmetric, with the same threshold level, or asymmetric, with different thresholds. The terms and conditions of the CSA will depend to a great extent on the negotiating power of both parties. But from market experience, it has usually been the case that banks manage to have the upper hand in securing favorable terms in these agreements. The lack of sophistication on the corporate side leads to situations in which banks not only impose unilateral CSAs favorable to them but also ignore these asymmetries when it comes to pricing derivative transactions.

From a bank's perspective, trading desks usually hedge commodity derivatives on a back-to-back (BTB) basis or by entering into a replicating portfolio of trades with other banks. The transactions between banks are usually fully collateralized. Hence, when the MTM of a fuel hedger becomes negative, the bank is required to post collateral to its BTB counterparty. When a unilateral CSA between the bank and the fuel hedger is in place, the bank receives collateral from its client that helps compensate for the collateral posted to the BTB counterparty. However, when the client's MTM is positive, the bank receives collateral from the BTB counterparty but does not post it to the fuel hedger under the unilateral CSA. In other words, these unilateral CSAs are a source of cheap funding for the banks (Figure 7.8).

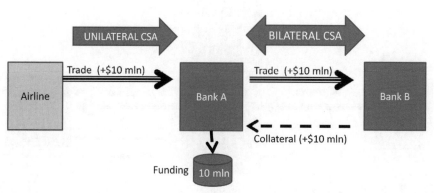

FIGURE 7.8 Asymmetric CSAs as a source of funding

FUNDING VALUATION ADJUSTMENT

Let us now consider the situation where there is no CSA in place between the bank and the corporate client. Depending on the MTM of the transactions, the bank will either receive funding, when the client has a positive MTM, or post funding to BTB counterparties when the client's MTM is negative. In the past, most derivatives were discounted at LIBOR, reflecting the fact that banks funded each other at LIBOR. This has changed since the credit crunch of 2008, as the funding costs of many banks have risen above LIBOR to reflect their creditworthiness. When the MTM of the client is negative, the bank might have to fund itself at a rate that is much higher than the interest earned on the collateral. The possible mismatch between derivative-related funding costs and benefits forced many banks to look for ways to adjust derivatives pricing accordingly.

Earlier, the interest on collateral (CSA rate) was close to LIBOR, which was the funding rate for most banks. However, as funding rates started reflecting the creditworthiness of each bank more accurately, many trading desks began feeling the pain when the funding rate required by the bank's internal treasury started getting wider than LIBOR. The prevailing risk aversion and liquidity crunch within the banking sector saw the average interbank borrowing rate decouple from the CSA rate.

To give a good intuition about the funding valuation adjustment (FVA), let's consider a simple example of an uncollateralized derivative in which the client pays a cash flow CF in a year. The trading desk needs to post collateral equivalent to the PV of the cash flow CF. At the end of 1 year, the client pays the cash flow CF to the trading desk. This is equivalent to giving a loan to the client, as seen in Figure 7.9. This loan is funded by the bank's treasury department. If the trading desk was only trading on a collateralized basis, such a situation would not arise as liquidity is just passed from one counterparty to the other under the CSAs. To price the uncollateralized derivative, the trading desk adjusts the price of the collateralized derivative by adding the costs of such loan. The cost of the loan is driven by two components – the cost of funding from the treasury department and the credit risk of the client.

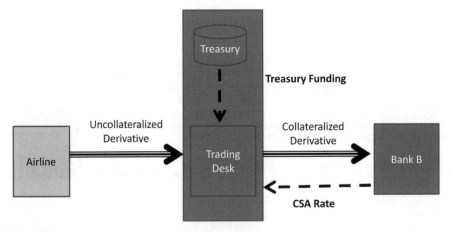

FIGURE 7.9   Funding costs when no CSA is present

The FVA accounts for the impact of the funding component to make sure that the trading desks compensate for the mismatch between the funding rate and the CSA rate. This impact can be positive or negative, and both cases need to be taken into account. This can be simplified as follows:

$$FVA = FVA_{cost} - FVA_{benefit}$$

where FVA_{cost} is calculated based on the expected positive exposure (EPE, the same as the EE) and $FVA_{benefit}$ is calculated based on the expected negative exposure (ENE).

Fuel Hedgers and FVA

FVA is not a big concern for fuel hedgers entering into zero-cost structures as the difference between the funding cost and the funding benefit tends to be small, as long as the EPE and the ENE have similar profiles. FVA becomes significant in three cases.

1. *Mismatch in expected cash flows*

We explained that for most structures with similar EPE and ENE profiles, the FVA is not significant but when a structure contains a cash-flow time spread, it is equivalent to lending, and this gives rise to FVA. For example, an airline sells 12-month put options to finance the purchase of 6-month call options. The strikes and notional are optimized to make the structure zero cost at inception.

The hedging counterparty is advancing a cash flow in 6 months equivalent to the payout of the call options to receive a cash flow in 12 months equivalent to the payout of the put options, as shown in Figure 7.10. At inception, the trading desk of the hedging counterparty expects to advance in 6 months an expected amount equal to the undiscounted price of the call options and receive in 12 months an expected amount equal to the undiscounted price of the put options. Traders would find it fair to charge for the expected funding cost associated with this situation.

In contrast, if the airline opts to finance the purchase of 12-month call options by selling 6-month put options, the situation is reversed and the trading desk of the hedging bank will enjoy a funding benefit that is seldom passed back to the fuel hedger.

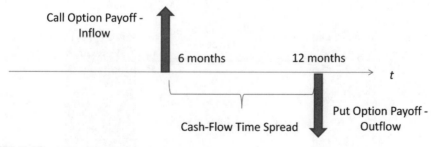

FIGURE 7.10 FVA caused by cash-flow time spreads

2. *Restructuring and extension of tenor*

Very often, hedgers try to restructure their OTM transactions to postpone their payments and wait for better market conditions. In 2009, many airlines managed to restructure transactions originally executed in 2008, by extending the tenor to 2010 or even further. This was done either by spreading the notional of the transaction over a longer tenor or by postponing the contingent cash flows. The restructuring of these transactions helped some of these airlines wait until the oil market recovered, albeit at some cost due to the prevailing market conditions. Firstly, the pricing of the new structures was impacted by the steep contango at that time (which reflected the lack of liquidity and the challenge faced by arbitrageurs to access funds required for cash-and-carry trades). Secondly, the tenor extension was very costly as banks charged heavily for the funding costs.

3. *Off-market trades*

Off-market transactions arise for different reasons. Some fuel hedgers combine hedging and financing using the same derivative instrument in what are called "prepaid structures." In a prepaid structure, the fuel hedger and the bank enter into a hedging structure that is OTM with a negative MTM for the hedger. This negative MTM for the hedger is compensated by an upfront payment made by the bank, as in Figure 7.11.

These structures are equivalent to a loan plus a zero-cost hedging structure and have the advantage of netting the credit exposure of the loan against gains on the hedge. However, these structures should not be executed in a manner that undermines transparency with regard to the liability of the company or with the objective of circumventing the covenants imposed by existing creditors.

Off-market trades can also arise from the novation or restructuring of trades done by the fuel hedger with other hedge providers. In such cases, the trades might be OTM for the fuel hedger and the new hedging counterparty needs to account for the funding cost. The old hedging counterparty benefits from getting rid of such exposure, which is costly to fund and the price of which may not have been accounted for at the inception of the trade as a zero-cost structure.

In a fair world, if the fuel hedger were to be charged the FVA by the new hedging counterparty, he/she should also be paid by the old hedging counterparty for the FVA benefit after the exposure is removed. It is important to bear in mind that the two FVAs are likely to be different, as both banks would not have the same funding costs. Moving from a bank with low liquidity to a more liquid bank should lead to an FVA benefit.

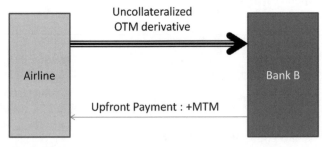

FIGURE 7.11   Off-market transactions or prepaid structures

The FVA Debate

There has been a huge debate within the financial markets community with regard to FVA, as it is considered equivalent to discounting derivatives at rates different from the risk-free rate to account for the bank's funding costs. Many experts consider FVA to be irrational and against the fundamentals of financial markets theory. This stems from the fact that investment decisions should be judged based on the risks and merits of the investment opportunity and not on the financial strategy/gearing of the investor. In the example discussed earlier, an airline might find it counterintuitive that it deserves a funding benefit for moving from a liquidity-constrained counterparty to one with better liquidity.

FVA can be considered as a fix for an organizational mistake in cost allocation on the banks' side, as they set up a treasury department that manages funding decisions on an aggregate basis. In other words, treasury departments offer one funding rate for all trading desks without taking into account the riskiness of transactions entered into by the desk. This means that the funding rate offered by the treasury department reflects the average risk taken by the bank. For example, if the funding rate given by the treasury department is LIBOR + 100 bps and a trader comes across an opportunity that is almost risk-free, yielding LIBOR + 30 bps, the trader would not be able to take advantage of this risk-free opportunity that is yielding higher than the risk-free rate. On the contrary, the trader is incentivized to enter into riskier transactions.

Imposing a funding spread throughout the whole bank is a backward-looking strategy that is antithetical to the fundamentals of efficient markets as funding rates become dependent on past decisions and transactions on the bank's books at the time. In other words, charging the FVA means that new transactions are priced based on old transactions and that new transactions are likely to be riskier. If all new transactions must have returns higher than the funding rate, then the bank would be avoiding safe trades and moving toward riskier ones, and the funding rates should increase further. This can lead to a vicious cycle of increasing risk and funding costs. A forward-looking strategy would be one where, if the bank enters into less risky transactions, its funding spread would be likely to tighten.

THE PRICE OF COUNTERPARTY CREDIT RISK

Counterparty risk has previously been discussed by contrasting the exposures under a derivative transaction with the exposure assumed by a bond investor. We noted that the exposure under the bond is predetermined, while that under a derivative is subject to market price fluctuations and the measurement of such exposure uses statistical methods (EE and PFE). That said, rational market participants require a return for assumed risks.

In the case of bonds or loans, the price of credit risk is generally given by the spread between the bond yield and the risk-free rate. In other words, if a bond is liquid enough, the bond yield gives an idea of the premium required by investors to compensate for the credit risk that they assume. Increasing interest in fixed-income investments and the need for more tailored credit investment vehicles contributed to the phenomenal development of OTC credit derivatives, which helped bring together yield seekers and credit protection buyers. If credit derivatives can be used to hedge the credit risk associated with bonds and loans, then these instruments can also be helpful in mitigating counterparty credit risks that are faced by hedgers and hedge providers.

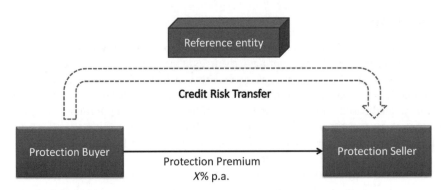

FIGURE 7.12 CDS payments when no credit event has occurred

Credit Derivatives and Credit Default Swaps

Credit derivatives are instruments that allow investors to express views on credit, in either direction, without being constrained by the ownership of the underlying bond or loan. These contracts have the ability to achieve a "pure" credit risk transfer, isolating credit risk from other risks such as interest rate risk and foreign exchange risk. The basic, most popular, form of credit derivatives are called credit default swaps (CDSs).

A CDS is a bilateral OTC derivative contract that transfers the risk of the loss of the face value of a reference debt over a specified period of time. The two parties involved in a CDS are

- the protection buyer (seller of credit risk)
- the protection seller (buyer of credit risk).

Once the CDS contract is executed, the protection buyer becomes short credit and the protection seller becomes long credit. The CDS contract defines the relevant credit by clearly stating a reference entity. As long as there is no credit event, the protection buyer typically pays a protection premium on a quarterly basis to the protection seller, who agrees to assume the credit risk associated with a reference entity (Figure 7.12).

The most important terms and conditions of a CDS contract are shown in Table 7.1.

TABLE 7.1 Important terms and conditions of a CDS contract

Term	Definition
Reference Entity:	The entity whose credit risk is transferred
Notional Amount:	Dollar amount of credit protection traded, e.g., $10 mm
Term:	Maturity of the credit protection. Standard contracts mature on IMM dates: March 20, June 20, September 20, and December 20
Premium (spread):	Compensation paid by the protection buyer to the protection seller. Paid quarterly, but expressed as an annualized percentage of the notional
Credit Events:	Predetermined events that, when suffered by the reference entity, "trigger" the contract. Common credit event definitions include bankruptcy, failure to pay, obligation default or acceleration, repudiation/moratorium, or restructuring
Settlement:	Once the contract is triggered, the process by which the protection seller compensates the protection buyer for the loss caused by a credit event

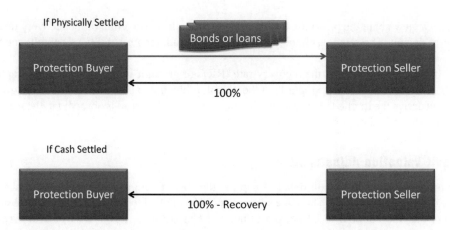

FIGURE 7.13 Settlements under a CDS contract in the case of a credit event occurring

If a credit event occurs, the protection buyer ceases to pay the protection premium and demands compensation. The compensation can be cash-settled or physically settled, as agreed in the CDS contract, with settlements as shown in Figure 7.13.

If the CDS is physically settled, the protection buyer will have to deliver a basket of deliverable obligations with an aggregate face value equal to the notional in exchange for the notional amount. Most CDS contracts were initially documented in a physically settled manner but as the volume of OTC CDS contracts around the world surged, the aggregate notional of certain CDS contracts far exceeded the notional of the issued bonds. This implied that if a default event were to occur, a protection buyer would have to rush to buy the defaulting bonds. It was then possible to see the value of a bond increasing after a default event occurred because of the way that CDS contracts were settled. To address this issue, cash settlements were introduced, allowing the settlement of CDS contracts by paying the difference between par and the recovery rate, which is typically based on the price assigned to the reference obligation (generally via an auction).

The most important aspect to note in a credit derivative is the definition of the credit event. The recent crisis in Greece has shown how the definition of credit events can be a central point of debate as distressed parties struggle to circumvent them. The most common definitions of credit events include bankruptcy, failure to pay, restructuring, obligation default, obligation acceleration, and repudiation/moratorium. These are legal terms that need to be checked before purchasing protection. For example, does "bankruptcy" apply in the case of a government as the reference entity? Similarly, how can "failure to pay" be determined?

There have been cases of traders who managed to "hedge" their counterparty risk on commodity derivatives by buying CDS protection with a notional corresponding to their expected exposure, only to realize later on that the CDS protection they bought would be useless in the case of the counterparty's default on the derivatives transaction. This is mainly due to the fact that most CDS contracts define "failure to pay" based on borrowed money, bonds, or loans but do not include derivative claims. In other words, if the counterparty keeps honoring his/her obligations under issued bonds and loans, the credit event under these CDS contracts is not triggered even if he/she defaults on the derivatives contract.

The CDS market for certain names is quite liquid and provides valuable information about the market's perception of the creditworthiness of these entities. The CDS spread reflects the market's view about the probability of default (PD) and the expectation of the recovery rate in case of default. The relationship between the CDS spread, the probability of default, and the recovery rate is very rigid.

If the CDS spread and the recovery rate (RR) are given, it is easy to derive the implied probability of default (PD). Similarly, if the default probability and the CDS spread are given, one can derive the implied recovery rate. In practice, the CDS spread is observed in the market, which helps calculate corresponding combinations of RR and PD.

Credit Valuation Adjustment

Premiums paid under a credit default swap are the cost of hedging the credit risk related to the exposure under a bond. The same concept could be applied to hedge derivatives exposures except that the notional to be hedged is not fixed in advance. In the case of a derivative, the exposure can only be hedged in a dynamic way. However, the cost of hedging the credit exposure must be accounted for on the pricing date (at the inception of the trade). Nowadays, most banks charge their corporate clients a CVA to account for the cost of hedging the counterparty credit risk.

CVA is the market price of counterparty credit risk, which can be estimated using Monte Carlo simulations of the MTM and the hazard rate (default intensity) implied from market CDS. The CVA calculated can be simplified by assuming no correlation between interest rates and the MTM of the portfolio. In such a case, we can write

$$ \text{CVA} = (1 - R) \int_{t=0}^{\infty} D(t).EE(t).P(t)_{\text{cpty}} dt $$

where R: recovery rate
       $D(t)$:   discount factor from 0 to t
       $EE(t)$:   expected (positive) exposure conditional on counterparty default
       $P(t)_{\text{cpty}}$: counterparty's default probability density function, which is derived from
                   the survival probability that is usually boot-strapped (derived) from CDS
                   spreads for different tenors (CDS term structure)

Probabilities of default can be derived from the following.

1. CDS spreads. This remains the best approach when the CDS on the counterparty's name is traded in the market. In practice, most fuel hedgers don't have an actively traded CDS.
2. Bond spread. This alternative is the second-best approach when the counterparty has an issued bond that is actively traded. The bond spread can be approximated by the difference between the bond yield and the risk-free rate. If there is a concern about the liquidity of the bond, it is advisable to take into account the repo rate of the bond, as it includes some of the liquidity cost. This helps isolate the credit spread from the risk-free rate and the liquidity premiums.

   The bond spread is a good approximation of the CDS spread, as both correspond (theoretically) to the price of the credit risk. The convergence between the two spreads is assured by two arbitrage strategies.
   - Long bond + buy CDS protection, when the bond spread is wider than the CDS spread.
   - Short bond + sell CDS protection, when the CDS spread is wider than the bond spread.

The second arbitrage strategy requires selling short the bond, which is not always easy and would depend on the repo rate, which reflects the liquidity of the bond. For this reason, the basis between the CDS spread and the bond spread is generally positive. This should be taken into account when deriving the probabilities of default.

3. Rating transition matrices can be used to calculate default probabilities as defined by rating agencies.
4. CDSs of comparable companies can also be used to arrive at default probabilities.

Calculating the EE conditional on default requires good knowledge of the correlation between default events and the underlying of the derivatives, and is a challenging task. If the underlying of the derivatives is uncorrelated with the market CDS, one can assume that the EE conditional on default is equal to the EE as discussed earlier in this chapter.

Common CVA Mis-steps

The introduction of CVA changes the way derivative transactions should be conducted, but many market participants have not managed to adapt to the new reality, either due to the lack of proper awareness and training on CVA for employees, resistance to change, or a reluctance to invest in new infrastructure and processes. The following are a few of the major facets of CVA calculation that are still not well appreciated, giving rise to arbitrage opportunities and sub-optimal structured transactions.

- CVA should not be calculated on a deal-by-deal basis. Charging for CVA of a deal on a standalone basis overestimates the credit charges. CVA should be calculated on a portfolio basis and only incremental CVA should be charged.
- CVA calculation should take into account existing CSAs and the nature of the collateral.
- The value of a trade is no longer a function of the market conditions alone. The value of a trade will depend on the counterparty and the existing trade portfolio.
- The portfolio effect in the calculation of the CVA will depend on the bilateral netting in place and on the enforceability of netting (jurisdiction risk).

Fuel hedgers should fully understand the drivers of their credit charge so that they can negotiate and optimize the way in which they distribute their hedge portfolio across hedge providers.

Gap Options and Collateralization Agreements

Credit charges can be reduced significantly by executing a CSA. The reduction of credit charges will depend to a certain extent on the threshold and the frequency of collateral calls. The CVA is lowest when the collateral is of good quality, the threshold is close to zero, and the frequency of collateral calls is high. We can say that the counterparty is fully collateralized if the collateral calls are daily and the threshold and minimum transfer amounts are equal to zero.

Many CVA desks don't charge any CVA for fully collateralized transactions as they assume that the credit risk is reduced to zero. This is far from the truth if the close-out risks are significant, as discussed previously when calculating the PFE and the gap risk. The gap risk stems from the fact that when a counterparty defaults, the value of the trades can move during the time required by the desk to close the client's positions (margin period of risk). This

CVA related to gap risk can be calculated as a gap option, taking into account the correlation between the default and the asset price. This is especially important when an announcement of a default prompts a jump in price.

DEBT VALUATION ADJUSTMENT

The concept of debt valuation adjustment (DVA) is the mirror image of the concept of CVA. When party A enters into a trade with party B, party A charges a CVA to take into account the cost of hedging against potential losses arising from default of party B. However, party A can also default while its MTM is negative. When pricing the transaction, party A adds a CVA charge to the risk-free pricing to take into account the positive payments it would not receive in case of default of party B, but should also deduct a DVA benefit representing the amounts it wouldn't pay in case of its own default.

In summary, DVA is a price discount equal to the CVA from the counterparty's perspective:

$$DVA = CVA_{counterparty}$$

$$DVA = (1 - R) \int_{t=0}^{\infty} D(t).ENE(t).P(t)_{own} dt$$

where R: recovery rate
       $D(t)$:   discount factor from 0 to t
       $ENE(t)$: expected negative exposure conditional on own default
       $P(t)_{own}$: own default probability density function

Fuel hedgers, including airlines and shipping companies, should familiarize themselves with the concept of DVA and try to account for it when negotiating new transactions or unwinding old ones. When the debate about DVA first started in the market, many participants showed reluctance in implementing such benefit in the valuation of trades as it was counterintuitive to account for benefits arising from their own default. Today, many major banks have reported billions in profits after accounting for DVA, especially after the crisis of 2008.

The DVA concept was also challenging from a trading perspective because traders found it difficult to monetize DVA. In the case of CVA, trading desks could buy CDS protection to hedge counterparty risk and the CVA would be the expected cost of such a hedging strategy. In the case of DVA, the only way to recover this pricing discount is by selling CDS protection on oneself. However, a bank cannot sell protection on itself (a self-referencing CDS). This leaves trading desks with other alternatives, such as

- selling a CDS index that is very correlated with the credit of the bank, or
- buying back the bank's own debt.

Fuel Hedgers and Debt Valuation Adjustments

Fuel hedgers have generally been inefficient in negotiating credit charges with their hedging banks. Moreover, levying exhaustive credit charges might have been unfair in situations when the bank was also as risky as the corporate hedger. Airlines and shipping companies seldom challenged these charges by asking for the bank's DVA to be included in the pricing. Including the bank DVA would have reduced the credit charge.

Instead of accepting the charged CVA, airlines should ask to apply a bilateral CVA:

$$\text{Bilateral CVA} = \text{CVA} - \text{DVA}$$

The airline should also keep track of its CVA and DVA with each bank:

$$\text{DVA}_{\text{airline}} = \text{CVA}_{\text{bank}}$$
$$\text{CVA}_{\text{airline}} = \text{DVA}_{\text{bank}}$$

Furthermore, when airlines sought to unwind their positions with many banks, they generally did not receive any CVA benefit. Many of these airlines were charged CVA at the inception of the trades but when they unwound the transactions, the bank would release CVA reserves and liquidate CVA hedges but keep these amounts as profit. Fuel hedgers seldom ask to get some of these reserves or the value of the CVA hedge portfolio. The credit benefit an airline would get from unwinding its transactions with a bank can be described as the airline's DVA.

This helps us define DVA in another way:

DVA is the discount of your liabilities to the other party that can only be monetized upon unwind of the transactions

In other words, if an airline has a negative MTM on a transaction, and it decided to unwind the transaction and pay the negative MTM, the airline should enjoy a discount corresponding to the cost of credit that gets waived from the bank's books (the CVA from the bank's perspective).

The Case for Bilateral CVA

If two counterparties do not use bilateral CVA, they would not agree on the pricing of their transactions because each party is only accounting for the counterparty's credit charge. Bilateral CVA helps keep track of the MTM and minimizes disagreements during the unwinding of transactions. Airlines and other fuel hedgers should push for the implementation and reporting of bilateral CVA so that they can keep track of the expected discount if trades are unwound. Airlines should not be surprised if they find out that banks are accounting for it. Let us consider the following situation.

An airline enters into a hedging swap at a fixed price X, which has been adjusted up to account for credit charge (CVA) of about \$1 million. After a significant rise in WTI price, the swap MTM is +\$30 million for the airline. The airline would like to unwind the transaction and cash in the MTM gain. In this case, the bank is likely to charge the airline for the DVA, which corresponds to the expected liability the bank wouldn't pay conditional on its own default. This means that if the bank is accounting for DVA, the airline should get some benefit on day one and not just when it is favorable to the bank.

Hedgers should also be mindful of the impact of bilateral CVA on pricing. Banks with bad credit will be more aggressive in pricing derivatives, while creditworthy banks would be less competitive because of their lower DVA.

WRONG-WAY RISK

Wrong-way risk (WWR) occurs when the exposure to the counterparty is negatively correlated with its credit quality. This happens when the exposure to the counterparty increases along with its probability of default. For example, an airline entering into a short WTI swap gives rise to WWR, especially when the airline cannot pass on increases in fuel costs to end customers. Right-way risk (RWR) is the opposite of WWR. WWR and RWR have considerable impact on the calculation of credit risk measures as well as CVA charges. We previously calculated CVA charges as

$$\text{CVA} = (1 - R) \int_{t=0}^{\infty} D(t).\text{EE}(t).P(t)_{\text{cpty}} dt$$

We defined EE(t) as the expected exposure conditional on default. The standard EE(t) is often used, assuming no correlation between the hazard rate and the exposure. This simplifies the calculation of the CVA tremendously but does not account for the WWR. To appropriately account for the WWR, it is important to use the conditional expected exposure (CEE).

Legal and compliance departments usually discourage traders from entering into transactions that are not suitable for clients. In the case of an airline, short WTI swaps would be considered as inappropriate transactions. But there can be cases where the airline justifies entering into a short fuel position to offset some of the existing hedges that it has with other hedge providers. This can be the case if the airline wants to decrease its hedged volume. While such a transaction can be justified from the airline's perspective, they are still a source of WWR for the trading desk. In fact, positive correlation between the probability of default and fuel price increases the CEE. Moreover, credit lines should be based on conditional PFE, which is higher in the case of WWR.

COUNTERPARTY CREDIT RISK HEDGING

When introducing CVA, we briefly noted that counterparty credit risk hedging needs to be dynamic. We now introduce tailored derivative contracts that incorporate this dynamic hedging and are used for counterparty risk management.

Contingent CDS

In a normal CDS, the amount of protection is fixed and clearly defined by a notional. For this reason, a CDS cannot be used as a static hedge for counterparty credit risk, as the exposure changes, but can only be used as part of a dynamic counterparty risk hedging portfolio. A contingent CDS (CCDS) addresses this issue by linking the amount of protection to the MTM of a hypothetical derivative transaction. For example, to hedge the counterparty risk with party A on a swap transaction T, one can enter into an OTC CCDS with party A as reference entity and the amount of protection determined by the MTM of a swap with the same terms as transaction T. The CCDS protection is linked to two conditions: the credit event and the MTM being positive. It is similar to a KI option on the MTM of the swap with the KI event linked to the default of counterparty A.

CCDSs provide a static hedge for the specified derivatives transaction, and are theoretically cheaper than normal CDSs, as the payout is conditional on both the credit event and a market price benchmark being higher than a certain trigger value. In practice, the benefit is reduced by conservative parameters assumed by traders offering such products.

In the case of WWR, the CCDS spread captures the correlation effect. The CCDS is wider in the case of WWR than in the case of RWR.

Capped Exposure Derivatives

Exposures can be capped by having the counterparty buy OTM options, which can be costly in the case of fuel. A cheaper way to cap the PFE of a transaction is by adding a target redemption feature on top of the whole transaction. This ensures that the sum of the amounts payable by the counterparty would never exceed the target.

Another example of a strategy to cap the exposures is to use some of the exotic techniques discussed in Chapter 6, such as cancellable structures. For example, by adding a Bermudan cancellable feature to the transaction, the airline can have the right to cancel a hedging transaction on a periodic basis by paying a pre-specified unwind amount. In this case, the airline knows that it has the right to exit the transaction by paying an amount not exceeding the pre-specified unwind amount and that the MTM would never exceed the pre-specified unwind amount on cancellable dates.

SUMMARY

New capital requirements have applied tremendous pressure on financial institutions to manage credit exposures, either by clearing derivatives through a CCP, executing bilateral CSAs or using credit risk mitigants. CVA and FVA charges have been passed on to clients and this has made derivative pricing less attractive for hedgers. To reduce credit charges in order to remain competitive, many derivatives traders are now attempting to deduct the DVA from CVA charges and optimize CVA calculations by recognizing netting effects (changing their calculation methodologies to execute calculations on a portfolio basis). In a later chapter, we will see how bundling financing and hedging transactions helps reduce total credit costs and can aid in monetizing the benefits of hedging.

CHAPTER 8

Conducting Scenario Analysis

"Give me six hours to chop down a tree and I will spend the first four sharpening the axe."

—Abraham Lincoln

S ometimes, it is worth planning the contingency plan's contingency plan. In the case of fuel hedging, derivatives transactions might only provide limited protection under certain scenarios or even give rise to downside risks that are not always matched with an upside in the business performance of a firm. In this chapter, we will look at how scenario analysis, as a useful pre-trade and post-trade tool, can help derivative users to better understand the behavior of derivatives structures under various price and volatility regimes. Scenario analysis can be used to estimate the value of products, both in terms of mark-to-market impact and in terms of payout, under certain assumptions about future price movements. This helps in identifying the worst-case outcomes from holding a particular hedging product and in selecting derivative contracts that are appropriately customized to a party's risk appetite and expectations of market movements.

Scenario analysis should not be confused with back-testing, which is the valuation or calculation of the payout from a product based on historical market price movements. Scenario analysis is a forward-looking approach that aids derivative users in visualizing potential payouts from holding a product. A scenario analysis should be balanced in terms of price scenarios in order to give a reasonable view of possible future outcomes. Historical price movements can comprise one scenario in the overall analysis but should not be given too much weight in determining potential gains or losses from a derivative transaction.

We will first look at how to conduct scenario analyses for vanilla products. Once the basics of developing price and volatility scenarios are understood, we will progress to performing scenario analysis for more complex products as well as a mark-to-market scenario analysis. Finally, we will look at scenario analysis and its usefulness in determining hedge effectiveness from an accounting standpoint.

SCENARIO ANALYSIS FOR VANILLA PRODUCTS

Let us begin with a scenario analysis for a swap product. For a derivative product that only depends on a single price such as the closing price on a particular day (a bullet fixing), conducting a scenario analysis is a simple matter of calculating the payout under the product for different values of the closing price. As we have seen in preceding chapters, average price swaps and swaps with multiple settlements are very common in the commodity markets. So, we shall consider swaps in this instance instead of bullet/European vanilla products (which are simpler in terms of fixings). Using swaps will also help us incorporate scenarios where prices move in different directions over the life of the swap. These scenarios are particularly useful when considering the calculation of MTM valuations for different price paths, as well as in the valuation of path-dependent derivatives.

We consider the swap in Example 8.1.

EXAMPLE 8.1: WTI CRUDE OIL SWAP

Underlying:	NYMEX WTI Crude Oil
Reference Price:	Daily closing price of the front-month futures contract of the underlying
Tenor:	Jan 2015–Jun 2015 (6 months)
Notional:	10,000 barrels/month
Calculation Periods:	Monthly, from and including the first business day of the month up to and including the last business day of the month
Position:	Long (bought)
Swap Price:	65 USD/bbl
Settlements:	Asian (average price), monthly
Settlement Dates:	5 business days after the end of each Calculation Period

---

Scenario analysis can be based on the price on each business day but, for simplicity, the monthly average price will be used instead. We can construct three basic scenarios for vanilla products.

1. A scenario where the price generally moves in favor of the holder of the swap over the life of the trade.
2. A scenario where the price remains around the swap price (i.e., does not deviate largely from expectations of forward prices at inception of the trade).
3. A scenario in which the price of the underlying moves against the swap holder.

For the trade described above, a scenario analysis table is shown in Table 8.1.

The same scenarios can be represented graphically, as in Figure 8.1.

The payouts under these scenarios and the aggregate payout (excluding the effect of discounting) are shown in Table 8.2. The payout for each month is obtained by calculating

TABLE 8.1   Price scenarios used for a vanilla swap

Price scenario (price in USD/bbl)	1. Price moves in favor of holder	2. Price remains around swap	3. Price moves against holder
Jan 2015	66	64	63
Feb 2015	69	67	59
Mar 2015	73	66	56
Apr 2015	72	63	52
May 2015	75	64	50
Jun 2015	78	65	48

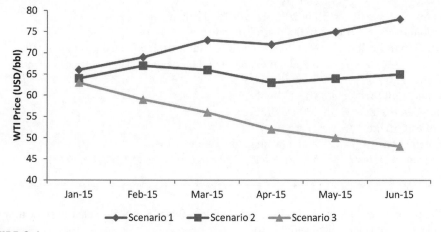

FIGURE 8.1   Three price scenarios used for a vanilla swap

the difference between the price for that particular scenario and the swap price (65 USD/bbl), multiplied by the monthly notional quantity.

These scenarios illustrate the monthly payout and the aggregate payout that can be expected under various market conditions. The price scenarios can be designed using either historical volatility or market implied volatility parameters, or even extreme volatility scenarios, depending on the purpose for which they are used. In fact, Monte Carlo analysis, which is

TABLE 8.2   Payouts (USD) under price scenarios used for a vanilla swap

Month	1. Price moves in favor of holder	2. Price remains around swap	3. Price moves against holder
Jan-15	10,000	(10,000)	(20,000)
Feb-15	40,000	20,000	(60,000)
Mar-15	80,000	10,000	(90,000)
Apr-15	70,000	(20,000)	(130,000)
May-15	100,000	(10,000)	(150,000)
Jun-15	130,000	—	(170,000)
Aggregate	430,000	(10,000)	(620,000)

used to price more complex structures, is nothing but an extension of scenario analysis, using an appropriately large number of paths following the market distribution of prices.

Similarly, we can conduct scenario analysis for a three-way structure specified in Example 8.2.

EXAMPLE 8.2: WTI CRUDE OIL THREE-WAYS STRUCTURE

Underlying:	NYMEX WTI Crude Oil
Reference Price:	Daily closing price of the front-month futures contract of the underlying
Tenor:	Jan 2015–Dec 2015 (12 months)
Notional:	10,000 barrels/month
Calculation Periods:	Monthly, from and including the first business day of the month up to and including the last business day of the month
Position:	Long (bought)
Bought Call Strike:	90 USD/bbl
Sold Call Strike:	100 USD/bbl
Sold Put Strike	77 USD/bbl
Settlements:	Asian (average price), monthly
Settlement Dates:	5 business days after the end of each Calculation Period

We present the three scenarios in separate tables (Tables 8.3–8.5) to clearly show how the settlement amounts are calculated.

The price scenarios used are shown in Figure 8.2. It can be seen that the scenarios incorporate some mean reversion of commodity prices over the life of the trade.

TABLE 8.3   Scenario 1: Price moves in favor of holder

Month	Monthly average price (USD/bbl)	Payout from the bought call (USD/bbl)	Payout from the sold call (USD/bbl)	Payout from the sold put (USD/bbl)	Net payout (in USD)
Jan 2015	88	0	0	0	—
Feb 2015	92	2	0	0	20,000
Mar 2015	95	5	0	0	50,000
Apr 2015	98	8	0	0	80,000
May 2015	104	14	−4	0	100,000
Jun 2015	109	19	−9	0	100,000
Jul 2015	115	25	−15	0	100,000
Aug 2015	112	22	−12	0	100,000
Sep 2015	110	20	−10	0	100,000
Oct 2015	103	13	−3	0	100,000
Nov 2015	96	6	0	0	60,000
Dec 2015	94	4	0	0	40,000
Aggregate					850,000

TABLE 8.4   Scenario 2: Price remains around the forward price

Month	Monthly average price (USD/bbl)	Payout from the bought call (USD/bbl)	Payout from the sold call (USD/bbl)	Payout from the sold put (USD/bbl)	Net payout (in USD)
Jan 2015	88	0	0	0	—
Feb 2015	86	0	0	0	—
Mar 2015	89	0	0	0	—
Apr 2015	92	2	0	0	20,000
May 2015	93	3	0	0	30,000
Jun 2015	89	0	0	0	—
Jul 2015	86	0	0	0	—
Aug 2015	83	0	0	0	—
Sep 2015	80	0	0	0	—
Oct 2015	76	0	0	−1	(10,000)
Nov 2015	79	0	0	0	—
Dec 2015	86	0	0	0	—
Aggregate					40,000

Alternate scenarios, which are a combination of one or more of these scenarios, can be constructed. For example, a scenario can be constructed where the price does not move significantly for the first few months and then rallies through the end of the year. Obviously, there could be innumerable scenarios that the commodity price could follow, and any information on price drivers or expected price movements can be used in the development of a scenario. However, as mentioned earlier, a good scenario analysis should consider both positive and negative developments in prices and volatility.

TABLE 8.5   Scenario 3: Price moves against the holder of the structure

Month	Monthly average price (USD/bbl)	Payout from the bought call (USD/bbl)	Payout from the sold call (USD/bbl)	Payout from the sold put (USD/bbl)	Net payout (in USD)
Jan 2015	86	0	0	0	—
Feb 2015	84	0	0	0	—
Mar 2015	80	0	0	0	—
Apr 2015	73	0	0	−4	(40,000)
May 2015	67	0	0	−10	(100,000)
Jun 2015	64	0	0	−13	(130,000)
Jul 2015	58	0	0	−19	(190,000)
Aug 2015	54	0	0	−23	(230,000)
Sep 2015	59	0	0	−18	(180,000)
Oct 2015	65	0	0	−12	(120,000)
Nov 2015	68	0	0	−9	(90,000)
Dec 2015	72	0	0	−5	(50,000)
Aggregate					(1,130,000)

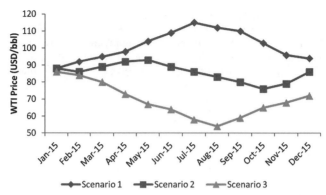

FIGURE 8.2   Three-ways structure – scenarios used

SCENARIO ANALYSIS FOR PATH-DEPENDENT PRODUCTS

In the previous section, we looked at a rudimentary approach to scenario analysis. Since we were dealing with linear products, constructing price scenarios where prices either rise, remain stable, or fall addresses positive and negative scenarios for payouts under these products. However, when we begin dealing with non-linear or exotic products, designing appropriate scenarios becomes trickier. This problem is magnified when we deal with developing scenarios for an entire portfolio. To commence the discussion on developing scenarios for path-dependent products, let us take the case of an extendible swap whose terms are described in Example 8.3.

EXAMPLE 8.3: WTI EXTENDIBLE SWAP

Underlying:	NYMEX WTI Crude Oil
Reference Price:	Daily closing price of the front-month futures contract of the underlying
Notional:	10,000 barrels/month
Guaranteed Period:	Jan 2015–Jun 2015 (6 months)
Extendible Period:	Jul 2015–Dec 2015 (6 months)
Extendible Date:	June 30, 2015
Extendible Option:	On or before the Extendible Date, the Counterparty (Hedge Provider) has the right but not the obligation to extend the transaction over the Extendible Period
Calculation Periods:	Monthly, from and including the first business day of the month up to and including the last business day of the month
Position:	Long (bought)
Swap Price:	80 USD/bbl
Settlements:	Asian (average price), monthly
Settlement Dates:	5 business days after the end of each Calculation Period

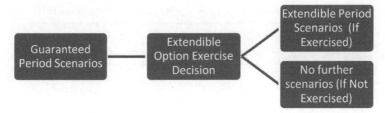

FIGURE 8.3 Decision tree for extendible swap

An extendible swap includes a guaranteed period, where the settlements are akin to a vanilla swap transaction, and an extendible period, which is subject to the exercise of the extendible option by the counterparty. Upon exercise of the swaption, the transaction becomes equivalent to a vanilla swap over the guaranteed and extendible periods. Thus, in developing the scenarios for this transaction, we will need to consider cases where the option is exercised as well as those scenarios where the extendible option is not exercised. The exercise of the swaption would be based on prevailing market conditions at the time of exercise, which in this case refers to the value of the swap over the extendible period. When looking at scenario analysis, we will consider only the payout and not the market conditions that determine exercise. Market variables are considered in the next section, dealing with developing MTM scenarios.

One approach to creating scenarios for path-dependent products is to use a decision tree, where the nodes represent the points at which option exercise decisions need to be made and the branches represent various price scenarios. For example, the above transaction can be represented in a decision-tree framework as in Figure 8.3. There is only one decision node, where the swap is either extended or not extended. Based on the decision, further price scenarios may be required.

The decision tree contains three price scenarios (bullish, bearish, and stable, as before) for the guaranteed period and nodes representing the swaption exercise decision. On the swaption exercise date, there could be additional price scenarios to be considered based on whether the option is exercised or not. Again, we use three price scenarios over the extendible period. This leads to a total of nine scenarios, which need to be developed to give a reasonably complete picture of the payout scenarios. In practice, to make the analysis more tractable, we omit certain scenarios based on assumptions on the change in shape of the forward curve. For example, if we assume that the shape of the forward curve does not change significantly, we can remove the branches of the tree where the price goes up during the guaranteed period. This is because the option to extend the swap would not be exercised by the counterparty if their MTM is negative upon exercise. These assumptions can be relaxed in the MTM-based scenario analysis.

Let us look at some of the scenarios for this product (Table 8.6).

The scenario in Table 8.6 is similar to the scenario described for the vanilla swap over the guaranteed period, as the swap is not extended over the extendible period. Tables 8.7 and 8.8 describe scenarios where the extendible option may be exercised.

We now look at another important path-dependent product where the payout is not just dependent on the current market fixing but also on previous market prices. The target

TABLE 8.6   Extendible scenario 1: price moves in favor of the holder

Month	Monthly average price (USD/bbl)	Payout from the extendible swap (USD)
Jan-15	86	60,000
Feb-15	89	90,000
Mar-15	93	130,000
Apr-15	92	120,000
May-15	95	150,000
Jun-15	98	180,000
Extendible option not exercised		
Jul-15	102	—
Aug-15	105	—
Sep-15	101	—
Oct-15	95	—
Nov-15	98	—
Dec-15	93	—
Aggregate		730,000

redemption transaction described in an earlier chapter is a prime example of this type of product. Barrier options are also similar structures, which can depend on past fixings of market prices. We consider the sample target redemption collar transaction on crude oil in Example 8.4.

TABLE 8.7   Extendible scenario 2: price moves against the holder and the extendible option is exercised

Month	Monthly average price (USD/bbl)	Payout from the extendible swap (USD)
Jan-15	86	60,000
Feb-15	84	40,000
Mar-15	80	—
Apr-15	73	(70,000)
May-15	67	(130,000)
Jun-15	64	(160,000)
Extendible option is exercised		
Jul-15	58	(220,000)
Aug-15	54	(260,000)
Sep-15	59	(210,000)
Oct-15	65	(150,000)
Nov-15	68	(120,000)
Dec-15	72	(80,000)
Aggregate		(1,300,000)

TABLE 8.8   Extendible scenario 3: price remains around the swap level and the extendible swap is exercised/not exercised

Month	Monthly average price (USD/bbl)	Payout if swap is extended (USD)	Payout if swap is not extended (USD)
Jan-15	88	80,000	80,000
Feb-15	86	60,000	60,000
Mar-15	89	90,000	90,000
Apr-15	92	120,000	120,000
May-15	93	130,000	130,000
Jun-15	89	90,000	90,000
Extendible decision		**Extended**	**Not extended**
Jul-15	86	60,000	—
Aug-15	83	30,000	—
Sep-15	80	—	—
Oct-15	76	(40,000)	—
Nov-15	79	(10,000)	—
Dec-15	86	60,000	—
Aggregate		670,000	570,000

EXAMPLE 8.4: WTI TARGET REDEMPTION COLLAR

Underlying:	NYMEX WTI Crude Oil
Reference Price:	Daily closing price of the front-month futures contract of the underlying
Tenor:	Jan 2015–Dec 2015 (12 months)
Notional:	10,000 barrels/month
Calculation Periods:	Monthly, from and including the first business day of the month up to and including the last business day of the month
Position:	Long (bought)
Bought Call Strike:	80 USD/bbl
Sold Put Strike:	72 USD/bbl
Target Profit:	30 USD/bbl (USD 300,000)
Knock-Out:	When the sum of positive payments made to the call option holder reaches the Target Profit, the transaction is terminated and no further payments are made
Settlements:	Asian (average price), monthly subject to Target Profit
Settlement Dates:	5 business days after the end of each Calculation Period

Unlike the extendible swap, where the extension is at the discretion of the extendible option holder, the target redemption trade early terminates depending on the path that the underlying price takes, with the trade being automatically terminated based on whether the target profit is reached. Thus, instead of there being only one node in the decision tree

TABLE 8.9 Target redemption scenario 1: price moves in favor of the holder and the target profit is reached early

Month	Monthly average price (USD/bbl)	Calculated monthly payout (USD)	Calculated positive accumulated payout (USD)	Actual monthly payout (USD)	Cumulative positive payout (USD)
Jan-15	86	60,000	60,000	60,000	60,000
Feb-15	89	90,000	150,000	90,000	150,000
Mar-15	93	130,000	280,000	130,000	280,000
Apr-15	92	120,000	400,000	20,000	300,000
May-15	95	Cumulative positive payout reaches the target profit and the structure is terminated			
Jun-15	98				
Jul-15	102				
Aug-15	105				
Sep-15	101				
Oct-15	95				
Nov-15	98				
Dec-15	93				

where a decision needs to be taken, continuation of the trade is evaluated at every fixing date. This is illustrated in the scenarios shown in Tables 8.9–8.11.

As can be seen from the scenario in Table 8.9, in the case where the price moves sharply in favor of the call option holder, the structure is knocked out and the call option holder receives the target profit. The call option holder no longer benefits from any price movements that would otherwise have been favorable for the corresponding vanilla structure.

TABLE 8.10 Target redemption scenario 2: price moves against the holder

Month	Monthly average price (USD/bbl)	Calculated monthly payout (USD)	Calculated positive accumulated payout (USD)	Actual monthly payout (USD)	Cumulative positive payout
Jan-15	86	60,000	60,000	60,000	60,000
Feb-15	84	40,000	100,000	40,000	100,000
Mar-15	80	—	100,000	—	100,000
Apr-15	73	—	100,000	—	100,000
May-15	67	(50,000)	100,000	(50,000)	100,000
Jun-15	64	(80,000)	100,000	(80,000)	100,000
Jul-15	58	(140,000)	100,000	(140,000)	100,000
Aug-15	54	(180,000)	100,000	(180,000)	100,000
Sep-15	59	(130,000)	100,000	(130,000)	100,000
Oct-15	65	(70,000)	100,000	(70,000)	100,000
Nov-15	68	(40,000)	100,000	(40,000)	100,000
Dec-15	72	—	100,000	—	100,000

TABLE 8.11   Target redemption scenario 3: price remains around the swap level

Month	Monthly average price (USD/bbl)	Calculated monthly payout (USD)	Calculated positive accumulated payout (USD)	Actual monthly payout (USD)	Cumulative positive payout
Jan-15	88	80,000	80,000	80,000	80,000
Feb-15	86	60,000	140,000	60,000	140,000
Mar-15	83	30,000	170,000	30,000	170,000
Apr-15	81	10,000	180,000	10,000	180,000
May-15	76	—	180,000	—	180,000
Jun-15	78	—	180,000	—	180,000
Jul-15	72	—	180,000	—	180,000
Aug-15	70	(20,000)	180,000	(20,000)	180,000
Sep-15	75	—	180,000	—	180,000
Oct-15	81	10,000	190,000	10,000	190,000
Nov-15	83	30,000	220,000	30,000	220,000
Dec-15	84	40,000	260,000	40,000	260,000

For the scenario described in Table 8.10, the target profit is not reached over the tenor of the trade and the settlements are akin to the settlements for a vanilla collar transaction.

Finally, in the price scenario shown in Table 8.11, the price does not move significantly in either direction. The cumulative positive payout is less than the target profit and the target redemption is not knocked out.

MTM-BASED SCENARIO ANALYSIS AND POTENTIAL FUTURE EXPOSURES

In addition to helping us understand the behavior of a derivative product under different price conditions, scenario analysis can also help us understand the evolution of the MTM of a transaction under different market scenarios. Until now, we have only considered the payout of a derivative under varying price scenarios. An MTM analysis depicts the possible mark-to-market of a transaction under some assumption on the evolution of prices as well as forward curves, implied volatilities, and/or correlations. Mark-to-market scenarios can be useful to determine the maximum exposure to a counterparty for OTC transactions or the potential margin requirements in the future for exchange-cleared trades. Scenario analysis is used extensively in the calculation of PFE and EE, which are critical to capital calculations for derivatives businesses at banks and financial institutions.

Calculating the future MTM of a transaction requires assumptions on multiple market parameters and there can be many methods to simulate future MTM values. In addition to the distributional assumptions on price that we briefly touched upon earlier, assumptions also need to be made to describe the evolution of forward curves, volatilities, and covariances. The most common approach is to assume that prices are normally distributed and forward contracts are perfectly correlated. Volatilities and correlations are also assumed to remain constant and are calculated based on historical data.

Alternatively, statistical techniques can be used to model prices so that other distributional assumptions such as non-normality can be accounted for. This enables prices and other variables to be modeled more accurately, but the complexity of generating price scenarios increases. Furthermore, there is always the risk that market prices do not follow the same distribution in the future. A third approach could be half-way between these two methods, whereby the forward curves are not set as static but modeled tractably using techniques like principal component analysis, which explain a majority of curve shapes.

By using a sufficient number of scenarios, the PFE for a transaction can be calculated. The PFE is defined as the maximum exposure to a counterparty for a given confidence level; it is usually defined for high confidence levels of 95%, 97.5%, or 99% (depending on the conservativeness required) for use in credit exposure calculations. Thus, a 95% PFE for a transaction is the level that the MTM would not be expected to exceed 95% of the time. By generating a large number of scenarios and calculating the 95th percentile of the MTM at any point in time, we can arrive at the PFE for that point in time. Calculating the 95th percentile of the MTM at each point in time gives us the PFE profile for a particular transaction.

In addition to calculating the PFE for a trade, we can also calculate the EE of a transaction. The EE or EPE is the average of positive exposures under a derivative contract. Using the same methodology of generating scenarios and calculating MTMs, we can estimate the EE of a transaction.

The VaR measure gives a statistical expression of potential losses on a trade or a portfolio of trades. The calculation methodology is the same as that used for the PFE, except that VaR is usually calculated over a short timeframe (up to 10 days). However, hedgers can use the same statistical technique to get VaRs for longer tenors, which would be equivalent to the PFE from the perspective of the other counterparty.

BEYOND PAYOFFS AND MTMs – COLLATERALIZATION AND FUNDING REQUIREMENT ANALYSIS

Most fuel hedgers and hedge providers conduct derivatives cash-flow analysis and MTM analysis separately, and seldom pay attention to the link between the two – even if a CSA is in place. This is mainly due to the fact that, historically, most OTC hedging transactions were uncollateralized. However, while an increasing number of banks have been pushing for the use of CSAs with their corporate clients, scenario analyses have not been adjusted to account for the impact of CSA contracts on the cash flow of hedges.

Until recently, when an airline or a shipping company executed a CSA with a hedging bank, the annex was usually taken for granted by front-office personnel, who considered its details to be a back-office/operations matter. However, since the financial crisis of 2008, more attention has been focused on CSAs and their economic impact. In fact, a CSA can be viewed as a derivative contract and must be taken into account when scenario analysis is conducted. For example, in the previous cash-flow analysis, the payments were based on the derivative hedges alone, without taking into account any collateral posting required.

Before entering into hedging transactions, fuel hedgers should conduct scenario analysis that accounts for all cash payments, including those under the CSA (accounting for all liquid collateral as cash). This helps identify funding liquidity risks that can be summarized in a profile of potential funding requirements, as inferred from the PFE profile from the counterparty's perspective. If a CSA is in place, the fuel hedger should, at the very least, maintain the PFE of its trades (from the hedging bank's perspective) in line with its funding capacity. For example, if an airline has CSAs with N counterparties, the potential funding requirement at time t under its CSAs is calculated as

$$\sum_{i=1}^{N} \left(\text{PFE}_i\left(t\right) - \text{Threshold}_i \right)$$

This shows that payments under the CSA can be much higher than monthly payments under long-dated derivatives, as the CSA payments (collateral posted) are calculated based on the present value of all expected future payments.

Thus, scenario analysis is useful not only for determining potential payoffs but also for market risk, credit risk, and liquidity risk management. We now look at how scenario analysis can help in achieving hedge accounting treatment for derivatives.

HEDGE EFFECTIVENESS

In this section, we present an overview of hedge accounting intended to provide readers with an appreciation of the issues involved in implementing hedge accounting. We deal with this topic here mainly in order to explain how scenario analysis can be used to demonstrate hedge effectiveness. Hedge accounting treatment is highly dependent on the jurisdiction and interpretation of prevailing laws and accounting standards, and is also susceptible to change from regular updates of accounting standards. Thus, practitioners should consult with legal and accounting domain experts while adopting hedge accounting for derivatives.

Hedge accounting is governed by the Statement of Financial Accounting Standards No. 133 "Accounting for Derivative Financial Instruments and Hedging Activities" (SFAS 133) in the USA and the International Accounting Standard 39 "Financial Instruments: Recognition and Measurement" (IAS 39) internationally. Individual countries/regions have their own versions of the international accounting standard. For instance, the European Union has its own version of the IAS 39 standard.

SFAS 133 and IAS 39 deal mainly with fair-value accounting and hedge accounting of financial instruments, although there are some differences. Fair-value accounting means that all derivatives should be carried on the books of a company at their fair value or mark-to-market value (which can be very different from the value at inception, as a number of instruments like futures and swaps have zero cost when transacted). Fair-value accounting can result in a mismatch between the value of derivative contracts and the underlying physical contracts they are meant to hedge. Underlying contracts may be carried at book value while derivatives are marked to market, resulting in artificial earnings volatility when, in actual fact, the changes in the underlying contract's value and the value of the hedging instrument should offset each other. Hedge accounting aims to match gains or losses in derivative contracts to the gains or losses in the underlying hedged items. In order to allow hedge accounting, a derivative instrument must be shown to be effective in offsetting changes in the value of the hedged item.

Hedge accounting treatment can be applied for the hedging of fair-value exposures, cash-flow exposures, or net foreign investments. Fair-value exposures include exposures to the changes in fair value of existing assets, liabilities, or future commitments. Gains and losses from fair-value exposures and related hedges are recognized in income. Cash-flow exposure refers to changes in cash flow from a balance sheet item or future transaction, while net foreign investment exposure relates to the exposure to change in net foreign operations due to fluctuations in exchange rates. Gains or losses from cash-flow hedges and foreign investment hedges are reported in other comprehensive income and entered into income when the underlying hedged cash flows are recognized.

In order for a derivative instrument to qualify for hedge accounting treatment, the underlying exposure being hedged should be clearly identified and matched to the derivative designated for hedging. The relationship between the hedged item and the derivative needs to be documented and the objective and strategy of the hedge clearly stated. It must also be demonstrated that the hedge is expected to be highly effective, that is, the hedge cash flows effectively offset the cash flows of the hedged item, and this effectiveness must be reliably tested. Hedge effectiveness needs to be demonstrated before entering the hedge (ex-ante) and on an ongoing basis after the hedge is executed (ex-post).

It is in this regard that scenario analysis can be used to demonstrate the effectiveness of a derivative. Hedge effectiveness can be assessed qualitatively by matching the terms of the hedged item and the derivative contract, known as the "critical terms" method. Alternatively, a statistical analysis using historical data on the hedging relationship or a scenario analysis modeling the effectiveness of the hedge under different price scenarios can be used. The suggested rule for verifying hedge effectiveness proposed by the Financial Accounting Standards Board (FASB) is the 80/125 rule, that is, the gains or losses on the derivative contract should fall within 80% to 125% of the hedged item's gains or losses. The ratio of changes is calculated as follows:

Ratio $= -$ Change in fair value of the hedging instrument / Change in fair value of the hedged item

When the ratio is between 80% and 125%, the hedging is deemed effective. In the event that hedge effectiveness cannot be demonstrated retrospectively, the entity has to discontinue hedge accounting unless the breakdown in the hedging relationship is expected to be a one-off event and will not impact effectiveness going forward.

The weakness with the ratio analysis method is that it may show ineffectiveness when the fair-value changes involved are small. A fix for this issue would be to use the cumulative change in fair value as opposed to the change in fair value in one period.

Among the statistical methods that are used to determine the relationship between hedging instruments and hedged items, regression analysis and scenario analysis are the most common ones.

Regression analysis, as described earlier, involves determining the relationship between historical changes in fair value of the hedged item and a hypothetical hedging instrument used over that historical period. The least-squares method of fitting a line between the two variables (changes in fair value of instrument and hedged item) is used to determine the relation between them. Regression statistics are used to determine the effectiveness of the hedge. The R-square of the regression indicates the degree of variability of the hedged item that is explained by the variation of the hedging instrument. R-square values of over 80% indicate that the relationship has good explanatory power. This is corroborated by the t-statistic or F-statistic, which indicates statistical significance of the regression. The slope of the regression is analogous to the ratio described above, and a slope of -0.8 to -1.25 is deemed acceptable for prospective hedge accounting.

Scenario analysis can be used to determine how the hedging instrument's fair value behaves over different market scenarios. However, as described earlier, the ratio calculation may fail for certain scenarios where the price does not move by much. By using appropriate scenarios or a high number of scenarios, we can improve the reliability of the scenario analysis to determine whether hedge accounting can be applied.

SUMMARY

In this chapter, we stressed the importance of scenario analysis in the risk management of market risks as well as ancillary derivative risks, including credit risk and funding risks. We touched upon the impact of derivatives collateralization on the cash management of a firm and demonstrated how MTM analysis can be extended to model the impact of derivatives on the liquidity position of a firm, when CSAs are in place. In Chapter 10 we will revisit these aspects when we discuss a hedge restructuring case, where multiple considerations including appropriateness, credit risk, market risk, CSAs, CVA, and funding costs are intertwined and scenario analysis can be of great importance.

CHAPTER 9

Financing and Risk Management: Bundled Solutions

"The whole is greater than the sum of its parts."

—Aristotle

T he equity value of a highly levered airline can be completely annihilated by relatively small losses, exposing its lenders to loan/bond default risk. In previous chapters, we described hedging strategies that can be utilized by consumers to reduce risks related to fuel prices, ranging from vanilla strategies to exotic trades. As we mentioned earlier, hedging market risks has the effect of reducing volatility in stock prices and lowering credit costs. In this chapter we look at practical examples, which can help companies monetize the benefits that accrue from commodity hedging by combining their funding management with market risk hedging. Before elaborating on how firms can achieve these synergies, we begin with a review of the different modes of financing prevalent in the aviation business.

STRUCTURED AVIATION FINANCE OVERVIEW

In Chapter 1 we discussed the costs and profitability of airline companies. After flight costs including fuel expenses and staff costs, ownership costs form a large part of the cost structure for airlines, especially newer airlines. We also noted the fact that when considering return on invested capital by sector, the airline industry is among the lowest in terms of return on capital; most companies in the industry fail to earn their weighted average cost of capital (WACC). In addition, aviation is also a cyclical industry, having long alternating periods of high growth and oversupply. Despite these facts, financing for the airline industry is plentiful and there are multiple sources of funds. This may be due to the fact that there is still a reasonable amount of government involvement in and/or implicit support available to the industry. It may also be due to the fact that asset-backed finance as a means of funding has been increasing in use over the last few years.

There are numerous modes of financing for airline companies. Aside from the traditional use of cash and retained earnings, airlines can also borrow from banks and other financial institutions. Additionally, over the last decade and particularly after the credit crisis, airlines have been looking at more non-traditional modes of financing and new investors have been entering these markets. The major sources of aviation finance are as follows.

1. Cash and retained earnings. This is the simplest means of financing the purchase of aircraft but is also the least likely to be used. This is due to the fact that many airlines do not have large reserves of cash on their balance sheets over long periods, due to their low profitability. Airlines are also penalized with high borrowing costs during down-cycles and thus can better deploy cash elsewhere rather than purchasing long-term capital assets outright.
2. Bank debt or finance leases. Airlines can either take medium-term loans from banks for purchasing aircraft or enter into finance leases. Under a finance lease, the bank purchases aircraft from the airline and leases it back to the airline in return for monthly lease rental payments and at the end of the lease, the airline retains the aircraft or purchases it at a nominal cost.
3. Operating leases. Operating leases are similar to finance leases but for the fact that the airline does not get to own the aircraft at the end of the lease. Operating leases are offered by banks or specialized leasing companies. We will look at leases in more detail in the next section.
4. Export Credit Agency (ECA) guaranteed loans. These are mainly loans made by banks, which are guaranteed by export credit agencies like the US Ex-Im Bank or COFACE in France, which do so in order to support local manufacturers. These agencies can also lend directly to aircraft purchasers.
5. Manufacturer support. Alternatively, manufacturers can support airlines by financing purchases of their aircraft by means such as sale-and-leaseback or by guaranteeing residual values at the end of a lease term.
6. Tax leases. These are leases that companies enter into with airlines in order to profit from beneficial tax treatment of the purchase of new equipment. The companies may only invest a portion of the capital required to purchase the aircraft and receive financing for a large part of the purchase price and, hence, these leases are also called leveraged leases.
7. Capital market financing. Airlines can finance aircraft purchases by issuing debt in the capital markets or through securities called enhanced equipment trust certificates (EETCs) or asset-backed securities (ABS). EETCs are a form of securitization that is popular among US carriers, whereby a special purpose vehicle (SPV) raises money from the capital markets to purchase aircraft and leases them to an airline, which makes regular rental payments. Equity issuances may also be used to finance purchases of aircraft, but they are generally not used.
8. Islamic finance. With the growth in Middle Eastern carriers, there has been more impetus to use Shariah (Islamic law)-compliant financing.

The share of these financing modes in aviation finance globally is estimated to be as shown in Figure 9.1.

Many airlines now provide data on the breakdown of their financing by mode as well as their fleet composition by means of finance. The fleet composition (number of airplanes) by means of finance for prominent airlines by region is shown in Table 9.1.

The aviation finance market consists of banks and financing organizations, export credit agencies, and operating lessors, in addition to manufacturers and airlines.

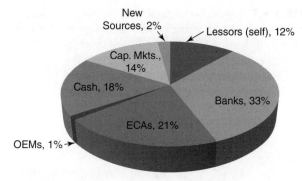

FIGURE 9.1   Share of financing modes in aviation finance (2013)
Data Sources: Boeing, Avolon.

Banks can either lend on unsecured terms or engage in secured lending on a fixed or floating-rate basis. An airline's purchase of aircraft can be financed by a single bank or, more commonly, by a syndicate of banks, with the fees going to individual banks in proportion to the quantum of financing provided. Some of the prominent banks in the airline financing business are listed in Table 9.2.

The major export credit agencies are the US Ex-Im Bank, the Export Credits Guarantee Department in the UK, Compagnie Française d'Assurance pour le Commerce Exterieur (COFACE) in France, and Euler Hermes in Germany. Export credit agencies provide financing for the portion of the aircraft produced in a country. Thus, ECGD, COFACE, and Hermes

TABLE 9.1   Fleet composition by means of financing

Region		Airline	Self-owned	Finance	Operating	Total
				Leases		
Asia						
	1.	China Eastern	——305——		160	465
	2.	Air China	242	137	182	561
	3.	Emirates	6	63	128	197
	4.	Cathay Pacific	71	63	58	192
Europe						
	1.	Lufthansa	562	37	23	622
	2.	Ryanair	216	30	51	297
	3.	Air France KLM	85	48	113	246
	4.	British Airways	——240——		38	278
North America						
	1.	American Airlines	475	28	467	970
	2.	Delta Air Lines	592	94	57	743
	3.	United Airlines*	431	——834——		1265
	4.	Southwest Airlines	516	——164——		680

* Includes capacity purchase under leases.
Source: Company balance sheets as of 2013.

TABLE 9.2   Prominent banks in the airline financing market

1.	BNP Paribas
2.	Crédit Agricole
3.	Citigroup
4.	Commonwealth Bank of Australia
5.	DVB Bank
6.	Goldman Sachs
7.	J.P. Morgan
8.	KfW IPEX-Bank
9.	Natixis
10.	Bank of Tokyo-Mitsubishi UFJ

would provide portions of the financing for the purchase of an Airbus aircraft with financing amounts proportional to the national manufacturer's share in the production of the aircraft. They also provide insurance and guarantees for financing.

Aircraft leasing companies raise money in the public markets to purchase aircraft and place them with airlines. They usually focus on popular aircraft like the Airbus A320 and the Boeing B737, as these are the main aircraft used by most airlines and are therefore easy to lease out. Leasing companies can either purchase new aircraft outright, or through sale-and-leaseback, or transact in the used aircraft market for assets. Leasing companies have geographically diversified portfolios to manage cyclicality in individual airline markets. The aircraft leasing market is dominated by two major lessors, the International Lease Finance Corporation (ILFC) and General Electric Capital Asset Services (GECAS), although their market share has been dropping in recent years. A list of prominent lessors in the market is shown in Table 9.3.

AIRLINE FINANCING VIA DEBT AND AIRCRAFT LEASES

In this section we take a deeper look at the mechanics of debt financing for the purchase of aircraft. As mentioned earlier, bank loans and ECA-guaranteed debt and leases are the largest sources of financing for the industry. With the new Basel III regulations coming into effect, the lending capacity of banks is likely to be curtailed and the share of leasing in aviation finance is likely to grow over the next few years. Let us first take a look at term loans offered by banks.

TABLE 9.3   Prominent aircraft lessors

1.	GECAS
2.	ILFC
3.	Air Lease Corporation
4.	CIT
5.	Aviation Capital Group
6.	BBAM
7.	BOC Aviation
8.	SMBC Aviation Capital
9.	AWAS
10.	AerCap

Term Loans

Banks and other financial institutions can offer term loans for the purchase of aircraft on a bilateral basis or on a syndicated basis for larger deals. The lead bank that arranges the loan is usually one that has a close relationship with the borrower. Loans can be unsecured, but in practice most loans are secured by the aircraft purchased as well as additional collateral or credit enhancements where necessary. Banks can also impose covenants on the purchaser in terms of metrics, which may include the debt service ratio, debt-to-equity ratio, and liquidity ratios.

Loans made available to airlines can have different payment profiles, which can be structured based on the needs of the airline. For example, payments may need to be made in advance of the purchase of an aircraft and, thus, a grace period for repayment needs to be incorporated into the loan. Airlines may also have different usage levels for the asset over its life, which can affect the cash flows used to repay the loan. In such cases, the amortization profile for the notional or the net payment profile can be adjusted to the airline's requirements.

One of the most common types of payment profiles for loans is a fixed repayment profile over the life of the loan. Another common type of term loan is one where the notional amortizes in a straight line. A popular feature is to have interest rates kept floating, usually linked to a benchmark rate such as LIBOR. Based on the repayment frequency and currency of borrowing, the benchmark reference could be a 1-month, 3-month, or 6-month rate. Fees paid to arrange a loan are also significant and include documentation/facility fees and agency fees for syndication, in addition to charges on undrawn balances (commitment fees). We look at an example of a loan of 100 million USD used for the purchase of new aircraft. The main parameters of the loan are the notional amount, the payment profile (assumed to be fixed payments), the total interest rate (fixed here at 4%), the frequency of payments (annual for ease of reference), and the tenor of the loan (10 years). The schedule of annual payments and the outstanding notional at the start of each year are shown in Table 9.4.

The preference for fixed or floating interest rates depends on the view taken by the airline's treasurer on interest rates. In an environment where interest rates are expected to be lower than the prevailing forward interest rates over the loan tenor, the treasurer may choose to use floating interest rates. In cases where interest rates are expected to increase, airlines may want to lock in fixed rates. In addition to the exposure to benchmark interest rates, airlines are also exposed to economic and credit conditions at the time of financing. Thus, the timing of entering the borrowing market is also important for airlines in terms of reducing their borrowing costs.

TABLE 9.4 Outstanding notional schedule and annual payments for a loan with fixed repayments

Year	Outstanding notional (USD)	Annual payment (USD)
1	100,000,000	12,325,000
2	91,675,000	12,325,000
3	83,017,000	12,325,000
4	74,012,680	12,325,000
5	64,648,187	12,325,000
6	54,909,115	12,325,000
7	44,780,479	12,325,000
8	34,246,698	12,325,000
9	23,291,566	12,325,000
10	11,898,229	12,325,000

Export Credit Agency Debt

Export credit agency guarantees are useful when the credit markets are tight and banks are not willing to lend to risky borrowers. In the wake of the credit crisis, ECA-backed financing was an important source of funds for airlines. After the credit crisis, ECAs increased their share of support in aircraft financing from 15–20% of total deliveries to 30–40%. ECA guarantees are governed by an arrangement called the Large Aircraft Sector Understanding (LASU). Prior to 2011, airlines in countries that were not manufacturers of large aircraft (i.e. countries other than the USA, UK, France, Germany, and Spain) were the only ones with access to ECA-backed financing, and while this was not an issue before 2007, the cost of ECA financing after the credit crisis was seen to be much cheaper than traditional financing. This resulted in the amendment of the LASU in 2011 to reduce the importance of ECAs in financing decisions. Additionally, there has been uncertainty in the USA with regard to the Ex-Im Bank's charter expiring in 2015, further reducing the viability of ECA financing. The 2011 LASU requires ECAs to classify borrowers based on credit rating and prescribes minimum spreads and upfront payments for these structures, which are updated regularly. ECAs are also required to include risk mitigants based on the rating of the borrower. An example of LASU-prescribed rates is shown in Table 9.5.

The US Ex-Im Bank provides guarantees for up to 85% of the US cost of aircraft. The same is the case for ECGD, while COFACE and Hermes only cover 95% of the principal and interest on 85% of the aircraft cost. Maximum repayment tenors are 10 to 12 years although under exceptional cases, the tenor can be up to 15 years. Repayments are usually on a quarterly basis. A sample ECA-backed financing transaction structure is described in Figure 9.2.

Leases

The transportation industry is one of the largest users of leasing as a means of finance. Passenger cars, commercial vehicles, rail, aviation, and shipping are some of the biggest industry segments that use leasing as a means of finance. Lease finance is provided by specialized asset finance companies (lessors), which could be subsidiaries of banks, capital goods manufacturers, or independent leasing finance companies. Leases can be differentiated from rentals by their duration; for example, rentals are usually for short durations of two years or less while leases are typically for longer durations.

TABLE 9.5 2011 ASU Table 5 – minimum premium rates as of October 15, 2014 (12-year repayment term, asset-backed transactions)

		Minimum premium rates	
Risk category	**Risk classification**	**Per annum spreads (bps)**	**Upfront (%)**
1	AAA to BBB−	89	4.98
2	BB+ and BB	126	7.09
3	BB−	144	8.12
4	B+	166	9.39
5	B	185	10.50
6	B−	195	11.08
7	CCC	217	12.38
8	CC to C	222	12.67

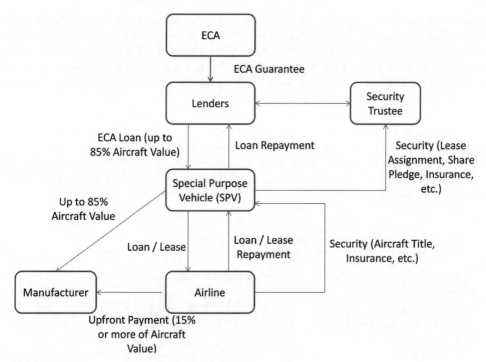

FIGURE 9.2   Sample ECA-backed financing structure

The basic principle of leasing is as follows. The lessor purchases the asset for leasing and rents it to the lessee in return for rental payments, which should cover the capital outlay for the purchase of the asset and related financing costs, in addition to generating a reasonable rate of return. The lessor can purchase the asset directly or enter into a sale-and-leaseback arrangement with the equipment user who already owns the asset or who can arrange to procure the asset initially. Under some leases, the equipment reverts to the lessor at the end of the lease period while in other cases, the lessee retains the asset by making a nominal payment if necessary.

Leases can be categorized under two main types – finance/capital leases and operating leases. A finance lease is a lease that transfers substantially all the risks and rewards incidental to the ownership of an asset from the lessor to the lessee. An operating lease is defined as a lease that is not a finance lease. Thus, in terms of returns, finance leases are those leases where the lessor generates almost all of their income from the rental payments and not from the disposal of the asset at the end of the lease term (as per US GAAP, where the present value of rental payments received by the lessor exceeds 90% of fair market value of the asset less investment tax credits retained by the lessor). Conversely, operating leases are true leases where the proceeds from the sale of the asset comprise a significant portion of the income of the lessor. Leases where ownership of the asset is transferred to the lessee at the end of the lease term, or where the lessee has a bargain purchase option, are general indicators of a finance lease. Also, if the lease term is for a major part of the asset's economic life (defined as 75% or more under US GAAP), the lease is classified as a finance lease.

Under a finance lease, the asset is owned by the lessor but if, at the end of the rental period, the asset can be purchased by the lessee, the lessee can claim any depreciation or other capital allowances associated with the asset. Usually, finance leases are capitalized on the balance sheet of the lessee, with the equipment shown as an asset and a financial liability toward the lessor, while operating leases can be off-balance sheet. However, the distinction between these two types of lease has become increasingly blurred and international accounting rules are in the process of being amended to bring more transparency to company balance sheets by including commitments under operating leases explicitly.

The main terms of a lease include the asset under lease and the ownership of the asset, the lease period, lease rentals, options upon termination, and early-termination features. Rental payments are influenced by many factors, chief among which are the interest rate and the credit risk associated with the lessee. The residual value of the asset at the end of the lease period is also important in determining the rental charged. The sample terms for a leasing transaction are described in Example 9.1.

EXAMPLE 9.1: SAMPLE TERMS OF A LEASE

Lessor:	Airline Finance Company
Lessee:	ABC Airlines
Aircraft Type:	Airbus A320 aircraft with 2 x IAE V2500 engines
Delivery Location and Date:	London, UK on June 1, 2015
Lease Term:	5 years from Delivery Date
Lease Rental:	USD 450,000 per month, fixed, paid monthly in advance
Maintenance Reserves:	Lessee shall pay to Lessor monthly, as follows. Airframe Check: USD 25,000 per month Engine Maintenance: USD 300 per engine block hour Landing Gear Overhaul: USD 20 per block hour APU Refurbishment: USD 50 per block hour
Security Deposit:	USD 1,000,000
Operation and Maintenance:	As per Aviation Authority approved program
Insurance:	Lessee to maintain insurance coverage for the aircraft
Lessee Covenants:	As agreed between Lessor and Lessee

Some of the benefits of leasing are as follows.

a. Leasing is a good source of medium-term finance, where the quantum of finance could be as high as 100% of the value of the asset and the security required under the transaction could be limited to the asset itself.
b. It could cost less than bank loans or other forms of financing, as leasing firms can pass on bulk discounts that they receive on aircraft purchase to lessees.
c. It helps corporations to maintain liquidity.
d. Rental payments can be tailored to suit individual users' requirements.
e. It removes residual risk of aircraft values from the balance sheet in addition to enabling airlines to run fleets of newer, more efficient aircraft.

Taxation plays a big role in determining whether to opt for leasing or financing through a loan or other conventional methods. Leasing can provide tax benefits, as rentals are allowed costs against taxable income and can provide for more savings than claiming capital allowances on an asset's cost. It could also be advantageous to use leasing when there are differences in tax rates between lessors and lessees, and when lessees do not have sufficient profits to claim all allowances due to them. This feature led to the development of leasing structures such as the Japanese leveraged leases, whereby Japanese investors invested 20% or more as the equity share in an SPV and leveraged it using bank debt to purchase and lease out aircraft to foreign airlines. These leases allowed both foreign airlines and Japanese investors to claim tax credits but were withdrawn in the late 1990s and replaced by Japanese operating leases, where only local investors received tax credits. Similar structures have been replicated in the USA, the UK, Germany, and other jurisdictions. In general, leveraged leases are the product of investment credits allowed for accelerated depreciation of equipment, combined with an airline industry that needs large quantities of equipment but does not have the profits to claim credits against. However, tax-driven transactions have dropped significantly in volume as tax authorities changed the rules to allow only economic owners to claim depreciation on assets.

RATIONALE FOR COMBINING HEDGING AND FINANCING

We have studied modes of financing for airlines in previous sections. In most cases, decisions on the funding mix for an airline are made in isolation, independent of other risk management decisions. However, the risks arising from financing and operations are interrelated. When investing in leasing or purchasing an aircraft, airlines are making assumptions based on a forecast of future demand. Demand for air travel is generally related to the rate of economic growth, and assumptions on the rate of growth are embedded in these forecasts. In order to generate the cash flow required to pay off the cost of the aircraft, airlines need to ensure that their costs are kept under control. Fuel costs are the largest and most volatile component of costs, and there is limited visibility on fuel expenses without the use of hedging. In scenarios where oil prices rise in tandem with GDP and air traffic, increased demand can help airlines tide over the rise in costs. However, when there is an oil-price shock that is independent of economic growth, airlines can be squeezed with respect to servicing their debt. Hedging structures, when combined with financing, can cushion cash flows against the impact of oil-price shocks and guarantee a rate of return on the use of the aircraft.

Hedging to protect the cash flows required to service debt repayments or lease payments, when combined with new borrowings, can also reduce the cost of debt for airlines. This is because banks are willing to accept lower rates of return when the risk of repayment is reduced by fuel hedging. Although there is a theoretical basis for hedging helping to reduce financing costs, airline companies in general do not monetize this efficiently. Unlike financing in other industries like mining or construction, where factors such as the predominance of bank financing and the lack of transferable collateral can compel companies to hedge price risks to secure financing, the ready availability of easily transferable collateral (in the form of aircraft) can preclude integrated risk management. The asset-specific nature of most airline financing can distract both lenders and airlines from considering risks in totality.

In this section we will consider the quantification of the reduction in credit risk arising from commodity hedging. In the next section we will look at structures that link commodity risk and funding risk and can be used to reduce borrowing costs.

Reduction of Default Risk through Hedging

To examine the reduction in credit risk arising from hedging, we return to the case of the US airline industry. In Chapter 1, we described how the negative correlation between airline stock prices and fuel prices can be utilized to reduce equity volatility by means of hedging. We now attempt to describe a similar reduction in the probability of default by considering the overall volatility of the assets of an airline. Demonstrating a reduced probability of default can result in a reduction in borrowing costs.

One measure of the riskiness of a firm is the "distance to default" (Figure 9.3). Distance to default combines information on asset values, business risk, and leverage into a single metric that compares the net worth of an entity with the size of a one-standard-deviation move in the value of its assets:

$$\text{Distance to default} = \frac{(\text{Market value of assets} - \text{Default point})}{(\text{Market value of assets}) * (\text{Asset volatility})}$$

Theoretically, the default point for a company is when the market value of assets drops below the book value of liabilities. However, in reality, companies continue functioning even when their market value drops below their book value. An accurate estimate of the default point would be somewhere between the level of short-term liabilities and long-term liabilities. In our simplified analysis, we make the assumption that the default point is fixed at the level of total debt.

The market value of assets and the asset volatility can be calculated based on equity prices, debt, and equity price volatility using the fact that equity value behaves like a call option on the asset value struck at the level of debt. To simplify our analysis, we assume a constant debt for each airline and model asset volatility based solely on equity volatility (the two are

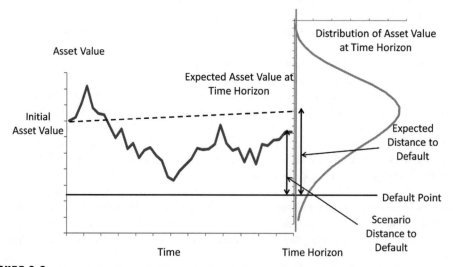

FIGURE 9.3   Expected and actual distance to default for a particular asset value scenario

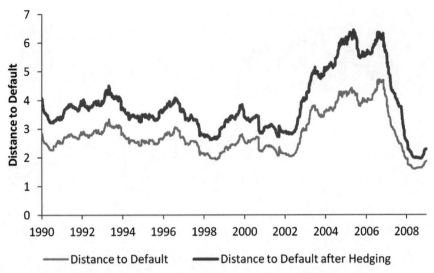

FIGURE 9.4   Distance to default for Southwest Airlines before and after hedging

proportional to each other, although they can be very different based on the capital structure of the firm). Assuming that the debt value is constant allows us to calculate asset volatility by de-levering equity volatility as follows:

$$\text{Asset volatility} = \text{Equity volatility} * \frac{\text{Equity}}{\text{Asset value}}$$

Under these simplifying assumptions, it becomes clear that Distance to Default is inversely related to equity volatility. As we observed a drop in equity volatility with hedging, we can expect a rise in the distance to default with hedging. We assume that 40% of equity value is hedged using WTI Crude Oil as in our earlier illustrations. Based on these assumptions, we plot the distance to default for a couple of US airline firms over time in Figures 9.4 and 9.5.

Although our assumptions regarding asset volatility are simplistic, they serve to illustrate how the distance to default rises with hedging of fuel price risks. A higher distance to default should result in lowered borrowing costs for airlines. This can be manifested during the issuance of bonds, as a lower spread or lower costs can be negotiated with banks at the time of arranging loan or lease financing.

We now describe some structures that can help airlines reduce their debt servicing costs while simultaneously protecting against fuel price increases.

OIL-LINKED FINANCING STRUCTURES

There are two types of strategies for combining hedging with financing products. They achieve similar goals but differ in approach. While one type of structures embeds financing costs and commodity risk management into a single structure, another type of structures links traditional loans or debts with hedges where sold optionality finances the reduction in interest costs. We begin by describing a structure called a hedged lease or a flexible oil-insulated lease.

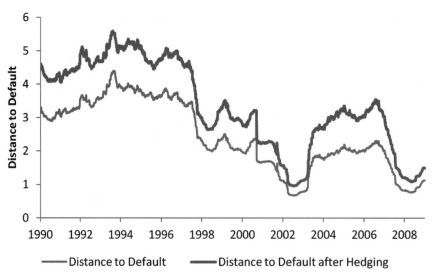

FIGURE 9.5   Distance to default for American Airlines before and after hedging

Flexible Oil-Insulated Lease

A flexible oil-insulated lease structure is a combination of a hedging structure and an operating lease. This structure can be offered by banks or financial institutions that have the capability of offering an oil-price hedge. By linking the hedging structure with a particular asset that is being financed (an aircraft in this instance), the cost of the lease can be reduced. Based on the asset being financed, the projected usage of the aircraft and the fuel consumption rate, the amount of fuel used can be estimated. We can construct the hedge based on the constraint that the total amount hedged should not exceed the projected usage. In practice, we would also allow some leeway due to the fact that there is uncertainty in demand and, hence, uncertainty in the actual usage of the aircraft.

We estimate the fuel consumption of an aircraft as follows:

$$\text{Annual fuel consumption (1)} = \frac{\text{Operating hours p.a.} * \text{Average speed}\left(\frac{\text{km}}{\text{h}}\right)}{\text{Fuel economy}\left(\frac{\text{km}}{\text{l}}\right)}$$

Let us take the case of a long-haul aircraft that is expected to be used for about 4000 hours a year (roughly 12 hours/day after allowing for a few weeks of maintenance). If it travels at an average speed of 850 km/h and has a fuel economy of 0.06 km/l, the annual fuel consumption works out to nearly 360,000 barrels of oil (converted from liters to barrels at the rate of 158.987 liters/barrel). This amounts to 30,000 barrels of oil on a monthly basis.

Let us assume that the adopted hedge ratio is 50% and that the monthly rental payments due under the operating lease are 450,000 USD. One way to make these lease payments variable and linked to fuel prices is illustrated in the structure described below, with sample terms listed in Example 9.2.

EXAMPLE 9.2: HEDGED LEASE TERMS WITH LINEAR REDUCTION IN LEASE RENTALS

Underlying Commodity:	WTI Crude Oil
Tenor:	Jan 2015–Dec 2019 (60 months)
Settlement Price:	Monthly average of daily settlement prices of the WTI front-month futures contract
Rental Payments:	USD 450,000 + (80 – Floating Price) * 15,000, floored at 0 and capped at 900,000 USD

Rental payments rise by 15,000 USD for each dollar that the WTI price settles below 80$/bbl, and vice versa. The level of 80$/bbl is close to the prevailing swap rate for the tenor at the time of entering the trade.

Thus, under this structure, lease rental payments can vary between 0 and 900,000 USD/ month; that is, up to twice the level of rental payments assuming a fixed payment schedule. However, when combined with changes in the cost of fuel, the total payments can be much lower than cases where the airline is unhedged. The diagrams of the payments to be made under this hedged lease structure, and the total monthly payments (including fuel cost) for different levels of fuel price, are shown in Figures 9.6 and 9.7.

Thus, as can be seen from the diagrams, the net cash outflow under leases and fuel purchase is smoothed across different levels of oil price. This predictability of cash flows can be very valuable to treasurers at airline companies. The benefits of the flexible oil-insulated lease structure can be summarized as follows.

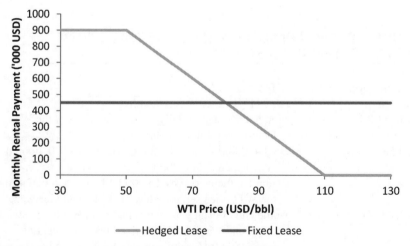

FIGURE 9.6 Payments to be made under hedged lease and fixed leases

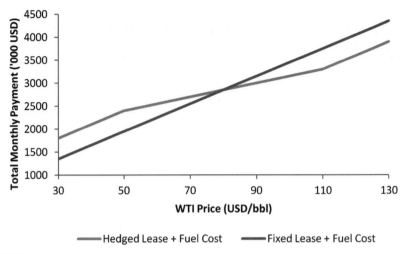

━━━ Hedged Lease + Fuel Cost   ━━━ Fixed Lease + Fuel Cost

FIGURE 9.7   Total lease and fuel payments for hedged leases and fixed leases

Benefits of Flexible Oil-Insulated Leases

1. Combine funding management and fuel price risks.
2. Allow airlines to raise asset-based financing at cheaper rates by using embedded hedging to reduce risk.
3. Stabilize overall cash flow of the airline, enabling better capital budgeting.
4. Minimize the distraction from periodic hedging decisions and are suited to firms that maintain strategic hedges.

The embedded hedging structure used in this example is a swap with a cap and a floor. Another variation of the previous structure is described in Example 9.3.

EXAMPLE 9.3: SWITCHABLE FLEXIBLE LEASE TERMS WITH LINEAR REDUCTION IN LEASE RENTALS

Underlying Commodity:	WTI Crude Oil
Tenor:	Jan 2015–Dec 2019 (60 months)
Settlement Price:	Monthly average of daily settlement prices of the WTI front-month futures contract
Rental Payments:	USD 450,000 + (75 − Floating Price) ∗ 15,000, floored at 0 and capped at 900,000 USD
	Rental Payments rise by 15,000 USD for each dollar that the WTI price settles below 75 \$/bbl, and vice versa
Switchable Option:	At the end of each year, the bank has the option to switch the counterparty back to a fixed lease payment of USD 450,000 for the remaining tenor

This structure is similar to the previous structure except that the airline counterparty grants the bank options to switch the lease rental payments from floating back to fixed payments. This structure contains Bermudan extendible/cancellable options like those discussed earlier. The value of these cancellable options is passed to the airline in the form of reduced rental payments, as can be seen in Figure 9.8.

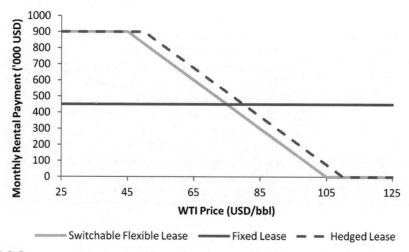

FIGURE 9.8 Payments to be made under hedged leases and fixed leases

Finally, in addition to lowering credit costs by reducing volatility, an airline can also reduce their lease costs at inception by selling optionality on fuel price. This is usually accomplished by selling OTM put options or put spreads on crude oil. However, the quantum of options to be sold to receive a meaningful reduction in lease rentals can be quite significant. Such a sale of options should be considered in the context of overall hedging for the airline and depending on the view of fuel prices. An example of a structure where initial lease costs are reduced is described in Example 9.4, and the lease and option payments to be made are shown in Figures 9.9 and 9.10, respectively.

It is to be noted that this structure differs from the previous flexible leases in that the sale of options impacts on the hedge ratio of the airline as a whole. Unlike the previous flexible lease structures, which are self-contained, initiation and risk management of this transaction requires an understanding of existing hedges and potential hedges in the future. Although this structure achieves a reduction in lease rental costs, the disadvantage of having to consider sold options under this structure in hedging and accounting decisions can reduce the attractiveness of the structure. In all the flexible lease structures, the airline can benefit from lowered credit costs (in terms of equivalent credit spread, assuming a fixed lease) and this is imputed in the pricing of the hedged leases.

Another way to achieve a reduction in upfront interest costs is through the use of cancellable structures.

EXAMPLE 9.4: FLEXIBLE OIL-INSULATED LEASE TERMS WITH PROGRESSIVE REDUCTION IN LEASE RENTALS

Underlying Commodity:	WTI Crude Oil
Tenor:	Jan 2015–Dec 2019 (60 months)
Settlement Price:	Monthly average of daily settlement prices of the WTI front-month futures contract
Rental Payments:	If Settlement Price is between 60$/bbl and 85$/bbl, USD 225,000
	If Settlement Price is above 85$/bbl, USD 225,000 + (85 – Floating Price) * 15,000, floored at 0
	If Settlement Price is below 60$/bbl, USD 450,000
	Rental Payments are halved between 60$/bbl and 85$/bbl and reduce by 15,000 USD for each dollar that the WTI price settles above 85$/bbl
Sold Options:	Airline sells put spread options with strikes of 50$/bbl and 35$/bbl for 100,000 bbl/month

Cancellable Hedged Loans as Interest Cheapeners

As opposed to flexible leases, where the quantum of interest cost reduction is determined by the hedge ratio for that particular aircraft, a cancellable hedged loan fits well with a traditional hedging program. The solution introduces the cancellable feature to existing hedges to generate optionality, instead of selling vanilla put options. This is useful for airlines that

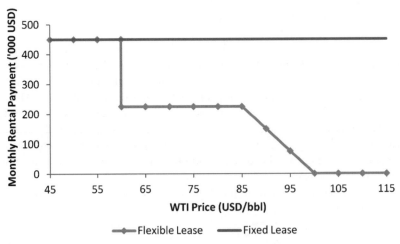

FIGURE 9.9 Payments to be made under flexible lease and fixed lease

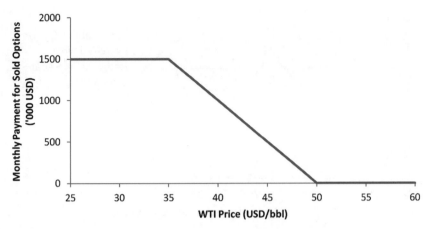

FIGURE 9.10 Additional payments to be made under sold put/spread options

have an established hedging program and maintain a minimum long-term hedge ratio as part of their strategy. Similar to the previous structure, the extent of cost reduction is determined by the amount of fuel hedged by the airline and this can be independent of the actual fuel consumed by the particular aircraft being financed.

The cancellability feature works as follows. The airline borrows money in the form of a loan or a lease to acquire an aircraft. In addition, the airline also enters into hedges during their normal course of business, which can be linked to this loan. The airline gives the loan and hedge provider (assumed to be the same) the right to cancel the hedges together with the loan repayment obligations at any point in time in the future; that is, if the hedge provider elects to cancel the hedge, no further payments under the loan would be required from the airline. Such a situation would only arise if the mark-to-market value of the hedge in favor of the airline is higher than the present value of the remaining principal and interest payments due on the loan.

Sample terms for a cancellable hedged loan are presented in Example 9.5.

EXAMPLE 9.5: CANCELLABLE HEDGED LOAN TERMS

Underlying Commodity: WTI Crude Oil
Tenor: Jan 2015–Dec 2019 (60 months)
Floating Price: Monthly average of daily settlement prices of the WTI front-month futures contract
Loan Payments: USD 450,000/month for 10 years
Underlying Hedge: Airline bought Asian swap at 70 USD/bbl for 50,000 bbl/month for 5 years
Cancellability: At the end of each year, the bank has the option to cancel both the hedge and the outstanding loan. Upon cancellation, no further payments are required or due from either party with respect to the hedge or the loan

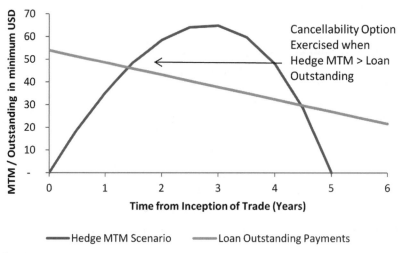

FIGURE 9.11 Cancellable option exercise scenarios

For this structure, a scenario where the cancellable option may be exercised is shown in Figure 9.11.

DVA and Cancellable Hedged Loans The cancellable structure can be more effective in terms of managing cash flows at an airline. In cases where the hedge is cancelled, the airline owns the asset and benefits from not having to pay loan payments or lease rentals. However, the airline would then be fully exposed to high fuel prices prevailing at the time. Nevertheless, the funding liquidity benefit for the airline is significant, as high fuel prices are typically accompanied by high interest rates and high financing costs for airlines. The high financing costs of the airline have an impact on the PV of the loan, which brings the "strike" of the cancellable option lower and increases the chance of exercise of the cancellable. In such a scenario, if the loan is cancelled along with the hedge, the airline would have monetized its own DVA. In other words, the loan would be cancelled at a lower price due to the airline's own risk of default.

SUMMARY

From a fuel consumer's perspective, hedging helps keep costs under control and stabilizes profits but also involves the payment of hedging costs or forgoing equity upside when fuel prices drop. While equity holders might be willing to assume increased volatility to reap higher expected returns, debtholders are short optionality on the asset value of the company and are willing to compensate for the company's hedging by lowering financing costs. In this chapter we have shown how fuel consumers can monetize some of the benefits of hedging by negotiating their financing and hedging deals as bundled transactions.

CHAPTER 10

Applied Fuel Hedging – Case Studies

In this section, we examine some case studies that will illustrate the hedging and risk management concepts that have been discussed in previous chapters. The case studies are based on actual hedging problems and risk management challenges faced by fuel consumers. We use the examples of a container shipping company and an airline to demonstrate the establishment and management of a hedging program. The case study focusing on a shipping company's fuel price exposure clarifies facets of the discussion related to the identification of risks and the choice of instruments for hedging. The study of an airline company's hedging strategy provides an overview of an existing hedge portfolio of an airline and addresses important questions related to market and credit risk aspects of portfolio management in adverse price scenarios. We discuss the novation and restructuring of the hedge portfolio along with associated credit risk, funding risk, and market risk management.

CASE STUDY 1: YM CARGO INC.

YM Cargo Inc. (YMC) is an Asia-Pacific-focused shipping company that offers cargo services worldwide. YMC mainly provides container shipping services and has also begun to offer wet freight shipping. YMC owns and charters vessels for the movement of cargo and is also developing a logistics business, offering end-to-end transport services including customs clearance, last-mile transportation over land, and integration with customers' systems to provide a seamless logistics experience. YMC's business can broadly be divided into three business segments.

- Container shipping services, which is the largest segment.
- Logistics services, including rail or road transportation for shipment of goods over land.
- Wet freight services, which include the transportation of energy commodities like crude oil and oil products using appropriate tankers.

Business Risks

YMC faces a difficult business environment and multiple business risks, the most significant of which are as follows.

A Challenging Economic Landscape   The demand for shipping is closely connected to global GDP growth and, after the financial crisis of 2008, the uneven pace of the recovery in global growth has increased the volatility in earnings for shipping companies. The container shipping and dry freight markets have been hardest hit, as benchmark indices like the Baltic Dry Index collapsed in 2008 and have not recovered significantly. The industry's gross margins have historically been in single digits and have even been negative for extended periods over the past few years.

The Race for Market Share   After the financial crisis, the trend among corporate users of shipping has been toward lowering costs and this has significantly affected the demand for YMC's services. This unforeseen elasticity in demand has also impacted the long-term plans of YMC and other industry players. Many shipping companies projected their growth rates based on their performance in the early 2000s, and placed orders for additional ships. As demand growth has not kept up with expectations, the industry is also suffering from overcapacity. This has led to companies losing pricing power over customers and many firms have resorted to pricing at marginal cost to retain market share.

Market Risk Factors

- On the cost front, fuel costs have risen in importance over the last decade and currently account for 20–30% of operating costs for large shipping companies. Fuel costs are, by far, the most volatile part of operating costs as well. YMC has forecast that fuel cost volatility is likely to persist over the next few years, coupled with an upward trend in prices as oil prices recover from their fall in late 2014.
- Capital costs also constitute a significant fraction of operating costs and with the reduction in capacity utilization, there is added pressure on the cash flows of shipping companies. YMC bears interest rate risk due to the floating-rate nature of financing used to purchase or lease vessels.
- YMC also has exposures to FX risks due to the multinational nature of its business and the fact that costs are denominated in different currencies.

Operational Mitigants

To date, YMC has mainly used operational techniques to manage its rising cost base.

- Negotiating with ports and terminals for better fees.
- Shipping route optimization by investing in sophisticated technology to determine minimal-cost routing strategies.
- Passing on fuel costs to customers. Until recently, YMC could pass on some of its fuel cost increases to its customers via a bunker fuel surcharge but, with increasing competition, it is unlikely that they would continue to be able to do so.

YMC's management needs to develop a risk management strategy that gives due importance to the volatility of individual costs and manages the ones that can significantly impact profitability. Fuel costs are the prime candidate for the implementation of a risk management strategy due to their magnitude and impact on YMC's margins.

Risk Appetite

YMC, like many other shipping companies, has traditionally been conservative in their management of fuel costs. YMC has entered into fixed-price contracts with bunker fuel suppliers or passed on costs to its customers. After identifying the business and market risks that can be hedged, the next step in setting up a risk management program involves quantifying the risk appetite of the company. YMC's risk management preferences are as follows.

- YMC can allow for variability of margins up to 4% of revenues. With fuel costs accounting for almost 30% of costs and fuel price volatility of 30–40%, the variation in margins with change in fuel prices is significantly higher than that allowed by YMC's management.
- Management has very low tolerance for cost fluctuations on committed contracts.
- With the prevailing market situation where margins have shrunk, YMC is open to new methods of managing fuel prices.
- FX rate volatility is also a significant risk factor for YMC in the current market environment. YMC operates in many emerging economies in the Asia-Pacific region that are vulnerable to sudden and sharp exchange rate movements, while a big part of its costs are denominated in USD. However, as future revenues (estimated through extrapolation techniques) are becoming less reliable, caution should be exercised with regard to long-term FX hedging.
- YMC is comfortable with the level of interest rates that it currently pays on long-term liabilities.

Hedge Program Objectives and Scope

Based on their risk management preferences, YMC's management arrives at objectives for the hedging program. The agreed objective of the hedging program is to limit the volatility in operating income arising from fuel price and FX rate movements. In addition, the developing logistics segment at YMC needs to make commitments on transportation costs to its customers over the medium term and this necessitates fixing of fuel prices to protect margins. Strategic hedging is not prevalent in the shipping industry and if YMC can gain comfort with hedging fuel exposures regularly, this can become a source of competitive advantage for the company.

A risk governance committee is constituted to be responsible for the oversight of the hedging process and to institute policies and limits to be adhered to by a competent execution team. The committee includes an independent Director/Board Member and senior management including the Managing Director/CEO, Chief Financial Officer, and Company Secretary. The risk governance committee ensures that the execution team complies with all procedures and reviews the risk policies on a regular basis. The execution team consists of the Chief Financial Officer, Company Secretary, Treasury Manager, a designated Fuel Hedging Manager, and a Procurement Manager. The execution team should have the necessary knowledge base to understand the physical aspects of fuel procurement and the financial markets, specifically fuel markets and derivatives. Involvement of senior managers like the Chief Financial Officer is critical to ensuring that appropriate and effective hedging decisions are taken and that they do not expose the firm to significant additional risks.

YMC's management sets out the scope in terms of exposures that can be hedged as follows:

- A large fraction of fuel costs (over 45%, but not exceeding 80%) to be fixed as and when the demand picture becomes clearer. YMC has allowed for up to 13% movement in total fuel costs calculated based on the margin variability allowed.
- Long-term FX hedges not to exceed 50% of the forecasted FX exposure, but exposures can be hedged up to 100% as and when forecasted exposures materialize.
- A minimum of 30% of interest-rate exposure on long-term liabilities to be hedged and additional contingent hedging of at least 30% if rates fall by 50 bps or more.
- Fuel hedging costs are not allowed to exceed 5% of the prevailing fuel cost. That is, YMC is not allowed to commit more than 5% of fuel cost as premium or transaction costs at the inception of a transaction.
- Hedging instruments should be at least 80% correlated to underlying exposures. YMC's underlying bunker fuel purchase price is very close to the price of High Sulfur Fuel Oil.
- To minimize situations of large hedging losses, the downside on the derivatives hedges should never be leveraged.
- The maximum fuel and FX hedge tenor allowed for under the program is 18 months forward.

Implementation of Hedging

After the objectives of the risk management program are clarified and shared among relevant stakeholders within the firm, YMC's hedging execution team can plan the structuring and placement of hedges.

Choice of Underlying   To select the underlying to be used for hedging bunker fuel exposure, YMC conducts an analysis of the correlation and regression between fuel oil price returns and other underlying price returns. YMC can directly use a local fuel oil benchmark like the HSFO 380 CST or other fuels whose price is correlated to fuel oil. A regression analysis shows that WTI Crude Oil, Brent Crude Oil, and Dubai Crude Oil prices are highly correlated with the HSFO. For instance, the correlation between WTI Crude Oil monthly returns and HSFO 380 CST returns over a 10-year period was 0.72, while the corresponding correlation between Brent Crude Oil and HSFO returns was 0.81.

Choice of Instruments and Tenors   Based on the scope of the hedging program, YMC's risk managers determine that financial hedging is the best means for managing fuel price risks. Physical fuel markets are illiquid beyond 3 to 6 months and pose logistical challenges related to taking delivery of cargos. Financial markets, in contrast, are much deeper in terms of liquidity and the number of counterparties available. Options and other derivatives are also more liquid in financial markets. Therefore, using financial hedging allows YMC to access different hedging instruments across a wider range of tenors and minimizes unwanted risks like counterparty risk.

HSFO 380 CST swaps are reasonably liquid for 6 months. Beyond tenors of 6 months, Brent Crude Oil and WTI Crude Oil are proposed to be used. In addition, options are liquid mainly in WTI and Brent markets, and these underlyings are to be used in any option-based transactions in order to minimize transaction costs (capped at 5% of total fuel costs). Hedging tenors of a maximum of 18 months are allowed as specified under the scope of hedging.

In addition to swaps, options, and option structures, as well as extendible swaps, the execution team can enter into spread swaps to hedge the differential between prices. For example, a HSFO CST 380 vs. WTI Crude Oil spread swap may be overlaid on an existing WTI swap to hedge the spread exposure.

Hedging Strategy   The team should endeavor to time its hedging strategy in an optimal way while abiding by the scope of the hedging program. For example, the following rationale can be used when selecting a hedge structure.

- When prices are historically low, swaps should be favored over options strategies. To lock in a longer tenor, the first 6 months can be hedged using a HSFO CST 380 swap and subsequent months can be hedged using WTI swaps. Alternatively, the HSFO CST 380 swap's level can be enhanced by making it extendible into a 6-month WTI swap.
- When prices are historically high, call options should be favored over swaps. The cap on the premium that can be spent on the options (5% of fuel cost) implies that lower volumes will be hedged when prices are high.
- Collars and other zero-cost option structures can be considered when prices are close to historical averages or are expected to settle within ranges over an extended period.

Before entering into a hedging trade, a scenario analysis should be conducted to make sure that potential hedging losses and aggregate cash payments are manageable, especially when the hedging counterparty requires the collateralization of derivative transactions.

Hedging Counterparty   Credit risk exists on OTC transactions and, depending on YMC's credit limits, transactions can be maintained as bilateral trades or they can be cleared through a central counterparty. For example, if the aggregate exposure to a hedge provider exceeds a certain threshold, or if the total notional hedged with a counterparty exceeds 50% of the outstanding hedge notional of YMC, the company can elect to clear the transactions by placing margins with a clearing counterparty.

To minimize counterparty risk, hedging is to be conducted with at least three counterparties, with no single counterparty having more than 50% of the outstanding hedges of YMC. These counterparties are to be selected after an appraisal of their creditworthiness, either based on past dealings or existing market information such as credit ratings and CDS spreads.

Legal Documentation   YMC sets up a financial hedging program by agreeing on margins and credit lines with brokers and OTC hedge providers, in addition to negotiating ISDA Master Agreements where necessary. It is common to kick-start a hedging program by entering into a plain vanilla transaction like a fixed-price swap. YMC can request sample terms and confirmations from its hedge providers to understand the settlement terms for a swap trade. A sample term sheet for such a swap transaction is detailed in Table 10.1.

This transaction is customized for YMC in terms of the notional amounts applicable for each calculation month. The notional amounts are chosen based on the demand pattern forecast by YMC. Operationally, the calculation of the settlement amount based on the floating price (which depends on the reference commodity and the specified price), the settlement dates, and business days are significant details of the transaction.

A hedging strategy that can be useful when the contango is steep and costly (in terms of fixed-price hedging levels) is a three-ways structure, as documented in Table 10.2. The trade is

TABLE 10.1   Transaction terms for a swap

Party A:	Hedge Provider A
Party B:	YMC Cargo Inc.
Trade Date:	20 November, 2015
Effective Date:	1 January, 2016
Termination Date:	30 June, 2016
Commodity:	Singapore High Sulfur Fuel Oil 380 CST
Total Notional Quantity:	88,000 MT
Notional Quantity per Calculation Period:	For each monthly Calculation Period, according to the table below

Monthly calculation period	Notional (MT)
January 2016	15,000
February 2016	13,000
March 2016	18,000
April 2016	14,000
May 2016	13,000
June 2016	15,000

Calculation Periods:	Monthly periods, from and including the Effective Date to and including the Termination Date, for a total of six Calculation Periods
Settlement Dates:	5 Business Days following the end of each Calculation Period, subject to adjustment in accordance with the Modified Following Business Day convention
Settlement Business Days:	Singapore, New York
Fixed-Amount Details	
Fixed-Price Payer:	Party B
Fixed Price:	380 USD/MT
Floating-Amount Details	
Floating-Price Payer:	Party A
Floating Price:	For a particular Calculation Period, the unweighted arithmetic mean of the Commodity Reference Price for each Pricing Date over the Calculation Period
Commodity Reference Price:	"FUEL OIL-380 CST SINGAPORE (CARGOES)-PLATTS ASIA-PACIFIC" means that the price for a Pricing Date will be that day's Specified Price per metric ton of fuel oil with a viscosity of up to 380 centistoke, stated in US dollars, published under the heading "Singapore: HSFO 380 CST" in the issue of Platts Asia-Pacific that reports prices effective on that Pricing Date
Specified Price:	Mean of Platts Singapore, which is the arithmetic average of High and Low Prices published for that Pricing Date
Pricing Dates:	Each Commodity Business Day during the relevant Calculation Period
Calculation Agent:	Party A
Documentation:	Confirmation under ISDA Master Agreement

TABLE 10.2   Transaction terms for a three-ways

Party A:	Hedge Provider
Party B:	ABC International Logistics Co.
Trade Date:	20 November, 2015
Effective Date:	1 July, 2016
Termination Date:	31 December, 2016
Reference Commodity:	OIL-WTI-NYMEX
Total Notional Quantity:	300,000 barrels
Notional Quantity per Calculation Period:	50,000 barrels/month
Calculation Periods:	Monthly periods, from and including the Effective Date to and including the Termination Date, for a total of six Calculation Periods
Settlement Dates:	5 Business Days following the end of each Calculation Period, subject to adjustment in accordance with the Modified Following Business Day convention
Settlement Business Days:	Singapore, New York
Premium:	0 USD/bbl

Floating-Amount Details
Upper Cap

Floating-Price Payer:	Party B
Cap Price:	80 USD/bbl

Lower Cap

Floating-Price Payer:	Party A
Cap Price:	66 USD/bbl

Floor

Floating-Price Payer:	Party B
Floor Price:	58 USD/bbl

Terms Applicable to Each Cap and Floor

Floating Price:	For a particular Calculation Period, the unweighted arithmetic mean of the Commodity Reference Price for each Pricing Date over the Calculation Period
Commodity Reference Price:	"OIL-WTI-NYMEX" means that the price for a Pricing Date will be that day's Specified Price per barrel of West Texas Intermediate light sweet crude oil on the NYMEX of the Futures Contract for the Delivery Date, stated in US dollars, as made public by the NYMEX on that Pricing Date
Specified Price:	Official Settlement Price
Delivery Date:	First nearby month
Pricing Dates:	Each Commodity Business Day during the relevant Calculation Period
Calculation Agent:	Party A
Documentation:	Confirmation under ISDA Master Agreement

structured to be zero-cost at inception. The underlying used here is WTI Crude Oil, as required under the hedging program when options are used.

As the transaction gets closer to pricing, the liquidity for fuel oil increases. The basis risk can then be managed using spread swaps as follows. The execution team can enter into a crack/spread swap as the structure above matures, in order to lock in the differential between WTI Crude Oil and fuel oil price. The transaction is structured as documented in Table 10.3.

Thus, long-dated hedging with a liquid underlying using option structures, coupled with spread hedging closer to pricing dates, can provide YMC with a viable, lower-cost option than hedging with a straight swap. However, YMC does take on the risk of the crack spread changing prior to the execution of the spread swap.

Portfolio Monitoring

Once these trades are executed and properly documented, the hedging portfolio should be monitored to ensure that it is providing the expected protection from fuel prices. This includes ensuring that physical procurement prices do not deviate significantly from financial benchmarks that are hedged (i.e., physical discounts or premiums are not volatile), actual volumes consumed are in line with hedged notionals (to ensure there is optimum hedging and no over-hedging), and the settlement calculations are accurate and reflect the economics of trades entered into. Portfolio risk metrics for YMC's financial derivative portfolio can then be calculated.

In order to ensure that their measurement of sensitivities and valuations is accurate, YMC can request for weekly or monthly valuations to be provided for their hedge portfolios. Weekly updates on portfolio values can significantly improve YMC's response time for restructuring or adding trades to their portfolio and is recommended when market volatility is high.

In addition, CSAs negotiated between YMC and its hedge counterparties (if any) need to be optimized for managing YMC's funding liquidity. The team must try to execute bilateral CSAs where possible, or require the threshold for top-up of margins to be reasonably high so that there are no immediate liquidity requirements once a trade is executed. Periodic reviews of counterparty creditworthiness are also recommended. Additionally, the team should also consider capping the potential downside using capped MTM or capped payment structures whenever such features are available cheaply.

Finally, YMC's management should review the risk management program periodically (at least annually) and take an inventory of risks facing the firm to identify new risks or trends that can affect the firm's profitability going forward.

CASE STUDY 2: WORLDWIDE AIRLINES

Worldwide Airlines (WWA) is a large airline company primarily based in Europe. WWA is an international carrier with a competitive presence across many routes. WWA serves destinations worldwide by implementing a hub-and-spoke model, with a European hub catering to both traffic within Europe as well as travelers between the Americas and the Asia-Pacific region. WWA is a well-established airline and has been managing its fuel price risks proactively since the mid-1990s.

TABLE 10.3   Transaction terms for a spread swap

Party A:	Hedge Provider
Party B:	ABC International Logistics Co.
Trade Date:	20 May, 2016
Effective Date:	1 July, 2016
Termination Date:	31 December, 2016
Reference Commodities:	FUEL OIL-380 CST SINGAPORE (CARGOES)-PLATTS ASIA-PACIFIC; OIL-WTI-NYMEX
Total Notional Quantity:	300,000 barrels
Notional Quantity per Calculation Period:	50,000 barrels/month
Calculation Periods:	Monthly periods, from and including the Effective Date to and including the Termination Date, for a total of six Calculation Periods
Settlement Dates:	5 Business Days following the end of each Calculation Period, subject to adjustment in accordance with the Modified Following Business Day convention
Settlement Business Days:	Singapore, New York
Fixed-Amount Details	
Fixed-Price Payer:	Party B
Fixed Price:	−7.0 USD/barrel
Floating-Amount Details	
Floating-Price Payer:	Party A
Floating Price:	For a particular Calculation Period, the unweighted arithmetic mean of the Reference Spread for each Pricing Date over the Calculation Period
Reference Spread:	The difference between Commodity Reference Price 1 and Commodity Reference Price 2, expressed in USD/barrel
	That is, (Commodity Reference Price 1/6.35) – Commodity Reference Price 2, where 6.35 is the Conversion Factor between MT and barrels
Commodity Reference Price 1:	"FUEL OIL-380 CST SINGAPORE (CARGOES)-PLATTS ASIA-PACIFIC" means that the price for a Pricing Date will be that day's Specified Price per metric ton of fuel oil with a viscosity of up to 380 centistoke, stated in US dollars, published under the heading "Singapore: HSFO 380 CST" in the issue of Platts Asia-Pacific that reports prices effective on that Pricing Date
Specified Price (for Commodity Reference Price 1):	Mean of Platts Singapore, which is the arithmetic average of High and Low Prices published for that Pricing Date
Commodity Reference Price 2:	"OIL-WTI-NYMEX" means that the price for a Pricing Date will be that day's Specified Price per barrel of West Texas Intermediate light sweet crude oil on the NYMEX of the Futures Contract for the Delivery Date, stated in US dollars, as made public by the NYMEX on that Pricing Date
Specified Price (for Commodity Reference Price 2):	Official Settlement Price
Delivery Date:	First Nearby Month
Pricing Dates:	Each Commodity Business Day during the relevant Calculation Period
Calculation Agent:	Party A
Documentation:	Confirmation under ISDA Master Agreement

Evolution of WWA's Hedging Strategy

WWA's hedge program has changed significantly over the previous decade, moving from primarily physical price risk management to using futures and OTC exotic transactions for hedging.

From Supplier Counterparty Risk to Liquidity Shortage   Initially, WWA managed commodity price risks by entering into fixed-price contracts with their fuel suppliers in advance of their purchases. Fixed-price contracts with fuel suppliers might appear to be straightforward, as they help hedge the price risk for both the supplier and the consumer at the same time without involving third parties that would require margins. However, with the high volatility of fuel prices, counterparty risk considerations make these contracts quite risky. When a physical fuel trader defaults due to mark-to-market losses, the airline can also suffer disruption of physical supply, which can be a major issue. To mitigate this risk, WWA resorted to dissociating physical supply from price hedging, thereby moving their counterparty credit exposure from physical suppliers to more creditworthy counterparties. WWA started entering into futures contracts linked to crude oil and diesel on financial exchanges.

Over time, the airline realized that mitigating its counterparty risk had given rise to liquidity risk. In the past, the fixed-price contracts with suppliers did not require upfront payments. This was great for the airline as it was able to enter into long-term contracts. However, fully collateralized futures contracts required significant margins to be placed, restricting the airline's ability to enter into long-term and high-volume hedges out of concern for cash-flow shortage if and when volatility picked up. Higher volatility translates to higher initial margins in addition to increasing the possibility of high MTMs, which require high variation margins.

Lost in Contango   As liquidity in the commodity markets increased and banks began offering commodity hedging services, WWA started hedging in the OTC market with banks. This was advantageous to WWA, as they were not required to post initial margins with banks, thus freeing up capital that would otherwise be stuck with an exchange clearing house. It also allowed WWA to enter into more customized contracts like average-price (Asian) swaps. Initially, the instruments favored by WWA for hedging were mainly Asian swaps and options linked to WTI Crude Oil and Jet – North West Europe. With the increase in liquidity of Brent Crude Oil, WWA also started hedging using Brent and ICE Gasoil.

As oil prices started moving upwards in 2005, WWA increased their hedge volumes and began exploring other derivatives for risk management. However, the crude oil futures term structure moved from backwardation to contango in 2006, reflecting the hedging pressure from fuel consumers and revealing interesting behaviors of fuel hedgers. Like other fuel hedgers, WWA's Fuel Risk Management Officer was comfortable entering into swaps when the curve was backwardated, mainly due to the expected positive cash flow at the start of the trade (positive carry). Backwardation implies that the front end would be higher than the swap price, resulting in a positive cash flow at the start of the trade. This sweetener was encouraging to fuel risk managers, as they could show early positive results from hedging to their firm's management. The effect was also amplified by rising front-month prices. The switch to a contango shape of the forward curve completely changed the expected cash-flow schedule of simple hedges like swaps. When using swaps, risk officers had to expect to incur cash outflows at the start of the hedging period, which might not be easy to explain to top management due to their lack of familiarity with commodity curves. Moreover, the contango experienced in

2006 was a normal contango that usually involves rolling costs. From WWA's perspective, the roll would be costly as the expected future price is lower than the forward price.

Dealing with the Costs of Contango   As competition surged between banks providing fuel hedging services, WWA approached sophisticated banks to tailor solutions that could cope with the contango by mitigating the negative-carry issue, thus enhancing the expected cash-flow profile of hedging structures. Many banks suggested selling optionality to compensate for the contango costs. One of the proposed structures was a three-ways, where the airline is short a put and long a call spread. The sale of the call with a higher strike was used to enhance the odds of positive cash flow at the start of the transaction, if the crude price remained unchanged. The airline also started using an extendible swap structure, which was commonly used in the market at the time. The extendible swap structure allowed WWA to get better hedge levels for their swaps, in comparison with vanilla swaps, while giving their hedge providers an option to extend the swap. However, with the trend in prices being upward, extendible swaps were not extended by hedge providers as it was not advantageous for them to do so. This left WWA unhedged over the extendible period, but the structure was more profitable for them compared with vanilla swaps for the guaranteed period. The initial success of these structures piqued the airline's interest in more exotic hedging strategies.

The economics of the structure (for the guaranteed period) were further enhanced by the introduction of Bermudan extendible structures, but these structures were again cancellable at the hedge provider's discretion. As the market was trending upwards at the time, these extendibles were usually early-terminated.

Getting Addicted to the Medicine   To combat the negative effects of contango, airline risk managers were drawn toward using structured hedges and WWA was not an exception. Structured hedging methods were used more frequently by risk managers, even after the oil market switched to backwardation in 2007. This was primarily due to the fact that the economics for the hedger in these hedging strategies were further enhanced by the backwardation. Attracted by the profitability of these structures, WWA started using TAR structures toward the second half of 2007 (Figure 10.1). These structures were new to the commodities market, while having

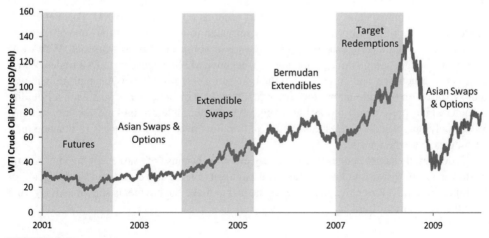

FIGURE 10.1   Crude oil price and derivatives usage by WWA

been used in other markets like FX for some time. These structures capped the total payout (the target) to the hedger prior to an early termination, if any. In fact, the termination of these structures was dependent on the payments accrued to the hedger, thus removing the discretionary element involved in extendible structures. Target redemptions work well for consumers when prices are stable or trending upwards. Consequently, through 2007 and the first half of 2008, WWA entered into more TAR structures as and when the previous structures knocked out, which was at relatively short intervals of a few months. From a credit usage perspective, TARs were also much more interesting for exotics trading desks than extendibles, as TAR trades were recurrent and trading desks earned high margins for every new trade. However, with each new structure, the hedge level ratcheted upwards as fuel prices rose. At the same time, WWA also increased the use of leveraged notional amounts (i.e., they sold put options with higher notional quantities than the options purchased by them).

Hedging Transactions Executed by WWA

WWA executed extendible and TAR transactions from 2007 to mid-2008, which were usually not extended or were early-terminated by their hedgers. However, during the second half of 2008, oil prices reversed direction and began to tumble, affecting the expected life of their outstanding hedges at that time.

Trades Executed Pre-Global Financial Crisis (GFC)   In mid-2008, the crude oil market had been trending upwards strongly, making new highs on a weekly basis. At the time, many market observers and oil market researchers were envisaging even higher prices, making predictions for crude oil to rally further to levels close to 200$/bbl. In July 2008, WWA entered into a TAR hedge transaction with its hedge counterparties with the terms described in Table 10.4.

Trades Done Post-GFC   From July 2008 onwards, oil prices started dropping and oscillated significantly in September 2008 due to the turmoil caused by the bankruptcy of Lehman Brothers. For October 2008, WWA was required to pay out on their hedge as the floating price fixed below the put strike. In order to preserve liquidity, WWA entered into additional TAR transactions with ITM calls and low target profit parameters, which were expected to provide short-term cash inflows and knock out in short order as oil prices stabilized. This belief was guided by the fact that oil prices had already retreated to levels seen at the start of the year. As fuel prices continued to drop precipitously and economic conditions worsened, WWA was locked into hedges at high prices, showing high negative MTM values for its TAR trades. WWA explored restructuring and unwinding of the transactions. However, WWA's management was more focused on operational matters arising from a drop in customer demand and a liquidity crunch, which pre-empted the airline from paying to completely unwind the transactions. WWA only purchased a modest amount of put options over short durations to manage their cash flows in the near term.

However, these put hedges were not very effective because of market timing and as soon as they expired, the airline had to make full payments on the target redemption hedges. For example, for the TAR detailed here, the airline had to make the payments shown in Table 10.5 over the last quarter of 2008.

TABLE 10.4 Transaction terms for a target redemption collar

Party A:	Hedge Provider
Party B:	Worldwide Airlines (WWA)
Trade Date:	10 July, 2008
Effective Date:	1 August, 2008
Termination Date:	31 January, 2011, subject to the Knock-Out Event
Reference Commodity:	OIL-WTI-NYMEX
Calculation Periods:	Monthly periods, from and including the Effective Date to and including the Termination Date, for a total of 30 Calculation Periods
Settlement Dates:	5 Business Days following the end of each Calculation Period, subject to adjustment in accordance with the Modified Following Business Day convention
Settlement Business Days:	New York
Business Day Convention:	Modified Following
Floating-Amount Details	
Cap	
Floating-Price Payer:	Party A
Cap Price:	112 USD/bbl
Total Cap Notional Quantity:	1,500,000 barrels
Cap Notional Quantity per Calculation Period:	50,000 barrels per month
Floor	
Floating-Price Payer:	Party B
Floor Price:	95 USD/bbl
Total Floor Notional Quantity:	1,500,000 barrels
Floor Notional Quantity per Calculation Period:	50,000 barrels per month
Terms Applicable to Both Cap and Floor	
Floating Price:	For a particular Calculation Period, the unweighted arithmetic mean of the Commodity Reference Price for each Pricing Date over the Calculation Period
Commodity Reference Price:	"OIL-WTI-NYMEX" means that the price for a Pricing Date will be that day's Specified Price per barrel of West Texas Intermediate light sweet crude oil on the NYMEX of the Futures Contract for the Delivery Date, stated in US dollars, as made public by the NYMEX on that Pricing Date
Specified Price:	Official Settlement Price
Delivery Date:	First nearby month
Pricing Dates:	Each Commodity Business Day during the relevant Calculation Period
Settlement Amounts, subject to the Knock-Out Event:	For a particular Calculation Period, subject to the Knock-Out Event not occurring and the Target Profit level not being reached
	If the Floating Price for the Calculation Period is higher than the Cap Price:
	Party A pays (Floating Price – Cap Price) * Cap Notional Quantity for such Calculation Period

(continued)

TABLE 10.4   *(Continued)*

	If the Floating Price is between the Cap Price and the Floor Price, neither party makes any payments If the Floating Price is lower than the Floor Price: **Party B pays (Floor Price – Floating Price) * Floor Notional Quantity for such Calculation Period** The sum of all payments made by Party A will be subject to a maximum of the Target Profit. If the Settlement Amount calculated above, when added to previous payments made by Party A, would cause the sum of payments to exceed the Target Profit, the Settlement Amount would be adjusted such that the sum of all payments made by Party A does not exceed the Target Profit. For clarity, if the Target Profit is reached during a particular period, a Knock-Out Event is said to have occurred
Knock-Out Event:	A Knock-Out Event is said to occur on a Settlement Date if the calculated Settlement Amount for that period, when added to previous settlements in favor of Party B, equals or exceeds the Target Profit If a Knock-Out Event occurs, the settlement due from Party A to Party B will be reduced such that the sum of all payments made to Party B does not exceed the Target Profit. For clarity, in case of a Knock-Out Event occurring: **Party A pays Party B (Target Profit – Sum of previous positive settlements to Party B)**
Target Profit:	25 USD/bbl * Cap Notional Quantity per Calculation Period (i.e., 25 * 50,000 USD = 1,250,000 USD)
Calculation Agent:	Party A
Documentation:	Confirmation under ISDA Master Agreement

TABLE 10.5   WTI price fixings and settlements under the target redemption

	WTI price	Payment (USD/bbl)	WWA payment (USD)
Oct-08	77.129	17.871	893,550.00
Nov-08	57.792	37.208	1,860,400.00
Dec-08	41.751	53.249	2,662,450.00

Wrong-Way Risk Transactions   Burdened by these high hedge payments, WWA looked to manage their cash flows by entering into directionally opposite transactions. In late 2008, WWA entered into producer-side TAR structures, that is, structures where the hedger benefits when prices fall. It was hoped that these transactions would hedge the airline against falling prices, while the settlement amounts due under these trades compensated, in part, for the losses under the original TAR trades. One of the wrong-way transactions entered into by WWA is described briefly in Table 10.6.

It was expected that the wrong-way transactions would provide some relief on the settlements to be made to its counterparties, in addition to knocking out early. This thinking was

TABLE 10.6   Abridged terms for a producer target redemption swap

Party A:	Hedge Provider
Party B:	Worldwide Airlines (WWA)
Tenor:	24 months, subject to Knock-Out
Reference Commodity:	OIL-WTI-NYMEX
Total Notional Quantity:	4,800,000 barrels
Notional Quantity per Calculation Period:	200,000 barrels per month
Calculation Periods:	Monthly periods, from and including the Effective Date to and including the Termination Date, for a total of 24 Calculation Periods
Fixed-Amount Details	
Fixed-Price Payer:	Party A
Fixed Price:	80 USD/bbl
Floating-Amount Details	
Floating-Price Payer:	Party B
Target Profit:	60 USD/bbl * Notional Quantity per Calculation Period (i.e., 60 * 200,000 USD = 12,000,000 USD)

encouraged by the steep contango that helped achieve TAR strikes well above the spot price. Initially, this strategy worked well with the first transactions getting knocked out.

Oil prices bottomed in early 2009 and began to creep upwards again. At this point, WWA continued to be burdened by high outflows from their initial TAR hedges, while the new "wrong-way" hedges did not effectively offset these payments as prices had risen closer to the sold option strikes.

WWA was stuck in a situation where there would be net outflows irrespective of the direction of oil price movement. This was a cause of concern for both WWA and its hedge counterparties. WWA's top management requested a full analysis of the hedging transactions from a cash-flow perspective from its hedge provider, BM Capital (BMC).

Hedge Portfolio Analysis

A simplified portfolio view of outstanding hedging transactions is shown in Table 10.7.

TABLE 10.7   WWA hedge portfolio

	Direction	Notional (bbl/month)	Leverage	Trade type	Tenor (months)	Strike prices	Remaining target (if any)
1	WWA buys	50,000	1 × 1	Target redemption collar	15	112c/ 95p	21
2	WWA buys	50,000	1 × 1	Target redemption collar	20	85c/ 75p	40
3	WWA sells	250,000	1 × 1	Target redemption swap	30	78c/ 65p	45

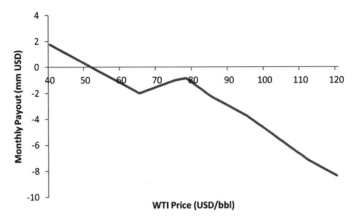

FIGURE 10.2   Monthly payout for WWA assuming no knock-outs

BMC began the analysis of the portfolio by aggregating the payouts from all the outstanding trades. Developing the portfolio payout helps in understanding the cash flows at different levels of fuel price and can make potential restructuring transactions apparent. For the portfolio of trades discussed earlier, the portfolio payout profile for WWA for a particular month before a KO event is graphed in Figure 10.2.

However, a payout profile only displays the payout calculated for a particular month. For exotic products with KO features, like TAR structures, the settlement for a particular month depends on the path that prices have taken from the beginning of the trade. Specifically, the total payout is capped under a target redemption. One way to better visualize this total payout is to aggregate the notionals under a transaction to determine the payout at a constant price level (Figure 10.3). For example, the payout for a consumer collar with a target can be displayed as the payout for the sold put added to the payout from a bought call, which is capped at the target profit level.

Additional granularity in payoff profiles can be obtained by constructing the payoffs for a particular interval of time. For example, the payoffs for the first year can be different from

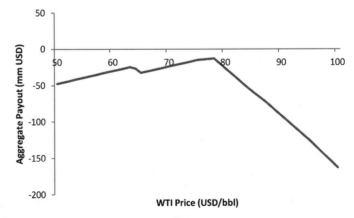

FIGURE 10.3   Aggregate portfolio payout for WWA, assuming WTI price stays at a particular level

those for the second year, as some trades expire earlier. This can also be applied to the Greeks of a transaction – referred to as "bucketing."

From the payout graph, it is fairly obvious that WWA is exposed to both rising and falling fuel prices outside a range. In other words, WWA is short volatility. If oil prices were to move rapidly in either direction, WWA would be faced with having to pay out large amounts under their hedges. Given the management view that oil prices would continue to rise, it would be prudent to address the sold call options under the TAR structure promptly.

How Did the Portfolio Become So Unfavorable? To sum up, looking at the payout analysis, the payout is likely to be negative most of the time. This can give the impression that the banks have executed unfair trades with the airline. However, if the same analysis is done at the inception of each trade, the situation would look different. Here is a summary of the events that led to this payout profile.

1. Executed right-way hedging transactions (consumer TARs).
2. Market turned against the hedges and cash payments were required from the airline.
3. Partial (but inefficient) immunization of the existing long position carried out with a positive-carry transaction.
   a. Short WTI position to limit the impact of dropping prices.
   b. Short volatility – sold optionality to collect short-term cash to cover payments required under existing TARs.
4. The payout enhancement of the early months (due to the positive cash flow from the producer TAR) was matched by a leveraged deterioration of subsequent months' payouts. This is similar to the case of an option seller in the sense that, once an option premium is received, there is no further upside as only cash outflows can occur.

The downside of the portfolio can be likened to that of a straddle, composed of

- a short up-and-out put and
- a short down-and-out call.

Credit Lines and Collateralization Issues

After further analysis, it was also found that the existing hedging structures were not only unfavorable from a cash-flow perspective but also very inefficient from a credit standpoint. The trades were executed with different hedging counterparties. For example, the producer (sold) TAR was split across three banks with exactly the same terms but the other two consumer TARs were traded with a single counterparty. Moreover, WWA executed CSAs with all hedging banks except BMC, with whom they had a good relationship and substantially better credit terms.

Analysis of the executed CSAs showed that they were all unilateral with very low thresholds. This was very costly for WWA from a funding perspective, as they had to place collateral with the banks with which they had negative MTM, but never benefited from the positive MTMs. This could have been entirely avoided if the CSAs were two-way CSAs, allowing WWA to receive collateral on its positive MTM positions and post it with other banks.

To understand the impact of the CSAs on their funding liquidity, WWA should have conducted a proper MTM analysis of the portfolio at different price levels, making suitable assumptions about forward and volatility curve dynamics. Such analysis could have given a clear picture of the potential funding need when entering into these hedging transactions.

Portfolio Novation   As it was too late and time-consuming to renegotiate the CSAs with relevant banks, the solution that came to mind was to make sure that all these trades were netted against each other.

The management of WWA took a decision to novate (replace the counterparty to their hedges) and restructure their hedge portfolio; they approached their hedging counterparty BMC for an analysis of their hedge portfolio and possible restructuring ideas. While WWA's hedges were executed with different banks, it was preferable to approach BMC due to the strength of their relationship and, more importantly, the significant credit line that it had advanced WWA, which allowed for uncollateralized transactions. The novation would help unlock a significant amount of cash posted as collateral with other hedging banks (Figure 10.4).

In the absence of a CSA, a hedge portfolio that is underwater for WWA (has negative MTM from WWA's perspective) would have to be financed by the hedge provider. This is because BMC would have matching positions with third parties that are collateralized. Therefore, the novation of transactions is not a costless exercise and funding costs are incurred by BMC's trading desk to hold these positions. The novation is similar to BMC's trading desk extending a loan to WWA. BMC's trading desk will have to take into account its costs of funding from their treasury (that gives the FVA) as well as the credit charge (CVA). However, as the trades will be restructured, it is better to calculate these charges based on the new restructured portfolio

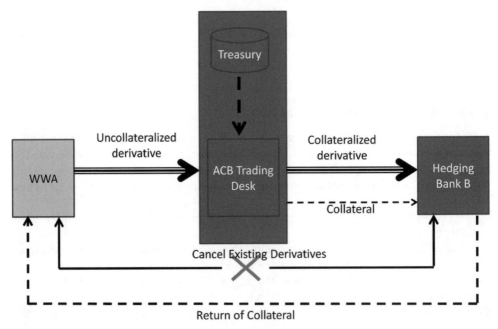

FIGURE 10.4   Novation from hedging bank B to BMC

to take into account the change in the expected exposure profile and how the cash flows might be extended.

Restructuring WWA's Portfolio

There are multiple options to be considered when restructuring a hedge portfolio. These include the method of restructuring, the final payout desired, and the cost of restructuring.

Overlay Structure   Once all trades with third parties are novated to BMC, it is tempting to present the restructuring as an overlay to the existing trades. In other words, the existing structures are kept as is and a derivative is added to change the payout to a desirable one. Since both the TAR trades are OTM for WWA, they behave more like vanilla structures. The use of a vanilla overlay might be a solution assuming no TAR knock-out.

However, adding a vanilla overlay may not have the desired effect due to the presence of exotic options in the portfolio. This could be remedied by including knock-out features in the overlay structure to offset the knock-outs under the TAR structures, although the transaction would be quite complex and unnecessary.

Instead of unwinding a target redemption that is deeply OTM for WWA, the airline can choose to keep all the upside on the exotics, as they are cheap and can be thought of as lottery tickets. For example, a consumer target redemption can be restructured in such a way that the target knock-out only affects the downside (the put). In other words, the TAR contract can be restructured so that only the put gets terminated when the target is reached, but the call option remains alive. Such a restructuring would be cheap and very effective.

To restructure the sold call options (under the producer TAR), one solution would be to replace them with put options such that the mark-to-market of the structure is the same. This is almost equivalent to unwinding the sold target redemption. Another solution would be to unwind the producer TAR and transfer the MTM to a swap structure.

In summary, once WWA's management agrees about its ideal payout profile, the overlay will just be a derivative that is the difference between the ideal payout and the existing payout. The important factor to consider is the cost of such an overlay. The current profile is far from a long WTI position and moving to a long position will imply crossing the bid/offer spread. Moreover, the current short-volatility position is very unstable and WWA should avoid a negative-convexity situation, especially when it is due to being short lottery tickets (cheap OTM optionality).

Unwind and Replace   The overlay method can be a very cumbersome exercise that makes the documentation of the new portfolio extremely complicated, with multiple offsetting legs in place. This exposes both parties to unnecessary legal risks. Moreover, there could be concerns about the enforceability of netting agreements in WWA's chosen jurisdiction. It was therefore advisable to keep the book clean by replacing all existing trades with new simple trades that are documented as a single contract.

As WWA expects oil prices to rebound, the optimal trade would be to enter into a swap transaction, taking full advantage of price increases. As WWA faces high cash outflows under the existing transactions over the first few months, it can restructure the portfolio to a longer-term swap, minimizing the additional cash flows that would have to be paid out on the derivative.

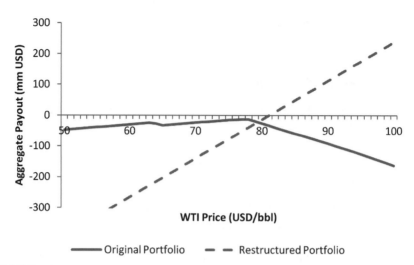

FIGURE 10.5　Original and restructured portfolio payoffs

　　WWA chose to restructure its portfolio into a longer-dated swap transaction. WWA cancelled their existing portfolio and purchased a swap for 36 months on a notional of 350,000 barrels per month. An initial indicative pricing of the swap, ignoring funding and credit costs, showed that the unwind price of the existing portfolio can be achieved using a swap at 81 USD/bbl for 36 months and a notional of 350,000 bbl/month (Figure 10.5). This indicative pricing assumed that the netting benefits of the Greeks are not significant.

Counterparty Risk and Funding Considerations for BMC

Upon restructuring a transaction, the MTM of the portfolio does not change significantly. However, the expected exposure and potential future exposure profiles can be very different. In the old portfolio, the PFE was driven by the downside associated with high WTI prices. This was a wrong-way risk and the PFE should have been calculated conditional on default to take into account the correlation between the MTM changes and the probability of default of the airline. In the new simple structure, the PFE is associated with dropping WTI prices. This constitutes right-way risk and it is conservative to use standard PFE and EE to evaluate the counterparty risk. In the case of the restructured portfolio, the potential future exposure to WWA for a hedge counterparty can be much higher if fuel prices dropped compared with the initial portfolio (Figure 10.6). This is due to the added notional on the downside from the long-term swap that replaced the TARs.

　　Similarly, the expected exposure profiles prior to and after restructuring the transaction can also be plotted. The PFE and EE profiles are derived using the standard calculation that is not conditional on default. In other words, the profiles discussed above assume no correlation between the probability of default of the counterparty and the mark-to-market changes. The peak PFEs for the old portfolio and the new portfolio are $217 million and $362 million, respectively. The peak is reached in about 8 months for both portfolios, which does not change the shape of the exposure significantly.

　　It is also worthwhile noting that the PFE and the EE profiles coincide on the starting date. This is an important characteristic that should always be checked to avoid erratic exposure calculations. At $t = 0$, we should always find EE = PFE = MTM. If we use the same observation

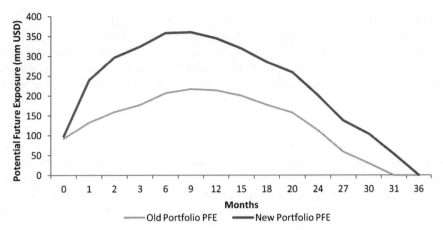

FIGURE 10.6   Portfolio PFE before and after restructuring

on the new portfolio, we can infer that the MTM of the new portfolio (which is equal to the EE and PFE at $t = 0$) is higher than that of the old portfolio. This difference in MTM is mainly due to the costs of restructuring, which include those related to the hedging of the residual delta and vega profiles.

It is important to ensure that the exposure profiles are being calculated accurately. Many counterparties do not calculate exposures on a portfolio basis but on a transaction basis, due to logistical constraints. For example, in the case of the old portfolio, the PFE and the EE should not be calculated by adding up the PFE and the EE of the three TARs. This is mainly due to the offsetting effect between the producer and the consumer hedges (an increase in the MTM of the producer TAR because of a rise in price is accompanied by a decrease in the MTM of the consumer TARs).

Note on PFE Comparison   The use of the PFE profiles above is an oversimplification of the counterparty risk analysis because the standard PFEs and EEs do not reflect the impact of the wrong-way risk, which is inherent in the old portfolio. If the PFE and the EE were calculated conditional on default, the number would look different and the PFE of the old portfolio would look much higher than what is shown in the profile above. The use of the standard PFE in our analysis is a conservative approach, as we are restructuring a wrong-way risk to a right-way risk. But one should bear in mind that the peak PFE conditional on default might be a multiple of the standard PFE, depending on the volatility of the counterparty credit spread and its correlation with fuel price. This is especially the case for short positions for which the exposure can theoretically be unlimited compared with long positions that are capped at the committed purchase price (as the underlying price cannot be lower than zero).

Credit and Funding Charges   As discussed earlier, the novation of all the trades to BMC should incur charges related to funding and counterparty risk. We also explained that the non-collateralization of the derivatives between WWA and BMC is equivalent to BMC extending an unsecured loan to WWA. When the trade is initially uncollateralized, the new counterparty would typically require a novation fee from the existing hedging bank. The existing hedging bank should be willing to pay a fee not exceeding the FVA and the CVA of the transaction (or whatever reserves were kept for this purpose). However, while most banks would agree about the CVA (which only depends on the creditworthiness of the counterparty), the FVA is specific to the hedging bank. It is very likely that the FVA calculated by BMC is different from that calculated by the existing hedging bank, depending on the internal funding cost of each bank. This is not the case in our example, as all existing derivatives have been collateralized, which means that existing hedging banks will be unwilling to pay for the funding and credit charges of BMC. It is only fair that the airline WWA covers these costs, as it is the ultimate beneficiary of the release of collateral under the existing CSAs with other banks.

The FVA and the CVA of the novated portfolio can be calculated from the EE of the old portfolio by applying a funding spread and a CDS spread to the EE profile. For example, assuming a funding spread of 100 bps and a CDS spread of 200 bps (ignoring the recovery rate), we could say that the charges would be approximately $4 million for the CVA and $2 million for the FVA. However, this rough calculation does not take into account the wrong-way risk. In fact, the CVA should be based on the expected exposure conditional on default. The wrong-way risk CVA can be much higher than $4 million and WWA might not be willing to pay cash to cover for these costs.

A good solution is to combine both the novation and the restructuring into one transaction. In this way, WWA avoids paying for high wrong-way risk CVA because the ultimate hedge is a consumer swap, which is a right-way transaction. Moreover, the final CVA and FVA costs can be charged by adjusting the swap level without requiring WWA to pay cash. From BMC's perspective, the transaction will incur CVA and FVA charges that can be calculated either from the EE of the new portfolio (the swap) or by adding incremental CVA and incremental FVA to the numbers calculated earlier. The incremental CVA and FVA are calculated based on the incremental EE profile (Figure 10.7).

The total FVA charge is roughly around $2.9 million and the CVA charge is roughly about $5.8 million. This is calculated assuming constant funding and CDS spreads of 100 bps and 200 bps for the bank and the hedger, respectively, and neglecting the recovery rate effect on the CVA calculation. We also assume that there is no correlation between the MTM and the funding or CDS spreads.

To justify the high costs of restructuring, some traders may present a restructuring as two transactions, an unwinding of the original transaction and entering into a new transaction. By doing so, the hedger is given the impression that the trading desk will incur the costs of

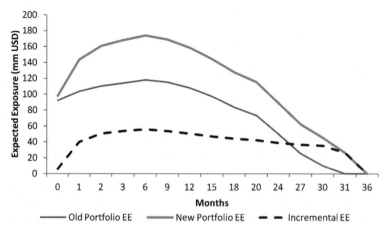

FIGURE 10.7 Original and restructured portfolio expected exposures and incremental expected exposure

unwinding the position and the costs of entering into a fresh transaction. This is usually wrong! Fuel hedgers should only be charged the hedging costs of the incremental derivative:

Incremental transaction = New derivatives portfolio – Old derivatives portfolio

This means that only the incremental risk is hedged and the closer the risks of the old and the new transactions are, the lower is the incremental risk (and the restructuring costs). It is important to remember that the novated portfolio is already hedged on a back-to-back basis and BMC is just sitting in the middle, as we described earlier.

To restructure the existing portfolio into a swap, BMC will need to hedge (Swap – Old portfolio). This can be achieved by immunizing the Greeks of the incremental derivative (Swap – Old portfolio). The incremental derivative is exotic by nature as it contains target redemptions, which implies that the hedging will be dynamic. No matter how restructuring is done, it boils down to calculating the Greeks' profiles of the incremental portfolio and estimating the cost of immunizing the risks.

The execution of this novation and restructuring has to be documented carefully to make sure that there is no misunderstanding between all involved parties and that the information about the existing trades with third parties is accurate. WWA should also require details such as the credit spread used, the PFE profile, EE profile, funding spread, delta profile, and vega profile. With the help of a derivatives expert, these numbers can be cross-checked for any discrepancy. If the CVA and FVA charges are high, WWA should ask BMC to include these charges in the periodic valuation reports and request that in the case of an unwind of the trades by WWA, the CVA and FVA need to be accounted for in the unwind price. Also, BMC should agree that if WWA decides to execute a CSA, the reduction in CVA and FVA should be paid back to the airline.

A checklist of items to consider when restructuring the portfolio as discussed is shown in Table 10.8.

TABLE 10.8   Restructuring checklist

	Existing portfolio	New portfolio	Incremental (New portfolio – Old portfolio)
Instruments	Portfolio of TARs	Swap	
MTM	Portfolio MTM	Swap MTM	Theoretically 0, but bid/ask spreads and credit charges are added on
Delta profile	Portfolio delta profile	Swap delta	Net delta profile: most of the delta is not offset because the old portfolio was a short position at prevailing price levels
Vega profile	Portfolio vega profile	0	Net vega profile = − Old portfolio vega
Potential future exposure	Portfolio PFE	Swap PFE	Incremental PFE
Expected exposure	Portfolio EE	Swap EE	Incremental EE
Funding and credit costs	To be charged upon novation but prefer to be included in the restructured portfolio	CVA and FVA calculated	Incremental CVA is difficult due to wrong-way risk in novated trades. Therefore, charge full CVA and FVA of the new portfolio

SUMMARY

In this chapter, we have described the practical application of commodity hedging techniques introduced over previous chapters in different corporate settings. We aimed to present the salient points from our discussion on hedge program development, implementation, and risk management in these case studies.

We began our discussion of fuel hedging with an introduction to the energy markets, focusing on price formation in Chapter 1. This was followed by an overview of fuel-consuming industries including airlines, shipping firms and industrial consumers and the basics of physical and financial trading of commodities. With this foundation on commodity markets and market participants, we then discussed a framework for setting up a hedge program, covering important steps including risk identification and assessment, risk appetite determination, hedge objective setting, implementation, and monitoring. In the first case study of this chapter, we revisited many of these discussions as we developed a risk management program for a shipping company. During our discussion on the implementation of the program, we introduced simple hedging structures as well as basic portfolio management issues.

The second part of this book has dealt with popular derivative products used by commodity consumers, beginning with vanilla derivatives including forwards, futures, options, and swaps and their valuation and sensitivity calculations. We then introduced more structured derivatives like collars and swaptions, and concurrently discussed models for explaining commodity forward curve shapes. Finally, we considered exotic hedging structures like extendibles and target redemption structures, and explained the valuation methodologies used in these cases, in addition to providing quick shortcuts for checking prices quoted for these instruments. We utilized these discussions in our second case study, where we studied the hedging portfolio of an airline that transacted multiple structured derivatives.

The final section of the book discussed market risk management and ancillary issues, including counterparty risk measurement and management using derivatives and legal recipes. We also discussed scenario analysis and its importance as a pre-trade and post-trade tool for determining market, credit, and liquidity risks. Finally, we described some popular financing structures used by airline companies and introduced bundled hedging and financing products that can help these companies perform holistic risk management in an effective manner. The second case study in this chapter drew extensively on the discussions related to credit risk and scenario analysis to explain hedge portfolio analysis and restructuring for a distressed airline, in addition to displaying the benefits and downside of different hedging strategies.

In this book we have spent considerable time dealing with hedging issues from the perspective of transportation companies, which are major users of energy commodities. While market conventions and types of participant differ across commodity markets, commodity cost management concerns are similar across most consumers. The hedging frameworks and instruments described here have been used successfully by consumers across metals and agricultural commodity markets as well. As we conclude this book, we hope that readers have developed an appreciation of the finer points of structuring and risk managing hedge portfolios. Commodity markets have moved and evolved at a rapid pace over the last two decades, and we trust that this work has gone some way to helping readers understand these markets and trade in them with confidence.

Bibliography

CHAPTER 1

ASTM International website (http://www.astm.org/Standards/D323.htm). Retrieved June 2015. *BP Statistical Review of World Energy*. 2014.

Canadian Centre for Energy Information website (http://www.centreforenergy.com/AboutEnergy/ONG/OilsandsHeavyOil/Overview.asp?page=1). Retrieved July 2014.

Energy Intelligence. 2008. *The International Crude Oil Market Handbook*, 8th edn, June.

Gorton, G. and K. Geert Rouwenhorst. 2005. Facts and Fantasies about Commodity Futures. Yale ICF Working Paper, February 28.

International Energy Agency. 2014. *Key World Energy Statistics*. IEA.

International Gas Union. 2014. *Wholesale Gas Price Survey* – 2014 Edition. A global review of price formation mechanisms 2005–2013. IGU.

Kumins, L. and Bamberger, R. 2006. Oil and Gas Disruption from Hurricanes Katrina and Rita. CRS Report for Congress, April 6.

Lai, H. 2009. *Asian Energy Security: The Maritime Dimension*. Basingstoke: Palgrave Macmillan.

OPEC website (http://www.opec.org/opec_web/en/data_graphs/330.htm). Retrieved August 2014.

Quick, H. 1995. Physical characteristics and refining. Chapter 2 in *Oil Trading Manual*. D. Long (ed). Cambridge: Woodhead Publishing.

Schofield, N.C. 2007. *Commodity Derivatives: Markets and Applications*. Chichester: John Wiley & Sons.

Society of Petroleum Engineers. 1997. *Petroleum Reserves Definitions*. Retrieved from website (http://www.spe.org/industry/docs/Petroleum_Reserves_Definitions_1997.pdf).

Tang, K. and Xiong, W. 2012. Index investment and the financialisation of commodities. *Financial Analysts Journal*. 68(6), 54–74.

World Coal Association website (http://www.worldcoal.org/coal/uses-of-coal/coal-to-liquids/). Retrieved August 2014.

CHAPTER 2

Accenture and United Nations Global Compact. 2012. Sustainable Energy for All: Opportunities for the Metals and Mining Industry. Accenture.

AP Møller Mærsk. 2013. A/S. Annual Report.

Baffes, J. 2011. *Commodity Futures Exchanges: Historical Evolution & New Realities*. The World Bank, Washington, DC.

Belobaba, P., Odoni, A., and Barnhart, C. 2009. *The Global Airline Industry*. New York: John Wiley & Sons.

Canadian Fuels Association. 2013. *The Economics of Petroleum Refining*. Canadian Fuels Association, December.

CME Group. WTI Crude Oil Future Contract Specifications. Retrieved from website (http://www.cmegroup.com/rulebook/NYMEX/2/200.pdf).

Dijkman, J.E.C. 2010. Medieval market institutions: The organisation of commodity markets in Holland, c. 1200–c. 1450. Dissertation, University of Utrecht, June.

Energy Efficiency Exchange website (http://eex.gov.au/industry-sectors/mining/). Retrieved June 2015.

Hooper, W.R. 1876. The tulip mania. *Harper's New Monthly Magazine*. April, LII(CCCXL).

IATA Economics. 2010. IATA Economic Briefing – Airline Fuel and Labour Cost Share. February.

International Air Transport Association. 2014. *Annual Review 2014. Tony Tyler, Director General & CEO, IATA. 70th Annual General Meeting, Doha, June*.

International Air Transport Association. 2014. *Economic Performance of the Airline Industry*. Mid-Year Report.

International Energy Agency. 2011. *World Energy Outlook*. IEA.

International Energy Agency. 2014. *Key World Energy Statistics*. IEA.

Moss, D. and Kintgen, E. 2010. *The Dojima Rice Market and the Origins of Futures Trading*. Harvard Business School, Boston, MA.

Petchey, R. 2010. End use energy intensity in the Australian economy. Australian Bureau of Agricultural and Resource Economics – Bureau of Rural Sciences Research Report 10.08, September.

Stopford, M. 2009. *Maritime Economics*, 3rd edn. Routledge:, London.

Tordo, S., Tracy, B.S., and Arfaa, N. 2011. National oil companies and value creation. World Bank Working Paper No. 218.

US Commodity Futures Trading Commission website (http://www.cftc.gov/About/HistoryoftheCFTC/history_precftc). Retrieved June 2015.

CHAPTER 3

Campello, M., Lin, C., Ma, Y., and Zou, H. 2011. The real and financial implications of corporate hedging. *Journal of Finance*. 66(5), 1615–1647.

Carey, S. and Gonzalez, A. 2012. Delta to buy refinery in effort to lower jet-fuel costs. *Wall Street Journal*. April 30.

Carter, D.A., Rogers, D.A., and Simkins, B.J. 2006. Does hedging affect firm value? Evidence from the US airline industry. *Financial Management*. 35(1), 53–86.

Chiu, J. and Fujikawa, M. 2015. Asian aviation sector to benefit from fuel-price plunge. *Wall Street Journal*. January 27.

Damodaran, A., Garvey, M., and Roggi, O. 2012.*Risk Taking: A Corporate Governance Perspective*. International Finance Corporation, June.

DeMarzo, P.M. and Duffie, D. 1995. Corporate incentives for hedging and hedge accounting. *Review of Financial Studies*. 8(3), 743–771.

Morrell, P. and Swan, W. 2006. Airline jet fuel hedging: Theory and practice. *Transport Reviews*. 26(6), 713–730.

Popova, I. and Simkins, B.J. 2013. *Introduction to Energy Risk Management*. Chapter 16 in Simkins, B. and Simkins, R (eds), Energy Finance and Economics: Analysis and Valuation, Risk Management and the Future of Energy. New York: John Wiley & Sons.

Smith, C.W. and Stulz, R.M. 1985. The determinants of firms' hedging policies. *Journal of Financial and Quantitative Analysis*. 20(4), 391–405.

Wall, R. 2014. European airlines miss full benefit of lower fuel costs. *Wall Street Journal*, October 27.

CHAPTER 4

Black, F. 1976. The pricing of commodity contracts. *Journal of Financial Economics*. 3, 167–179.

Black, F. and Scholes, M. 1973. The pricing of options and corporate liabilities. *Journal of Political Economy*. 81(3), 637–654.

Hakala, J. and Wystup, U. 2001. *Foreign Exchange Risk*, Chapter 1. London: Risk Publications.

Hull, J.C. 2006. *Options, Futures, and Other Derivatives*, 6th edn. Englewood Cliffs, NJ: Prentice-Hall.

ISDA Commodity Definitions. 2005. International Swaps and Derivatives Association.

Kemna, A.G.Z. and Vorst, A.C.F. 1990. A pricing method for options based on average asset values. *Journal of Banking and Finance*. 14, 113–129.

Levy, E. 1992. Pricing European average rate currency options. *Journal of International Money and Finance*. 11, 474–491.

Raychaudhuri, S. Introduction to Monte Carlo simulation. Oracle Crystal Ball Global Business Unit. Proceedings of the 2008 Winter Simulation Conference, Broomfield, CO.

Turnbull, S.M. and MacDonald Wakeman, L. 1991. A quick algorithm for pricing European average options. *Journal of Financial and Quantitative Analysis*. 26(3), 377–389.

CHAPTER 5

Gabillon, J. 1991. The term structures of oil futures prices. Oxford Institute for Energy Studies, Working Paper.

Gibson, R. and Schwartz, E.S. 1990. Stochastic convenience yield and the pricing of oil contingent claims. *Journal of Finance*. 45(3), 959–976.

Haseeb, H. 2013. A comparison of models for oil futures. Department of Mathematics, Uppsala University, June.

Hilliard, J.E. and Reis, J. 1998. Valuation of commodity futures and options under stochastic convenience yields, interest rates, and jump diffusions in the spot. *Journal of Financial and Quantitative Analysis*. 33(1), 61–86.

Schwartz, E.S. 1997. The stochastic behavior of commodity prices: Implications for valuation and hedging. *Journal of Finance*. 52(3), 923–973.

CHAPTER 6

Dodd, R. 2009. Exotic derivatives losses in emerging markets: Questions of suitability, concerns for stability. IMF Working Paper, July.

Dupire, B. 1994. Pricing with a smile. *Risk Magazine*, January. Retrieved from http://www.risk.net/data/risk/pdf/technical/2007/risk20_0707_technical_volatility.pdf.

Dupire, B., Dempster, M.A.H., and Pliska, S.R. (eds). 1997. *Pricing and Hedging with Smiles. Mathematics of Derivative Securities*. Cambridge University Press, Cambridge.

Heston, S.L. 1993. A closed-form solution for options with stochastic volatility with applications to bond and currency options. *Review of Financial Studies*. 6(2), 327–343.

Longstaff, F.A. and Schwartz, E.S. 2001. Valuing American options by simulation: A simple least-squares approach. *Review of Financial Studies*. 14(1), 113–147.

Ludlow, K. 2011. Misselling allegations dismissed as High Court holds the line. Linklaters. July.

Marsh, J. 2009. Asia oil hedging. Sovereign hedging lessons. *Asia Risk*. March. Retrieved from http://db.riskwaters.com/data/energyrisk/EnergyRisk/Energyrisk_0409/asia_oil.pdf.

CHAPTER 7

Bruyère, R. 2006. *Credit Derivatives and Structured Credit: A Guide for Investors*. Chichester: John Wiley & Sons.

Gregory, J. 2010. *Counterparty Credit Risk: The new challenge for global financial markets*. Chichester: John Wiley & Sons.

O'Kane, D. and Turnbull, S. 2003. Valuation of credit default swaps. Lehman Brothers Quantitative Credit Research Quarterly. April.

Zhu, S. and Pykhtin, M. 2007. A guide to modeling counterparty credit risk. *GARP Risk Review*. 37, 16–22.

CHAPTER 8

CME Group. 2012. Derivatives and Hedge Accounting. March 2.

Pazzula, D.J. 2006. *PFE Simulation Methodology*. SAS Institute, Cary, NC.

Ramirez, J. 2007. *Accounting for Derivatives, Advanced Hedging under IFRS*. Chichester: John Wiley & Sons.

CHAPTER 9

Airfinance Journal website. Retrieved June 2015 from http://www.airfinancejournal.com/resources/whatis-aviation-finance.html.

Boeing. 2013. Current Aircraft Finance Market Outlook 2014–2018. Boeing Capital Corporation, December.

Bohn, J. and Crosbie, P. 2003. Modeling default risk – modeling methodology. Moody's KMV, December 18.

Coyle, B. 2000. *Leasing*. Glenlake Publishing, Oxford.

Croke, K. 2011. Accounting developments in aircraft finance. Chapter 22 in R. Murphy and N. Desai (eds), *Aircraft Financing*, 4th edn. Euromoney Institutional Investor, London.

Forsberg, D. 2012. *Airfinance Annual 2012. Euromoney Institutional Investor, November.*

Gerber, D.N. 2011. The 2011 Aircraft Sector Understanding: Calming the turbulent skies. *Air and Space Lawyer*, 24(1).

International Accounting Standard 17 – Leases & UK, Statement of Standard Accounting Practice 21 "Accounting for Leases and Hire Purchase Contracts."

Lease Europe. 2013 Leasing Facts & Figures. Retrieved from Lease Europe website, June 2015 (http://www.leaseurope.org/index.php?page=key-facts-figures).

Morrell, P.S. 2013. *Airline Finance*, 4th edn. Farnham: Ashgate Publishing.

OECD Trade and Agricultural Directorate website (http://www.oecd.org/tad/xcred/latestdocuments/).

Index

Index compiled by Indexing Specialists (UK) Ltd